Ready for English

Teacher's Book 2

Klett und Balmer Verlag Zug

Ready for English Neubearbeitung
Teacher's Book 2

Autorenteam
Franz Andres Morrissey
Hansruedi Fäs

Umschlaggestaltung
Christa und Heinz Waldvogel, Zürich

Bilder
Tony Stone: Chris Craymer, Erich Larrayadieu

Korrektorat
Andrea Grigoleit, Thalwil
Terminus textkorrektur, Luzern

Redaktion
Irene Schüpfer, Barbara Wuthier

Satz
GU-Print AG, Stefan Imhof, Urdorf

Druck
Rheintaler Druckerei und Verlag AG, Berneck

Gesamtherstellung
IB-Print AG, Zug

© Klett und Balmer AG, Zug 2002
1. Auflage 2002
Alle Rechte vorbehalten.
Nachdruck, Vervielfältigung jeder Art oder Verbreitung
– auch auszugsweise – nur mit schriftlicher Genehmigung
des Verlages.

ISBN 3-264-83321-2

Printed in Switzerland

Die Überarbeitung basiert auf dem Lehrwerk
Ready for English, Teacher's Book 2 Part 1

Projektleitung
Franz Andres, Bern

Autorenteam
Franz Andres, Bern
Hansruedi Fäs, Neuhausen
Denise Marchini, Solothurn
Daniel Stotz, Zürich

Redaktionelle Leitung
Marcel Holliger

Besuchen Sie unsere Homepage unter www.klett.ch
oder kontaktieren Sie uns per E-Mail: info@klett.ch
oder redaktion@klett.ch

Inhaltsverzeichnis

Vorwort

Kommentar zum Student's Book (blaue Seiten)   **10**

Kommentar zum Workbook Basic (gelbe Seiten)   **71**

Kommentar zum Workbook Intensive (grüne Seiten)   **127**

Kopiervorlagen

Inhaltsverzeichnis   **183**

Anweisungen   **185**

Kopiervorlagen   **187**

Einführung

Zum Teacher's Book

Rolle des Teacher's Book

Der Einsatz von *Ready for English* in der Praxis zeigt, dass viele Lehrkräfte (**L**) das *Teacher's Book* als sinnvolle Hilfestellung für den Unterricht empfinden. Das *Teacher's Book* enthält Informationen
- zur optimalen Verwendung der Einführungstexte (vor allem wenn diese nicht ganz im herkömmlichen Sinn zu verwenden sind),
- zur Vernetzung der einzelnen Lernschritte,
- methodischer Art,
- zu Ergänzungen und Auflockerungen,
- zum binnendiffenenzierenden Unterricht mit *Ready for English* (siehe auch unten).

Zur Methode

Das Lehrmittel

1. *Ready for English* ist für eine möglichst flexible Vermittlung des Stoffes konzipiert. Deshalb enthält es Zusatzunterlagen, die nach Bedarf eingesetzt werden können.
2. *Ready for English* soll in der Progression auf aktive Sprachverwendung ausgerichtet sein. Konkret heisst das:
Wie bereits in der Einleitung von Band 1 erläutert wurde, ist *Ready for English* nicht einer bestimmten Methode verpflichtet, sondern will möglichst verschiedene Lehr- und Lerngelegenheiten bieten. Folgende Punkte wurden berücksichtigt:

Strukturell / funktional:
In Band 2 geht der grammatikalische Aufbau prinzipiell von strukturell und funktional häufiger verwendeten Formen zu solchen, die für einen unmittelbaren kommunikativen Grundstock nicht mehr von so zentraler Bedeutung sind. Die drei letzten *Units* (18–20) behandeln anspruchsvollere Themen.

Lexikalisch / thematisch:
Was uns interessiert, davon sprechen wir. Ein wichtiges Auswahlkriterium für Themen und Texte ist das Interesse der Schülerinnen und Schüler (**S**). Der Wortschatz ist auch darauf ausgerichtet und deckt sich deshalb nicht immer mit offiziellen Worthäufigkeitslisten.

Neu im Band 2: Reading Corners

In Band 2 werden einige Kapitel mit einem *Reading Corner* an Stelle der Rubrik *Time for a Change* abgeschlossen. Das Vokabular der *Reading Corners* ist – wie auch dasjenige von *Time for a Change* – lehrbuchunabhängig und wird später nicht vorausgesetzt. Diese Rubriken sollen die **S** dazu anregen, fremdsprachige Texte sinngemäss zu erfassen. Die Texte eignen sich bei stärkeren Klassen auch für eine vertiefte Bearbeitung und bieten Stoff für Diskussionen. **L** steht somit ab Band 2 noch mehr Textmaterial zur Verfügung, das je nach Bedarf in der ganzen Klasse eingesetzt oder von guten **S** einzeln bearbeitet werden kann. Die Texte können auch nur auszugsweise verwendet oder für spätere Lektionen aufgespart werden.

Zur Binnendifferenzierung

Im Student's Book Das *Student's Book* ist grundsätzlich auf zwei Niveaus aufgebaut. Die Texte und Übungen für erweiterte Ansprüche sind mit dem Piktogramm *freiwillig* gekennzeichnet. Je nach Gutdünken können natürlich auch als freiwillig markierte Texte und Übungen für das tiefere Niveau ausgewählt werden bzw. in Klassen oder Gruppen mit höherem Niveau weggelassen werden. Dabei gilt es allerdings allfällige Konsequenzen für grammatische Strukturen und für das Vokabular zu beachten.

Im Workbook Das *Workbook Basic* ist auf die obligatorischen Teile im *Student's Book* abgestimmt; das *Workbook Intensive* stützt sich neben den obligatorischen auf die zusätzlichen, als freiwillig markierten Texte und Übungen des *Student's Book*.
Jede der zwei *Workbook*-Ausgaben ist ebenfalls wieder auf zwei Niveaus aufgebaut; wie im *Student's Book* kann **L** aus den zusätzlichen Übungen wiederum je nach Gutdünken einige oder alle für die Klasse / eine Gruppe auswählen.

Im Vocabulary-Teil des Student's Book Bei der Auswahl des Vokabulars ist der doppelten Binnendifferenzierung Rechnung zu tragen. Dies wird erstens durch die zweifache Auflistung des *Vocabulary*, je für *Basic* (gelber Streifen) und *Intensive* (grüner Streifen), ermöglicht. Für *Basic* sind die Wörter in den zusätzlichen Texten und Übungen des *Student's Book* nicht aufgelistet. Sie können aber an entsprechender Stelle im *Vocabulary* für *Intensive* nachgeschlagen werden; dort sind sie mit einem Stern markiert. Ebenso sind die Wörter aus den freiwilligen Übungen in den *Workbooks* in beiden *Vocabularies* mit Stern markiert.
Für beide *Vocabularies* gilt, dass die fett gedruckten Wörter vorwiegend zum Aktivwortschatz und die nicht fett gedruckten Wörter zum Passivwortschatz der **S** gehören.

Die Niveaus von Ready for English Durch die doppelte Binnendifferenzierung entsteht ein Lehrmittel mit vier Niveaus. Diese seien hier kurz aufgelistet.

Niveau 1:
Obligatorische Texte und Übungen im *Student's Book*, obligatorische Übungen im *Workbook Basic*.
Aktivwortschatz: gelber Teil, nur fett gedruckte Wörter ohne Stern.

Niveau 2:
Obligatorische Texte und Übungen im *Student's Book*, obligatorische und ausgewählte freiwillige Übungen im *Workbook Basic*.
Wortschatz: gelber Teil, alle Wörter. Ausnahmen sind möglich für die Wörter von *Time for a Change* und der *Reading Corners* sowie für einige nicht fett gedruckte Wörter, die nach Gutdünken weggelassen werden können.

Niveau 3:
Obligatorische und freiwillige Texte und Übungen im *Student's Book*, obligatorische Übungen im *Workbook Intensive*.
Wortschatz zum *Student's Book*: grüner Teil, alle Wörter ohne Stern und die fett gedruckten Wörter mit Stern. Ausnahmen sind möglich für die Wörter von *Time for a Change* und der *Reading Corners* sowie für einige nicht fett gedruckte Wörter, die nach Gutdünken weggelassen werden können.
Wortschatz zum *Workbook Intensive*: alle Wörter ohne Stern.

Niveau 4:
Obligatorische und freiwillige Texte und Übungen im *Student's Book*, obligatorische und ausgewählte freiwillige Übungen im *Workbook Intensive*.
Wortschatz: grüner Teil, alle Wörter. Ausnahmen sind möglich für die Wörter von *Time for a Change* und der *Reading Corners* sowie für einige nicht fett gedruckte Wörter, die nach Gutdünken weggelassen werden können.

Zur Binnendifferenzierung

Einführung

Zusätzliche Flexibilität des Einsatzes von *Ready for English* ergibt sich durch das Dazunehmen oder Weglassen der *Time for a Change*- und *Reading Corner*-Seiten und durch die Kopiervorlagen im *Teacher's Book*, die sich auch gut für Hausaufgaben und zur Individualisierung des Unterrichts eignen.

Welches Niveau für welche Stufe?

Die Sekundarstufe I ist in der Schweiz von Kanton zu Kanton verschieden gegliedert. Das für einen bestimmten Schultypus zu wählende Niveau von *Ready for English* muss daher von den verantwortlichen Stellen entsprechend der Gliederung im eigenen Kanton ausgewählt werden. Mischformen der vier eigentlichen Niveaus sind selbstverständlich möglich.

Vorschläge

Einige in der Praxis gewählte und erprobte Beispiele:
- Für Progymnasien und Mittelschulen Niveau 4 mit allen Textteilen inklusive *Reading Corners* und *Time for a Change* und mit dem entsprechenden Vokabular.
- Für höhere Sekundarschulen (z.B. „E" in gegliederten Sekundarschulen, Bezirksschulen) Niveau 3–4: Im *Student's Book* werden die *Reading Corners* als Lesetexte bzw. mit passiver globaler Wortschatzerschliessung und im *Workbook Intensive* die meisten freiwilligen Übungen dazugenommen, beim Vokabular hingegen die nicht fett gedruckten Wörter mit Stern grundsätzlich weggelassen.
- Für Sekundarschulen (z.B. „G" in gegliederten Sekundarschulen) Niveau 3.
- Für Realschulen oder den untersten von drei Sekundarschultypen Niveau 2.
- Für Oberschulen, Kleinklassen, Werkklassen etc. Niveau 1.

Das Lehrwerk *Ready for English* lässt sich also jeder beliebigen Gliederung der Sekundarstufe I anpassen.

Allgemeine Hinweise

Vorschläge zur Arbeit mit den verschiedenen Lehrwerksteilen und Projekten finden sich in der Einführung zu Band 1, Abschnitte 3, 4 und 5, Seite 9 bis 14.

Abkürzungen

EA = Einzelarbeit
PA = Partnerarbeit
GA = Gruppenarbeit
GU = Gesamtunterricht, ganze Klasse beteiligt
WT = Wandtafel
S = Schülerinnen und Schüler
L = Lehrerin / Lehrer
OHP = Hellraumprojektor (Overhead Projector)

Sprachkompetenz nach Abschluss von *Ready for English 2*

Die folgenden Hinweise sollen den Lehrkräften und Schülerinnen und Schülern helfen, dem Lernprozess eine langfristige Perspektive zu geben. Sie erlauben ihnen, sich am Europäischen Referenzrahmen zu orientieren, der ein europaweit anerkanntes Instrument bietet, mit dem sich Lernende selbst einschätzen oder ihre Kenntnisse von Lehrpersonen oder Prüfungsinstitutionen bewerten lassen können. Der Referenzrahmen umfasst sechs Niveaus von A1 über A2, B1 und B2 zu C1 und C2. Das bekannte Cambridge First Certificate situiert sich etwa auf Niveau B2.

Die unten stehenden Kompetenzbeschreibungen *(can-do's)* stammen aus den Checklisten der Schweizer Version des **Europäischen Sprachenportfolios** (www.sprachenportfolio.ch). Mit A1 wird das erste von insgesamt sechs Sprachniveaus bezeichnet. Dieses sollten gute Schülerinnen und Schüler am Ende von *Ready for English 1* erreicht haben.
Als Globalbeschreibung der Sprachkompetenz auf der nächsten Stufe A2 kann man dort lesen: («Ein Lerner / eine Lernerin …)

- kann Sätze und häufig gebrauchte Ausdrücke verstehen, die mit Bereichen von ganz unmittelbarer Bedeutung zusammenhängen (z.B. Informationen zur Person und zur Familie, Einkaufen, Arbeit, nähere Umgebung);
- kann sich in einfachen, routinemässigen Situationen verständigen, in denen es um einen einfachen und direkten Austausch von Informationen über vertraute und geläufige Dinge geht;
- kann mit einfachen Mitteln die eigene Herkunft und Ausbildung, die direkte Umgebung und Dinge im Zusammenhang mit unmittelbaren Bedürfnissen beschreiben.»

Am Ende von *Ready for English 2* sollten die Schülerinnen und Schüler nach gründlicher Durcharbeitung der 10 *Units* in den rezeptiven Fertigkeiten (Hör- und Leseverstehen) den Ansprüchen des Niveaus A2 genügen. In den mündlichen produktiven Aktivitäten (zusammenhängend sprechen, an Gesprächen teilnehmen) wird Niveau A1+ angestrebt. Die Schreibfähigkeit wird auf dem Können von *Ready for English 1* weiter ausgebaut und sollte am Ende des zweiten Bandes auf Niveau A1 ausgebildet sein, vorausgesetzt, die Schreibaufgaben werden seriös durchgeführt und die Lernenden erhalten konstruktives Feedback.

Die allermeisten der im Portfolio aufgelisteten Sprechhandlungen sind in *Ready for English 2* vertreten. Das Zielniveau A2 bedingt allerdings, dass die im Lehrbuch dargestellten Szenen und Situationen immer auch auf den eigenen Lebensbereich übertragen werden. Einige wenige Checklisten-Einträge wurden weggelassen (z.B.: „Ich kann beschreiben, wo ich wohne": schon in Band 1 abgedeckt; oder: „Ich kann jemanden einladen und reagieren, wenn mich jemand einlädt": in *Ready for English 2* durch keine Übungen abgedeckt).
In der folgenden Liste kursiv gedruckte Kann-Beschreibungen wurden der Portfolio-Checkliste beigefügt; sie betreffen zusätzliche Fähigkeiten, die entweder altersspezifischer sind als diejenigen im Portfolio oder im Lernkontext der schulischen Oberstufe eher zu erwarten sind.
Ausblick: Am Ende des dritten Bandes sollten die Zielstufen B1 für rezeptive und A2+ für produktive Fertigkeiten erreicht sein.

Einführung

Vergleich der Kompetenzbeschreibungen im Sprachenportfolio (Europäischer Referenzrahmen) mit den Aktivitäten in RfE1

Niveau	Fertigkeit	Kann-Beschreibung	Units in RfE 2
A2	Hören	Ich kann verstehen, was man in einfachen Alltagsgesprächen langsam und deutlich zu mir sagt; es ist möglich, sich mir verständlich zu machen, wenn die Sprechenden sich die nötige Mühe machen können.	U11–U20
		Ich kann im Allgemeinen das Thema von Gesprächen, die in meiner Gegenwart geführt werden, erkennen, wenn langsam und deutlich gesprochen wird.	U11–U20
		Ich kann Sätze, Ausdrücke und Wörter verstehen, wenn es um Dinge von ganz unmittelbarer Bedeutung geht (z.B. ganz grundlegende Informationen zu Person, Familie, Einkaufen, Arbeit, näherer Umgebung).	U13, U19, U20
		Ich kann die Hauptsache von dem, was in kurzen, einfachen und klaren Durchsagen oder Mitteilungen gesagt wird, mitbekommen.	U13, U16
		Ich kann Geschichten und kurze Berichte verstehen, wenn sie einfach formuliert sind und ich sie mehr als einmal hören kann.	U12, U14, U16, U17, U18
A2	Lesen	Ich kann Meldungen oder einfachen Zeitungsartikeln, in denen Zahlen und Namen eine wichtige Rolle spielen, die klar gegliedert sind und mit Bildern arbeiten, wichtige Informationen entnehmen.	U12, U16, U17, U19
		Ich kann einen einfachen persönlichen Brief *oder ein E-Mail* verstehen, in dem mir jemand von Dingen aus dem Alltag schreibt oder mich danach fragt.	U14, 19
		Ich kann einfache schriftliche Mitteilungen von Bekannten oder Mitarbeitern verstehen (z. B. wann man sich zum Fussballspielen trifft).	U15, U20
		Ich kann in Informationsblättern über Freizeitaktivitäten, Ausstellungen usw. die wichtigsten Informationen finden.	U13, U15, U16
		Ich kann kurze Erzählungen und Berichte verstehen, die von alltäglichen Dingen handeln und in denen es um Themen geht, die mir vertraut sind, wenn der Text in einfacher Sprache geschrieben ist.	U11, U12, U14, U16, U17, U18, U19
A1+	An Gesprächen teilnehmen	Ich kann in Geschäften, auf der Post oder Bank einfache Erledigungen machen.	U20
		Ich kann mir einfache Informationen für eine Reise beschaffen.	U15, U16
		Ich kann mit anderen besprechen, was man tun oder wohin man gehen will, und kann vereinbaren, wann und wo man sich trifft.	U19, U20
		Ich kann sagen, was ich gerne habe und was nicht.	U20
		Ich kann eine andere Person zu einem Geschehen oder Sachverhalt befragen.	U11, U12, U13, U14,
A1+	Zusammenhängend sprechen	Ich kann mich selbst, meine Familie und andere Personen beschreiben.	U11–U20
		Ich kann kurz und einfach über ein Ereignis berichten.	U11, U12, U13, U14, U17, U18
		Ich kann in einfacher Form über meine Hobbys und Interessen berichten.	U13, U14, U16, U19
		Ich kann über vergangene Aktivitäten und persönliche Erfahrungen berichten (z. B. das letzte Wochenende oder meine letzten Ferien).	U16, U19
A1	Schreiben	Ich kann auf einem Fragebogen Angaben zu meiner Person machen (Beruf, Alter, Wohnort, Hobbys).	U11
		Ich kann eine einfache Postkarte (z. B. mit Feriengrüssen) schreiben.	U16
		Ich kann einen Notizzettel schreiben, um jemanden zu informieren, wo ich bin oder wo wir uns treffen.	U16, U20
		Ich kann in einfachen Sätzen über mich schreiben, z. B. wo ich wohne und was ich mache.	U19, U20
		Ich kann eine kurze, einfache Beschreibung über einen Gegenstand oder eine Region verfassen.	U15, U16

Warm-up

Stars and Memories

Einstimmung mit Musik Kurze Musikstücke von U2, Madonna, Presley und den Beatles einspielen; die S raten lassen, wer zu hören ist.

Bilder U2, Charles Lindbergh mit Frau, Madonna, Diana und Charles, Elvis Presley, die Beatles, Präsident John F. Kennedy.

Warm-up

Hinweise/Ideen Die S sollen herausfinden, wer auf den Bildern zu sehen ist. In der Klasse dazu einen Wettbewerb veranstalten (möglicherweise in Gruppen).

Vorgehen Was wissen die S über die verschiedenen Personen?
Mögliche Fragen: *Where is she/he from? Do you know any of her/his/their songs? What are they famous for? Are they alive today? Are they famous today?*

Ausbau/Varianten
1) Die S suchen gruppenweise zu einzelnen Personen oder Bands im Internet Informationen (oder Adressen für mögliche spätere Projekte) und stellen diese für die Klasse zusammen.
2) Während der gesamten Zeit, in der man die Unit 11 behandelt, könnte das Schulzimmer mit Postern von U2, Madonna, Presley und den Beatles illustriert werden und die WT oder ein schwarzes Brett könnte als "Protokollunterlage" dienen, wo Schlüsselwörter und Verbformen festgehalten werden. Somit kann während der Arbeit immer wieder darauf zurückgegriffen werden.

Unit 11 Focus

Music, Music, Music ...

I Madonna

1. Madonna Louise Ciccone was born in Bay City, Michigan, on 16 August 1958. Her dream was to be a star and New York was a good place for a career in the music business. At first, she was a dancer in a number of dance
5. companies, then she was a background singer. Her first album "Madonna" (1983) wasn't very successful, but her second album "Like a Virgin" (1984) was a big hit. This was the beginning of her career as an international pop star.
10. Her videos were a bit like short films and her concerts were great shows with dancers and lights and Madonna in a lot of different dresses. But were her films a success? No, most of them weren't. Her role in the film musical "Evita" wasn't bad, but she isn't a great actress. In the
15. early days Madonna was just a singer, but her new videos show that she is also a good entertainer.

II U2

1. It was the year 1976, the time of punk and of loud aggressive music and a time of young people with no future. Larry Mullen Jr. was 14 years old. He lived in Dublin and his interest was music, rock
5. music. He was a drummer and he wanted to play in a band. So he looked around for other musicians at his high school in Dublin. Three students joined him: Paul Hewson (Bono) was a singer, David Evans (The Edge) was a guitarist and Adam Clayton was a
10. bass player.
The new band needed a good name. A friend suggested U2. Why did they like it? Because it sounded like "you, too" or "you two" and it was the name of a submarine and a spy plane.
15. Most punk groups copied other bands but U2 tried to find a new style. The four school-friends loved music, but they were also interested in politics.
Their first albums were good, but their first big hit was "Sunday, Bloody Sunday" in 1983, a song about
20. the conflict in Northern Ireland.
Who listened to the music of this new Irish band? At first, mostly people from Ireland, but soon people from all over the world were interested in U2. "Pride (In the Name of Love)", a song about the mur-
25. der of Martin Luther King, was a big success.
Did their style change in the last years? Yes, experiments with electronic music and dance music were important for U2. Not all their fans liked the changes, but nobody can say that U2 is a boring band.

Above: Clayton, Evans, Mullen and Hewson (left to right)
Left: Paul Hewson (Bono Vox) on stage

Unit 11

Sprachfunktionen:	Themen:
Über Vergangenes sprechen	Jahreszahlen; Rückblick auf die Popmusik; Biografie von Stars
Strukturen: Einfache Vergangenheit von *to be*, bejahend, Frageform, einfache Vergangenheit von regelmässigen Verben bejahend, Frageform (nur rezeptiv)	**Mögliche Abfolge:** Focus I → First Step → Exercise 1 → Exercise 2 → Focus II → Second Step → Third Step → Exercise 3 → Exercise 4 → (Focus III)) → (Focus IV) (Fourth Step)
Grammatik: § 21, 22, 24	→ (Fifth Step) → Exercise 5 → Stepping Out → (Exercise 6) → Exercise 7 → (Exercise 8)

Focus I: Madonna

Hinweise/Ideen	Der strukturelle Schwerpunkt von Focus I (und III) liegt auf der einfachen Vergangenheit von *to be*.
Material	CD
Vorgehen	Hören (mitlesen) und global verstehen. • Den Text mit offenem Buch *(Basic)* oder ohne Buch *(Intensive)* hören. Rückfragen: Woran (Namen, Zahlen) können sich die S erinnern? • Heraussuchen der Vergangenheitsformen von *to be*. • Lesetraining in PA
Wichtig	Bei beiden Focustexten geht es grundsätzlich um das globale Textverständnis. Die S sollten die Details der Texte anhand der Übungen im Training und im Workbook erschliessen, müssen aber vorerst noch nicht jedes Wort verstehen. L sollte je nach Leistungsstärke der Klassen entscheiden, inwieweit der Focustext bereits hier als Lautlesetext behandelt werden soll.

Focus II: U2

Hinweise/Ideen	In Focus II (und IV) werden regelmässige Verben mit *-ed*-Vergangenheit eingeführt sowie *did* als Frageform.
Material	CD, OHP-Folie
Vorgehen	Hören (mitlesen) und global verstehen. • Heraussuchen der regelmässigen Vergangenheitsformen. • Entwicklung der Regel „verb+ed" an WT.

Erweiterungen

Kopiervorlagen
Fill in the Gaps I (1)

Ausbau
1) Die S stellen Grössen aus der Film-, Musik- und Sportwelt vor.
2) Spiel "Musikerquiz": Die S suchen in Popzeitschriften Bilder von Musikern/Bands und stellen ein Musikquiz zusammen, indem sie die Bilder der Köpfe auf Karten kleben. S1 hält eine Karte hoch: *What's her/his name/ Where is she/he from? What does she/he play?* S2 antwortet.
Richtige Antworten können mit Punkten honoriert werden.
3) Musical Geography: Die S suchen Stars aus Zeitschriften, wobei sie auch herausfinden müssen, woher die Stars stammen. Dann mit einer Amerika-Karte oder einer Karte von UK die Gesichter der Stars bei den Ortschaften aufkleben.

Material
Bilder aus Popzeitschriften, grossformatige Landkarten

Student's Book, p. 2

Unit 11

Siehe Hinweise auf Seite 2.

Erweiterungen

Kopiervorlagen
Fill in the Gaps II (2)

III Elvis Presley

1. For the Beatles, for Bruce Springsteen and for many young people in his day he was "The King".
For American parents he was shocking, bad for their sons and their daughters, a terrible danger for the clean
5. American life style.
Elvis Aaron Presley was born in Tupelo, Mississippi in 1935. He was a truck driver. His first record was "My Happiness", a song for his mother's birthday.
10. Elvis Presley's music was a mixture of black music like gospel and blues and white music like Country and Western, and his style was aggressive and sexy. Elvis was the first really big rock'n'roll star, the first teenage rebel ...
15. In the sixties Presley was a soldier in the US army. Then, in his later life there were problems: his huge success wasn't good for him. At the age of forty Elvis wasn't a good-looking singer any more. He was very fat. His death in August 1977 was the result of too many
20. cheeseburgers and too many drugs.

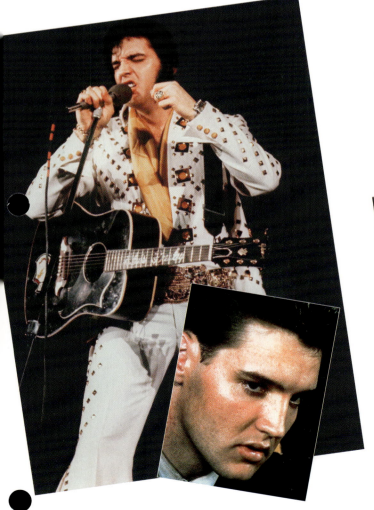

IV The Beatles

1. They were four young men from Liverpool and they were full of new ideas. Teenagers George Harrison, Paul McCartney, John Lennon and Ringo Starr liked American rock'n'roll. But the beginning wasn't easy:
5. the Beatles started to play in Liverpool, then in Hamburg. They worked hard and learned a lot. Lennon and McCartney were also good songwriters. Back in England they started to work with manager
10. Brian Epstein. He liked their music but he also liked the four young men and helped them a lot in their career.
After their first single "Love Me Do" almost all their singles were top hits. The sixties were the time of
15. Beatlemania: Teenage girls all over Great Britain and the United States started to go wild at their concerts. In 1966 the Beatles were tired of touring. There was only one more concert in 1969 for the film "Let It Be" but the police stopped that.
20. For the next four years the Beatles released a lot of albums, all different in style and music. In 1970 there was trouble between Paul McCartney and John Lennon because of Lennon's new wife Yoko Ono. That was the end of the Beatles as a group. In 1980
25. Mark Chapman killed John Lennon in New York. George Harrison died in 2001.

(§ 21, 22, 24a, 24b, WB Ex 1, 2, 3)

Training

First Step (§ 21a, 21b, 21c)

The Madonna Quiz

a) Answer the questions.

1. Where was Madonna born?
2. What was her dream?
3. Was she successful as a background singer?
4. What was the name of her first album?

b) True or false?

5. Her films were a great success.
6. In the film musical "Evita" she was a great actress.
7. In her early days she was just a singer.
8. Her concerts were great shows.

Second Step (§ 21a)

The U2 Quiz

a) What is correct?

1. U2 are from Ireland/England/Scotland.
2. They are a group of three/four/five school-friends.
3. It was the time of rock 'n' roll/beat/punk music.
4. U2 were interested in music and in sports/politics/the theatre.
5. Their first big hit was in 1973/1983/1993.

b) Complete.

6. "Sunday, Bloody Sunday" was a song about ...
7. There was a big hit about the murder of ...
8. People all over the world ...
9. There were experiments with ...

Above: Madonna at a concert and Madonna in her role as Evita
Left: The Edge and Bono on stage

Unit 11

Training

First Step

Hinweise/Ideen	Die Übung zum Textverständnis kann von den S still vorbereitet werden. Hier sind auch Kurzantworten ohne Verb möglich. Vor allem bei der Stufe *basic* sollte man nicht auf ganzen Sätzen insistieren.
Vorgehen	Nach dem Erarbeiten des Focustextes stellen die S in PA/GA die Antworten auf die Fragen zusammen.
Ausbau	Die S könnten die Antworten der Trainingsübungen schriftlich (in einem Heft oder auf einer Grosscollage im Schulzimmer) festhalten und erhalten auf diese Weise eine Zusammenfassung über Madonna, U2, (Elvis, die Beatles).
Intensive	Gute S tragen zu b weitere *true/false*-Aussagen zusammen und legen diese dem Rest der Klasse vor.

Second Step

Hinweise/Ideen	Kann wie oben bearbeitet werden.

Erweiterungen

Kopiervorlagen
Verb Training (3)
Beachten Sie dazu die Anweisungen.

Ausbau
In PA Aussagen zu den Focustexten ausformulieren, wobei z.T. bewusst falsche Aussagen gemacht werden.
Danach spielen zwei Paare als Teams gegeneinander.
Ziel ist es, die falschen Angaben zu korrigieren.

Student's Book, p. 4

Unit 11

Third Step

Hinweise/Ideen Hier geht es um die Einübung von Fragen, vorerst mit *to be*, dann mit regelmässigen Verben. Bei schwächeren Klassen sollte die Frageform zuerst mit den Beispielen aus dem Focustext an der WT erarbeitet werden.

Vorgehen In PA die Übung erarbeiten.

Ausbau/Varianten Die S formulieren in PA weitere Aussagen, die sie zu Fragen umwandeln. Die Fragen werden daraufhin dem Rest der Klasse gestellt. Hier müssten evtl. auch die Kurzantworten (samt Verneinung) eingeführt werden *(yes, he did; no, they didn't)*.

Fourth Step

Hinweise/Ideen Kann auch als EA verwendet werden: Die S erarbeiten die Fragen zusammen mit den beiden freiwilligen Focustexten.

Fifth Step

Hinweise/Ideen Eignet sich als EA für einen kurzen mündlichen Vortrag oder für einen Kurzaufsatz.

Erweiterungen

Kopiervorlagen
Verb Training (3)
Beachten Sie dazu die Anweisungen.

Ausbau
Die S stellen in EA oder in GA weitere Starporträts zusammen und hängen diese im Klassenzimmer auf. Bei „Musikermüdung" Film- oder Sportgrössen dazu nehmen.

Third Step (§ 21c, 22c)

a) Make questions and/or give answers.

1. – Was Madonna born in Italy?
   – No, she ...
2. – ... a love story?
   – No, "Evita" was a film musical.
3. – Did Larry Mullen live in Dublin?
   – Yes, he ...
4. – Where did Larry Mullen look for other musicians?
   – He ...
5. – ...?
   – Yes, the four school-friends loved music.
6. – ...?
   – The band U2 lived in Ireland.

b) Make questions and give answers.

Example: Madonna / be / born in 1985
– Was Madonna born in 1985?
– No, she was born in 1958.

U2 / start / in London
– Did U2 start in London?
– No, they started in Dublin.

1. Madonna / be born / in New York
2. „Like a Virgin" / be / Madonna's first album
3. U2 / start / in 1976
4. Paul Hewson / live / in England
5. U2 / be / the name of a spy plane
6. Their first big hit / be / about Martin Luther King
7. Their style / change / in the last years
8. Their fans / like / the changes

Fourth Step (§ 21c, 22c)

Quiz: Elvis and the Beatles

Here are some correct answers. What did the quiz-master ask?

Example: – Where did the Beatles start?
– They started in Liverpool.

1. – ...?
   – It was a song for his mother's birthday.
2. – ...?
   – In Liverpool, then in Hamburg.
3. – ...?
   – Brian Epstein.
4. – ...?
   – He liked the four young men.
5. – ...?
   – He was a lorry driver.
6. – ...?
   – Mark Chapman.

Fifth Step (§ 21, 22)

What can you say about ...

... "The King"? (music, jobs, films, death)
... The Beatles? (beginning, concerts, end, ...)
... U2 (texts, hits, music styles, ...)
... Madonna (family, music, films, ...)

Stepping Out

History Quiz

What happened in ...

... 1963?
– Charles Lindbergh crossed the Atlantic in a small aeroplane.
– The Spice Girls had their first number 1 hit.
– Lee Harvey Oswald killed John F. Kennedy.

... 1969?
– The Americans landed on the moon.
– The Second World War ended.
– Edmund Hillary and Sherpa Tenzing climbed Mount Everest.

... 1981?
– The Reggae guitarist Bob Marley died in Miami.
– Martina Hingis played her first tennis match.
– "Harry Potter" was a big hit in the cinema.

... 1789?
– The French Revolution started.
– William Shakespeare was born.
– Thomas Edison invented the electric guitar.

When did terrorists destroy the World Trade Center?
1985   1998   2000   2001

When were the first modern Olympic Games?
1896   1933   1980   2000

When did the 'Titanic' start her journey?
1712   1812   1912   1971

When did Graham Bell invent the telephone?
1450   1776   1876   1976

When did the First World War end?
1848   1914   1918   1945

When did Mark Chapman kill John Lennon?
1815   1915   1980   2001

When did Princess Diana marry?
1957   1997   1949   1981

When did Columbus "discover" the New World?
1291   1492   1815   1989

*Top to bottom:
Charles Lindbergh,
Titanic,
World Trade Center*

cross, destroy, die, discover, invent, journey, kill, land, marry, moon, Olympic Games, World War

Unit 11

Stepping Out

Hinweise/Ideen Vorgängig sollten die Jahreszahlen und Daten eingeführt bzw. gefestigt werden (Grammatik § 24). Als Beispiele das gegenwärtige Jahr, das Geburtsjahr der S, den Eintritt in die Schule usw. verwenden.

Vorgehen Die S spielen in Teams gegeneinander. Für richtige Antworten wird ein Punkt vergeben. Das Team mit der höchsten Punktzahl erhält einen Preis.

Lösungen
1963: Lee Harvey Oswald killed John F. Kennedy
  (Spice Girls: 1996; Charles Lindbergh: 1927)
1969: The Americans landed on the moon
  (2nd World War: 1945; Hillary and Sherpa Tenzing: 1953)
1981: Bob Marley died of cancer
  (Martina Hingis: In 1989 – at the age of 9 – she became Swiss Junior Champion;
  Harry Potter: 2001)
1789: The French Revolution started
  *(William Shakespeare: 1564; Edison invented **the phonograph** in 1877)*

*Terrorists destroyed the WTC in **2001**.*
*The first modern Olympic Games were in **1896**.*
*The Titanic started her journey in **1912**.*
*Graham Bell invented the telephone in **1876**.*
*The First World War ended in **1918**.*
*Mark Chapman killed John Lennon in **1980**.*
*Princess Diana married in **1981**.*
*Columbus "discovered" the New World in **1492**.*

Erweiterungen

Kopiervorlagen
History Quiz (4)

Ausbau
Die S schreiben Lebensläufe berühmter Person (mit Daten) auf, ohne deren Namen zu nennen und hängen diese im Schulzimmer auf. Die Klasse versucht zu erraten, um wen es sich handelt.

Student's Book, p. 6

Unit 12

Unit 12

Sprachfunktionen: Über Vergangenes sprechen und Fragen stellen.	Themen: Geschichte: Ermordung von Präsident Kennedy
Strukturen: Einfache Vergangenheit der unregelmässigen (starken) Verben, Aussage-, Frageform und Verneinung; Ordnungszahlen und Daten Grammatik: § 22, 23, 24	Mögliche Abfolge: Focustext I → First Step a → Second Step → WB Ex 1 → WB Ex 2 → (Focustext II) → (First Step b) → WB Ex 3 → Third Step → (WB Ex 4) → WB Ex 5 → (Fourth Step) → WB Ex 6 → Stepping Out → WB Ex 7 → (WB Ex 8) → (Reading Corner)

Focus I: Elm Street

Warm-up	a) Die S sollen erzählen, was sie über John F. Kennedy wissen (evtl. kennen Einzelne den Film von Oliver Stone). b) Alternativer Einstieg mit konkreten Fragen: *Do you know John F. Kennedy? Where was he from? What was his job? When did he die? Do you know other American presidents? Were other American presidents killed? Who?*
Hinweise/Ideen	Bei den Texten zuerst nur auf das globale Verständnis eingehen, das mit der Einführung (oben) erleichtert wird; Verständnisfragen können vom Einstieg übernommen und mit weiteren Fragen ergänzt werden: *What was the name of Kennedy's wife? There were some shots. At what time? Where did the shots come from? Who did the police arrest? When did the police arrest him?*
Material	CD
Vorgehen	Text hören, mitlesen und global verstehen.
a) Basic	1) Den Text mehrmals abspielen und die S still mitlesen lassen. 2) Die Zeichnung mit den Beschriftungen als Verständnishilfe einsetzen *(car park, Elm street, big building, Oswald's position).* 3) Verständnisfragen (siehe oben) stellen. Noch nicht auf die unregelmässigen Verben eingehen. Bei schwächeren Klassen können die Verbformen jedoch vorgängig an der WT notiert werden.
b) Intensive	1) Der Text kann zuerst in stiller Einzelarbeit gelesen und danach angehört werden. Noch nicht auf die unregelmässigen Verben eingehen. Nur bei Bedarf die Verbformen suchen und daraus die Gegenwart erraten lassen. 2) Verständnisfragen (siehe oben) stellen.
Bemerkungen	Die S sollen ermuntert werden, den Text (mit Hilfe der Einführung und der Illustrationen) sinngemäss zu erfassen und sich nicht an einzelnen unbekannten Wörtern aufzuhalten.

Focus II: The Dallas Police Department

Hinweise/Ideen	Im zweiten Teil "The questions" wird die Problematik des weitgehend ungelösten Falles angesprochen. Hier ergäben sich Querverbindungen zum Geschichtsunterricht.
Vorgehen	Siehe oben.

Erweiterungen

Kopiervorlagen *Two Days in Novmber (5)* *Fill in the Gaps (6)*	Ausbau Ausschnitte aus der DVD "JFK" mit deutschen Untertiteln könnten die Geschichte filmwirksam illustrieren.

Unit 12   Focus

Two Days in November ...

I Elm Street

1 On 22 November 1963 President John F. Kennedy and his wife Jackie came to Dallas, Texas. It was a normal visit, but then ...
   On their tour through Dallas the president and his wife sat
5 in an open limousine. The limousine turned from Houston Street into Elm Street and went past a small hill. But what happened next? We know some things because a man had a film camera with him and made a film of the scene:
10 At 12.31 there were three or four shots. Some people said that the shots came from a big building. Other people said that the shots didn't come from the building, but from a car park.
   One bullet hit Kennedy in the head; he brought his hands
15 up to his neck and fell forward. The limousine took the president to Parkland Hospital at great speed. Doctors at the hospital worked very hard to save Kennedy's life, but it was too late. Kennedy died in hospital and Vice President Johnson became America's new president
20 ninety-nine minutes after the shots.
   At about 14.30 the police arrested a man called Lee Harvey Oswald. He worked in the big building on Elm Street. In the building the police found Oswald's gun ...

Who was Lee Harvey Oswald?

1 Lee Harvey Oswald had an unhappy life. He was a soldier and he was always in trouble in the army and later with the police. He was also a communist and that was a problem in America in those days. Perhaps he didn't like
5 President Kennedy's policies towards Cuba because at that time the Americans had problems with communist countries like Russia and Cuba.
   Early in 1963 Oswald bought two guns. His wife took a photograph in their garden. On it he wore a black uniform
10 and he held his new guns up in the air.

Kennedy's car after the shots

II The Dallas Police Department

1 Two days after his arrest the police got Oswald out of his cell in the Dallas Police Department. They wanted to take him to another cell. A man called Jack Ruby walked up to Oswald and the policeman.
5 He took a gun out of his pocket and killed Oswald. Millions of Americans saw this on television. Nobody knew how Jack Ruby got into the building ...

The questions

1 There are a lot of questions about President Kennedy's death. Did all the shots come from the big building on Elm Street? Did some of them come from a car park? How many shots were there? Did Oswald act
5 alone? Kennedy was a popular president but some conservative politicians didn't like his ideas. The Mafia didn't want him as a president because he and his brother Robert were very anti-crime. Some people think that Oswald didn't work alone or that he didn't
10 kill the president. They think that a big organisation wanted President Kennedy dead. Was this the Mafia or an anti-Communist group? And why did Jack Ruby kill Oswald? Some people think that Ruby had connections with the Mafia. Others say that he didn't ...
15 What really happened on 22 November 1963? There are still a lot of questions and not many good answers.
(§ 22b, 23, WB Ex 2, 3)

Training

First Step (§ 22b, 23)

True or false?
a) *Read these sentences and give an answer.*

Examples:　　John F. Kennedy and his wife
　　　　　　 came to Dallas.
　　　　　　 – *That's true, they came to Dallas.*

　　　　　　 John F. Kennedy and his family
　　　　　　 came to Houston.
　　　　　　 – *That's false, they didn't come to Houston.*

1. The president and his wife sat in an open sports car.
2. The limousine went past a mountain.
3. A man made a film of the scene.
4. All the shots came from a big building.
5. Kennedy died in Parkland hospital four hours after the shots.

NEW WORD

mountain

b) *All the following information is false; correct the sentences.*

Example:　　Jack Ruby took a gun out of his jacket.
　　　　　　 – *He didn't take a gun out of his jacket, he took a gun out of his pocket.*

1. In 1963 Oswald bought two revolvers.
2. Oswald's wife took a photograph in their house.
3. Oswald wore a red uniform and held his guns in the air.
4. Three days later the police got Oswald out of Alcatraz.
5. Everybody knew how Jack Ruby got into the building.

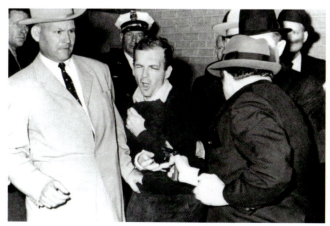

Above: Jack Ruby (right) shoots Lee Harvey Oswald.
Right: Kennedy's funeral

Second Step (§ 23, WB Ex 1, 2)

These verbs are in the past tense.
a) *Find out what the present tense is.*

– became　　– brought
– bought　　– swam
– came　　　– made
– went　　　– wrote
– did　　　　– sat
– fell　　　　– took
– had　　　　– got
– knew　　　– saw

– found　　　– gave
– held　　　 – wore

b) *Use the verbs to form sentences in the past tense.*

Examples:　– *Madonna became a background singer.*
　　　　　　– *My friend didn't bring the workbook.*

Unit 12

First Step

Hinweise/Ideen	• Erster Umgang mit der Vergangenheitsform der starken Verben. Ein Hinweis auf Ähnlichkeiten mit dem Deutschen (*singen – sang / kommen – kam*) kann für den Einstieg hilfreich sein.
	• Da die S nicht umhin kommen, von nun an bei vielen Verben zwei Formen zu lernen, könnte man ein spezielles Vokabelheft *(The Verb Booklet)* anlegen lassen (evtl. mit drei Kolonnen, damit man später das Partizip einfügen kann).
Vorgehen	Übung still vorbereiten lassen und danach überprüfen.
a) Basic	Die S bestätigen zuerst alle richtigen Sätze. Danach verneinen sie die falschen Sätze.
b) Intensive	Die S bereiten sich in PA vor. L ruft die Zahlen 1–5 auf, die S bejahen oder verneinen die Aussagen und stellen entweder die falschen Aussagen gleich richtig oder tun dies in einer zweiten Phase.
Ausbau	• Die S machen weitere Aussagen über den Text, die von der Klasse als richtig oder falsch beurteilt werden.
	• Die Übung schriftlich machen lassen, sodass eine Zusammenfassung des Textes über den Kennedy-Mord entsteht.

Second Step

Hinweise/Ideen	Hier geht es darum, anhand der noch unbekannten Vergangenheitsformen den Infinitiv bereits bekannter Verben zu finden. Diese Übung kann auch als Vorentlastung für ein Detailverständnis der Focustexte verwendet werden.
Ausbau	Kurztexte zu den Verben schreiben oder sprechen lassen.

Erweiterungen

Kopiervorlagen
Verb Training I (7)
Verb Training II (8)
The Past Crossword (12a, b)

Ausbau
S machen Verbkärtchen, die im Lauf des Kurses kontinuierlich ergänzt werden. Variante a: Auf der Vorderseite steht die deutsche Bedeutung, auf der Rückseite das englische Verb mit den drei Formen *infinitive - simple past - participle* (Leerraum für die dritte Form lassen). Variante b: Auf der Vorderseite steht der englische *infinitive*, auf der Rückseite *simple past - participle* (Leerraum lassen). Diese Kärtchen dienen als Lernhilfe und als Vorlage für Spiele.

Verb-Tennis:
S1 zieht eine Karte und liest das Verb, das darauf steht, im Infinitiv vor, S2 muss die korrekte Vergangenheitsform finden, erhält die Karte und zieht die nächste. Ist die Antwort von S2 falsch, so behält S1 die Karte und zieht die nächste. Wer die meisten Karten hat, gewinnt.

Reaktionsspiel:
Klasse und Wandtafel werden geteilt. Eine Anzahl regelmässiger und unregelmässiger Verben werden im *simple past* gleichmässig auf beide Tafelhälften verteilt. L ruft die Grundform eines Verbes. Das Team, in dessen Hälfte das Verb steht, ruft *"we've got it"*. Eine richtige Reaktion gibt einen Punkt, eine falsche einen Abzug für das entsprechende Team.

Student's Book, p.8

Unit 12

Third Step

Vorgehen	Partnerübung (evtl. mit Vorbereitung in EA oder GU)
a) Basic	Bei schwächeren Klassen zuerst die *prompts* besprechen, damit klar ist, dass Sätze ohne Fragewörter mit *did* anfangen und eine *yes/no*-Antwort verlangen. Die Antworten können auch als EA schriftlich gelöst werden (evtl. als Hausaufgabe zur Vorentlastung oder Nachbereitung). Die Dialoge nach der Ausformulierung durchspielen lassen.
b) Intensive	Die S führen ein Interview in ansprechendem Tempo; die Übung eignet sich auch als *milling exercise* (die S wandern im Zimmer umher und befragen sich gegenseitig).

Fourth Step

Hinweise/Ideen	Die Bildergeschichte kann in PA oder GA ausformuliert werden. Gute S können weitere Abenteuer von Secret Agent 009 beschreiben oder sogar als Comic-Projekt bearbeiten.

Erweiterungen

Kopiervorlagen
Question Cards (9)
Verb Diagram (10)

Ausbau
Spiel I: *"Find someone who ..."*
Aufgrund der Fragen im *Third Step* und *WB Ex 6* stellen die S einen Fragebogen zusammen, der nachher als *milling exercise* in der Klasse behandelt wird. Beispielfragen: *Did you come to school before 7 yesterday? Did you have lunch in a restaurant on Sunday?* etc.

Spiel II: *Jig Saw Story*
Die Bildergeschichte im *Fourth Step* ohne Text fotokopieren und die Einzelbilder ausschneiden.
Die S (evtl. in GA) erhalten die Einzelbilder und müssen diese zusammenfügen und die entsprechende Geschichte selber neu formulieren. Dabei kann die Geschichte auch erweitert werden.

Third Step (§ 22, 23, WB Ex 6)

Yesterday ...
Ask your friends questions and let them answer.

Example: Where / sit / your friend / yesterday?
– Where did your friend sit yesterday?
– He sat on the red chair behind the desk.

1. When / come / to school / yesterday?
2. bring / something / for lunch / yesterday?
3. Who / watch TV / yesterday?
4. go / home / during the morning break?
5. Where / have lunch / yesterday?
6. like / your lunch?
7. When / do / your homework?
8. work / at the cinema / after school?

Fourth Step (§ 22, 23)

secret agent, boss, jump (vb. reg.), flight, palace, fall over, famous

Tell the short story.

A Hard Day for Secret Agent 009.

At midnight Secret Agent 009 (get) a phone call from his boss.

After the call 009 (jump) out of bed and into his car.

At one o' clock 009 (be) at the airport and (buy) a ticket for the next flight to Belonia.

In Belonia he (take) a taxi to a big park.

There 009 (give) his friend, Agent 008, a letter with instructions from M., their boss.

10 minutes later the two agents (make) their way to the king's palace.

Near the palace Agent 008 (fall) over something.

009 (look down) and (know) at once: this (be) the work of Black Harry, the famous terrorist.

But Agent 009 always (do) the right thing at the right moment ...

Then he (see) Black Harry and (hit) him on the head.

What a day! 009 (be) very tired when he (come) home.

the End

Stepping Out

Portrait: Lady Diana – "Princess of Wales" (§ 22, 23, 24, WB Ex 7)

Make sentences in the past.

1961   1 July: born near Sandringham, Norfolk, England. She has two older sisters and a younger brother.

1967   Her parents separate; she lives with her father. At school Diana shows a talent for music.

1977   She leaves England and goes to the Institut Alpin Videmanette in Rougemont, Switzerland. After school Di works as a kindergarten teacher in London.

1981   She marries Prince Charles at St.Paul's Cathedral.

1982   She gives birth to Prince William.

1984   She has her second son Prince Henry. Lady Diana does a lot for homeless and disabled people, children and people with AIDS. She visits many Third World countries to help people.

1992   December: Prince Charles and Princess Diana separate.

1995   She gives a television interview where she speaks of her unhappiness in her personal life.

1996   The Prince and Princess of Wales are divorced.

1997   June: Princess Diana speaks at the landmines conferences of the American Red Cross organisation.

31 August: Princess Diana dies in a car accident in Paris. (Her companion Mr Dodi Fayed and the driver of the Mercedes also die; her bodyguard is injured.) Diana is buried on an island in the centre of a lake at Althorp, England.

> **NEW WORDS**
> separate, give birth, homeless, disabled, unhappiness, divorced, landmines, conference, accident, companion, injured, buried, island, lake, wedding

Top to bottom: Diana as a child and at her wedding, Diana with a girl injured by a landmine, Diana's son Prince William

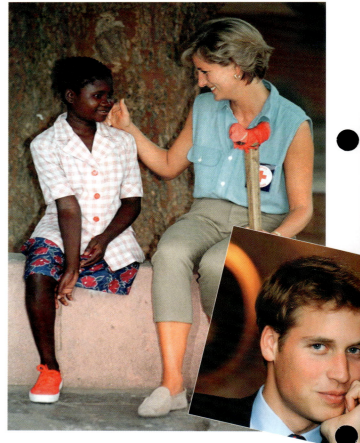

Unit 12

Stepping Out

Hinweise/Ideen	Hier geht es darum, dass die S die Biografie von Princess Diana in der Vergangenheitsform wiedergeben.
Vorgehen	• Die unbekannten Wörter erklären. • Den Text von den S still lesen lassen. • Die S geben den Text mündlich oder schriftlich im *past simple* wieder.
a) Basic	1) Die S lesen das Porträt und schreiben unbekannte Wörter an die WT. Diese werden nachher in der Klasse besprochen (wenn möglich einsprachig). 2) Die S schreiben in PA oder GA den stichwortartigen Lebenslauf um, indem sie daraus ganze Sätze im *past simple* machen. 3) Die Texte werden in der Klasse vorgelesen oder in *cross-group reporting* mit anderen Gruppen verglichen. Korrektur zuerst durch die S, erst in letzter Instanz durch L.
b) Intensive	Nach dem Lesen in EA bereiten die S in PA eine mündliche Präsentation von Dianas Leben vor. Möglicherweise Niederschrift als EA oder Hausaufgabe.
Ausbau	Im Vortrag werden absichtlich inhaltliche Fehler eingebaut. Der Rest der Klasse muss diese finden und richtigstellen. Somit wird nochmals die Verneinung geübt.

Erweiterungen

Kopiervorlagen
The Club of Dead Rock'n'Roll Stars (13)

Ausbau
1) Hotseat
Jemand aus der Klasse verkörpert in einem Interview Diana oder einen Journalisten, der ihre Lebensgeschichte geschrieben hat. Die Klasse stellt Fragen anhand des Porträts.

2) Die S schreiben einen freien Text über Diana. (Wer kann zusätzliche Informationen beisteuern?)

Variante 1: Die S schreiben einen Text aufgrund folgender Reizwörter (oder einer Auswahl davon): *AIDS, Althorp, Charles, landmines, Paris, Prince William, Sandringham, St Paul's Cathedral, second son, separation, Switzerland, unhappiness.*
Variante 2: L gibt eine Liste mit Verben aus dem Text vor. Die S schreiben dazu Sätze zu Dianas Biografie.

3) Collage (siehe auch WB Ex 8)
Die S stellen in PA oder GA eine Collage mit Bildern einer Berühmtheit ihrer Wahl zusammen und stellen diese mündlich anhand der Bilder in einem Kurzvortrag der Klasse vor.

Student's Book, p. 10

Unit 12

Reading Corner

Hinweise/Ideen Der *Reading Corner* ist als Leseecke für interessierte S gedacht. Aus diesem Grund gilt für alle Texte dieser Rubrik:
1. Das Vokabular ist lehrbuchunabhängig und wird später *nicht* vorausgesetzt.
2. Die Texte basieren auf authentischen Vorlagen. Die S sollen lernen, diese Texte sinngemäss zu erfassen.
3. Sie sind nicht obligatorisch.

Möglichkeiten Text in EA lesen lassen.
Die S formulieren Verständnisfragen und fragen einander in PA ab.
Die S suchen zu spezifischen Themen weitere Informationen, z.B. geografische Informationen zu den *Confederate States*, Informationen zum Sezessionskrieg, zur Sklaverei in den Südstaaten und zu den Bewegungen zur Abschaffung der Sklaverei (Abolitionismus).

Erweiterungen

Video/DVD zur Geschichte des Sezessionskrieges und der Sklaverei, z.B. *Gone with the Wind*, *Uncle Tom's Cabin* oder Buster Keaton's *The General*

Reading Corner

Abraham Lincoln, another murdered president

John F. Kennedy was the fourth president killed during his presidency. The first was Abraham Lincoln. On 14 April 1865 John Wilkes Booth, an actor, shot Lincoln in the back of the head. A day later Lincoln died.

John Wilkes Booth was a famous actor at that time. He was from the Southern States and hated Lincoln and his political ideas. With some of his friends he wanted to kidnap the president during a visit to a hospital, but Lincoln didn't come to the hospital as planned.

Why did the Southerner Wilkes Booth hate Lincoln so much?

The background: slavery and the war between the South and the North

In 1861, one month after Lincoln became president, a war broke out between the South and the North. The Southern States (Alabama, Arkansas, Florida, Georgia, Louisiana, Mississippi, North Carolina, South Carolina, Tennessee, Texas and Virginia) wanted to form a separate state, the Confederate States of America (CSA). They didn't want to be part of the United States of America (USA) any more.

The reason for this war was slavery. The government of the United States wanted to make slavery illegal. But for the big plantations and farms in the South, slavery was very important. The white masters on these farms and plantations held large numbers of black people as slaves and they bought and sold them, very much like farm animals. Some of these white masters had sexual relationships with black women, and the women had children from their white bosses. There were whites who beat their black slaves or even killed them, because they thought a black life wasn't worth very much.

Of course, not all the white masters were brutal monsters. On some of the farms the slaves had to work hard, but they had a home and they had religion. Therefore people in the South thought that there was nothing wrong with slavery: blacks were there to work, they were not much more than animals, not intelligent and very primitive.

You can read about slavery in the South in a famous book called "Uncle Tom's Cabin" by Harriet Beecher Stowe. The book came out in 1852. It played an important role in the history of slavery in America. The people in the North were shocked when they read about the life of the slaves in the South. They wanted the Southern masters to free their slaves.

Abraham Lincoln was against slavery. When he became president, the Southern States knew that Lincoln would do everything to stop slavery in the United States of America. Therefore they wanted to form a separate state with a separate law.

Lincoln's death

On 9 April 1865 the South capitulated. Lincoln said that he wanted to make peace with the South and to be president of a united nation.

Five days later, on 14 April he went to the theatre with his wife and some friends. It was a comedy called "An American Cousin". There his killer, the actor John Wilkes Booth, waited for him. As always Lincoln sat in the president's box. When the officer in front of the box went for a drink, Booth waited until the people in the theatre laughed because of a joke. Then he opened the door of the box, got behind Lincoln and shot him. After that he jumped over three metres down onto the stage and ran away. As an actor he knew the theatre well and found his way out.

Lincoln died the next day. Booth tried to get away, but the police found him. He died in a gun fight with the police.

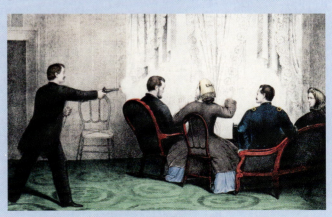

John Wilkes Booth shoots President Lincoln in the theatre

Lincoln and Kennedy

Can a history teacher explain all this?

Abraham Lincoln became a member of Congress in 1846.

John F. Kennedy became a member of Congress in 1946.

Abraham Lincoln became president in 1860.
John F. Kennedy became president in 1960.

In both names, Lincoln and Kennedy, there are seven letters.

Both wives lost a child while they lived in the White House.

Both murders were on a Friday.

Both killers shot the presidents in the head.

Both killers came from the South of the USA.

Lincoln's secretary was called Kennedy.
Kennedy's secretary was called Lincoln.

A man called Johnson became president after Lincoln.
A man called Johnson became president after Kennedy.

Andrew Johnson, the president after Lincoln, was born in 1808.
Lyndon Johnson, the president after Kennedy, was born in 1908.

John Wilkes Booth, the killer of President Lincoln, was born in 1839.
Lee Harvey Oswald, the killer of President Kennedy, was born in 1939.

Both killers had three names.

Lincoln was shot in a theatre called 'Kennedy'.
Kennedy was shot in a car called 'Lincoln'.

Booth ran from a theatre. The police caught him in a warehouse.

Oswald ran from a warehouse. The police caught him in a theatre.

Unit 12

Hinweise siehe vorhergehende Seite.

Hinweise siehe vorhergehende Seite.

Student's Book, p. 12

Warm-up

What's Going On?

Einstimmungsbilder In diesem Kapitel geht es um das *present progressive,* die Verlaufsform in der Gegenwart. Mit Hilfe der Fotos kann die Verwendung der Form eingeführt werden, bevor man zum Focus-Text übergeht. Die Form selbst ist aus RfE Band 1, Unit 10, bereits bekannt.

Warm-up

Hinweise/Ideen
- Mit der Klasse besprechen, was es auf den Bildern zu sehen gibt.
- Die Verben an die WT schreiben (lassen) oder im Brainstorming sammeln:
  He's riding a motorbike. She's eating an ice cream. He's riding a mountain bike. She's swimming in the pool. She's feeding animals / kangaroos. He's riding a horse. He's selling drinks. They're playing music. Some people are dancing.

Ausbau
- Handlungsabläufe im Schulzimmer vorführen lassen und kommentieren.
- Die Beispiele an der WT sammeln.
  What are you doing now? Oh, you're sitting on your chairs / in the English class. I'm standing in front of the class. Now I'm writing on the blackboard. Can you open the window, please? Look, Marc is opening the window. He isn't opening the door.

Bemerkung   Das *present progressive* wird im Englischen nicht so häufig gebraucht, wie dies traditionelle Kurse suggerieren, vor allem nicht in dieser Form (eine soeben ablaufende Handlung beschreiben). In der Alltagssprache wird es viel häufiger verwendet, um über Pläne und Vorhaben in der Zukunft zu sprechen (siehe RfE Band 1, Unit 10).
Um zu verhindern, dass die S die Verlaufsform überall dort verwenden, wo man im Deutschen einen Satz in der Gegenwart findet (ein Fehler, den Fremdsprachige häufig begehen), wird das *present progressive* daher erst hier eingeführt.

What's Going On?

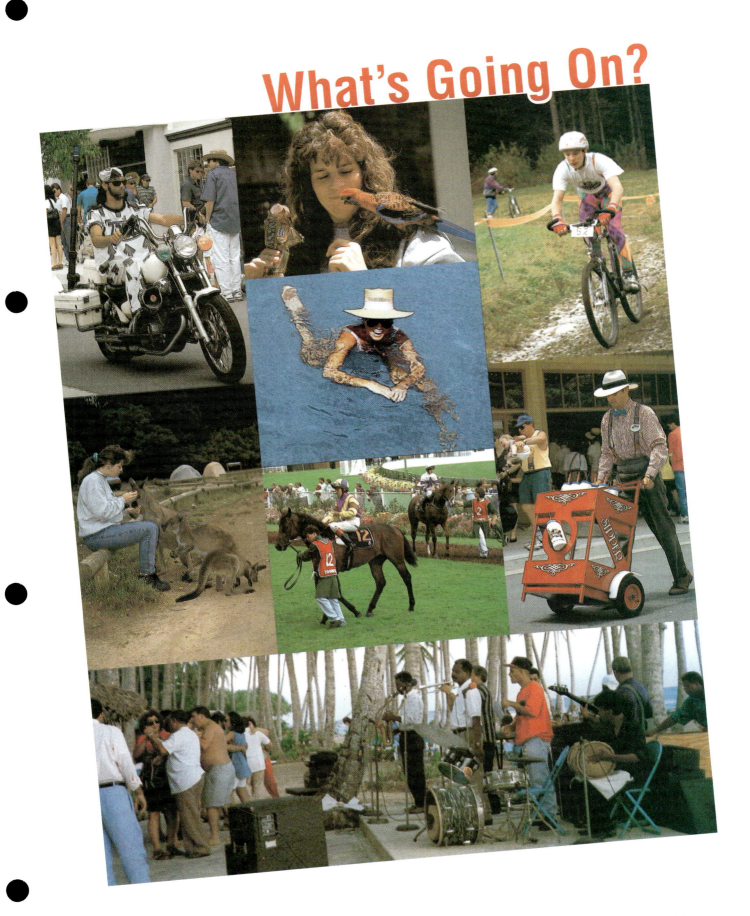

Unit 13 Focus

A School Fete

I Let's dance

1 Hello and welcome to the Bedford Park School Fete.
It isn't raining any more, it's clearing up and the sun is shining. It looks like a nice day, doesn't it?
So what's going on? The school band is playing. A lot of
5 people are listening to the music and they're having a really good time. But there aren't many people dancing yet.
So go over there, have a good time and DANCE!
And please don't forget our coffee shop. At the moment
10 some people are sitting at the tables in front of the coffee shop and only a few people are waiting in the queue.
Are you hungry? Go over there and eat something. There aren't any hot meals but Christina and Tony have got a lot of sandwiches and ice creams too, in many different fla-

1 vours. Is there anything else? Oh, yes, they are selling home-made cakes, too. They're something special!
Go and taste them!
Or is anybody thirsty? Our sixth formers Cathy and
5 Brian aren't serving any alcoholic drinks, but there are a lot of different fruit juices and there is tea.
Wait a minute! Two boys are smoking behind the toilet. Stop it right there, boys!
By the way, Greg and Sharon are taking pictures.
10 So smile!
And what is going on in the sports field? Some people over there are laughing and making a lot of noise.
Ah yes, the three girl finalists are running the 80 m race and Danny, our school champion is riding his
15 bicycle over the first part of the obstacle course ...
(§ 25a, 25b, 27)

Unit 13

Sprachfunktionen:	Themen:
Beschreiben, was gerade vor sich geht	Festivitäten, Wetter, Esswaren
Strukturen:	**Mögliche Abfolge:**
Verlaufsform der Gegenwart (bejahend, verneint und Frageform) *a lot of, much, many*	Focus I → First Step → Second Step → Third Step → WB Ex 1, 2, (Fourth Step, WB Ex 3, WB Ex 4) → (Focus II) → WB Ex 5 → (Fifth Step) Stepping Out → WB Ex 6 → (WB Ex 7, 8)
Grammatik:	
§ 25, § 27	

Focus I: Let's dance!

Hinweise/Ideen — Über Lautsprecher werden die Ereignisse eines Schulfestes für die Besucher kommentiert. Dieser Text sollte daher von den S zuerst nur übers Ohr aufgenommen werden. Nebst dem *present progressive* enthält dieser Focustext auch die unbestimmten Mengenangaben *a lot of* und *many* (*much* kommt im Focus II vor). Darauf soll aber in der Einführungsphase noch nicht explizit eingegangen werden.

Material — CD, OHP-Folie

Vorgehen — Hören und (mit Bildvorlage) verstehen.
Den Inhalt beim ersten Durchgang global erfassen.

Variante I
1. Hörtext abspielen und parallel dazu die Handlungen im Bild auf der Folie vorzeigen oder durch die S zeigen lassen.
2. Die S lesen den Text ruhig und bearbeiten in EA/PA die Kopiervorlage *True or false?* zum globalen Textverständnis. Die KV kann auch als Folie aufgelegt werden.
3. Die Lösungen werden im GU präsentiert.
4. Die Aussprache des ganzen Textes üben (Nachsprechen in verschiedenen Unterrichtsformen, evtl. Walkman/Discman einsetzen).
5. Die S simulieren die Rolle des Platzsprechers und lesen den Text laut in PA/GA vor, wobei die S sich gegenseitig bei der Aussprache kontrollieren und korrigieren.

Variante II — Den Inhalt beim ersten Durchgang vollständig erfassen.
1. Folie auflegen und Fragen stellen (siehe KV *Questions and Answers*).
2. Hörtext abspielen.
3. Den Text mit dem Buch erarbeiten und festigen. (Die S lesen den Text in EA ruhig durch und notieren unverständliches Vokabular, schwierig auszusprechende Strukturen werden an der WT notiert).
4. Im GU das Vokabular klären und die Strukturen einüben.
5. Leseübung (EA/PA): Die S üben die Rolle des Platzsprechers.

Bemerkung — Für die Stufe *basic* genügt es, auf die Varianten *a lot of* und *many* hinzuweisen, ohne auf die Differenzierung (§ 27) einzugehen. Bei der Stufe *intensive* wird im Focustext II *At the coffee shop* auf die unterschiedliche Verwendung von *a lot of, many* und *much* eingegangen, man kann aber schon hier die Beispiele besprechen.

Erweiterungen

Kopiervorlagen
A School Fete (14)
Check Your Vocabulary (15)
Questions and Answers (16a, b)
True or False (17)

Folie
Nr. 3

Student's Book, p. 14

Unit 13

Focus II: At the coffee shop

Hinweise/Ideen	Das Interview des Reporters sollte als Radioreportage zuerst übers Ohr aufgenommen werden, bevor die S den Text aufschlagen und mitlesen. Zentrales Thema in diesem Text sind die unbestimmten Mengenangaben *a lot of/many/much*.
Material	CD/Folie
Vorgehen Variante I	Hörverständnisübung. Einführung der unbestimmten Mengenangaben mit Hilfe des Textes. 1. Den Hörtext abspielen und die Folie dazu auflegen. 2. Den Hörtext nochmals abspielen und dabei nach jeder Rolle kurz anhalten, um unbekanntes Vokabular zu erläutern. 3. Den Text mit den S im Buch durchgehen und die Aussprache üben. (Nachsprechen in verschiedenen Unterrichtsformen, evtl. Walkman/Discman einsetzen). 4. Gegenüberstellung der unbestimmten Mengenangaben an der WT. (Siehe dazu Grammatik § 27; WB Ex. 5). Als Hilfe kann auch die Folie benutzt werden, indem man anhand der Auslage des *coffee shop* auf die zählbaren und unzählbaren Nomen hinweist: *bread, a loaf of bread; milk, a bottle of milk; cake, a piece of cake etc.*
Variante II	1. Mit der Folie das Thema einführen *(What can you see? What are they doing?)* und die unbestimmten Mengenangaben *a lot of, many* und *much* erarbeiten *(a lot of pupils in the queue ..., not many bottles of milk on the table ..., not much milk in the bottles ...)*. 2. Den Hörtext abspielen. 3. Die S lesen den Text im Buch still nach und erarbeiten das neue Vokabular selbstständig. 4. Die Aussprache üben (Nachsprechen in verschiedenen Unterrichtsformen, evtl. Walkman/Discman einsetzen). 5. Die unbestimmten Mengenangaben mit der Grammatik und mit den Übungen im WB festigen (§ 27/WB Ex. 5) Als Hilfe kann auch die Folie benutzt werden, indem man anhand der Auslage des *coffee shop* auf die zählbaren und unzählbaren Nomen hinweist: *bread, a loaf of bread; milk, a bottle of milk; cake, a piece of cake etc.*

Erweiterungen

Kopiervorlagen	**Folie**
Dialogue Snap (18)	Nr. 4

II At the coffee shop

1 Reporter: Now, here we are at Christina and Tony's coffee shop. Christina, how is business?
Christina: We're doing fine. Look at the queue!
Tony is just making some fresh sandwiches.
5 Hey, Tony, don't put so much butter on the bread!
Tony: OK, OK. There isn't much bread left, anyway.
Christina: Of course, there is. It's over there.
Two loaves of brown bread and one big loaf
10 of white bread.
Reporter: I can see you've got a lot to do and not much time for an interview. Is there anything important you'd like to say?
Christina: Well, yes. Hello everybody! We've still got
15 a lot of fruit cake and some apple pie.
There isn't much chocolate cake left,
I'm afraid, but you can have chocolate-chip biscuits. Or you can try one of Tony's sandwiches in a minute. So, come to the
20 coffee shop, sit down and have a cup of tea or coffee, or a milkshake ...
Tony: Christina, there isn't much milk left, so they can't have any milk shakes or milk in their tea ...
25 Christina: Tony! There are five bottles of milk right behind you! ... Really!
Reporter: Yes, well ... I can see business is going well for Christina and Tony. They're a great team. Thanks for the interview.

(§ 27, WB Ex 5)

Training

First Step (§ 25)

You are at the school fete. Look at the pictures and tell your partner what you can see.

Example: — A man is eating an ice cream.

Second Step (§ 25)

Here is another picture of the school fete at Bedford Park. What is different? Ask your partner and find out.

Example: — Is the sun shining?
— No, it isn't (shining).

— Are the girls running the 80 m race?
— Yes, they are (running the 80 m race).

USE

dance, have, listen, make, play, run, sell, serve, sit, wait, smoke, take pictures, laugh, ride

Unit 13

Unit 13

First Step

Hinweise/Ideen Ziel: Die Verlaufsform mündlich anwenden.

Vorgehen Partnerübung: **S1** spricht, **S2** kontrolliert (übernimmt die Rolle der *language police*).

Variante I **S1** spricht, **S2** zeigt auf die entsprechende Person oder Personengruppe: *That's him/her/them* (Repetition der Personalpronomen).

Variante II **S1** spricht und **S2** antwortet mit Zusatzinformation. **S1**: *A man is eating an ice cream.* **S2**: *Oh yes, that is the man with the red cap.*

Variante III **S1** und **S2** sprechen abwechslungsweise, wobei es keine langen Pausen geben sollte (**S2** überlegt sich – während **S1** spricht – bereits den eigenen nächsten Satz).

Second Step

Hinweise/Ideen Üben der Verlaufsform durch einen Bildvergleich (Bild S. 14 und S. 16).

Vorgehen Partnerarbeit: **S1** hat das Bild zum Focustext (S. 14) vor sich, **S2** das Bild zum Second Step (S. 16). Die **S** fragen einander, wie sich die Aktivitäten der Personen auf den beiden Bildern unterscheiden.

Variante I **S1** stellt möglichst viele Fragen hintereinander, **S2** reagiert mit Kurzantworten.
S1: *Is the sun shining?* **S2**: *No, it isn't.*
S1: *Are the boys smoking behind the toilet?* **S2**: *No, they aren't.*
S1: *Is the school band playing?* **S2**: *Yes, it is.*

Variante II **S1** stellt eine Frage, **S2** antwortet und fragt direkt zurück.
S1: *Is the sun shining?* **S2**: *No, it isn't. Is the man in front of the band taking a picture?*
S1: *No, he isn't. Are the pupils dancing?* **S2**: *No, they aren't. Is a girl eating an ice cream?*

Variante III Statt Kurzantworten liefern die **S** ausformulierte Antworten:
No, the sun isn't shining, it is raining.

Erweiterungen

Ausbau
Memory: Die **S** betrachten das Bild zum *Training Second Step* während etwa 2 Minuten.
Nachher wird das Bild zum Focustext auf S. 14 als Folie aufgelegt. Die **S** nennen so viele Unterschiede wie möglich (oder schreiben sie auf).

Student's Book, p. 16

Unit 13

Third Step

Hinweise/Ideen	Die S bilden in EA/PA aus den vorgegebenen *prompts* vollständige Sätze. Bei eher leistungsschwachen Klassen kann diese Übung zur Vorentlastung als Hausaufgabe schriftlich gelöst werden.
Vorgehen	Bei der Übung a nicht nur mit den *prompts* Sätze formulieren, sondern auch Fragen stellen: *What is John drinking? He is drinking a glass of water.*
	Bei der Übung b ordnen die S in PA/GA die *prompts* den entsprechenden Bildern zu und bilden Sätze im *present progressive*.
	Bei der Übung c ordnen die S alle Posten aus a und b nach eigenem Gutdünken und reportieren.
Lösung b)	*John is riding his bicycle around the black box.* *John is jumping over the chair.* *John is climbing over the wall.* *John is trying to catch three balloons.* *John is writing his name on the poster.* *John is running across the finishing line.*

Erweiterungen

Kopiervorlagen
What Are You Doing? (19)
Verb Training (20)

Folie
Nr. 5

Ausbau
Zu Übung c: Die S lesen ihre Version als Reportage vor, der Rest der Klasse skizziert oder zeichnet den Parcours oder bringt die kopierten, einzeln ausgeschnittenen Bilder aufgrund der Reportage in die richtige Reihenfolge.
Die S bauen in PA/GA einen Hindernislauf in einer ihnen sinnvoll erscheinenden Abfolge von Posten (in der Turnhalle) und reportieren.

Zum *present progressive:* Die S stellen pantomimisch Handlungen dar, der Rest der Klasse versucht, den zugehörigen Satz im *present progressive* zu bilden (evtl. als Team-Spiel).

get / his bicycle

drink / a glass of water

sit / on the red chair

get / ready for the race

carry / his bicycle along the red line

eat / three biscuits

Third Step (§ 25, WB Ex 1, 2, 4)

What is John doing?

a) You are a reporter. Use the prompts under the pictures to make a report about the obstacle race.

Example: get ready / for the race
– John is getting ready for the race.

b) Look at the pictures below and make sentences.

... his bicycle around the black box
... over the chair
... over the wall
... to catch three balloons
... his name on the poster
... across the finishing line

USE
climb, jump, ride, run,
try, write

box, balloon, climb, finishing line, poster

c) Create another obstacle course.
Use the prompts to make a report about it.
Start again with:

– John is getting ready for the race. He's ...

Fourth Step (§ 25, WB Ex 3)

Listen to the CD. Which sound is which?

a) Someone's taking a photo.
b) Someone's reading the paper.
c) A girl's getting up.
d) Someone is cleaning a window.
e) Someone is opening an umbrella.
f) A woman is singing in the shower.
g) A baby is laughing.
h) Someone is cutting a piece of paper.
i) Someone is eating corn flakes.
j) Someone is chewing gum.
k) A man is laughing.

Now do Ex 3 in the Workbook.

NEW WORDS

tape, sound, someone, paper, clean (vb.), shower (vb.), cut (vb.)

Fifth Step

Here is an interview with the head teacher at Bedford Park. There were some problems with the tape. Listen to the interview and try to complete it.

– Excuse —. Can I ask you — questions?
– Yes, of —.
– How — people were there at — fete?
– Oh, I — know the number, but — were a —. I — about 250 to 300.
– — visited the fete?
– Oh, there were the — of our school, of course, their parents and also — brothers and sisters.
– Did you have — problems during the fete?
– Oh, this year we — very lucky. There weren't — problems. We just had a — phone calls because of the loud music...
– Thank you very — for the interview.
– It was a —.

Unit 13

Fourth Step

Vorgehen
1. Die Sätze mit der Klasse lesen und die neuen Wörter erklären.
2. CD abspielen. Die S ordnen die Sätze in PA/GA den Geräuschen zu.
3. CD ein zweites Mal abspielen. Die S ordnen die Geräusche in EA im WB Ex 3 zu.
4. Die Geräusche werden nochmals eingespielt und die S präsentieren die Lösungen. Dabei verwenden sie das *present progressive: Here someone's taking a photo. I think a man is laughing here. ...*

Lösung
1) k
2) i
3) e (braucht etwas Fantasie)
4) f
5) h
6) j
7) d
8) a
9) b
10) c
11) g

Fifth Step

Hinweise/Ideen
Die S sollen aus dem lückenhaften Interview einen sinnvollen Text herstellen, indem sie die unverständlichen Stellen ergänzen. Wichtig ist dabei, dass die S das Interview zuerst hören und erst danach mit der Textvorlage arbeiten.

Vorgehen
Das Interview als Hörübung abspielen und danach den Lückentext ergänzen lassen.

a) Basic
1. Die S hören das Interview *ohne* Textvorlage. Was fällt ihnen beim ersten Abspielen auf? Welche Informationen bekommen sie allenfalls mit?
2. Das Interview *mit* Textvorgabe Satz für Satz nochmals abspielen. Die S überlegen sich dabei, was in den Lücken stehen könnte.
3. Die S diskutieren in PA/GA ihre Varianten.
4. Mögliche Lösungen werden im GU geliefert.
5. Zur Festigung wird das Interview in PA gelesen und ev. geschrieben.

b) Intensive
1. Die S hören das Interview *ohne* Textvorlage mit der Aufgabe, Fragen bzw. Antworten herauszuhören. Dies kann auch als GA gelöst werden, wobei sich eine Gruppe auf die Fragen konzentriert, eine andere auf kurze Antworten, eine weitere auf die beiden Schlusssätze und sehr gute S auf die Informationen in längeren Sätzen.
2. Lösungen und Vermutungen an der WT sammeln.
3. Das Interview nochmals abspielen, diesmal Satz für Satz; die S liefern (in PA/GA/GU) sinnvolle Ergänzungen zur Vervollständigung der Sätze.
4. Mit der Textvorlage vergleichen und die Lücken ergänzen.
5. Das Interview wird in PA gelesen.

Lösung
Excuse me. Can I ask you a few questions?
Yes, of course.
How many people were there at the fete?
Oh, I don't know the number, but there were a lot. I think about 250 to 300.
Who visited the fete?
Oh, there were the pupils of our school, of course, their parents and also their brothers and sisters.
Did you have any problems during the fete?
Oh, this year we were very lucky. There weren't any problems. We just had a few phone calls because of the loud music.
Thank you very much for the interview.
It was a pleasure.

Erweiterungen

Kopiervorlagen
What Are You Doing? (19)
Verb Training (20)

Ausbau Fourth Step
L oder Gruppen von S nehmen Geräusche auf (oder imitieren sie). Die übrigen S versuchen herauszufinden, worum es sich handelt. Wichtig ist, dass die Lösungen als Sätze im *present progressive* präsentiert werden (siehe oben).

Student's Book, p. 18

Unit 13

Stepping Out

Hinweise/Ideen Die S sollen die Wetterkarten mit Hilfe der Piktogramme interpretieren.
Mit den Piktogrammen wird auch das neue Vokabular erschlossen, sodass man ohne Übersetzungen auskommen sollte. (Selbstverständlich kann man in leistungsschwachen Klassen zur Kontrolle die Vokabeln übersetzen lassen.)
Bei dieser Übung geht es darum, den *aktuellen* Wetterbericht für die einzelnen Orte zu erstellen, also Sätze im *present progressive* zu machen.

Material OHP-Folie

Mögliche Einstimmung
1) Wetterbericht einer englischsprachigen Fernsehstation auf Video aufnehmen und der Klasse vorführen. Bei leistungsstarken Klassen auf die Informationen eingehen und auf diese Weise einen Teil des Vokabulars einführen.
2) Klassengespräch über das Wetter: *What's the weather like today? Is it hot? What do you think the weather is like in Australia/in Hawaii ....?*

Vorgehen
1. Die Wettersymbole und die *expressions for the weather* mit den entsprechenden Piktogrammen (Folie) besprechen.
2. Die S bilden Sätze nach der Vorgabe im SB (EA/PA/GU).

Mögliche Lösungen
Australia (December): It's hot in Alice Springs and the sun is shining. In Perth it is cloudy and the temperature is 22° Celsius, strong winds are blowing from the south. ... It is summer in Australia.

New Zealand (July): It's freezing in Alexandra, the temperature is minus 1° Celsius and it is snowing. .... It is winter in New Zealand.

Great Britain (October): It's warm in Edinburgh, the temperature is 15° Celsius. In London it's cloudy and it's raining. ... It is autumn in Great Britain.

USA (March): It's hot in Los Angeles and the sun is shining, but in Chicago it is cold and it's raining. ... It is the beginning of spring in the USA.

Bemerkung Achtung! Bei jedem Wetterbericht muss den S vermittelt werden, dass sie mitten im Geschehen sind. Also: *It is December and we are in Australia. What is the weather like?* Auf keinen Fall dürfen Sätze entstehen wie "im Dezember scheint in Sydney die Sonne und die Temperatur beträgt 20 Grad", da in diesem Fall das *present simple* verwendet werden müsste.

Erweiterungen

Folie
Nr. 6

Ausbau
Anhand von Atlanten, englischsprachigen Zeitungen oder Satellitenbildern aus dem Internet bereiten die S selber einen Wetterbericht vor und tragen dies der Klasse vor.

Die andern S schreiben auf, wie das Wetter an den präsentierten Orten aussieht. Achtung! Nur das aktuelle Wetter soll vorgestellt werden – keine Prognosen, da man sonst das Futur verwenden müsste.

Umrechnung
Fahrenheit in Celsius: [(Fahrenheit - 32) : 9] x 5

Stepping Out

The Weather Across the World (WB Ex 6, 7)

Here are some expressions for the weather:
- 🟥 It's hot.
- 🟨 It's warm.
- 🟩 It's cold.
- 🟦 It's freezing.

- ☀ The sun is shining.
- 🌧 It's raining.
- 🌨 It's snowing.
- ☁ It's cloudy.
- 〰➤ Winds are blowing from the east/south/west/north.

Look at the maps and form sentences like this:
Examples:
Australia (December): *It's hot in Alice Springs and the sun is shining.*
New Zealand (July): *It's freezing in Alexandra and ...*
Great Britain (October): *It's warm in Edinburgh ...*
USA (March): *It's hot in...*

blow, cloudy, cold, east, freezing, north, snow (vb.), south, warm, weather, west, wind

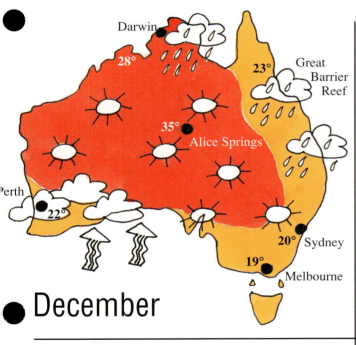

December

July

October

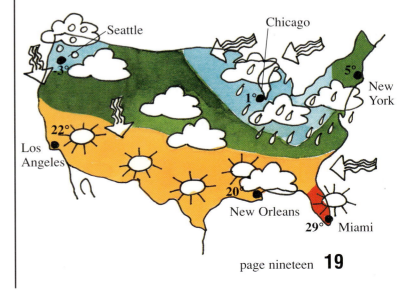

March

Unit 14 Focus

A Dream About New Zealand

Last night I had a dream …

1 I don't usually remember my dreams but I remember this one. I think a lot of things in my dream were wrong. But what are things in New Zealand really like? Can you help?

5 **Here's my dream:**
I'm sitting on the back of a Kiwi. We are flying over two big islands and a lot of small ones. It looks like a volcanic wonderland. There are a lot of craters and some
10 springs are boiling.
Where are we going, I wonder? The bird says: "Welcome to New Zealand. In five minutes we are landing in Dunedin, the capital. Its name is a combination of the two Scottish cities Dundee and
15 Edinburgh."
Now we are flying over a beach. A lot of people are lying in the sun. On the beach there are also some dogs. They are wearing straw hats and sunglasses. Some also have green cream on their noses.
20 "Dogs very often wear hats and sunglasses because of the sun," the bird says. "The green cream protects their noses. The ozone layer is very thin here, you see."
Now the Kiwi is landing on the beach. A man is coming towards us. He is holding a fish in his hands.
25 "This is Hohepa or Joseph in English. He's a Maori," says the Kiwi. What's happening? Hohepa is rubbing noses with me.
"That's normal," says the Kiwi, "Maoris usually rub noses when they say hello. It's called 'hongi'. And they dive into
30 the water and catch fish just with their hands. Isn't that clever? You know, some Maoris speak two languages. One is English, the other one is their old language, quite an interesting one. In Maori New Zealand is called Aotearoa: Land of the Big White Cloud. And there is a
35 Maori place name with 84 letters. That's a very long one, isn't it?"

Taumatawhakatangihangakoauauotamateaturipukaka

Unit 14

Sprachfunktionen:	Themen:
Gegenüberstellung der einfachen Gegenwart und der Verlaufsform; Beschreiben, was immer so ist bzw. was gerade vor sich geht	Reisen (Neuseeland), Alltagsgepflogenheiten, Fantasie und Realität
Strukturen:	**Mögliche Abfolge:**
Einfache Gegenwart und Verlaufsform der Gegenwart; die unbestimmten Pronomen *one/ones*	Focus → First Step → WB Ex 1 (2) → Second Step → WB Ex 3 → (Third Step) → Fourth Step → WB Ex 4 → (Fifth Step) → (WB Ex 5) → Stepping Out → (Reading Corner) → (WB Ex 6)
Grammatik:	
§ 26, 28	

Focus: A Dream About New Zealand

Bemerkung	Der Unterschied zwischen *present progressive* und *simple present* kann auch vorgängig mit den Fotos der Einstimmungsseite (SB, S. 13/ Folie Nr. 2) eingeführt werden: 1. Was spielt sich auf den Bildern ab? Beispiel: *Today, he's going to town on his motorbike.* 2. Was tun die Personen normalerweise? Beispiel: *Normally he goes by bus.*
Hinweise/Ideen	• Es handelt sich beim Focustext um einen Traum von einer ungewöhnlichen Reise nach Neuseeland. Der Text enthält Fehlinformationen über Neuseeland, welche die S herausfinden sollten (siehe SB, *Training First Step*, S. 22). • Einstimmung: L/S tragen Informationen zu Neuseeland zusammen. Den S sollte vorgängig klar sein, dass ein Kiwi eine Vogelart ist und dass Neuseeland aus Inseln besteht. Andere Angaben können sie sich z.T. mit Hilfe der Fotos im Buch zusammenreimen.
Material	CD, OHP-Folie
Vorgehen	Auch bei leistungsstarken Klassen empfiehlt es sich nicht, beide Textteile auf einmal einzuführen. Nach Zeile 36 sollte man unterbrechen. 1. Die S lesen still den Text (auch als vorgängige Hausaufgabe geeignet) oder hören ihn und lesen dabei mit. Sie haben den Auftrag, auf mögliche Fehlinformationen (was ist Traum, was Realität?) zu achten. 2. Die Bilder als Hilfe für die korrekten Aussagen zu Neuseeland beiziehen. Die S suchen dazu Textstellen, welche den Bildern entsprechen: *New Zealand looks like a volcanic wonderland. Maoris usually rub noses, when they say hello.* 3. Lösungen diskutieren. (Training *First Step*, S. 22, kann später in PA als Repetition eingesetzt werden.) 4. Vokabular erarbeiten: Die S schreiben unbekannte Wörter an die WT. 5. Lese- und Ausspracheübung der neuen Wörter, inhaltliche Festigung des Textes.

Erweiterungen

Kopiervorlagen	**Folie**
Fill in the Gaps (21a, b)	Nr. 7

Student's Book, p. 20

Unit 14

Hinweise/Ideen Vorgehen wie im ersten Teil. Es sollte unbedingt vermieden werden, den Text Satz um Satz anzugehen, da beim ersten Durchgang ein sinngemässes Verstehen genügt. Die Bilder tragen wiederum zum Verstehen bei.

Material CD, OHP-Folie

Erweiterungen

Kopiervorlagen	Folie
Fill in the Gaps (21a, b)	Nr. 7

1 Hohepa has got a "motopaika". That's the Maori word for motorbike.
I'm sitting on the back seat, Hohepa is driving it – on the left. "Don't worry, in New Zealand we drive on
5 the left," says the Kiwi. He is still flying over our heads.
As we are travelling along we see thousands of sheep. "There were about 12 sheep per person in 1999," says
10 the bird.
Oh, I need some money. There is a bank by the side of the road. The bank clerk looks very strange, I think: he is wearing a shirt and tie with – shorts and socks, white ones. He is very friendly: "Here are
15 your New Zealand pounds. Have a nice time in New Zealand, eh."
"This is very typical," says the Kiwi, "we often say 'eh' and bankers usually wear shorts in summer."
Now I'm flying on the back of the Kiwi again.
20 There is a skyscraper under us. Some people are jumping off ... and they survive!
"This is called rap jumping. A lot of tourists come here to walk down the walls," the bird says.
"Watch out! Two people are flying towards us!"
25 I shout.
"No problem, they are just paragliding," the Kiwi laughs, "don't you like tandem flights?"

Just then I hear a voice. "Come down Sheila, you're late for school …!"

(§ 26, 28, WB Ex 1, 2, 5)

Training

First Step (Focus)

a) Facts or a dream?

Of course, you can't sit on a Kiwi and fly. That is part of the dream.
What do you think is true? Ask questions and make a list of the facts.

Example: New Zealand looks like a volcanic wonderland.
– Does New Zealand look like a volcanic wonderland?
– Yes, I think that's true.

1. Kiwis can fly.
2. The name of the capital of New Zealand is Dunedin.
3. There are beaches in New Zealand.
4. Dogs often wear straw hats and sunglasses because of the sun.
5. Maoris speak two languages.
6. Maoris catch fish with their hands.

What else does the text say about New Zealand? Look at the information in the text and make sentences. What is true?

8. In New Zealand cars (and motorbikes) ...
9. Sheep: There were 12 ...
10. Bankers usually ...
11. Money: In New Zealand you pay in ...
12. Tourists come ...

b) What is happening?

Look at the pictures of New Zealand again.
What are the people doing?

USE
rub, boil, lie, jump, sit, drive

Second Step (§ 22, 26 WB Ex 4)

Ask questions. Look at the example first.

Example: it / rain in your town?
often   – Does it often rain in your town?
yesterday – Did it rain in your town yesterday?
right now – Is it raining in your town right now?

1. your English teacher / give you a test?
   often / yesterday / right now
2. you / ski?
   often / yesterday / right now
3. you and your friends / play cards?
   often / yesterday / right now
4. your teacher / write on the blackboard?
   often / yesterday / right now

Third Step (WB Ex 3)

Jane ist phoning her mother.
Read the text and put the verbs into the correct form.

– Hello, Mum. Guess where I am!
– ...
– No, I (sit) on the beach in the sun.
– ...
– Oh, (snow) in Scotland? Really? Here the sun (shine). We often (go) to the beach in the evening. During the day we usually (take) trips around the country. The hotel (have) special bus tours.
– ...
– Tom is fine. He (lie) right next to me. He (read) the guidebook about New Zealand. What you (do) at the moment?
– ...
– Oh? You just (get) up? Of course, you (be) twelve hours behind. Just a minute, Tom (say) something ... Oh, yes. This (be) expensive. So, bye for now! Have a nice day.

guess, guidebook

Unit 14

First Step

Hinweise/Ideen
- Bei dieser Übung sind nicht nur die inhaltlichen Aspekte (welche Aussagen sind richtig, welche falsch?) wichtig. Es geht auch darum, die Frageform zu üben. Wurden die Ungereimtheiten im Text geklärt, kann man sich auf die Fragestellung konzentrieren.
- Wurde der Inhalt noch nicht besprochen, sollte L die Fragen stellen, damit sich die S auf die Antworten konzentrieren können.

Vorgehen — Fragen stellen und antworten (diskutieren, mutmassen).

a) Basic — Die Fragen ungeordnet an der WT vorgeben und die Antworten zuordnen; anschliessend Frage um Frage entfernen und im GU/GA reproduzieren.

b) Intensive — Die Übung kann in PA erarbeitet werden, falls der Inhalt bereits besprochen wurde. Die S sollen die Antworten möglichst im freien Gespräch geben und durch weitere Informationen ergänzen.

Lösung
1. Kiwis can't fly, so they can't land on the beach.
2. Dunedin isn't the capital of New Zealand. Wellington is the capital of New Zealand.
3. Of course there are a lot of beaches in New Zealand; New Zealand is an island.
4. Dogs don't wear sunglasses or straw hats, but a lot of people wear hats and sunglasses because the ozone layer is so thin.

(Hinweis: *cream on their noses* stimmt hingegen. In Neuseeland müssen auch Hunde vor Sonnenbrand an unbedeckten Körperstellen geschützt werden.)

5. A lot of Maoris speak English and Maori (dialects).
6. That's true. A lot of Maoris fish things with their hands.

Ausbau Intensive — S stellen eigene Fragen nach dem Schema *Do you think it's true...?* (Fragen zu Ländern, Angaben aus dem Guinnessbuch der Rekorde usw.)

Lösung (Intensive)
8. In New Zealand cars and motorbikes drive on the left.
9. There were 12 sheep per person in 1999.
10. Bankers usually wear a shirt and a tie. Sometimes they wear shorts and white socks.
11. In NZ you don't pay with NZ pounds, you pay with NZ dollars.
12. Quite a lot of tourists come to walk down the walls.

Second Step

Hinweise/Ideen — Drillübung zu den Zeitformen, geeignet für PA oder GA mit 4 S.

Lösung
1. Does your English teacher often give you a test? Did your English teacher give you a test yesterday? Is he/she giving you a test right now?
2. Do you often ski? Did you ski yesterday? Are you skiing right now?
3. Do you and your friends often play cards? Did you play cards yesterday? Are you playing cards right now?
4. Does your teacher often write on the blackboard? Did he/she write on the blackboard yesterday? Is he/she writing on the blackboard right now?
5. Do you often read detective stories? Did you read a detective story yesterday? Are you reading a detective story right now?

Third Step

Hinweise/Ideen — In einem zweiten Schritt könnten die S die Gesprächsteile der Mutter ergänzen und den Dialog als PA durchspielen.

Lösung — *I am sitting; is it snowing; the sun is shining; we often go; we usually take; the hotel has; he is lying; he is reading; are you doing; you are just getting up; you are; Tom is saying; this is*

Student's Book, p. 22

Unit 14

Fourth Step

Hinweise/Ideen	Das erste Bild zeigt Aktivitäten, die gerade jetzt ablaufen *(present progressive)*, das zweite, was auf dem Pausenplatz normalerweise geschieht *(simple present)*. Die Übung bietet auch Gelegenheit, die Präpositionen des Ortes (Band 1, § 15) zu repetieren.
Vorgehen	1) Folie zeigen: Die **S** sollen herausfinden, welches Bild alltäglich und welches ungewöhnlich sein könnte (ein *football match* mit Helm und ein *cheeseburger* als Pausenmahlzeit sind eher ungewöhnlich). 2) Übung mit den Verben im Buch machen lassen.
Ausbau/Varianten	• PA/GA: **S1** macht Sätze und **S2** zeigt auf das Gesprochene im Bild. • **S1** macht Sätze zum ersten Bild im *present progressive*. **S2** reagiert darauf mit dem entsprechenden Beispiel im *simple present* im zweiten Bild. • Als zusätzliches Vokabular können *bench* und *fountain* eingeführt werden.
a) Basic	• **L** stellt Fragen zu den Bildern, die **S** antworten in der richtigen Zeitform. Beispiel: *Are they playing American football today? Yes, they are. Do they play American Football every day? No, they don't.* • **L** stellt Fragen nach Ortsangaben: *Where is the teacher standing? He is standing in front of the school/near the door.*
b) Intensive	Die Informationen zu den Ortsangaben (siehe *Basic*) quizartig ausbauen nach dem Muster: *I can see something in front of the door. It is black.*

Erweiterungen

Kopiervorlagen
Verb Training (22)

Fourth Step (§ 26, Revision Workshop 3)

Look at the two pictures. What is different? Find out and make sentences (picture 1: today; picture 2: usually, normally)

Example: – *Today, the teacher's wearing a pullover.*
           – *That's right, he normally wears a jacket.*

USE
clean, drink, eat, listen, read, sit, watch

Unit 14

Fifth Step (§ 26)

A letter from New Zealand

Read the text and put the verbs into the correct form.

29 December

Hi everybody,

As you can see, Greg and I (do) something different this year. We (have) a great time at the East Shore Activity Centre. People (come) here every summer to learn about the country and culture of New Zealand. I (take) a course in Maori language and another one in photography. Greg (take) sailing lessons and he also (do) sheep shearing. Together we (take) lessons in traditional dancing.
We (get up) at 7 a.m. every morning and (have) our early morning tea. From eight till twelve a.m. we (work) in our groups.
Then we usually (have) lunch. Sometimes there (be) more lessons in the afternoon, so it (be) pretty hard work, but we (like) it here. We (have) a super time.
It (be) half past seven p.m. now, and we (sit) in the park in front of the Centre. The weather (be) lovely and the sun (shine).
It rarely (rain) in New Zealand at this time of year, you know.
Stay cool and be good!

Love
Carol

NEW WORDS
culture, sailing, sheep shearing, pretty hard

Unit 14

Fifth Step

Hinweise/Ideen Die Übung kann mündlich oder schriftlich gelöst werden. Bei schwächeren Klassen sollte eine Kontrolle durch L stattfinden, bevor die S in EA/PA die Zeitformen eigenständig einsetzen/diskutieren. Für stärkere S kann die Übung als Test eingesetzt werden.
(Ein Grüppchen starker S bereitet den Brief in einem Nebenraum vor, während der Rest der Klasse im GU arbeitet, danach werden die Lösungen verglichen.)

Vorgehen
1) Die S lesen den Brief in EA.
2) In PA/GA wird diskutiert, warum das *simple present* oder *present progressive* einzusetzen ist (bei schwächeren Klassen auf Deutsch).
3) L liest den Brief bis zum Einsetzen der Verbformen laut vor, die S liefern die richtige Zeitform (evtl. gleichzeitig durch einen S die Verbform an der WT festhalten lassen.)

Ausbau/Varianten PA: Die Frageformen werden wiederholt, indem S1 einen bis drei Sätze vorliest, S2 Fragen stellt, S1 diese beantwortet.
Beispiel: *Who is doing something different this year? – Greg and I (we're) doing something different this year. Where are you staying? – We're staying at East Shore Activity Centre.*

Lösung *Greg and I are doing; We are having (at this point in time!); People come here every summer; I am taking a course; Greg is taking sailing lessons; he is also doing; we are taking lessons; We get up at 7; and have our early morning tea; we work; Then we usually have lunch; there are more lessons; so it is pretty hard work; we like it; We are having; It is half past seven; we are sitting; The weather is lovely; the sun is shining; it rarely rains.*

Student's Book, p. 24

Unit 14

Stepping Out

Hinweise/Ideen	Darauf hinweisen, dass der Geister- und Aberglaube in Grossbritannien seit jeher weit verbreitet ist. Zu fast jedem schottischen Schloss gehört ein Gespenst und seine Geschichte wird den Touristen mit Stolz an den Führungen erzählt. Fehden, Komplotte und das sündige Leben der ehemaligen Bewohner trugen zu dieser Legendenbildung bei. Die Erforschung übersinnlicher Erscheinungen ist eine ernste Sache und es gibt unzählige Bücher dazu. Meistens sind sie gleich in den *bookshops* der Schlösser zu kaufen. Sheila Batts Studien würden also von den meisten Briten keineswegs belächelt!
	Eines der berühmtesten Schlösser in Bezug auf Legenden ist *Glamis Castle* in Schottland. Es soll nicht nur Shakespeare als Schauplatz für *Macbeth* gedient haben, es hat auch eine stattliche Anzahl übersinnlicher Erscheinungen vorzuweisen. Nebst einer *Grey Lady* und einer *White Lady* taucht ab und zu ein bärtiger Kartenspieler auf, der seine Seele beim Spiel an den Teufel verlor. Auch ein Monster soll einst ein bis heute unentdeckt gebliebenes Zimmer bewohnt haben (es könnte sich dabei um einen missgebildeten Sohn eines früheren *Earl* gehandelt haben). Da die Mauern des Schlosses an gewissen Stellen bis zu vier Meter dick sind, könnte das Zimmer tatsächlich existieren. Um sein Geheimnis – und die damit verbundene Attraktion – zu erhalten, hütet man sich, das Gebäude allzu ernsthaft abzusuchen.
	Aber auch einsame Moorlandschaften, abgelegene Gasthöfe und Burgruinen sind ideale Schauplätze für Geistergeschichten, und mit solchen Bildern aus Grossbritannienführern könnte man die S für den Text über Sheila Batts und den nachfolgenden *Reading Corner* in die richtige Stimmung versetzen.
Material	CD
Wichtig	Auf der CD befindet sich der Bericht von Sheila Batts zum Teil b. Skript: siehe Kopiervorlagen. Der Text der E-Mail wurde nicht vertont.
Vorgehen	1) Die S lesen den Brief still und diskutieren anschliessend in PA/GU die Fragen: *Who is Pauline West? What is her profession? Why is she working 16 hours a day? What do you think of the White Lady? Who is Sheila Batts? Why is she at Kilmichael House?*
	2) Die S hören die CD (evtl. Skript zum Mitlesen abgeben). Diese Übung kann auch als PA gemacht werden, indem die S nach der Hörübung Informationen austauschen.
	3) Der zweite Teil der CD ist als vergnüglicher Abschluss gedacht. Um den Effekt zu verstärken, kann man das Klassenzimmer verdunkeln und Kerzen aufstellen.
Ausbau/Varianten	Die S in EA/PA/GA eine Zusammenfassung (mündlich/schriftlich) des Briefes machen lassen. Stichwörter als Hilfe an der WT sammeln: *letter from Scotland – hotel to open before Easter – 12 guests – a ghost, called the White Lady; lived 250 years ago in Kilmichael House – a guest, Ms Batts, is studying the ghost.*

Erweiterungen

Kopiervorlagen
Script: The White Lady (23)

Stepping Out

The White Lady (§ 26)

a) Read the e-mail.

To: Carol Evans <cevans@kiwi.net>
From: @ Pauline West <p.west@kilmichaelhouse.co.uk>
Subject: Quick Mail
Cc:
Bcc:
X-Attachments:

Hi Carol,
Sorry, this is a quick e-mail. We moved into "our" hotel last week, and now we're working about 16 hours every day to get it ready for the week before Easter. We're expecting 12 guests. Now we're buying food, painting the bedrooms, cleaning windows and and and ...
Don put the computer in the big "blue room" at the back of the house. I'm sitting here now, it's a nice quiet room and I like to write letters here. Kilmichael is a lovely place, you know. I'm happy that we bought it.
Now some really BIG NEWS: WE HAVE A GHOST! She's called the White Lady. She doesn't look very old, wears a white dress and has white hair. She lived in Kilmichael House about 250 years ago and there is a strange story about her. She sometimes appears at night outside the yellow bedroom on the first floor.
We also have our first guest. Her name is Sheila Batts and she works for the Supernatural Studies Institute in Glasgow. She's here to study our ghost. We think it's funny, but who knows? Have you got ghosts in New Zealand?
Write soon
Pauline

Pauline and Don West
Kilmichael House, Dundee
bookings@kilmichaelhouse.co.uk

b) What's the story of the White Lady? Listen to the report of Ms Batts about her.

NEW WORDS

ago, appear, bedroom, disappear, Easter, expect, food, ghost, guest, more into, news, paint (vb.), quiet, ready, suddenly

Reading Corner

Ghosts and Phantoms

Many people think of Great Britain as a country with a lot of rain and bad weather, old castles and, very often – ghosts. Perhaps that is true, perhaps not. One thing is true: ghosts are an important part of British folklore. There are not many castles or old houses without a ghost – if you believe the stories which people tell you.

There are two kinds of ghosts in Britain: there are the famous ones: kings, queens and heroes. You read about them in old stories, but not many people see them. But there are also the other ones: a lot of people see them, but nobody knows who they are.

The Ghosts of Sawston Hall

In Sawston Hall near Cambridge there is an example of the first kind. The story says that the Duke of Northumberland tried to kill Mary Tudor, later Queen of England. In 1553 he very nearly caught her in Sawston Hall – she slept there as a guest – and she only got away because she wore the clothes of a milkmaid. Some people say that the ghost of Queen Mary Tudor haunts the halls of this beautiful castle and that you can see her as she runs through the garden.

But there are also ghosts of the second type in Sawston Hall. One example is "the Lady in Grey". She appears in the Tapestry Room. A very polite phantom, she knocks on the door three times before she comes in. A student slept in the Tapestry Room some years ago. In the middle of the night he heard knocks on the door, and he felt that somebody tried to come in. There are also strange sounds in the castle: someone plays a spinet (an old-fashioned type of piano) and sometimes a girl laughs in the halls.

London Ghosts

Here are two examples of ghosts in London. One haunts Drury Lane Theatre when new plays are on. He looks like a gentleman and wears clothes from about two hundred years ago. Sometimes he walks along the seats on the second floor, sometimes he sits in one of the seats. He is not there all the time. In fact, he only appears if a play is a hit.

The second example is very strange: in 1966 two Canadian tourists stayed in Queen's House in Greenwich (London), now a part of a big museum. They did not, and still do not, believe in ghosts. One evening they took a photograph of the stairs up to the first floor. There was nobody on the stairs when they took the picture. On the photograph there are the stairs and some lamps. It is a normal picture of a normal staircase. But there are also two figures. They are not very clear but they are also not difficult to see. One is standing at the bottom of the stairs, the other has got one hand on the banisters. Both are wearing thick heavy coats. You can't see their faces. Experts say that there is nothing wrong with the picture ...

Unit 14

Reading Corner

Hinweise/Ideen Die S sollen die Texte global verstehen. Sie sind nicht als Aussprache- oder Textverständnisübung gedacht.
Hintergrundinformationen: siehe Hinweise zum *Second Step*.
Weitere Geschichten dieser Art finden sich in den Kopiervorlagen (siehe unten).

Erweiterungen

Kopiervorlagen
The Phantom on the Wall (25)

Student's Book, p. 26

Unit 15

Up North and Down Under

Einstimmungsbilder Im Uhrzeigersinn von links oben: Kanada *(Native Canadians)*, Kanada (Freilichtmuseum), Australien (Buntwaran, Reptil), Australien (tropische Pflanze), Australien (Koala), Kanada (Robbe); Australien *(Aborigine);* Australien (Verkehrsschild); Kanada (Elch); Mitte: Australien (Sydney Tower)

Landeskunde Kanada Nordamerikas Ureinwohner wanderten vor 10'000 bis 30'000 Jahren über die Bering-See ein. Sie lebten als Jäger, Fischer oder Bauern. Kein Lebensbereich der Indianer blieb unbeeinflusst, als es im 17. Jahrhundert zu den ersten Kontakten mit den Europäern kam. Ab 1830 wurden sie in Reservate im heutigen Ostkanada umgesiedelt.
Im Wettlauf um Territorien wurde die Ostküste Kanadas zuerst von den Franzosen verwaltet, während England Neufundland und die Gebiete um die Hudson Bay für sich beanspruchte. 1713 mussten die Franzosen im Frieden von Utrecht grosse Gebiete räumen und nach der Eroberung Quebecs durch die Engländer ganz Kanada den Briten überlassen.
Allerdings sicherten die Briten den französischen Einwanderern die Tolerierung ihrer Sprache zu. Die britische Königin ist bis heute Souverän des Landes, doch staatsrechtlich ist Kanada durch ein "Verfassungsgesetz" von Grossbritannien unabhängig. Französisch ist die zweite, gleichberechtigte Amtssprache, aber die französische Minderheit verlangt noch immer die Unabhängigkeit Quebecs oder zumindest einen Sonderstatus.

Landeskunde Australien *Down Under*, *Oz* oder *the Lucky Country* sind Namen, unter denen man den Kontinent auf der Südhalbkugel kennt. Offiziell heisst Australien jedoch *The Commonwealth of Australia*. Dazu gehören das Festland, die Insel Tasmanien sowie kleinere Inselgruppen.
Die australischen Ureinwohner kamen vor 40'000 bis 60'000 Jahren von Indonesien her. Europäische Werte wie hierarchische Strukturen, materielle Güterwirtschaft und Sesshaftigkeit sind ihnen bis heute fremd.
Die ersten europäischen Siedler waren Sträflinge, die Grossbritannien im 19. Jahrhundert verbannte, anstatt sie in Gefängnisse zu stecken. Viele blieben im Land, nachdem sie ihre Strafe verbüsst hatten, und die heutigen Bewohner sind meist stolz darauf, dass sie solche Vorfahren nachweisen können. Die Goldfunde, die 1850 einsetzten, zogen aber auch freiwillige Einwohner ins Land.
Über die Hälfte der Bevölkerung lebt heute im Südosten des Landes in der Gegend um die Grossstädte Sydney und Melbourne.

Warm-up

Hinweise/Ideen
- Die S versuchen herauszufinden, welche Bilder von Kanada und welche von Australien sind.
- Die S zeichnen die Umrisse von Australien auf ein Blatt und notieren möglichst viele Ausdrücke, die ihnen dazu in den Sinn kommen (wenn möglich auf Englisch, aber auch auf Deutsch). L kann auch Stichwörter an die WT notieren, um die Fantasie anzuregen. Beispiele: *kangaroo, dry, outback, Ayers Rock*.
- Dasselbe für Kanada machen lassen. Beispiele: *maple leaf, grizzly, huskies, Quebec (French)*.

Erweiterungen

Folie Nr. 9

Up North and Down Under

Unit 15   Focus

Which is the best way to travel in Australia?

Air safari

1 Cost: $A 4,260
   Australia is a huge island continent. It is larger than all the countries of Europe together. There are great distances between the cities, and the trains and roads are not as
5 good as in many European countries.

   An air safari is the fastest and most direct way to get to the Australian outback. You fly from place to place in a
10 small ten-passenger aeroplane. Our eight-day air safari takes you from Cairns to Sydney, Australia's most exciting and most beautiful city.

1 On the way from Cairns to Sydney you stay at farms and small but comfortable hotels. Our air safaris take you to the Great Barrier Reef, Escott Cattle Station, Lawn Hill National Park, Alice Springs, Ayers Rock, Birdsville and
5 Lightning Ridge.

Adventure camping tours

Cost: $A 919

1 Do you like adventure trips? This 10-day camping tour is a wonderful way to see Australia. Our special four-wheel drive coaches are tough enough to travel on the wildest bush roads. Our tours are open to tra-
5 vellers of all ages, but they are most popular with younger people (under 35).

   We travel in small groups (6 to 12 people) and passengers usually help with the camp tasks: they put up
10 the tents and cook the meals.

1 Comfortable clothes are important, and you can bring one suitcase of maximum 16 kg. The price includes touring, meals, sleeping bag and camping equipment.

   Our Red Centre Tour takes you from Melbourne or
5 Sydney to Alice Springs, via the Flinder Ranges and Ayers Rock (ca. 5,500 km).

Perth

Unit 15

Sprachfunktionen: Vergleiche anstellen, zustimmen und widersprechen	**Themen:** Reisen, Australien, Verkehrsmittel
Strukturen: Komparativ und Superlativ mit Endung -er/-est und mit *more*, *most* sowie Vergleiche mit *as ... as*; Fragewörter *what* und *which*	**Mögliche Abfolge:** Warm-up → Focustexte I-III → WB Ex 1 → First Step → Second Step → WB Ex 2 → Third Step → WB Ex 3 → (Fourth Step) → (WB Ex 4) → WB Ex 5 → (WB Ex 6) → Stepping Out → WB Ex 7 (WB Ex 8)
Grammatik: § 29	

Focus I: Which is the best way to travel in Australia?

Hinweise/Ideen	Die Texte basieren auf authentischen Reiseprospekten. Die S sollen verschiedene Arten zu reisen kennen lernen und vergleichen. Vorerst geht es darum, dass die Texte sinngemäss verstanden werden.
Material	CD, OHP-Folie
Vorgehen	1) Die S überfliegen die Texte wie einen Reiseprospekt und wählen ihre Reisevariante.
	2) Sie sitzen entsprechend zusammen, vertiefen sich in PA/GA in den gewählten Text und versuchen die Aufgaben zum Textverständnis (siehe KV *Yes or No?*) zu lösen.
	3) Die Informationen werden im GU vorgestellt. Bsp.: L liest vor, S antworten. **L:** *Australia is an island (right or wrong?).* **S:** *That's right, Australia is an island.*
Wichtig	Das passive Verständnis des Vokabulars soll hier im Vordergrund stehen. Erst später den aktiven Umgang (Einbettung in Sätze, Aussprache, Leseübung) angehen.
Variante	1) Die Klasse ist wiederum je nach Reisevariante in drei Gruppen eingeteilt und jede Gruppe liest ihren Textteil still durch.
	2) Die Textteile werden von der CD abgespielt, die ganze Klasse liest im SB mit; nach jeder Reisevariante wird gestoppt, die Folie *Yes or No?* eingeblendet und von der entsprechenden Gruppe ("Spezialisten") kommentiert.
a) Basic	Das Vokabular und die Aussprache satzweise oder abschnittweise mit Hilfe der CD erarbeiten. Die schwierigen Wörter an der WT auflisten.
b) Intensive	Die freiwilligen Textteile können auch erst in einer späteren Phase angegangen werden.
Bemerkung	Im Anschluss an die Textarbeit kann in leistungsstarken Klassen eine Diskussion durchgeführt werden, in der die S ihre bevorzugte Reiseart beschreiben und verteidigen. Da im Trainingsteil der Wortschatz gefestigt wird und Vergleiche geübt werden, kann diese Diskussion auch erst am Ende der Unit durchgeführt werden.

Erweiterungen

Kopiervorlagen
Map of Australia (29)
Yes or No? (30)
Fill in the Gaps (31, 32)

Folie
Nr. 10, 12

Ausbau
Die S bauen mit Reiseprospekten zu verschiedenen Ländern Ateliers auf, bereiten sich sprachlich auf Kurzreferate vor und präsentieren ‚ihr' Land mit ‚ihren' Reisevarianten.

Student's Book, p. 28

Unit 15

Hinweise siehe vorhergehende Seite.

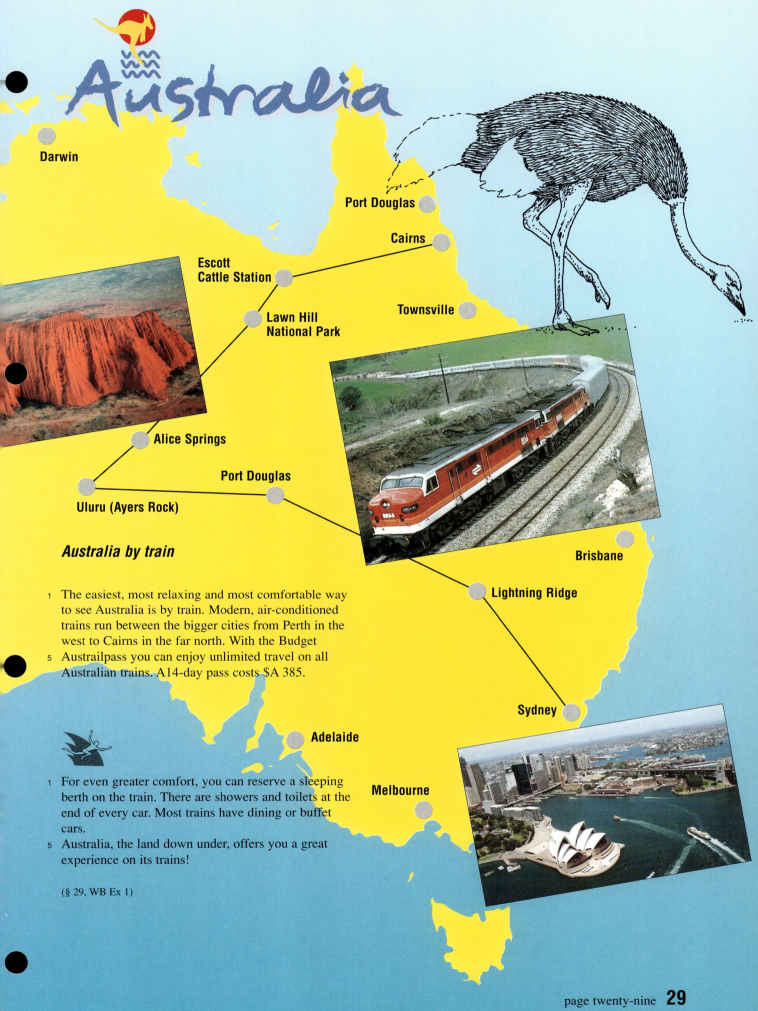

Australia by train

1 The easiest, most relaxing and most comfortable way to see Australia is by train. Modern, air-conditioned trains run between the bigger cities from Perth in the west to Cairns in the far north. With the Budget
5 Austrailpass you can enjoy unlimited travel on all Australian trains. A 14-day pass costs $A 385.

1 For even greater comfort, you can reserve a sleeping berth on the train. There are showers and toilets at the end of every car. Most trains have dining or buffet cars.
5 Australia, the land down under, offers you a great experience on its trains!

(§ 29, WB Ex 1)

Training

First Step (§ 29)

a) Compare the different ways of travelling in Australia.

Examples: cheap: adventure tour / air safari
– An adventure tour is cheaper than an air safari.

expensive: air safari / train trip
– An air safari is more expensive than a train trip.

fast: air safari / train trip
hard: adventure tour / train trip
easy: air safari / adventure tour
comfortable: train trip / air safari
exciting: adventure tour / air safari
dangerous: adventure tour / train trip
relaxing: train trip / air safari

b) Which is the best way to travel? Ask your partner.

Example: expensive
– Which is the most expensive way to travel?
– The most expensive way to travel is by air safari.

easy / fast / direct / wild / comfortable / relaxing

c) What about you?

Example: – I'd like to travel by train because it's more comfortable and easier than by air.

NEW WORD
compare

Second Step (§ 29, WB Ex 5)

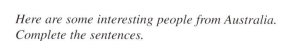
win, record, swimmer, Aborigine

Here are some interesting people from Australia. Complete the sentences.

– Ian Thorpe won three world records in three days. He was the (fast) ... swimmer at the Olympics 2000.

– At the age of 16 Lauren Jackson was the (young) ... player in the Australian basketball team.

– Cathy Freeman is one of the (interesting) ... women in Australia. She is an Aborigine and won a gold medal at the Olympic Games. She is also working for a (good) ... future for the Aborigines.

– In one of his (funny) ... films Paul Hogan played "Crocodile Dundee".

Unit 15

Unit 15

First Step

Hinweise/Ideen	• Mündliche Übung zur Einführung der Steigerungsformen. • Als Vorbereitung können die Adjektive und Komparative/Superlative aus den Focustexten gesammelt und nach Reisearten geordnet an der Wandtafel aufgelistet werden. Danach den Unterschied zwischen der Steigerung mit *more/most* und *-er/-est* erarbeiten. • Als Vorentlastung kann der *Language Focus* zu Exercise 1 im Workbook vorgezogen werden.
Vorgehen	1) Vorbereitung der Vergleiche in PA. 2) Präsentation im GU
Ausbau/Varianten	Die S formulieren eigene Beispiele mit weiteren bekannten Adjektiven. Beispiel: *nice, beautiful, wonderful, interesting, boring, hot*
a) Basic	Evtl. zuerst die Adjektive der Teile a und b nach Steigerungsart sortieren.
b) Intensive	Die Sätze in einem zweiten Durchgang ergänzen, indem eine Begründung hinzugefügt wird: *An air Safari is more expensive than a train trip because you fly from place to place.*

Second Step

Vorgehen	Die Übung eignet sich als EA.
Ausbau	• Die S betrachten die Sätze einige Sekunden lang und schreiben sie dann auswendig nieder. • Die S formulieren eigene Beispiele zu weiteren bekannten Personen (aus verschiedenen Ländern). • Die S suchen im Internet mehr Informationen zu den Personen und präsentieren diese in derselben Übungsform.
Lösung	▪ *fastest; youngest; most interesting; better; funniest*

Student's Book. p. 30

Unit 15

Third Step

Hinweise/Ideen	Die Lösungen sollen der Meinung der S entsprechen und können auch in PA diskutiert werden.
Vorgehen	Je nach Leistungsstärke der Klasse können die drei Vergleichsarten zuerst einzeln und erst danach gemischt geübt werden.
a) Basic	Die Formen der Adjektive *(better, higher etc.)* an WT, OHP oder Moltonwand (zum Auf- und Abdecken) vorgeben.
b) Intensive	In einem zweiten Durchgang kann man auch hier die S auffordern, persönliche Begründungen *(because ...)* anzufügen.
Ausbau/Varianten	Nur mit den Bildern arbeiten: PA. **S1** zeigt auf ein Bild, **S2** formuliert seine/ihre Meinung und verwendet dazu passende Adjektive.

Fourth Step

Hinweise/Ideen

- Die S müssen vor dieser Übung den Unterschied zwischen *what* und *which* kennen. Fragen mit *which* beziehen sich auf eine eingeschränkte Auswahl, Fragen mit *what* auf eine uneingeschränkte Zahl. Exercise 6 im WB könnte als Vorentlastung hier eingeschoben werden.

- Es geht in dieser Übung nicht nur um die Vertiefung der Steigerungsformen, sondern auch darum, die eigene Meinung mit Hilfe von einfachen Redemitteln auszudrücken.

Erweiterungen

Kopiervorlagen
Switzerland Quiz (33)
Cue Cards: Nonsense Comparisons (34)

Ausbau
1) Spiel "Kettenreaktion" (für stärkere Klassen):
S1 beginnt mit einem Vergleich, **S2** fügt einen zweiten Vergleich hinzu, **S3** einen dritten usw. Wichtig ist, dass jeder/jede S die bisher genannten Vergleiche wiederholen muss, bevor das eigene Beispiel hinzugefügt wird.

2) Wettbewerb
Zwei oder mehr Teams. **L** gibt zwei Substantive oder ein Adjektiv vor. Welches Team bietet zuerst eine vernünftige Lösung?

Third Step (§ 29, WB Ex 2, 6, 7)

Now compare these things.

Example: good / hamburger / hot dog
– A hamburger is better than a hot dog.
– A hamburger is as good as a hot dog.
– A hot dog isn't as good as a hamburger.

good / ice cream / banana
high / Ayers Rock / Matterhorn
bad / RTL / SF1
interesting / Australia / New Zealand
heavy / rucksack / schoolbag
beautiful / Switzerland / France
loud / guitar / drum
important / French / English
old / Rome / Sydney
small / Ireland / Scotland

Fourth Step (§ 29, WB Ex 3)

Ask your partner these questions. Do you agree with his or her answers?

Example:
Student A: What do you think? Which is more comfortable, a trip by car or a trip by train?
Student B: I think a trip by train is more comfortable.
Student A: I agree (with you).
Student B: What do you think? Which is ..., a ... or a ...?
Student A: I think a ...
Student B: I don't really agree (with you). I think a ...
Student A: What do you think? Which is easier, a ... or a ...?
Student B: I think a ... is as easy as a ...
Student A: I agree (with you).

exciting: a football match / a tennis match
easy: English / French
beautiful: Switzerland / Australia
fast: a mountain bike / a city bike
good: dinner in the dining car / dinner at a restaurant
bad: a day without TV / a week without the sun
dangerous: a wild dog / a wild cat
loud: a train / a coach
heavy: kiwi / kangaroo

Stepping Out

Quiz

1. The smallest continent in the world is ...
   - A ... Europe.
   - I ... Australia.
   - W ... Greenland.

2. The fastest rapper is Tung Twista with ...
   - A ... 597,
   - E ... 88 or
   - S ... 1,537 syllables per minute.

3. The biggest train station in Europe is in ...
   - M ... Leipzig.
   - A ... Zurich.
   - T ... Milan.

4. The world's longest river is ...
   - R ... the Rhine.
   - I ... the Amazon.
   - T ... the Nile.

5. The most expensive shoes (in 1999) cost ...
   - E ... US$ 937.
   - H ... US$ 23,800.
   - M ... US$ 7,500.

6. The highest point in the world (Mount Everest) is ...
   - F ... 8,888 metres above sea level.
   - R ... 7,000 m.
   - E ... 8,830 m.

7. The most expensive film (up to 2001) was ...
   - C ... Modern Times with Charlie Chaplin.
   - B ... Titanic with Kate Winslet and Leonardo di Caprio.
   - O ... Terminator II with Arnold Schwarzenegger.

8. The first comic was published in ...
   - O ... 1956
   - E ... 1896.
   - F ... 1786.

9. How many women did the greatest kisser in the world, A.E. Wolfram, kiss in 8 hours?
   - L ... 81
   - U ... 801
   - S ... 8,001

10. The biggest party in the world took place in London's Hyde Park with ...
    - T ... 160,000 children.
    - A ... 160,000 policemen.
    - S ... 160,000 punks.

NEW WORDS

point, publish, kiss (vb.), sea level, syllables, take place, up to, river

Unit 15

Stepping Out

Hinweise/Ideen Repetition der Superlativformen. Wer alle richtigen Antworten errät, erhält den Spruch *I AM THE BEST*.

Vorgehen
- Diese Übung kann in EA (auch als Hausaufgabe) gemacht werden. Anschliessend werden die Lösungen als mündliche Übung im GU ausformuliert.
- Wird die Übung in PA/GA angegangen, sollen die möglichen Lösungen zuerst diskutiert *(I think it's A)* und anschliessend auf einem Beiblatt festgehalten werden.
- Will man vom Lösungswort ablenken, kann man die S ohne Buch arbeiten lassen. L trägt dabei die drei Varianten diktatmässig vor und die S notieren sich die Sätze mit der richtigen Lösung.

Student's Book, p. 32

Unit 16

Sprachfunktionen:	Themen:
Über Pläne und Vorkehrungen sprechen; über Vergangenes berichten	Abenteuerreise in Kanada (Erlebnisbericht), Nationalparks in Kanada
Strukturen:	**Mögliche Abfolge:**
Modale Hilfsverben *must*, *have to* und *need to* sowie Vollverb *need*. Steigerung von *a lot of*, *(a) few*, *(a) little*	Focustext 1 → WB Ex 1 → Focustext II → First Step → WB Ex 2 → Second Step → WB Ex 3 → Third Step → WB Ex 4, 5 → Fourth Step → WB Ex 6, 7 → Stepping Out → WB Ex 8 → Time for a Change → WB Ex 9/10
Grammatik:	
§ 27b, c, § 30	

Focus I: Drifting down the Fraser River

Hinweise/Ideen	Warm-up: siehe Hinweise zu Seite 27 *(Up North and Down Under)*
	Die Radiosendung sollte zuerst als Hörtext (ohne Buch) aufgenommen werden. Der Text basiert auf einer tatsächlichen Flossreise einer Gruppe von Schweizerinnen und Schweizern.
Material	CD, OHP-Folie
Vorgehen	1) Einen Teil des Vokabulars mit Karte und Bild einführen: *river, source* (auf Karte zeigen); *raft, wooden, to drift* (Foto)
	2) Focustext I abspielen (die Folie als Hilfe auflegen und auf der Karte mitfahren). Buch zu.
	3) In GU zusammentragen, was die **S** verstanden haben. *Where is the radio station? What is the name of the reporter? What day of the week is it? Where did the Swiss start their trip? What is the name of the river? What did they use at the beginning?*
	4) Hören und mitlesen.
	5) Text laut lesen lassen.
a) Basic	Da der freiwillige Teil nicht sehr schwer ist, könnte man ihn passiv erschliessen. Die **S** bekommen z. B. die Aufgabe, möglichst viele geografische Namen herauszuhören und die Orte auf der Karte zu finden.
b) Intensive	Den freiwilligen Teil entweder gleich im ersten Durchlauf erschliessen oder separat angehen mit Einführung (siehe Hinweis bei *Basic*).

Focus II: Interview

Vorgehen	1) Text abspielen. Buch zu.
	2) Verständnisfragen: *How many oil drums did they use? Can they eat on their rafts? Can they sleep on them? How? What kind of material did they use for the rafts? What about insects? Is the raft trip dangerous? What is worse at the moment, the wind or the rapids?*
a) Basic	Vokabular als Vorentlastung einführen: *oil drum, tent, tree, forest, rain jacket, life jacket*
b) Intensive	Nach dem Erschliessen des freiwilligen Teils (Vorgehen wie bei Focus I) könnten die **S** den zweiten Teil abändern und eigene Interviewfragen schreiben.

Erweiterungen

Kopiervorlagen
Fill in the Gaps! (40)
Match the Questions and the Answers (42)

Folie
Nr. 13

Ausbau
Lektüre: Ausschnitte aus *The Adventures of Huckleberry Finn*, Easy Reader (z.B. Oxford Bookworm Green Series Stage 2).

Unit 16   Focus

I Drifting down the Fraser River

1 Hi folks! This is Joan Bensen from CHWK Radio, Chilliwack, with a Saturday afternoon special. A group of young people from Switzerland arrived in Chilliwack last night, but not by car or train. They are drifting down the
5 Fraser River on two wooden rafts.
   They started out near the source of the Fraser, in a place called Lucerne. That's near Jasper National Park. They had to use canoes at the beginning because the river is not
10 deep enough there. Then they built their rafts in Prince George. They took five weeks to get to Chilliwack.

1 But why come to Canada to drift down a river? It's a long story. Some years ago, a few friends went down the River Rhine in Europe on their own rafts. They liked it so much that they decided to travel down the St. Lawrence River in
5 Eastern Canada. They wanted to see the Great Lakes, Toronto with the CN Tower, Montreal and French-speaking Quebec City. But there were the Niagara Falls between Lake Erie and Lake Ontario. They were just a little too high for them. So the Swiss decided to come out
10 West.

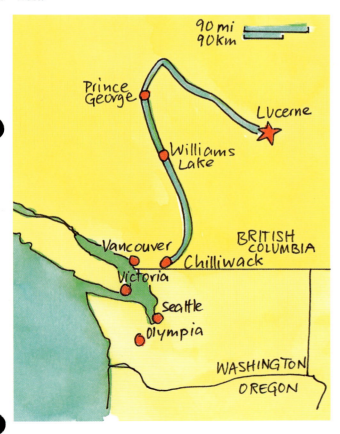

II Interview

1 JB: Hi Marco, welcome to Chilliwack. So what kind of material did you use to build your rafts? Did you cut down trees in the forest?
   M: No, we bought a lot of wood from a sawmill, and
5 we used 64 oil drums. There are two tents on one raft and a big table with a fireplace on the other. So we can cook our own meals while we are drifting.
   JB: And what did you bring from Switzerland? What are the most important things for you and your
10 friends?
   M: Anti-mosquito spray – just kidding… There are very few insects around here, actually. No, I think it is rain jackets and the good old Swiss Army knives.
   JB: Isn't the river quite dangerous in some places?
15 Do you wear life-jackets?
   M: Of course we do. And we must be good swimmers, too! In fact, it's less dangerous here than further north. There aren't as many rapids as up there. Sometimes we crash into the trees. Right now we're
20 having some problems with the wind. It's very strong.

1 JB: What can you do about it?
   M: Not much. We just have to wait and see. Perhaps we can drift a little further tomorrow.
   JB: And what are your plans for tonight?
5 M: We're going to Harrison Hot Springs. We all need a nice warm bath.
   JB: Oh, I see. You must meet a lot of interesting people on your trip.
   M: Yes, the people here are very friendly, but there
10 are far fewer people in British Columbia than in Switzerland.
   JB: Well, Marco, thank you very much for talking to us. I hope you have a good trip to Vancouver.
   M: Thank you.

(§ 30, 31, WB Ex 1, 2)

Training

First Step (Focus)

On Monday, there was an article in the **Chilliwack Post** about the group from Switzerland. Eight things are different from the radio interview. What are they?

CHILLIWACK POST

Tom Sawyer and Huckleberry Finn in Town!

But today they are Swedish, not American, and they are drifting down the Fraser River, and not the Mississippi. A group of young men and women arrived in Chilliwack on two big rafts on Friday. Their adventure trip began in Jasper National Park two months ago. Because the Fraser is very wild at the beginning, they

used canoes first. Later they cut down some trees and built two wooden rafts. Their first plan was to travel down the Yukon in Alaska, but that was too dangerous because of all the rapids and water falls. The rafts are not strong enough for a river like the Yukon. In fact they look very comfortable. There is a tent on one of them and a table on the other. The travellers can cook and eat their own meals, and sometimes they even have a dance at midnight.

At the moment, the adventurers from Switzerland have to wait in Chilliwack because of the strong wind. They are trying some of our pubs. However, they want to be in Vancouver in a few days. What are their plans for Vancouver? A big party in Stanley Park! *JCB*

NEW WORDS
Swedish, water fall

Second Step (§ 30, 31, WB Ex 3)

You want to go on a six-day canoe trip in Jasper National Park. Which of these things do you want to take with you?

a) Choose ten things.

Examples: *I need a hat.*
I must have my sleeping bag.
I have to take a compass.

1. air bed
2. anti-mosquito spray
3. book of comics
4. book of ghost stories
5. camera
6. camping chair
7. compass
8. hat
9. life-jacket
10. map
11. discman
12. rain jacket
13. rucksack
14. sleeping bag
15. suitcase
16. Swiss Army knife
17. tent
18. video camera

NEW WORDS
air bed, map

USE
I need ... I must have ...
I have to take ...

b) Discuss the ten things on your list. You can use some of these expressions:

USE
Oh yes, I agree.
Yes, I think you're right.
I think a ... isn't very good because ... .
Don't you think we need ... .
Oh no, I don't quite agree because ... .

USE
I think we must have ... because ... .
I think we have to ... because ... .
I think we need ... because ... .

Unit 16

Unit 16

First Step

Hinweise/Ideen Aufgabe zum Textverständnis

Vorgehen Zuerst als stille EA, dann Vergleich der Ergebnisse in PA, zuletzt Kontrolle in GU.

Basic
- Achtung! Die Übung lässt sich nur machen, wenn die freiwilligen Texte zumindest passiv erschlossen wurden (siehe Hinweise auf der vorhergehenden Seite), da der Zeitungsbericht auch solche Teile enthält.
- Alternative: Text nur bis *"... two wooden rafts"* bearbeiten. Vorgabe: Wer findet mindestens einen Fehler im Text?
- Wird der ganze Zeitungstext bearbeitet, da die S die freiwilligen Focusteile kennen, könnte man den Bericht abschnittweise mit dem Focustext vergleichen und die Fakten beider Texte an der WT nebeneinander auflisten (lassen).

Varianten
- Den Zeitungstext laut vorlesen, die S sollen beim Zuhören die Fehler erkennen.
- Der Zeitungsbericht wird laut gelesen, abschnittweise gleich beim Lesen korrigiert und mit den richtigen Angaben nochmals vorgetragen.

Lösung
1. *The rafters are Swiss, not Swedish.*
2. *The trip didn't begin in Jasper National Park, but near it.*
3. *They used canoes because the Fraser river isn't deep enough, not because it is wild.*
4. *They didn't cut down trees, they got wood from a sawmill.*
5. *Their first plan was to travel down St. Lawrence River, not the Yukon.*
6. *There are two tents on one raft, not only one.*
7. *They don't have dances on the rafts.*
8. *They are going to Harrison Hot Springs tonight, not to local pubs in Chilliwack.*

Eventuell erwähnen die S auch die Party in Stanley Park. Da Marco im Interview nichts dazu sagt, ist unklar, ob diese Information stimmt (kann als Fehler dazugerechnet werden).

Second Step

Hinweise/Ideen Die S sollen ähnlich wie bei *Unit 15, Third Step* argumentieren üben und ihre Meinung begründen. Siehe Strukturvorgabe in der *USE-Box*.

Variante Die S schreiben fünf bis sieben Dinge auf, die ihrer Meinung nach notwendig sind. L übt mit zwei starken S den Dialog vor der Klasse.

Ausbau Viererguppen mit je zwei Paaren machen. Aufgabe: Es dürfen nur 15 Sachen mitgenommen werden. Jedes Paar wählt aus und vergleicht seine Auswahl mit dem anderen Paar.

Erweiterungen

Kopiervorlagen
Is this Text Correct? (41)
Match the Questions and the Answers (42)

Student's Book, p. 34

Unit 16

Third Step

Hinweise/Ideen	• Die Grammatik § 27 *(a lot/a few/not much)* und/oder der *Language Focus* zu WB Ex 4 sollte man vor dieser Übung erarbeiten.
	• Der *Algonquin Provincial Park* liegt in der Nähe von Toronto und ist im Sommer oft überfüllt. Auch die im Westen gelegenen Parks *Jasper/Banff* sind bei den Touristen sehr beliebt. Auf *Vancouver Island* regnet es häufig. Die Zahlen zur Wetterstatistik sind jedoch erfunden.
Vorgehen	Einführung im GU. Bei leistungsstarken Klassen auch als PA oder GA geeignet.
a) Basic	An WT/OHP als Hilfe *a lot of, many, not much, few, little* aufführen und die Beispiele *(people, sunshine, rain, lakes, forest, mosquitoes)* nach dem Kriterium zählbar/unzählbar auflisten.
b) Intensive	Bei leistungsstarken Klassen können die Teile a und b der Übung von Anfang an gemischt werden.

Erweiterungen

Kopiervorlagen
Canada and Switzerland (43)

Third Step (§ 27)

Here is some information about three famous parks in Canada.
a) Talk about them.

Examples:
– *There are a lot of lakes in Algonquin Park.*
– *There are just a few lakes in Jasper/Banff National Park.*
– *There is not much sunshine on Vancouver Island.*

	Vancouver Island	**Jasper/Banff National Park**	**Algonquin Park**
Tourists	very few people	quite a lot of people	lots of people
Weather	rain nearly all the time; 3.5 hours of sunshine per day in July	some rain and snow in the summer; 7.8 hours of sunshine	not a lot of rain in the summer; often cloudy; 5.6 hours of sunshine
Lakes	13	3	178
Forest	65%	25%	80%
Insects	some mosquitoes in August	no mosquitoes	millions of mosquitoes from June to August

b) Now compare them.

Examples:
– *There are fewer people in Jasper and Banff than in Algonquin Park.*
– *There is less rain in Algonquin Park than on Vancouver Island.*
– *There is more rain on Vancouver Island than in Algonquin Park.*

c) Discuss:

– Which park is best for a canoe trip in August?
– Which park is best for a trip with young children?
– Which is the best season to visit the parks?
– What do you need to bring?

Fourth Step (§ 30, WB Ex 6)

Look at this picture. It is from the day full of adventures in Algonquin Park (Ontario). Some things went wrong!

a) Here is what some people said.
   Ask them. Make questions with 'have to'.

Example: – I had to go to hospital.
           – Why did you have to go to hospital?

NEW WORDS

bear, campfire, continue, dark, hospital

b) Here is what one traveller wrote about that day. Continue her report. Use "have to" with the underlined verbs.

Example: "What a day! First of all, it was still dark when we had to get up. Max didn't get up until seven. Then it began to ... and we didn't have any ... for ...."

1. rain / no coffee / breakfast
2. <u>walk</u> / long way
3. <u>carry</u> / heavy rucksacks
4. not have enough canoes / three people / <u>use</u> one canoe
5. Chris / fall into the water / <u>swim</u>
6. be / too much water
7. <u>leave</u> the river / <u>walk</u> through the bush / wind come at night
8. not tie the canoe to a tree / canoe drift away
9. best thing / campfire / evening
10. often / sing songs / make coffee and tea
11. one night / bear / come / eat all our food
12. <u>go</u> back to town / <u>buy</u> more food

36 page thirty-six

Unit 16

Unit 16

Fourth Step

Hinweise/Ideen Teil a: Übung zur Vergangenheitsform von *must/have to*. Repetition der Frageform im *simple past*.
Teil b: Bei den unterstrichenen Verben wird *have to* in die Vergangenheit gesetzt, bei den anderen das Vollverb.

Vorgehen Fragen üben und ein Interview erstellen.

a) Basic
1) Die **S** setzen die Sprechblasen in die Frageform. Jedes Fragewort soll mindestens einmal vorkommen. Die Fragen können schriftlich festgehalten werden.

2) Teil b in GU machen.

3) Zu Teil b formulieren die **S** drei bis vier Fragen (mit oder ohne Fragewort) und schreiben sie auf.

4) Mit diesen Fragen (oder einer Auswahl davon) machen sie in PA/GU ein Kurzinterview. Für die Antworten verwenden die **S** Aussagesätze aus den Teilen a und b.

b) Intensive
1) Die **S** setzen die Sprechblasen in die Frageform.

2) Die **S** machen in PA/GA mit den Sprechblasen ein Interview, wobei der Reporter bei gewissen Aussagen nachfragt und die Reisegruppe Begründungen oder Details dazu geben muss, also die Sprechblasen mit weiteren Aussagen ergänzt.

3) Teil b als EA (schriftlich) oder PA erarbeiten lassen.

Ausbau Teil b
- Die Übung kann man auch als schriftliche Klassenarbeit (PA/GA) angehen: **S1** formuliert einen der Sätze mündlich, **S2**, **S3** usw. korrigiert ihn oder segnet ihn ab, alle schreiben ihn auf. **S2** formuliert den nächsten Satz usw. Die Sätze können dabei gut untereinander zu einem Bericht verbunden werden und müssen nicht einzeln nummeriert sein.

- Die **S** ergänzen den Bericht mit weiteren Erlebnissen.

Lösung
> *Then it began to rain and we didn't have any coffee for breakfast. We had to walk a long way and some of us had to carry heavy rucksacks. We didn't have enough canoes, so three people had to use one canoe. Chris fell into the water and had to swim. In Mike's canoe there was too much water. Susan and Mike had to leave the river and had to walk through the bush. A strong wind came at night. Max didn't tie his canoe to a tree and it drifted away. The best thing was the campfire in the evening. We often sang songs and made coffee and tea. One night a bear came and ate all our food. We had to go back to town and buy more food.*

(Personennamen können nach Belieben eingesetzt werden)

Erweiterungen

Kopiervorlagen
Danger – Your Safety? (45)

Unit 16

Stepping Out

Hinweise/Ideen	Es handelt sich hier um eine Hörverständnisübung, wobei die S die Bilder den entsprechenden Nummern zuordnen müssen. Es sind je fünf Beispiele aus Australien und Kanada, welche das Kapitel *Up North and Down Under* bildlich abschliessen.
Vorgehen	• Die S betrachten die Bilder im Buch, der Hörtext wird nach jedem Bild angehalten, die Zuordnung erfolgt im GU/PA/GA.
	• Die S hören den Text und zeigen dabei auf die entsprechenden Bilder im Buch.
	• Die S ordnen die Nummern den Bildern während des Zuhörens (auf Notizzetteln) zu.
	• Die S ordnen die Bildnummern im Voraus den Überschriften zu, hören danach den Text und bringen evtl. Korrekturen bei ihrer Zuordnung an.
Ausbau	Die S erarbeiten einen eigenen Kommentar zu den Bildern und präsentieren diesen mündlich oder schriftlich. Diese Variante lässt sich auch quizartig ausbauen.

Stepping Out

The Best and the Greatest ... (WB Ex 8)

Listen to Mike and Tim. Which picture goes with which title?

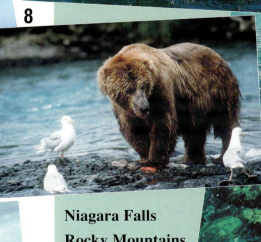

Barrier Reef
Ayers Rock
Koala Bear
Nullarbor Train
Sydney Tower

Niagara Falls
Rocky Mountains
Grizzly Bear
Transamerican Highway
CN Tower

page thirty-seven 37

Time for a Change

Experiment 1: How far away is the thunderstorm?

When you see lightning and then hear thunder, you can find out how far away the flash is. You see the lightning immediately because light travels fast. But sounds like thunder take about three seconds to travel one kilometre. Use a watch to count the seconds between the flash of lightning and the sound of thunder, or count out loud: one thousand, two thousand ...
Example: If you count nine seconds, the flash is three kilometres away. It is time to get out of the water!

Experiment 2: a strange lemon

Make something interesting with pieces of an old dry battery, the light bulb and socket of a torch or a bicycle lamp, two pieces of copper wire and a lemon.

1. First you have to take the battery to pieces. From the metal cover on the outside of the battery (zinc) you cut a bit off. Then you take out the black stick in the middle of the battery (it is made of carbon).

2. Now connect the wires to the socket of the light bulb. Tie the end of one wire around the black stick (carbon) and the end of the other wire around the piece of metal (zinc).

3. Then you push the black stick and the piece of metal into the lemon in two different places.
What happens next?

Experiment 3: Test your strength

Play this trick on a friend.
You need:
Three or four sheets of newspaper and a strong, flat ruler.

1. Put the ruler on a table. One end of the ruler has to be in the air. Cover the other end (the one on the table) with the newspaper (as in the picture).

2. Say to your friend: "This is a magic newspaper. I can make it very heavy. You can't lift it."
Move your hands over the newspaper and say:
"Abracadabra Cancandelabra".

3. Hit the free end of the ruler with one hand (do it fast!).

4. Ask your friend: "Are you stronger? Can you lift it? Try it. You must do it fast." He/she is not strong enough!

(WB Ex 9)

Time for a Change

Hinweise/Ideen   Die Experimente sind als Abwechslung gedacht, eignen sich aber auch für den fächerübergreifenden Unterricht oder für (immersive) Formen der Präsentation. Sie könnten zum Beispiel als Gruppenarbeit auf Englisch den andern in der Klasse vorgeführt oder in einer anderen Klasse präsentiert werden.

Vorgehen
1) Die entsprechenden Materialien bereitstellen.
2) Die Materialien Englisch benennen oder mit Kärtchen beschriften.
3) Die Experimente werden durchgeführt und je nach Leistungsstärke der Klasse auf Englisch oder Deutsch kommentiert.
4) In WB Ex 9 a und b finden sich die Erklärungen zu den Experimenten. Die S füllen (evtl. als Hausaufgabe) den Bericht aus.

Ausbau/Varianten
- Die Experimente 2 und 3 können getrennt durchgeführt und anschliessend gegenseitig erklärt werden. Dazu wird die Klasse in zwei Gruppen geteilt und die Experimente werden in zwei verschiedenen Räumen erprobt. Die S aus den beiden Gruppen führen einander anschliessend ihr Experiment vor.
- Die S überlegen sich, wie der Effekt zustande gekommen ist.

Warm-up

Mystery and Murder

Einstimmungsbilder Sie müssen nicht im Detail besprochen werden, sondern sollen die S auf die nachfolgenden Focustexte einstimmen: In Unit 17 geht es um die fiktive Gangsterbande Al Bigone.
In Unit 18 lösen die S als Detektive einen Kriminalfall.

Warm-up

Hinweise/Ideen L bringt Bilder von Hauptdarstellern in Krimi-Serien und lässt die S die Serien und ihre Figuren erraten.
Krimi-Klassiker, die immer noch recht bekannt sind:
Derrick mit Horst Tappert und Fritz Wepper
Columbo mit Peter Falk
Tatort mit diversen Kommissaren (26 Serien mit Schimanski)
Einige neuere Serien:
Ein Fall für zwei mit Claus Theo Gärtner als Josef Matula
Der Bulle von Tölz mit Ottfried Fischer
Die Kommissarin mit Hannelore Elsner
Kommissar Rex (Hauptdarsteller ist ein deutscher Schäferhund)
Polizeiruf 110 (Serie mit mehreren Kripo-Teams in deutschen Städten)
Grossstadtrevier (Kripo-Team)
Weitere Informationen und Bilder finden sich im Internet z.B. bei yahoo/Nachrichten und Medien/Fernsehen/Serien/Kriminal-und Polizeiserien.
Mit der Einstimmung über die deutschen Serien, die den S bekannt sind, lässt sich gut auf die Bilder im Buch überleiten und von da aus auf weitere Schriftsteller und Helden aus dem englischsprachigen Raum: *Sherlock Holmes (Arthur Conan Doyle), Hercule Poirot, Miss Marple (Agatha Christie)* usw.

Varianten
- Die S bringen selbst Bilder berühmter Filmhelden, Gangster und Detektive aus Büchern, Illustrierten oder dem Internet mit und stellen in PA/GA damit ein Quiz zusammen.
- Die S versuchen die Vorgeschichte und Hintergründe zu den Bildern auf Seite 39 zu erraten.
Mögliche Fragen: *What is the man on the left looking at? Why is the man dying? Who are the people on the series of photographs? Whose office door could that be?*

Mystery and Murder

Unit 17   Focus

The Chicago Mirror
Established 1879

Police Arrest Al Bigone's Gang

Yesterday at 10 p.m. Inspector Elliot Lomond and the Chicago police went into Al Bigone's headquarters. They arrested many members of the gang of Chicago's biggest crime boss.

Complete Surprise
The raid on the headquarters, a warehouse with a luxury apartment in the Docks, was a complete surprise. The gangsters were not expecting the police. Carla Del Monte did not hear anything: she was listening to Elvis Presley's Jailhouse Rock on her discman. Steve 'the Thinker' King was reading a book called "Crime and Punishment."
The Galton Brothers did not realise what was going on because they were playing monopoly on their computer. Ave‑

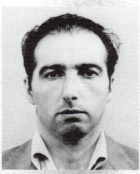

rell Galton was very angry. He said: "It's not fair. I was winning for the first time in my life."

Lucky Police
But the police were also very lucky. There was no shooting, perhaps because Ramona Zotti was cleaning her machine gun at the time of the raid. Her boyfriend, 'Big' Tony Lynch, did not have his gun ready because he was ironing Ramona's minidress. Even Johnny 'the Bulldozer' Walker was no problem. He was fil‑

ling bottles with smuggled Scotch whisky. A policeman said: "He was singing a very happy song when we took him to the police car."
Al Bigone and his wife were very surprised. "We were watching the *News at Ten* on television when we heard the noise. But we thought the boys were just having a good time."

Aeroplane and Helicopter Ready
Next to the apartment the police found a big hangar. There the service crew men were working very hard. Two mechanics, Fred Bull and George Sprite, were painting a new number on Al Bigone's aeroplane while Leonardo da Vicinity, the top technician, was servicing the helicopter.

(§ 32, WB Ex 1, 2, 3)

Unit 17

Strukturen: Bildung und Gebrauch der Verlaufsform der Vergangenheit (Past continuous) **Sprachfunktionen:** Erzählen, reportieren **Grammatik:** § 32	**Mögliche Abfolge:** Focus → First Step → Second Step → WB Ex 1 → (Third Step) → WB Ex 2 (Third Step) → WB (Ex 3, 4, 5) → Stepping Out → WB Ex 6 (→ WB Ex 7)

Focus: Police Arrest Al Bigone's Gang

Vorbemerkung — Beim Focustext handelt es sich um eine Parodie auf eine Razzia, wie sie im Gangsterfilm vorkommt. In Form eines fiktiven Zeitungsberichts wird der Moment, als die Polizei eindringt, beschrieben: Was taten die einzelnen Personen gerade, als sie von der Polizei überrascht wurden? = *past progressive form*.

Material — CD, OHP-Folie

Hinweise/Ideen — Als Einführung können die Personen vorgestellt werden und die *progressive form (present tense)* kann kurz repetiert werden, indem die OHP-Folie mit den Bildern aus dem *First Step* aufgelegt wird. Frage an die **S**: *What are these people doing?*

Vorgehen — Text still in EA lesen lassen und dann in GU/PA erarbeiten. *Past progressive* als Form einführen, aber noch nicht im Detail auf den Unterschied zum *simple past* eingehen (kommt in der nächsten Unit).

a) Basic
1) Eventuell Text auf Blätter kopieren und verteilen, damit die **S** beim Lesen anstreichen können, was sie nicht verstehen.
2) Den Text still in EA lesen lassen.
3) Die **S** lesen den Text in PA nochmals und suchen die Verben und beschriebenen Personen heraus.
4) Personen und Handlungen *(progressive form)* an der Tafel festhalten und im GU erläutern.
5) Text von CD abspielen. Die **S** lesen im Buch mit.

b) Intensive
1) Text still in EA lesen.
2) Das neue Vokabular in PA mit Hilfe der Wörterliste erarbeiten.
3) Tätigkeiten der verschiedenen Personen in PA festhalten.
4) Im GU *progressive form* erläutern.
5) Text von CD abspielen (mit oder ohne Buch).

Erweiterungen

Kopiervorlagen
Fill in the Gaps (46, 47, 48)
Is this Text Correct? (49)

Folie
Nr. 15

Ausbau
1) Bilder auf Seite 41 kopieren und verteilen. Aufgabe: Die **S** verfassen zu jedem Bild eine Legende (past progressive verwenden).
2) Spiel in 4er-Gruppen. *What were they doing on Friday 13th at 5 p.m.?* Handlungen werden aneinandergereiht, bis ein(e) **S** den Faden verliert. Beispiel: **S1**: *My brother was watching TV.* **S2**: *Sabina's brother was watching TV and I was playing football.* **S3**: *Sabina's brother was watching TV, Lukas was playing football and my cat was sleeping etc.*

Unit 17

First Step

Hinweise/Ideen	Übung zum Leseverständnis. Sie kann in EA/PA oder im GU gemacht werden.
Vorgehen	Die S suchen die Personennamen im Focustext und ordnen die Bilder zu.
Intensive	Die S formulieren danach Sätze wie: *Number 1 shows Carla del Monte, because the text says she was listening to Elvis Presley on her discman.*
Aubau/Varianten	Die S versuchen, die Namen der Figuren zu analysieren. *Al Bigone = the "Big one"* (basiert auf Al Capone, der im Chicago der 20er Jahre das Alkoholverbot unterlief); *Steve King* (amerikanischer Autor von Horrorgeschichten); *Ramona Zotti* (Anlehnung an Eros Ramazotti); *Johnny Walker* (schottischer Whisky); *Leonardo da Vicinity* (Anlehnung an Leonardo da Vinci); *Carla del Monte* (Anspielung auf Carla del Ponte); *Fred Bull and George Sprite* (Anspielung auf Red Bull und Sprite); *Galton Brothers* (Anspielung auf die Dalton Brothers, die Gangster aus dem Comic Lucky Luke); *Tony Lynch* (Anspielung auf die Lynch-Justiz nach einem berühmten Richter namens Lynch).

Second Step

Vorgehen	Die S machen Aussagesätze im *past progressive* (Singular und Plural)
Basic	1) Aufgrund der *prompts* festlegen, ob *was* oder *were* benötigt wird. 2) Die S erarbeiten in PA/GA anhand der Bilder im *First Step* die Sätze.
Lösung	*Tony Lynch was ironing Ramona's minidress.* *Fred Bull and George Sprite were painting a new number on Al Bigone's aeroplane.* *The Galton Brothers were playing monopoly on their computer.* *Carla del Monte was listening to Elvis Presley on her discman.* *Leonardo da Vicinity was servicing the helicopter.* *Johnny Walker was filling bottles with Scotch whisky.* *Ramona Zotti was cleaning her machine gun.* *Steve King was reading a book.* *Al Bigone and Mrs Bigone were watching the news on TV.*

Third Step

Vorgehen	Die S machen Sätze mit Hilfe der Bilder und der Vorarbeit im *1st Step* und *2nd Step*.
Ausbau	Mit der Klasse die Anachronismen erarbeiten. Der Focustext bezieht sich auf die USA der 20er oder 30er Jahre. Noch nicht zeitgemäss war: *Computer* (in dieser Form erst ab den Achtzigern); TV-Sendungen (in den USA ab 1940); *Jailhouse Rock* (in den 50er-Jahren, Elvis Presley wurde 1935 geboren, siehe Unit 11); *Discman* (seit den frühen 90er-Jahren); *Helikopter* (erste Modelle 1939); Minikleider und Maschinengewehre gab es bereits, Monopoly kam 1935 auf den Markt.

Erweiterungen

Kopiervorlagen	Folie
What Were They Wearing? (50)	Nr. 15

Training

First Step (Focus)

Who is who?

Read the text from the Chicago Mirror, look at these pictures, and make sentences.

Example: Al Bigone and Mrs Bigone
  – They are in picture number 8.

a) Steve King
b) Ramona Zotti
c) Johnny Walker
d) Leonardo da Vicinity
e) Carla Del Monte
f) Fred Bull and George Sprite
g) The Galton Brothers
h) Tony Lynch

Second Step (§ 32, WB Ex 1)

What were these people doing at the time of the raid?

a) Tony Lynch was ironing ...
b) Fred Bull and George Sprite were ...
c) The Galton Brothers ...
d) Carla Del Monte ...
e) Leonardo da Vicinity ...
f) Johnny Walker ...
g) Ramona Zotti ...
h) Steve King ...
i) Al Bigone and Mrs Bigone ...

Third Step (WB Ex 2, 3)

a) Make correct sentences with these prompts:

Example: Tony Lynch / eat an icecream
  – Tony Lynch wasn't eating an icecream.

1. Al Bigone and his wife / have lunch
2. Leonardo / drink a cup of tea
3. Ramona / iron her minidress
4. Steve / reading a newspaper

Now you go on.

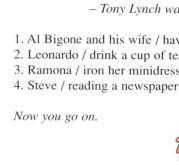

b) Here are some answers. Make the questions:

Example: *What was Al Bigone doing?*
  He was watching television.
– ...?
– Ramona wasn't listening to the Beatles.
– ...?
– They were playing monopoly on their computer.
– ...?
– He was filling whisky into bottles, not tea.
– ...?
– When they took him to the police car he was singing.

Now you go on.

page forty-one **41**

Stepping Out

Test Your Memory (§ 32, WB Ex 6)

Look at this picture for three minutes. Then close the book. What were the people doing?

Unit 17

Unit 17

Stepping Out

Hinweise/Ideen Mit schwächeren S *(basic)* kann hier auch das *present progressive* wiederholt werden, indem zuerst beschrieben wird, was auf dem Bild zu sehen ist. Danach werden die Sätze ohne Bildvorlage ins *past progressive* übertragen.

Material OHP-Folie

Vorgehen Die S betrachten das Bild (im Buch oder auf der Folie) während zwei bis drei Minuten und formulieren (mündlich oder schriftlich) möglichst viele Sätze zu den Personen und ihren Handlungen.

Erweiterungen
Folie Nr. 16

Student's Book, p. 42

Unit 18

Sprachfunktionen:	Themen:
Erzählen, Interviewen, Schlussfolgerungen ziehen	Kriminalfall
Strukturen:	**Mögliche Abfolge:**
Verwendung der Verlaufsform der Vergangenheit, Unterschied *past progressive/simple past*	Focus → WB Ex 1, (2) → First Step → (WB Ex 2) → Second Step → WB Ex (2), 3, 4 → Third Step → WB Ex (2), 5 → Fourth Step → WB Ex 6, 7 → Stepping Out (→ WB Ex 8)
Grammatik:	
§ 32, 33	

Focus: Who Killed Lady Mottram?

Wichtig! Dieses Kapitel ist als Projektarbeit aufgebaut: Die S sollen den Mordfall am Schluss lösen, die Hinweise sind in den *Steps* und *Exercises* versteckt. Da jeder *Step* Hinweise enthält, gibt es in Unit 18 keine Unterteilungen in freiwillige und obligatorische Übungen!
Die Ex 1 und 2 im WB sollen laufend ergänzt werden, sobald die S die nötigen Informationen erarbeitet haben.
Die Tabelle, in der die Tätigkeiten der Verdächtigen nach dem Focustext und den jeweiligen Übungen festgehalten werden, wird ebenfalls laufend ergänzt.
Die L können mit Hinweisen helfen und auf die Vermutungen der S entsprechend reagieren.
Einige Klassen kommen bereits beim Betrachten der Illustration auf die Tatwaffe, andere erst am Ende mit der Lösung des Kreuzworträtsels.

Lösung des Falls Professor Mottram hat seine Schwester mit einem Eiszapfen, den er in einer Thermosflasche mit kaltem Pfefferminztee in ihr Zimmer gebracht hat, ins Herz gestochen. Daher das Pfefferminzblatt in der Wunde! Als Professor der Anatomie konnte er den Stich so führen, dass dieser zum sofortigen Tod führte. Der Fall basiert auf der Kriminalgeschichte *The Tea-Leaf* von Edgar Jepson and Robert Eustace in *Great Tales of Detection*, herausgegeben von Dorothy L. Sayers.

Material CD, OHP-Folie

Vorgehen
1) Die S müssen die Einführung (Zeilen 1-11) verstehen, bevor der Dialogteil vorgespielt wird.
   Fragen dazu: *When did Lady Mottram die?*
   What was the wound like? Where was the wound? What do we know about the murder weapon? Where was the peppermint leaf?

2) Dialogteil abspielen. Die S den Text mitlesen lassen.

3) Vokabular erarbeiten.

4) Einige der folgenden Aspekte können herausgehoben werden:
   Lady Mottram only watches the Nine o'clock News.
   (Der Fernseher lief = Hinweis auf die Tatzeit).
   There was some blood on the front of her dress, but not much.
   (Hinweis auf anatomische Kenntnisse des Mörders).
   Professor Mottram's reading glasses on the table (macht ihn verdächtig).
   There were two thermos flasks: One had Earl Grey tea in it. The other one was full of cold peppermint tea. (Hinweis auf Eiszapfen).

Erweiterungen

Kopiervorlagen	Folie
Fill in the Missing Verbs (51)	Nr. 13
Fill in the Missing Words (52)	
What Are the Correct Questions? (53)	
Questions and Answers (54)	

Unit 18 Focus

Who Killed Lady Mottram?

1   Lady Penelope Mottram was dead. She died of a heart
    wound on 16th January between 6.30 p.m. and 11 p.m.
    The wound was very small, but it killed Lady Mottram
    immediately.

5   The murder weapon, a long pointed object, was nowhere.
    Mr Sanderby, the police expert, found a small piece of
    a peppermint leaf in the wound. There were two thermos
    flasks in Lady Mottram's room. One had Earl Grey tea in
10 it. The other one, next to Lady Mottram's chair, was full of
    cold peppermint tea. There was Earl Grey tea in her cup.

    *Inspector Bradley of Scotland Yard is talking to Isabella
15 Witherspoon, the household help. She found the body.*

    Bradley: How did you find the body?
    Ms Witherspoon: I was cleaning the hall. Then I
        heard the milkman. I was just carrying the
20   milk bottles in when I heard the television in
        Lady Mottram's drawing room.
    Bradley: Is that unusual?
    Witherspoon: Yes, Lady Mottram only
        watches the Nine o'clock News on
25   BBC 1 in the evening. She never watch-
        es anything else.
    Bradley: And what did the room look like?

    Witherspoon: Lady Mottram was sitting in her chair.
        First I thought she was sleeping, but then I saw
30   that her eyes were open. And there was some blood
        on the front of her dress, but not very much.
    Bradley: Did you notice anything unusual about
        the room?
    Witherspoon: Well, the television was on – BBC 1,
35   I think. Her reading light was on, but the fire in
        the fireplace wasn't burning.
    Bradley: This pair of glasses was lying on the table
        next to the thermos flask. Are they Lady Mottram's
40   glasses?
    Witherspoon: No, they are Professor Mottram's
        reading glasses.
    Bradley: I'm sorry, but I have to ask this question.
        What were you doing last night between dinner
45   and midnight?
    Witherspoon: Well, I brought Lady Mottram her
        evening tea, Earl Grey, at about a quarter to
        eight. I left the thermos flask on the
        little table next to her chair. She was
        talking to her friend Margaret on the
        phone. I said good night and then
        I went out to the cinema to see the new Tom
        Cruise film with – with a – friend. I came
        back at 11.30 and went straight to bed.

    (§ 32, 33, WB Ex 1, 2)

Training

First Step (§ 32, 33)

Inspector Bradley is talking about Ms Witherspoon with his colleague, Inspector Mailer. Can you form the questions and give the answers?

Mailer: Who found the body?
Bradley: Ms Witherspoon found the body.
Mailer: When / she / find ...?
Bradley: She ...
Mailer: Where / she / find ...?
Bradley: ...
Mailer: What / she / do / that morning before she found the body?
Bradley: ...
Mailer: Why / she / go / into the room?
Bradley: Because ...
Mailer: Where / Lady Mottram / sit?
Bradley: ...
Mailer: When / Lady Mottram / die?
Bradley: ...
Mailer: What / Ms Witherspoon / do / at the time of the murder?
Bradley: ...

Second Step (§ 32, 33, WB Ex 3, 4, 5)

Listen to the tape. Inspector Bradley's assistant, Detective Hopkins, is talking to Professor Mottram. Then answer these questions.

– Did Professor Mottram like his cousin?
– ...
– Were they talking to each other?
– ...
– What was he doing on the night of the murder?
– ...
– What did he hear that evening?
– ...
– Why did he wake up?
– ...
– What was he doing when Ms Witherspoon found the body?
– ...
– Did Professor Mottram go into the drawing room?
– ...

each, wake up

Unit 18

First Step

Hinweise/Ideen   Diese Übung zum Textverständnis ist zugleich eine Übung zur Verwendung von *simple past/past progressive*. § 33 der Grammatik sollte aus diesem Grund vorher behandelt werden.

Vorgehen   Fragen im *simple past* und *past progressive* formulieren und danach die passenden Antworten suchen.

1) Die S formulieren die Fragen (auch in GA möglich). Diese werden an WT/OHP notiert.
2) Im GU gemeinsam nach Antworten suchen.
3) Die S formulieren die Antworten in schriftlicher EA.
4) In PA mit wechselnden Rollen den Dialog durchspielen.

Lösung
> *When did she find the body? She found it in the morning.*
> *Where did she find it? She found it in Lady Mottram's drawing room.*
> *What was she doing that morning? She was cleaning the hall.*
> *Why did she go into the room? Because she heard the television.*
> *Where was Lady Mottram sitting? She was sitting in the chair.*
> *When did Lady Mottram die? After a quarter to eight.*
> *What was Miss Witherspoon doing at the time of the murder? She was watching a film in the cinema.*

Second Step

Hinweise/Ideen   Zur Lösung des Falles: Prof. Mottram gibt an, am Morgen nach der Tat nicht mehr im *drawing room* gewesen zu sein, doch seine Brille wurde dort gefunden!

Material   CD/Skript zum Text in den Kopiervorlagen

Vorgehen   Die S lesen die Fragen im Buch genau durch. Danach wird das Interview als Hörverständnisübung bearbeitet.

a) Basic
1) Die S lesen die Fragen im *Second Step*.
2) Das Skript wird als Vorlage abgegeben und der Text auf der CD abschnittweise abgespielt.
3) Die S arbeiten mit WB Ex 4 in PA/EA.
4) Im GU oder in PA werden die Fragen erarbeitet.

b) Intensive
1) Die S lesen die Fragen im *Second Step*.
2) Der Hörtext wird (abschnittweise) abgespielt. Aufgabe: Die S sollen sich auf die Fragen konzentrieren und die Antworten dazu stichwortartig auf einem Blatt notieren.
3) Im GU oder in PA werden die Fragen erarbeitet.
4) Das Skript kann abgegeben und der Dialog kann zusätzlich als Leseübung und Rollenspiel gemacht werden.

Erweiterungen

Kopiervorlagen
Script: Second Step (55)

Student's Book, p. 44

Unit 18

Third Step

Hinweise/Ideen Die S sollen in dieser Übung die Frageform von *simple past* und *past progressive* anwenden.
Zur Lösung des Falles:
Der Freund, mit dem Isabella Witherspoon ins Kino ging, war Archibald Plumley.
Professor Mottram hatte im *Second Step* behauptet, Archibald habe seiner Tante um 9 Uhr einen Tee gebracht.

Lösung
> *Did you like your aunt/Lady Mottram?*
> *What were you doing after dinner?*
> *When did Miss Witherspoon come into your room?*
> *Where was she going?*
> *Did she go out alone?*
> *Did you want to see the film?*
> *When did you leave the house?*
> *What were you doing this morning? What happened this morning?*
> *Did you go into your aunt's drawing room?*

Fourth Step

Hinweise/Ideen Die S diskutieren die Schlussfolgerungen von Inspektor Bradley und versuchen den Fall zu klären.

Lösung des Falles
- *Der Täter ist Professor Mottram. Sein Motiv war Geldnot. Hinweise dazu finden sich im Second Step, wo er sich darüber aufregt, dass seine Schwester ihr Geld Greenpeace und dem WWF hinterlassen will, und im WB, Ex 5, wo die Publikation seines Buches erwähnt wird.*

- *Die Mordwaffe war ein Eiszapfen, den Mottram in der Thermosflasche mit Pfefferminztee in Lady Mottrams Zimmer brachte. Hinweis dazu im Focustext: Der Earl-Grey-Tee war noch warm, der Pfefferminztee hingegen kalt.*

- *Die Mordzeit war zwischen 19 und 23 Uhr. Da Lady Mottram immer nur die 9-Uhr-Nachrichten hörte, dürfte der Mord eher in der Zeit danach geschehen sein. Hinweise finden sich im Focustext und im WB, Ex 5. Für diese Zeit haben Plumley und Witherspoon ein Alibi.*

- *Mottram machte folgende Fehler: Er wusste nicht, dass Plumley und Witherspoon zusammen ausgegangen waren. Er wusste zu viel über die Art der Wunde bzw. Todesursache, obwohl er behauptete, das Zimmer nicht betreten zu haben. Er vergass seine Brille am Tatort.*

Third Step

Inspector Bradley is talking to Archibald Plumley, Lady Mottram's nephew. Here are Archibald's answers. Can you form the question?

Bradley: ...
Plumley: Yes, I liked her. My aunt was very nice to me.
Bradley: ...
Plumley: After dinner I was working for my exams. Then Isabella came into my room. She was ready to go out.
Bradley: ...
Plumley: That was at ten to eight.
Bradley: ...
Plumley: She was going out to see the new Tom Cruise film.
Bradley: ...
Plumley: No, – erm – she didn't go out alone. I went with her ...
Bradley: ...
Plumley: No, I didn't really want to see the film but I wanted to go out with Isabella – Ms Witherspoon.
Bradley: ...
Plumley: I left at about five to eight.
Bradley: ...
Plumley: I was shaving when I heard Isabella – Ms Witherspoon – scream.
Bradley: ...
Plumley: No, I did not go into my aunt's drawing room after that.

exam, nephew, scream, shave, case

Fourth Step (§ 32, 33, WB Ex 5)

Inspector Bradley is thinking about the case. Look at the sentences. Ask questions and answer them if you can.

Example:
– Did Lady Mottram know the murderer?
– What was the murderer's motive?

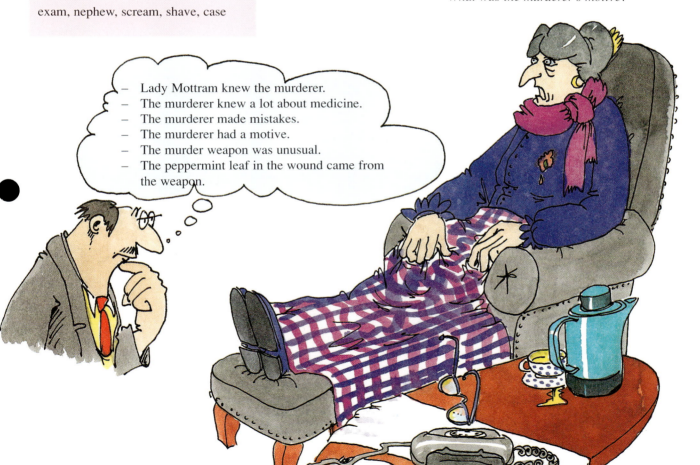

- Lady Mottram knew the murderer.
- The murderer knew a lot about medicine.
- The murderer made mistakes.
- The murderer had a motive.
- The murder weapon was unusual.
- The peppermint leaf in the wound came from the weapon.

Stepping Out

Strange Stories

These five stories are very strange. Can you find out why?

What a Game!

Our school basketball team was playing a very difficult game last Saturday. It was a hard match and they won it, but not one man scored a single basket.

An Easy Holiday

Last summer I was on holiday in Italy. I was having a great time and I took things easy. After my first day at the beach I switched off the light in my hotel room. I walked the 4 meters to my bed and was in bed before it was dark.

A Very Strange Story

A father and his son were going home by car. It was snowing and a strong wind was blowing. When they were going over a bridge, the father lost control of the car. It went over the side and fell into the river. The father died immediately. The son didn't die, and a helicopter took the boy to the nearest hospital. It was clear that a very difficult operation was necessary to save the boy's life. Then the doctor came in, looked at the boy and said: "I'm sorry. I cannot operate on this patient. He is my son."

Dangerous Trains

The train line between Thornington and Washam has two train tracks. But there is a high mountain with a tunnel on that line. In the tunnel there is not enough room for two tracks. One afternoon a train went into the tunnel. It was going from Thornington to Washam. Another train was travelling from Washam to Thornington. Both trains entered the tunnel, both trains were going in the opposite direction. Both trains were travelling very fast and – there was no accident.

A Slow Grand Prix

Bill Grates is very rich and a bit strange. He organised a Formula 1 Grand Prix with a prize of $100,000. But the prize was not for the fastest car in the race, it was for the slowest car.
One of the drivers said to Mr Grates: "How can we run this race? We'll all just go slower and slower and the race will never finish."
But Bill Grates had an idea. He told the drivers what to do and the race was as fast as any other, perhaps even a bit faster. What did Mr Grates think of?

NEW WORDS

score, switch off, save, operate, patient, tracks, travel, opposite direction, prize

Unit 18

Unit 18

Stepping Out

Hinweise/Ideen Es geht in dieser Übung nicht nur um das Lösen der Denkpuzzles, sondern auch um die Wiederholung der Frageformen. Die S sollen bei allen Geschichten Fragen ausarbeiten, die zur Lösung des Puzzles führen.

Vorgehen Zur Einstimmung die erste Geschichte *What a Game!* im GU erarbeiten: Den Text lesen lassen und gemeinsam Fragen ausarbeiten, die zur Lösung beitragen könnten.
Danach die Klasse in Gruppen aufteilen und die anderen Geschichten erarbeiten lassen.

1) Alle S lesen in EA einen der längeren Texte (*An Easy Holiday* vorerst weglassen).

2) Jene S, die dieselbe Geschichte gelesen haben, setzen sich zu einer Gruppe zusammen und beraten, was die Lösung sein könnte. L muss hier möglicherweise helfend eingreifen.

3) Dreiergruppen bilden, in denen je ein(e) S aus den drei Geschichtengruppen sitzen. Reihum werden die Geschichten von den jeweiligen "Experten" vorgelesen. Die anderen S stellen Fragen, die von den jeweiligen "Experten" beantwortet werden, und versuchen die Lösung zu verraten.

4) *An Easy Holiday* als Zusatzaufgabe für gute S. Wer die Lösung hat, wird von den anderen S ausgefragt.

Intensive Zu Punkt 3): Die S erzählen den anderen Mitgliedern der Gruppe ihre Geschichte in eigenen Worten, anstatt sie aus dem Buch vorzulesen.

Lösung

What a Game:	*It's a women's basketball team.*
An Easy Holiday:	*It was still daytime/daylight.*
A Very Strange Story:	*The doctor is the boy's mother.*
Dangerous Trains:	*The trains entered the tunnel at different times.*
A Slow Grand Prix:	*The prize goes to the slowest car, not the slowest driver.*
	If the drivers don't drive their own cars, they will go as fast as they can.

Erweiterungen

Kopiervorlagen
Puzzle Text (56)
Three Stories (57)

Unit 18

Reading Corner

Hinweise/Ideen   Im Zusammenhang mit dem Kapitel *Mystery and Crime* werden hier drei Autoren behandelt, die verschiedene Genres, Epochen und soziale Umfelder repräsentieren. Agatha Christie als Klassikerin aus der ersten Hälfte des 20. Jahrhunderts zeigt den britischen Mittelstand, meist in einer eng definierten Umgebung (Dorf, Herrschaftssitz etc.) und eine Welt, die durch die Lösung des Falles wieder ins Lot kommt. Die Amerikanerin Donna Leon lässt in der Lagunenstadt Venedig ihren Commissario Brunetti in einer korrupten Welt agieren, wo die Lösung des Falles meistens nur Auskunft über die Täterschaft gibt, ohne dass diese von der Justiz zur Rechenschaft gezogen wird. Ian Fleming verleiht seinem glamourösen, kosmopolitischen Helden James Bond übermenschliche Kräfte, damit er alle Bösewichte blutig zur Strecke bringen kann.

Eine Diskussion auf Deutsch könnte diese Aspekte und die Unterschiede zwischen den Autoren und ihren Stilen zum Thema haben.

Mögliche Bearbeitung
- Die S lesen die Texte in stiller EA und formulieren Verständnisfragen, die in PA/GA gestellt werden.
- Die S formulieren falsche und richtige Aussagen zu den Texten, der Rest der Klasse muss die Aussagen beurteilen und richtigstellen.
- Die S bekommen die Aufgabe, zu den Autoren und ihren Werken weitere Informationen zu suchen (Bücher, Filme, Internet).

Reading Corner

Agatha Christie: the Queen of Crime

Agatha Christie is the most famous writer of detective stories in the world. Her novels are very popular with sales of over a billion books in English and a billion in 45 other languages. Only the Bible and Shakespeare's works are more popular than Agatha Christie's stories of crime.

Agatha Christie was born Agatha Miller in Devon, England in 1890. She was the youngest of three children. Her family was wealthy and Agatha grew up in a large house. She never went to school but had a governess to teach her at home.

At the age of 24, she married Colonel Archibald Christie. During the First World War she worked at a hospital as a nurse. It was at this time that she started writing detective novels.

Archie and Agatha had a daughter, Rosalind, but they were not very happy and got divorced in 1928. In 1930 Agatha married Max Mallowan, a young archaelogist, who she met on a trip to Mesopotamia. This was a happy marriage, and Agatha often travelled with her husband to the Near East, where he worked with his team.

In over 50 years, Agatha Christie wrote 79 novels and short story collections. She also wrote a play called *The Mousetrap*. It opened in London on November 25, 1952 and it is still running today! It is the longest running theatre production in history.

Agatha Christie created two very unusual detectives. One is Hercule Poirot, a Belgian with a bowler hat and a small moustache. Poirot is very proud of his remarkable intelligence and says that he can solve every mystery with the help of his famous "little grey cells" (i.e. his brains).

Christie's other popular detective is an old lady, Miss Jane Marple. Miss Marple leads a very ordinary life: She lives in a small English village, drinks tea and chats with her friends and neighbours. But she knows more about people's characters than anybody else. That's why she is always the first person to find out the truth about a crime.

Many of Agatha Christie's books are also films. Two of the most successful are *Murder on the Orient Express* and *Death on the Nile*. In 1971, the Queen gave Agatha Christie the highest British honour, the Order of Dame Commander of the British Empire. Agatha Christie died on January 12, 1976.

Donna Leon: the Italian Connection

Donna Leon was born on September 28, 1942 in New Jersey, USA. She left the States in 1965 to work in Europe and in Asia. She lived and taught in Switzerland, Iran, China and Saudi Arabia.

Today Donna Leon lives in Venice, the "most beautiful city in the world" as she says. She moved to Italy in the eighties because she liked the Italian way of life, the food, the wine and the language. She has a teaching post as a professor of English Literature at the University of Maryland in Vincenza.

Donna Leon's detective is Commissario Guido Brunetti. He works at the Venice police headquarters. Brunetti is a very special Commissario, who loves Italian food and has a lot of friends. He is the father of two children, a boy and a girl, and his wife is a professor of English Literature like Donna Leon. Brunetti fights crime in Venice, but because so many criminals have friends in the government or are very rich, he can often only find out what happened but cannot arrest the criminals. This shows that Donna Leon's novels are very up-to-date and realistic.

Donna Leon's books, over 10 novels all together, are published in many languages, but not in Italian. She says that she does not want the Italians to feel that she is criticizing Italy because she is actually very happy with her life in Venice.

Ian Fleming: the Father of James Bond

His name was Fleming, Ian Fleming. The character he created was superhero James Bond, Secret Agent 007. Like his hero, Ian Fleming himself worked for the British secret service and master-minded several top secret operations.

Ian Lancaster Fleming was born on May 28, 1908. His father, Major Valentine Fleming, died in World War I when Ian was a boy. Ian went to elite English schools but didn't like them very much. Because he wasn't a good student, he didn't go to Oxford but became an officer at the army college of Sandhurst. He got very good marks there but felt that the army was not for him. After a period as a journalist in Moscow and as a banker in London, the British Secret Service MI5 offered him a chance to use his knowledge of languages and his flair for life in high society.

Fleming helped the Americans to set up the OSS (later the CIA). Like James Bond, he loved women and fast cars and was a man who was not afraid of doing dangerous things. During a training exercise he had to swim underwater and attach a mine to a tanker. This act was later the material for an exciting scene in *Live and Let Die* (1954).

During his travels for the secret service, Fleming visited Jamaica and fell in love with it. After the war he bought a holiday house there. In 1952 he married Anne Rothermere in Jamaica and shortly after his wedding he started to write his first James Bond novel, *Casino Royale* (1953).

In his last years, Fleming spent his winters in Jamaica writing. Books like *From Russia, with Love* (1957), *Goldfinger* (1959) and *You Only Live Twice* (1964) made Agent 007 a hero of the cold war.

But the father of James Bond had serious health problems because he smoked too much and drank a lot. He died in 1964. His last book, *The Man with the Golden Gun*, came out the next year, but several chapters were by a ghost writer.

Fleming never saw the great success of many of the James Bond films. In the eighties other writers started to write James Bond books, so that the popular series could go on.

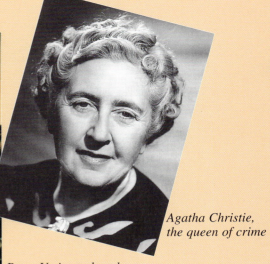

Agatha Christie, the queen of crime

Peter Ustinov played detective Hercule Poirot in several films.

Commissario Brunetti and his family

Ian Fleming, the man who created James Bond

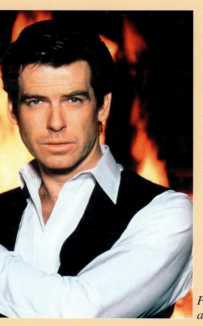

Donna Leon: an American writer in Venice

Pierce Brosnan, one of the many actors who were James Bond

48 page forty-eight **Unit 18**

Unit 18

Reading Corner

Hinweise/Ideen   Diese Seite illustriert die Texte auf Seite 47. Sie kann den Texten vorangestellt werden oder am Schluss als Ausklang dienen. Sie kann aber auch unabhängig von den Lesetexten besprochen werden.

Mögliche Aktivitäten   Die S beantworten folgende Fragen als GA:

Agatha Christie:
1) Do you know stories about Hercule Poirot and Miss Marple?
2) Are there any films from books by Agatha Christie? What are they called?
   "And Then There Were None", "Death on the Nile," "Murder on the Orient Express" (the most famous ones)
3) What are the titles of some of her books in German and/or in English?

Donna Leon:
1) Which of Brunetti's cases do you know?
   Death at la Fenice (Venezianisches Finale), Death in a Strange Country (Endstation Venedig), The Anonymous Venetian (Venezianische Scharade), A Venetian Reckoning (Vendetta), Acqua Alta (Acqua Alta), The Death of Faith (Sanft entschlafen), A Noble Radiance (Nobiltà), Fatal Remedies (In Sachen Signora Brunetti), Friends in High Places (Feine Freunde), A Sea of Troubles (Deutsch z.Zt. des Drucks noch nicht erschienen)
2) What are the members of his family called?
   Raffi, his son, Paola, his wife and Chiara, his daughter
3) Who does he often work with?
   Patta, his boss, Vianello, Signorina Elettra, his boss's secretary
4) What else do you know about him?

Ian Fleming:
1) What do you know about James Bond?
2) Which actors played James Bond?
   Sean Connery, Roger Moore, George Lazenby, Timothy Dalton, Pierce Brosnan
3) Do you know any of the baddies?
   Dr. No, Goldfinger, Blofeld, Scaramanga, Jaws (the most famous ones)
4) What is special about James Bond?
5) Can you remember some of the things James Bond always says?
   "My name is Bond, James Bond." "Shaken, not stirred." (his Martini)
6) Can you remember any other characters from James Bond?
   M, the boss, Q, the man who makes the clever gadgets, Miss Moneypenny, M's secretary

Student's Book, p. 48

Warm-up

Me, You and the Others

Warm-up

Diskussion

Die Einstimmungsseite eignet sich für eine Diskussion über Alter, Gruppen- und Cliquenzugehörigkeit. Man kann zu den unten stehenden Fragen auch ein Brainstorming machen, und das Resultat im Schreibanlass 2 (siehe unten) umsetzen.

Mögliche Fragen
Which three things do you like best about your age/your situation? Which three things do you hate most? Who are the most important people in your life? Do you like them and why? Do you hate them and why? What would you like to change in your life?
What do you like most about your friends, your family, your teachers, yourself? What do you hate most about your friends, your family, your teachers (yourself)?

Schreibanlass

Die folgenden kreativen Schreibanlässe sind unabhängig vom Lehrbuch und können auch zu einem späteren Zeitpunkt, z.B. nach *Time for a Change*, gemacht werden.

1) Prahl- oder Lobgedicht
   Die **S** verfassen von sich ein Prahlgedicht (Was kann ich so gut wie/besser als ...?) oder für einen Freund/eine Freundin ein Lobgedicht (Welche Eigenschaften bedeuten mir an ihm/ihr viel?).
   - Die ersten Versuche in GA machen lassen und ausdrücklich darauf hinweisen, dass der Text nicht "wahr" sein muss. (Jeder Text könnte sogar zwei Lügen enthalten).
   - Als Einführung tragen die **S** passende Adjektive zusammen und setzen diese dann im Gedicht um (Beispiele: *fast, clever, strong, good-looking, popular, intelligent, good at ..., sexy, cool, hip, etc*). Die Sprachform könnte so aussehen: *I am fast, as fast as a ... /I am faster than ...* oder *I am so clever, I can ... / I am cleverer than...*
   - Reime müssen nicht verwendet werden, da sie auf dieser Stufe einengen. Die Gedichtform kann sich daraus ergeben, dass die erste und die letzte Zeile des Textes identisch sind, dass jede Strophe mit den gleichen Worten anfängt, (Beispiel: *Look at me I am ...* oder *I need you because ...*), oder dass jede Strophe aus mehreren Vergleichen zum selben Adjektiv besteht oder dieselbe Anzahl Aussagen enthält

2) *What I love and what I hate*
   In PA ein Gedicht über die Schule und die eigene Situation verfassen, in dem eine Zeile mit *What I love about x is ...* und die nächste mit *What I hate about x is...* beginnt. **S1** beginnt mit Thema x (*What I love about x ...*), **S2** wählt Thema y (*What I love about y ...*). Beide notieren ihren Satz und tauschen dann die Blätter aus. **S1** schreibt nun zu **S2**s Satz *What I hate about y* und umgekehrt. Dann schreiben beide den nächsten Satz zu *What I love about ...*, wobei sie aus dem zweiten Satz ein Wort nehmen oder einen ganz neuen Satz formulieren usw.

Me, You and the Others ...

page forty-nine

Unit 19 Focus

Problem Page

"Help!?"
c/o Chill'n'Brill
24 Trestle Street
Manchester M15 9PN

Have you got a problem?
Write to "Help!?" and we can ask our readers what they think.

1 Hi there,
   My name is Andy and I've got a problem. I fancy this girl called Carla. She's not in my class but I see her in the computer lessons. She's great and I'd love to ask her out.
5 My problem: I am very shy. I always go red when I talk to people, especially girls. Sometimes I think of something clever to say, but when I talk to the girl, I can't get the words out. It may be because I'm not very good-looking: I'm skinny and my hair is very thick. I can't do anything
10 with it. My parents are old hippies and they like my hair long. I don't. I'd like it short. I'm also not very sporty. I'm only good at computer things and that's not very interesting for a girl, is it?
   Carla has got a lot of friends and she sometimes smiles
15 when I walk past. Perhaps I could say something to her, but there are always girls around her. I just can't talk to her alone.
   Can you help?   Andy, Lancaster

1 Dear Andy,
   You are good with computers, right? Can you send her a message in your computer class? Or could you ask one of her friends for Carla's e-mail address? Then
5 send her a funny e-mail and ask her to go out to the cinema. And you should talk to your parents about your hair.   Colin

1 Dear Andy,
   You don't like your hair? Well, what's the problem? I would go and have it cut. Your parents might not like it, but cut is cut, right?
5 And you think you are skinny. You shouldn't worry about that. You can go to a fitness club and work on your body.   Lisa
   (§ 34, WB Ex 1, 2)

1 Dear Andy,
   I had the same problem, but there is a way out: you must talk to her. Find out where she lives. Then you can wait for her and ask her out for an ice cream or something.
5 Jessica

   Dear Andy,
   I know a lot about computers and I find them interesting – and I'm a girl. You mustn't think that girls are not very
10 good with computers. Ask her for "help" with a computer problem. It could be a good start, you know ...
   Alice

Unit 19

Sprachfunktionen:
Gefühle ausdrücken, über Handlungsmöglichkeiten sprechen, Ratschläge geben, Erlaubnis oder Notwendigkeit ausdrücken

Strukturen:
Modale Hilfsverben *may, might, could, shall, must, should, would, would like* in der einfachen Gegenwart

Grammatik:
§ 34

Themen:
Beratungskolumne in einem Teenager-Magazin; verschiedene Sportarten und Regeln

Mögliche Abfolge:
Focus → First Step → WB Ex 1, 2 → Second Step → Third Step → WB Ex 3 → Fourth Step → WB Ex 4 → Fifth Step → (WB Ex 5) → WB Ex 6, 7 → Stepping Out → WB Ex 8 (→ WB Ex 9, 10)

Focus: Problem Page

Wichtig	In dieser Unit geht es um Modalverben. Sie sind ein problematisches Kapitel, weil ihre Wahl von den Kommunikationspartnern abhängig ist. Deshalb können Feinheiten im Gebrauch grammatikalisch nicht eindeutig festgehalten werden. Ob jemand *you must* oder *you should* sagt, beruht auf dem Autoritätsverhältnis zwischen den Kommunikationspartnern. Ob man *I might, I could* oder *I may* sagt, hängt davon ab, wie sicher man sich seiner Sache ist.
Material	CD
Vorgehen	
a) Basic	1) Die S lesen den Brief in EA und versuchen herauszufinden, was Andy's Problem ist. L kann wichtige Ausdrücke an die WT schreiben: *fancy, shy, not very good-looking, skinny, not sporty, she smiles, talk to her alone* 2) Brief ab CD spielen und still mitlesen. 3) Die S machen in PA/GA eine Liste von Andy's Problemen. 4) Die Klasse in drei Gruppen aufteilen, jede beschäftigt sich mit einem Antwortbrief und notiert stichwortartig, was Jessica, Alice und Colin vorschlagen. 5) Besprechung im GU.
b) Intensive	1) Die Klasse in zwei Teams aufteilen, die sich mit Andy's Brief (Team A) und mit Sue's Brief (Team B) beschäftigen. 2) Jedes Team hält die Hauptprobleme an WT auf OHP-Folie fest. 3) Die Präsentatoren von Team A und B erläutern anhand der WT/OHP-Folie das Problem. 4) Team A liest die Antwortbriefe zu Sue's Problem, Team B jene zu Andy's. Beide Teams halten wieder die Hauptaussagen fest. Diese werden mit dem Problem verglichen und kommentiert. 5) Texte als Hörübung ab CD spielen und evtl. als Leseübung vertiefen.
Bemerkungen	Achtung: Verwechslungsgefahr von "nicht dürfen" und "nicht müssen", wenn *mustn't* mit dem Deutschen verglichen wird. Man sollte versuchen vorerst ohne Übersetzung auszukommen, oder *mustn't* mit dem schweizerdeutschen Ausruf "Hey, muesch nöd!" vergleichen, der auch im Sinne von "nicht dürfen" gemeint ist.

Erweiterungen

Kopiervorlagen
Fill in the Verbs (58)
Fill in the Gaps (59)

Student's Book, p. 50

Unit 19

Hinweise siehe vorhergehende Seite: Vorgehen, Intensive

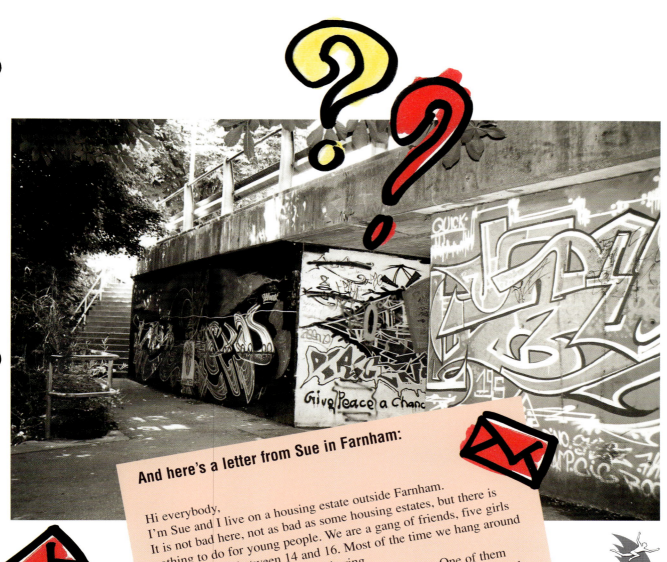

And here's a letter from Sue in Farnham:

Hi everybody,

I'm Sue and I live on a housing estate outside Farnham. It is not bad here, not as bad as some housing estates, but there is nothing to do for young people. We are a gang of friends, five girls and eight boys between 14 and 16. Most of the time we hang around the bus stop and talk, but it's so boring.

My problem is that I worry about some of the boys. One of them stole some cigarettes from a shop last week. Two others are in trouble with the police. They sprayed some pictures on a wall near the bus stop. I'm also worried about Joe, my boyfriend. He started to drink alcohol about a year ago and now he is drinking more and more. I think he might have problems with his parents (actually with his mother's boyfriend). I really want to help him.

Perhaps things would be better with a place for young people, a club or something.

Can you help?

Sue

1 Dear Sue,
You should try to find a place for a youth club. In a club you can do things and you don't have to hang around the bus stop every day. We have got our club now, a small
5 room at the back of a supermarket, and things are much better for all of us. It wasn't easy, and it took a lot of work. Try it!
Melanie, Pete and Simon

1 Dear Sue,
I understand that you want to help Joe, but you can't do very much for him. Can you talk to your parents about Joe? I think you should speak to them or to a
5 teacher. Joe has got a real problem, and he must stop: alcohol doesn't help, it makes everything worse.
Mary-Ann

Training

First Step (§ 34, Focus)

What do you think? Which of these things are possible? Which are necessary? Use may/may not and must/mustn't to complete the sentences.

Example:
– Carla's friends may help Andy.
– Carla may not think that Andy is too skinny.
– Andy must find out how Carla feels about him.

1. Carla ... like Andy because he's good with computers.
2. Andy ... think that his fitness is a problem.
3. Carla ... think that long hair is nice.
4. Some answers ... help Andy.
5. Carla ... want to talk to Andy.
6. Colin thinks that an e-mail to Carla ... be a start.
7. Andy ... think that girls are not interested in computers.
8. Carla ... like Andy.
9. Carla's friends ... think that Andy is an interesting person.
10. Jessica thinks that Andy ... talk to Carla.

Second Step (§ 34, Focus)

a) This is what Andy and Carla may think. Can you finish their dreams and thoughts?

Andy: I'd like to …
        But I …
        I could …
        Her friends …
        In the computer room …
        Perhaps I should …

Carla: I think Andy is …
        He seems to …
        He's got …
        I'd like to …
        Why doesn't he …?
        Perhaps I should …

b) What about Sue?

Sue thinks that ...
– the boys ... steal cigarettes from ...
– two of her friends ... spray ...
– Joe ... drink ...
– Joe ... with his parents because ...
– perhaps things ... place ... young people ...

Melanie, Pete and Simon think that ...
– Sue and her friends ... find ... youth club.
– a youth club ... be something for ...
– the group ... hang around ...
– they ... play things like basketball or ... in a youth club.
– a club ... bring a lot of fun.
– the boys ... be in trouble ...

Mary-Ann thinks that ...
– Sue ... do very much for Joe.
– she ... speak to ...
– Joe ... stop ...
– Joe ... go on like that.

USE
should, have to, must, may, might, can, could, shouldn't, mustn't

Third Step (§ 34, WB Ex 8)

a) This is Celia McDonald. She would like to go to St. Bernadette's School for Girls. But the school rules are very strict there. Can you remember them? Tell her what she should do or shouldn't do.

Example: – Celia, you shouldn't smoke; you must wear a school uniform ...

b) Give some information about your school.

Example: You mustn't smoke; you shouldn't be late for lessons; you can ...

USE
leave paper .../ chew .../ eat or drink .../ listen to .../ make a lot of ... / sit on ... / play the ... / wear jeans and ... / touch .../ bring ...

Unit 19

First Step

Hinweise/Ideen
- Übung zu *may/may not* und *must/mustn't*.
  Possibility = *may/may not* ("vielleicht", "es könnte sein, dass...")
  Necessity = *must/mustn't* ("muss", "sollte nicht" oder "darf nicht")
- Wenn möglich, sollte man nur mit den Begriffen *possibility* und *necessity* arbeiten und die deutsche Übersetzung nur beiziehen, wenn die S dies ausdrücklich verlangen.
- Die S darauf hinweisen, dass bei jenen Sätzen, wo der Text keine klare Auskunft gibt, *may* richtig ist, da es genau hier um Vermutungen und Möglichkeiten geht.

Vorgehen
1) Die S suchen im Focustext nach Aussagen zu den Sätzen.
2) In PA/GA: Welche Aussage ist eine Spekulation *(possibility)*, welche drückt eine Notwendigkeit *(necessity)* aus?

Lösungen
1. *Carla may (may not) like Andy because he's good at computers.*
2. *Andy mustn't think that his fitness is a problem.*
3. *Carla may think that long hair is nice.*
4. *Some answers may help Andy.*
   (Hier ist auch *must* möglich, wenn die S davon überzeugt sind.)
5. *Carla may want to talk to Andy.*
6. *Colin thinks that an e-mail to Carla may be a start.*
7. *Andy mustn't think that girls are not interested in computers.*
8. *Carla may like Andy.*
9. *Carla's friends may think that Andy is an interesting person.*
10. *Jessica thinks that Andy must talk to Carla.*

Second Step

Hinweise/Ideen

Die Übung könnte von Mädchengruppen für Andy und von Knabengruppen für Carla gelöst werden. Danach tragen die S in PA (Mädchen/Knabe) einander die Resultate vor.
Zur Vertiefung könnten die S einzelne Sätze auswählen und so lernen, dass sie diese der Klasse frei vortragen können.

Third Step

Hinweise/Ideen

Schulregeln aus Band 1, Unit 7. Es spielt jedoch für die Übung keine Rolle, ob sich die S daran erinnern. Für schwächere Klassen kann die OHP-Folie aus Unit 7 als Hilfe aufgelegt werden.
Verwendung von: *may, should, must, shouldn't, may not oder mustn't*.
Damit die S merken, dass es ein Unterschied ist, ob sie einer Freundin Ratschläge erteilen oder ein Verbot aussprechen, könnten stärkere S den Text als Klassenstreber oder Klassenbösewicht formulieren.

Erweiterungen

Kopiervorlagen
Can You Help Me? (62a, 62b)

Student's Book, p. 52

Unit 19

Fourth Step

Hinweise/Ideen Freie Diskussionsübung

Vorgehen Die S stellen in EA eine Liste zusammen mit ☺ für Dinge, die sie gern tun, ☺ für Dinge, die sie in Ordnung finden, und ☹ für Dinge, die sie nicht tun möchten. Für die beiden letzten Rubriken müssen sie auch Gründe notieren.
Die Klasse in Dreiergruppen aufteilen. Diese besprechen untereinander, was für ein Programm für sie in Frage kommt, und müssen sich dabei einig werden. Jene Dinge werden ausgeschlossen, die zwei Personen gar nicht passten.

Fifth Step

Hinweise/Ideen Gebrauch der Modalverben *may must* und *should* (evtl. noch *can*) bejahend und verneint.

Lösung
1. There <u>must</u> be eleven players in each team. The two teams <u>must / should</u> wear different colours. The goalkeeper shouldn't leave the penalty area. The players <u>mustn't / may</u> not stand in the penalty area during a penalty kick. The field players <u>mustn't / may</u> not touch the ball with their hands except when they throw it in from the sideline.
2. The ball <u>must</u> never touch the ground. After two passes you <u>must</u> play the ball into the other field. When you serve, you <u>mustn't / can't</u> play the ball with both hands. You <u>may / can</u> play the ball with your head. Girls and boys <u>may / can</u> play in the same team.
3. There <u>should</u> be twelve players in each team. Only seven <u>may / can</u> be on the field at a time. You <u>mustn't / may</u> not run with the ball in your hands, so you <u>should</u> pass it to another player. Only the goalkeeper <u>may / can</u> stand in the semi-circle. Field players <u>may / can</u> jump into the semi-circle around the goal as long as they throw the ball before they touch the ground. A new player <u>may / can</u> enter to throw a penalty.

Erweiterungen

Kopiervorlagen
What's the Name of the Game? (60)
The Story of an Escape (61)

Ausbau
1) Die S beschreiben weitere Sportarten.
2) Die S erfinden neue Sportarten und Regeln dazu.

Beispiel: Ice rugby: *Can you think of rules?*
Lösungsvorschlag: *You can play this game on an ice rink with a rugby ball. There must be five players in each team. They may carry the ball in their hands and skate. They may attack each other with their arms and hands, but they must not attack other players with their legs.*

Could, should, must/can may/might

Fourth Step (§ 34)

It's the last day on your school trip. You and your friend(s) are planning to go out this afternoon and evening. Discuss what to do.

Example:
Partner A: Shall we go to the beach? It is very hot today.
Partner B: I don't want to take a rucksack. But we could go to the cinema, there are some great films on this week.
Partner C: The cinema is too expensive. The Oldtimer Museum might be fun too and it is free.

USE
Shall we ...
We could ...
We might ...
I'd like to ...

USE
– open air museum
– indoor swimming pool
– concert at the rock cafe
– theatre
– open air cinema
– snackbar
– beach
– shopping
– park
– disco
– football match

Fifth Step (§ 34)

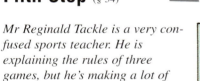

Mr Reginald Tackle is a very confused sports teacher. He is explaining the rules of three games, but he's making a lot of mistakes. What are the correct words: may, must or ... ?

Example: There may be eleven players in each team.
– *There must be eleven players in each team.*

NEW WORDS:
at the time, confused, except, explain, ground, semicircle

2. The ball must never touch the ground. After two passes you can play the ball into the other field. When you serve, you should play the ball with both hands. You can't play the ball with your head. Girls and boys must not play in the same team.

1. There may be eleven players in each team. The two teams can wear different colours. The goalkeeper must not leave the penalty area. The players shouldn't stand in the penalty area during a penalty kick. The field players must not touch the ball with their hands except when they throw it in from the sideline.

3. There must not be twelve players in each team. Only seven should be on the field at a time. You may run with the ball in your hands, so you should pass it to another player. Only the goalkeeper must stand in the semicircle. Field players can't jump into the semicircle around the goal as long as they throw the ball before they touch the ground. A new player should enter to throw a penalty.

Stepping Out

What do you think about school uniforms? (WB Ex 8)

British school children have to wear uniforms. So do a lot of pupils in other countries like Australia, India, Africa or America. It is a tradition there.

Some children like their uniforms, others hate them. A lot of people think that kids should wear a school uniform because these clothes don't show whether their family is rich or poor: all the children look the same.

Others think that uniforms take away their personal freedom. Most teenagers would like to dress in a more personal way. They'd prefer their own blouses or shirts, skirts and trousers.

Some school children say that a uniform is okay, but they could do without a tie and a hat.

Australia

India

Great Britain

As a test, a class in Germany wore school uniforms for two months. Some of the pupils liked it, others didn't. After the two months' test period 48 percent of the children at the school were against school uniforms and 34 percent were for school uniforms. In general, boys liked the uniforms better than girls.

Here are some opinions of the pupils that tested the uniforms:

Pro:
I can sleep longer in the morning because I don't have to decide what to wear.
You feel that you are part of a team.
Everybody can see that we go to the same school.
A lot of kids wear Nike, Reebok and Adidas clothes. These clothes are expensive. Kids should wear school uniforms, then they may have more money for other things.
I think the idea of a school uniform is good, but you should have two or three styles to choose from.

Con:
It is boring to wear the same clothes every day.
I don't like the colour of our school uniform.
I have to wear clothes that I don't like.
I can't choose the style of my clothes.
I didn't like our uniform because boys and girls had to wear the same clothes.
Two months is okay, but I don't want to wear the same clothes for years.
I don't feel comfortable in a uniform.

1. Would you like to wear a school uniform? Why? Why not?
2. Girls and boys have to wear a tie with their uniform. Would you like to wear a tie? Why? Why not?
3. In some European schools children have problems because their colleagues wear expensive designer clothes. What about your school? Are clothes important? (§ 34)

whether, rich, poor, look (vb.) the same, freedom, in general, opinion, decide (vb.), expensive, choose (vb.), boring

Unit 19

Stepping Out

Hinweise/Ideen	Kombination von Lesetext und Diskussionsübung
Vorgehen	1) Die S lesen die Texte zu den Schuluniformen in EA.
	2) Sie bilden zwei Teams. Team A trägt Argumente *für* Schuluniformen, Team B *dagegen* zusammen. Aufgabe für schwächere S: Sie wählen in den Kastentexten jene Argumente aus, die sie überzeugen, und versuchen weitere zu finden. Aufgabe für stärkere S: Sie lesen die Argumente im Buch durch, arbeiten aber danach ohne Buch und formulieren die Argumente selbst.
	3) Mit L als Moderator spielen die S eine Arena-Diskussion zum Thema "Schuluniformen" durch. L kann die drei Fragen zum Thema als Leitlinie für die Diskussion verwenden. Die S, die nicht mitdiskutieren, können als Punktrichter amtieren und am Ende der Debatte entscheiden, welche Seite die besseren Argumente eingebracht hat.
Ausbau	Repetition des Vokabulars zu Kleidern und Farben:
	• Die S suchen im Text alle Wörter zum Wortfeld "Kleider" heraus.
	• Die S beschreiben möglichst detailliert die Kleider auf den Bildern.

Student's Book. p, 54

Unit 20

Sprachfunktionen:	Themen:
Über die nahe Vergangenheit mit Hinblick auf die Gegenwart sprechen; Auskunft geben über den Stand der Dinge: was ist erledigt, was ist noch zu tun?	Eine Party organisieren, letzte Vorbereitungen treffen

Strukturen:
Present perfect (alle Formen); Unterschied *present perfect* – *simple past*

Grammatik:
§ 35

Mögliche Abfolge:
Focustext I → First Step → WB Ex 1,2 → (Focustext II) → Second Step → (WB Ex 3) → Third Step → WB Ex 4,5 → Fourth Step → (Fifth Step) → (WB Ex 6) → Stepping Out → (WB Ex 7) → Time for a Change → (WB Ex 8,9)

Focus I: A Week Before the End-of the-School-Year Party

Hinweise/Ideen	• Im Focustext I soll die neue Zeitform zuerst gefestigt werden. Erst im Focustext II werden *present perfect* und *past simple* einander gegenübergestellt. Diese Unterscheidung muss bei der Stufe *Basic* nicht vertieft behandelt werden. • Mögliche Einführung des *present perfect*: L erteilt einigen S vor der Lektion kleinere Aufträge (etwas holen, jemanden etw. fragen usw.) und fragt dann nach: *Have you asked Mr. ...? Have you brought...?*
Material	CD, OHP-Folie
Vorgehen	Möglicher Einstieg: Im GU an der WT eine Liste jener Sachen machen, die man für eine Party braucht (Vokabular einführen). Die Liste leitet zum Focustext über, der zuerst übers Ohr aufgenommen wird.
a) Basic	L lässt den Text abschnittweise abspielen und stellt Fragen: *Have they informed their neighbours? Have they got speakers? etc.* Die OHP-Folie mit der Checkliste zum Focustext I kann als Hilfe aufgelegt werden.
b) Intensive	OHP-Folie mit der Checkliste auflegen. Die S hören sich den Text ohne Buch an und haben die Aufgabe, jene Dinge auf der Liste abzuhaken, die erledigt worden sind.

Erweiterungen

Folie
Nr. 18

Ausbau
Spiel: Drei S gehen aus dem Schulzimmer und verändern je drei Dinge an Kleidern, Haar oder Gesicht (z.B. Entfernen der Ohrenclips, Pullover verkehrt anziehen). Die übrigen S müssen herausfinden, was die drei verändert haben (mündlich oder schriftlich).
Das Spiel kann auch in Gruppen gespielt werden: Je zwei oder drei S stehen einander gegenüber und betrachten einander genau. Dann gehen sie auseinander und ändern eine bestimmte Zahl von kleinen Details. Die Gruppe, welche die meisten Änderungen erkennt, hat gewonnen.

Unit 20   Focus

I A Week Before the End-of-the-School-Year Party

1 Penny: Where's Martin?
   Bridget: He's not here. Shall we wait?
   Roy: No, let's start. Right, I've informed the
            neighbours about our party. They should know
5   about the noise, I hope. I've also looked
            for a CD player and some big speakers.
            The good news is: we've got a very powerful
            CD player. The bad news is: my brother
10   hasn't agreed, so we can't have his big speakers.
            Sorry about that.
   Penny: That's no problem. I've asked my dad and we
            can have his. And I've asked our neighbour
            for the party lights. We can have them too.
15   But I haven't got any party decorations yet.
   Bridget: Oh, don't worry, I've organised that. I've bought
            lots of coloured paper and I've talked to my
            sister: we can have her old birthday party
            decorations. By the way, Roy, have you asked
20   Tanya to bring her dance CDs to the party?
   Roy: Yes, I have. That's all OK. She's bringing them
            and she's happy to be the DJ. And I've also
            organised a team to clean up after the party.
            It's Mike, Susan and Joe.

25 Penny: What about Martin's signs for the party,
            "bar", "toilets", "disco" and all that.
            Has he done that yet?
   Bridget: No, he hasn't painted any signs. But I don't
30   think we need them. We all know where
            the bar, the toilets and the disco are, don't we?
   Penny: And has Martin told the head teacher about
            the party?
35 Bridget: No, he hasn't. Could that be a problem?
   Roy: A problem? That's a catastrophe!
            I can't tell him. He really hates me.
   Penny: And me ...
   Bridget: Don't worry. I can ask him tomorrow.
40   Oh, what about the barbecue?
            Have you asked Mr Taylor, Roy?
   Roy: Yes, I have, it's all right. But we have to get
            some more gas bottles for it.
   Bridget: Right that's not a problem. Now, have you
45   invited the teachers to the party?
   Penny: The teachers? Are we inviting the teachers?

II The Afternoon Before the Party

1 Martin: Where's Roy?
Bridget: He's not here. Shall we wait?
Martin: No, let's start. Has Roy ordered the soft drinks?
Penny: No, he hasn't. That's your job. You agreed
5   to do that two weeks ago.
Martin: Oh no, you're right, and I haven't done it.
       Look, carry on, I'm doing it right now.
       Back in a minute.
Bridget: He's useless, isn't he?
10 Penny: Yes, he is. – Ah, here's Roy. Hi there.
Roy: Hello you two. Where's Martin?
Bridget: He's gone to order some soft drinks.
       He's forgotten to order them, you know.
Roy: That's typical. Last year he forgot to get the food.
15   He's great at the party but he can't organise
      one, can he? Right, I've bought the crisps
      and the peanuts and I've picked up the
      burgers and the sausages from the butcher's.
Penny: And I've got the plastic glasses and the
20   plates from the supermarket, so we're ready
       to go.
Bridget: Are we? Has Martin moved the tables out
       of the classroom? Has he brought the
       bar stools from the youth club?
25 Roy: I don't think so.
Bridget: But I've found some comfortable chairs
       for the chill-out room. My mother has just
       brought them in. So we can sit and watch
       Martin. He still has a lot of work to do
30   before the party starts ...
(§ 35, WB Ex 1)

Focus II: The Afternoon Before the Party

Hinweise/Ideen	Mit einer Beschreibung der Illustration (OHP-Folie) kann der Inhalt eingeführt und das *present perfect* gleich verwendet werden: *What have they just done?*
Material	CD/OHP-Folie
Vorgehen	• Der Text kann auch in PA/EA (mit Discman) bearbeitet werden und eignet sich für lautes Lesen und Rollenspiele.
	• Anhand des Textes den Unterschied *present perfect – past simple* einführen.
Bemerkung	Je nach Niveau der Klasse kann man auf den unterschiedlichen Gebrauch der Vorgegenwart in der Mundart und im Schriftdeutschen hinweisen sowie auf das *passé composé*. Die S sollen erkennen, dass jede Sprache *ihre* Grammatik hat und man eine bestimmte Struktur nicht einfach von einer Sprache auf die andere übertragen kann.

Erweiterungen

Kopiervorlagen	**Folie**
What Have They Done? (63)	Nr. 19

Student's Book, p, 56

Unit 20

First Step

Hinweise/Ideen
- Je nachdem, wie der Focustext bearbeitet wurde, kann diese Übung zur Einführung oder zur Vertiefung des *present perfect*, genutzt werden.
- Es wurde darauf geachtet, dass die Partizipformen alle gleich lauten wie die Formen des *simple past*. Man kann bereits an dieser Stelle darauf hinweisen, dass dem nicht immer so ist!
- Zur Vorentlastung können zuerst die Partizipformen der Verben im GU zusammengestellt werden.

Vorgehen
1) Folie auflegen (evtl. Partizipformen erarbeiten)
2) Im GU den Dialog durchspielen.
3) Die S machen den Dialog mit Hilfe der Folie nochmals als PA.

Aubau/Varianten
- Die Liste eignet sich auch, um das *present perfect* in allen Personen (auch verneint und fragend) durchzugehen.
- Die S erstellen eigene Listen über Partys, Hausaufgaben, Lagervorbereitungen etc. und stellen diese für analoge Übungen zur Verfügung.

Second Step

Hinweise
Die Partizipformen sind wiederum so gewählt, dass sie gleich lauten wie die Formen des *simple past*.

Vorgehen
Diese Übung kann sowohl bei der Erstbegegnung mit dem Focustext II oder als anschliessende Textverständnisübung eingesetzt werden.

Ausbau
Die S formulieren mögliche Begründungen für die versäumten Aufträge
(Martin hasn't ordered any soft drinks because ...).

Third Step

Hinweise
Inhaltlich knüpft die Übung direkt an den Focustext II an (Martin hat vergessen, Getränke zu bestellen). Sie kann aber auch gemacht werden, wenn die S diesen Text nicht bearbeitet haben (Stufe *Basic*).

Material
CD

Vorgehen
Die Übung kann nur mündlich (im SB) oder nur schriftlich (WB Ex 4) angegangen werden.

Basic
1) Die S arbeiten mit WB Ex 4.
2) Der Text wird abschnittsweise abgespielt und die Aussagen werden im GU vorgelesen und auf ihre Richtigkeit geprüft.

Erweiterungen

Kopiervorlagen	Folie
Fill in the Gaps (64)	Nr. 18
Kim's Game (65)	
Going to Camp (66)	

Training

First Step (§ 35, WB Ex 2)

A week before the party

Have they organised everything?
Look at the text on page 55 and at the list on the right.
Make questions and give answers.

Example: – Has Roy informed the neighbours?
– Yes, he has.

– Has Roy (look) for a good CD player?
– Yes, ...
– Has Penny (ask) the neighbours for the party lights?
– ...
– Have they (buy) decorations?
– ...

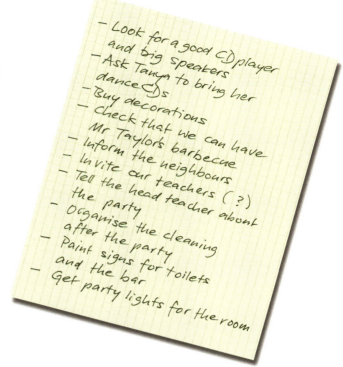

Second Step

The afternoon before the party

Look at the following list and compare it with the text.
What have they done? What haven't they done?

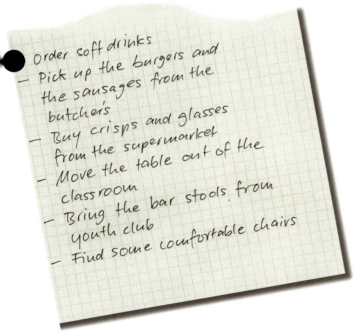

Third Step (WB Ex 4)

They haven't ordered any drinks yet.
Martin is phoning Duke's Drinks Delivery.
Listen to the conversation.

a) *Are these statements true or false?*

Martin has ordered
– ten bottles of Coke.
– some mineral water.
– four kinds of fruit juice.
– peanuts and crisps.
– tea and coffee.
– milk for milkshakes.
– party decorations.

b) *Correct the false statements.*

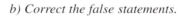
mineral water

Fourth Step

a) What have I done? When did I do it?

Example:
– I (find) my English book.
– I (find) it yesterday in my desk.
– I've found my English book.
– I found it yesterday in my desk.

1. I (do) my homework.   I (do) it yesterday before dinner.
2. I (put) all the CDs away.   I (put) them away last Sunday.
3. I (clean) my room.   I (clean) it two days ago.
4. I (make) my bed.   I (make) it early this morning.
5. I (take) out the rubbish.   I (take) it out late last night.
6. I (wash) the tea cups.   I (wash) them an hour ago.
7. I (bring) my friend all the comics back.   I (bring) them back on Wednesday.
8. I (phone) my grandmother.   I (phone) a week ago.

b) What have Steve and Monica done? When did they do it?

1. Steve (be) to Italy.   He (be) there last year for his holidays.
2. He (buy) a new Tomb Raider CD-ROM.   He (buy) it last week.
3. He (have) a hair cut.   He (have) a hair cut three days ago.
4. Monica (see) all Star Wars films.   She (see) the first one on television last Christmas.
5. She (bring) her dog to school today.   She (bring) it to the English class this morning.
6. She (read) all the Harry Potter books.   She (read) the last one last summer.

Fifth Step

What have they done?

NEW WORD
rubbish

Make sentences and match them with the numbers in the pictures.

– A girl (move) the comfortable chairs out of the room.
– Somebody (put) the big speakers in the car.
– ... (carry) in big ... for the rubbish.
– ... (bring) back Mr Taylor's barbecue.
– ... (move) ... back into the classroom.
– A girl (give) back the CD player.
– ... (finish) the ...
– ... (clean) ... and ...

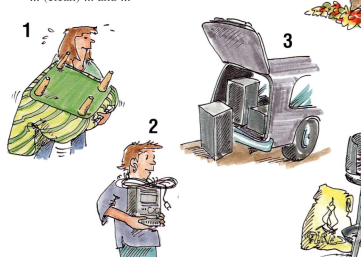

Unit 20

Unit 20

Fourth Step

Hinweise/Ideen Übung zu *present perfect/simple past*. Die beiden Zeitformen sind in der Übung klar getrennt, damit der Unterschied deutlich zu erkennen ist. Es geht hier also nicht darum, dass die **S** selber schon die Unterscheidung kennen und anwenden können. Hier sollen vor allem die Formen geübt und anhand der Beispiele die Anwendung und klare Trennung von *present perfect/simple past* vor Augen geführt werden.

Vorgehen Der Unterschied kann zusätzlich betont werden, indem eine Gruppe die Sätze im *present perfect*, eine andere jene im *simple past* abwechslungsweise im GU vorträgt.

Ausbau Die Beispiele können zusätzlich in die verschiedenen Personalformen gesetzt werden.

Fifth Step

Ausbau Die Übung eignet sich auch zur Repetition der bisher behandelten Zeitformen mit den entsprechenden Schlüsselwörtern.

A girl has moved the comfortable chairs out of the room.
A girl moved the comfortable chairs out of the room <u>yesterday</u>.
<u>Every week</u> a girl moves the comfortable chairs out of the room.
A girl is moving the comfortable chairs out of the room <u>right now</u>.
A girl is moving the comfortable chairs out of the room <u>tonight</u>.
A girl was moving the comfortable chairs out of the room <u>while</u> somebody was cleaning the windows.

Student's Book, p. 58

Unit 20

Stepping Out

Hinweise/Ideen
- Es geht darum, auf spielerische Art verschiedene Texttypen zu charakterisieren und ihre Funktion zu umschreiben. Ausserdem soll deutlich gemacht werden, dass das *present perfect* auch bei vergangenen Ereignissen, die sich auf die Gegenwart auswirken, verwendet wird.
- Zu a: Obwohl der Wortlaut der Texte identisch ist, drücken sie unterschiedliche Inhalte aus: Ein Gedicht wird anders gelesen und interpretiert als ein Zettel am Kühlschrank.
- William Carlos Williams (1883–1963) wurde in Rutherford, New Jersey (USA), geboren. Er besuchte Schulen und Universitäten in Genf und Pennsylvania und war während 40 Jahren praktischer Arzt an seinem Geburtsort. Er versuchte in seinen Gedichten unmittelbare Erfahrungen in Worte zu fassen. Dichterische Konvention wurde zugunsten einfacher, direkter und scheinbar formloser Gedichte verworfen.

Vorgehen

Zu a: Die erste Frage werden die S auf Englisch beantworten können, bei der zweiten sollen sie die Antwort auch auf Deutsch geben dürfen. Die Unterschiede der Textsorten lässt sich bei guten Klassen danach auch auf Englisch mit gezielten Fragen angehen:

What kind of a text is this? (A: short, quick note; B: poem)
Who reads text A? (One person, partner, husband, wife)
Who reads text B? (everybody can read it because it is in a book)
Did the writer have a lot of time to write the text? (A=no; B=yes)
What could the reaction of the reader be? (A: Possibly anger because the reader wanted the plums for breakfast; reader throws away the note. B: reader thinks about the text, closes the book, can read the text again in the future)

Zu b: Die möglichen Reaktionen auf den Text zuerst kurz im GU besprechen (negativ, gleichgültig, positiv). Die Antworten können danach von den S auf Post-it-Zettel geschrieben und untereinander ausgetauscht oder in die Bücher geklebt werden. Somit müssen sie sich kurz fassen. Eine Antwort könnte ja sogar nur aus einem Ausruf bestehen *(Oh, no!!)*

Zu c: Die S ordnen in EA/PA/GA die Mitteilungen nach Farben und geben an, wo sich die einzelnen Texte befinden könnten.

Ausbau/Varianten
- Die S schreiben weitere Mitteilungen für zu Hause/im Schulzimmer/im Schulhaus. Diese können auch englische SMS sein.
- Die Mitteilungen werden aufgelegt und in EA/PA (wettbewerbsartig) den Mitschülern und Mitschülerinnen zugeordnet.

Stepping Out

a) Where can you find these two texts (A and B)? In what way are they different?

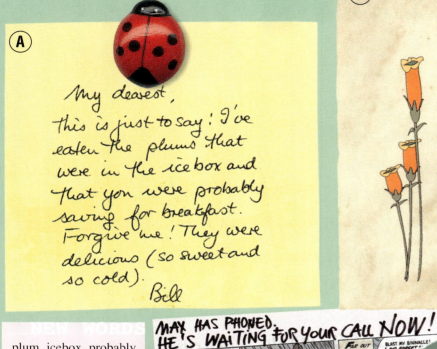

A

My dearest,
This is just to say: I've eaten the plums that were in the icebox and that you were probably saving for breakfast. Forgive me! They were delicious (so sweet and so cold).
Bill

B

THIS IS JUST TO SAY

I HAVE EATEN
THE PLUMS
THAT WERE IN
THE ICEBOX

AND WHICH
YOU WERE PROBABLY
SAVING
FOR BREAKFAST

FORGIVE ME
THEY WERE DELICIOUS
SO SWEET
AND COLD.

We've only taken the US dollar bills and the Euros...

NEW WORDS

plum, icebox, probably, save, forgive, delicious, sweet

b) You've just found the notice on the fridge door. Write a short answer.

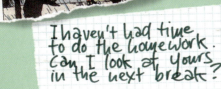

MAX HAS PHONED. HE'S WAITING FOR YOUR CALL NOW!

I haven't watched this yet. Please don't record over it!!!

I haven't had time to do the homework. Can I look at yours in the next break?

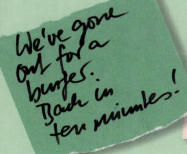

We've gone out for a burger. Back in ten minutes!

I've done my homework. Back for dinner.
Tom

I've fallen out of love with you. I'm leaving. Sorry.

More notices

c) Look at all these notices. Where would you find them?

Example: *The pink notice is on the door of Tom's room.*

Has anybody seen our cat FREDERICK? He is black, very small and disappeared on ~~June~~ 23 June. Please phone:

next to a telephone
on a blackboard
on a broken bank safe
on a shop door
on a small piece of paper during a lesson at school
on a video cassette
on the bathroom mirror
on the notice board in a block of flats or in a supermarket
(WB Ex 7)

page fifty-nine **59**

Time for a Change

How do you get on with the others in your gang?

Are you the centre of attention in your gang? Or are you a quiet person, happy in the background? This test tells you how you get on with the others in your gang …

1. There is trouble in your gang. Two of your friends are fighting. What do you do?
a) I say something like "Don't be so stupid" and try to stop them.
b) I don't do anything and let them get on with it.
c) I go home and stay away from the gang. When the problems are over, I come back again.

2. You're on holiday and it's raining. You are alone at home. What do you do?
a) I watch television or a video.
b) I phone some friends.
c) I look at the photos of my last holidays with my friends.

3. Read these statements. Which one is true for you?
a) I usually do what I want.
b) I like to get on with my friends, so I often do what they want.
c) I don't like it when I'm alone.

4. You have a serious problem. Who would you tell about it?
a) Nobody. I wouldn't tell anybody.
b) I would tell my best friend or my boyfriend/girlfriend.
c) I would talk about it with someone in my family.

5. Do you find it easy to get on with people?
a) No, I sometimes find it quite difficult.
b) Yes, I find it quite easy.
c) That's difficult to say. I think in some situations I find it easy and in some situations it's difficult for me.

6. Someone in your gang is feeling down because his girlfriend/her boyfriend doesn't want to go out with him/her anymore. What do you say?
a) "I'm not interested in your personal problems. You are getting on my nerves."
b) "I know how you feel. It happens to all of us sometimes …"
c) "Don't be sad, you can always find someone else. There are a lot of nice girls/boys in the world."

7. You want to impress the others in your gang. What would be the best way to do this?
a) I would like to impress the gang by being on a TV show.
b) I would like to impress them by going out with a really great (good-looking) boy/girl.
c) I don't want to impress the others in my gang.

(WB Ex 8)

Time for a Change

Hinweise/Ideen Die S sollten die Befragung möglichst ungestört in EA beantworten, sich die entsprechenden Buchstaben notieren und erst danach die Punktzahl im Arbeitsheft nachschlagen (WB Ex 8). An die Auswertung kann sich eine informelle Diskussion über Cliquen in der Schule oder am Wohnort (Quartier) anschliessen.

Notes

Workbook

Generelle Bemerkungen

New Words Im *Workbook* neu eingeführte Wörter sind gemäss der Kennzeichnung im *Vocabulary* im *Student's Book* zu behandeln.

Use-Box In vielen *Exercises* sind Wörter und Satzteile, die eingesetzt werden müssen, in der *Use*-Box aufgeführt. Je nach Leistungsstärke der Klasse und nach Einschätzung des Schwierigkeitsgrades der Aufgabe sollen die S mit Hilfe dieser Vorgaben arbeiten oder die *Use*-Box mit Post-it-Zetteln abdecken.

Language Focus Mit Hilfe des *Language Focus* sollen sich die S die Strukturen, die in der nachfolgenden Übung verlangt werden, nochmals vergegenwärtigen. Ein *Language Focus* kann aber auch nach dem Lösen einer Übung, nach dem Abschluss einer oder gar mehrerer *Units* eingesetzt werden, um alle behandelten Strukturen nochmals in Erinnerung zu rufen und zu wiederholen.

Structure Checklist Am Ende jeder *Unit* findet sich eine *Structure Checklist*. Sie dient den S als Überblick über die verlangten grammatischen Strukturen. Bereits behandelte Teilstrukturen werden in einigen Fällen nochmals aufgeführt. In den Kästchen können die S abhaken, welche Strukturen sie beherrschen.

Grammar Wie im *Student's Book* sind auch in den *Workbooks* die in Band 2 behandelten grammatischen Strukturen in der *Grammar* aufgelistet. Damit besitzen die S über den Schluss des Schuljahres hinaus eine ihren Kenntnissen entsprechende Englischgrammatik. Anders als im *Student's Book* wurden aber in den *Workbooks* die deutschsprachigen Erklärungen weggelassen, damit die S, in Anleitung durch L, handschriftlich eigene Erläuterungen und Beispielsätze einsetzen können.

Vocabulary Ebenso wie die Grammatik wird das alphabetisch geordnete Vokabular von Band 2 mit Angabe des Vorkommens in beiden *Workbooks* aufgelistet.

Unit 11

Exercise 1

Hinweise / Ideen zu a) Leseverständnisübung, die gleichzeitig auch die Einsicht in den Satzbau fördern soll.
Der Zugang zur Übung soll der Leistungsstärke der Klasse angepasst werden; er hängt auch damit zusammen, wie intensiv mit dem *Focus*-Text im *Student's Book* gearbeitet wurde.
Die S können sich in EA, PA oder GA an die Aufgabe machen. Die Zuordnung sollte mittels Kästchen und nicht durch Verbindungsstriche erfolgen, da die S bei b) die Aufgabe haben, alle Sätze richtig zusammengesetzt laut vorzulesen. Die Zuordnung in den Kästchen dient der Vorbereitung zur mündlichen freien Umsetzung.

zu b) auch als Kontrolle zu a) einsetzen

Bemerkung Bei schwächeren Gruppen den *Focus*-Text aus dem *Student's Book page 2* zu Hilfe nehmen.

Lösung zu a) 1c, 2e, 3b, 4f, 5g, 6d, 7a

zu b)
1. *Madonna Louise Ciccone was born in Bay City, Michigan in 1958.*
2. *At first, she was a dancer in a number of dance companies, then she was a background singer.*
3. *Her first album "Madonna" (1983) wasn't very successful.*
4. *Her second album "Like a Virgin" (1984) was a big hit and the beginning of her career as an international pop star.*
5. *Her videos were a bit like short films and her concerts were great shows with dancers and lights and Madonna in many different dresses.*
6. *But were her films a big success? No, most of them weren't.*
7. *In the early days she was just a disco singer, but her new videos show that she is a good singer and a good entertainer.*

Language Focus

Ziel *Past*-Formen von *to be*

Mögliche Lösung

I	was / wasn't	thirteen years old last year.
You	were / weren't	in England for your holidays.
He (my brother / friend)	was / wasn't	born in Neuhausen.
She (my mother / friend)	was / wasn't	born on 4 June 1958.
It (my dog, cat, etc.)	was / wasn't	in school last Monday.
We (my friend and I)	were / weren't	in a big city last week.
You (you and your friends)	were / weren't	in the disco at the weekend.
They (your friends)	were / weren't	tired last night.

Who	was	president of the USA in 2001?
How old	were	you in 1995?
What	was	her dream?
When	was	Madonna born?
Where	were	you yesterday?

Workbook Basic   Unit 11

Exercise 2

Hinweise / Ideen Leseverständnisübung, kann in stiller EA, in PA oder in GA gelöst werden. Obwohl auch einige Nomen und Adjektive eingesetzt werden müssen, geht es hier um Formen von *to be*. Auch dieses *Exercise* kann bei Bedarf als Hörübung angegangen werden. Den Tonträger entweder direkt zum Ausfüllen der Lücken oder zur Korrektur einsetzen.

Lösung *was born, was, music, was, was, successful, big, were, were, weren't, her, is, singer*

Language Focus

Ziel Frageformen von *to be*
Past-Formen der regelmässigen Verben

Mögliche Lösung

Yesterday	I	listen**ed**	to a CD.
Last week	you	play**ed**	football with a friend.
When I was 4,	my father	work**ed**	in Berne.
When I was 12,	my	mother lik**ed**	Günther Jauch.
Last night	my dog	lov**ed**	to go out for a walk.
In 1999	we	need**ed**	new school books.
Yesterday	you	cop**ied**	my homework.
Last week	they	tr**ied**	to find a good restaurant.

Were	you	at school yesterday?	Yes, / No,	I	was. / wasn't.
Was	she	at home on Sunday?	Yes, / No,	she	was. / wasn't.
Was	he	in Paris yesterday?	Yes, / No,	he	was. / wasn't.
Was	it	interesting?	Yes, / No,	it	was. / wasn't.
Were	you	happy with your last English test?	Yes, / No,	we	were. / weren't.
Were	they	at the cinema last Monday?	Yes, / No,	they	were. / weren't.

Did	you	listen to music last night?	Yes, / No,	I	did. / didn't.
Did	he	play the guitar yesterday?	Yes, / No,	he	did. / didn't.
Did	she	watch TV last Monday?	Yes, / No,	she	did. / didn't.
Did	it	rain last night?	Yes, / No,	it	did. / didn't.
Did	we	have homework on Tuesday?	Yes, / No,	you	did. / didn't.
Did	they	go to Zurich last weekend?	Yes, / No,	they	did. / didn't.

Exercise 3

Hinweise / Ideen zu a) Es geht darum, mit den vorgegebenen Elementen einen korrekten Satz zu formulieren. Das *Exercise* kann auch in PA als Sprech- und Schreibübung gelöst werden. Dabei werden die Sätze Nummer um Nummer zuerst mündlich und unmittelbar danach schriftlich formuliert. Schwächere **S** können diese Übung in PA / GA lösen. Vorgehen: Die **S** schreiben die einzelnen Satzelemente zuerst auf kleine Zettel und bringen diese anschliessend in die richtige Reihenfolge.

zu b) Dieser Übungsteil kann auch zur Lautleseübung ausgebaut werden.

Unit 11   Workbook Basic

Lösung zu a)
1. It was the time of young people with no future.
2. U2 were interested in music and politics.
3. Their first big hit was "Sunday, Bloody Sunday" in 1983.
4. "Pride (In the Name of Love)" was a big success.
5. There were always experiments with new styles.

zu b) good, name, U2, drummer, band, were, music, Sunday, song, Ireland, world, interested, experiments, dance, electronic, fans, band

Exercise 4

Hinweise / Ideen Diese Drillübung eignet sich als stille EA oder als Hausaufgabe, kann aber auch in der Klasse als Staffette durchgespielt werden: **S 1** liest den *Infinitive* (und ersetzt dabei die Symbole + / – / ? durch die entsprechenden Ausdrücke) oder die vorgegebene Verbform, **S 2** ergänzt den fehlenden Ausdruck.

Lösung

Infinitive	Present simple	Past tense
she / look / +	she looks	she looked
he / watch / +	he watches	he watched
we / love / –	we don't love	we didn't love
I / touch / –	I don't touch	I didn't touch
you / love / ?	Do you love ...?	Did you love ...?
we / play / –	we don't play	we didn't play
I / answer / –	I don't answer	I didn't answer
you / stop / +	you stop	you stopped
we / check / +	we check	we checked
they / brush / +	they brush	they brushed
she / spell / –	she doesn't spell	she didn't spell
he / walk / –	he doesn't walk	he didn't walk
she / turn / ?	Does she turn ...?	Did she turn ...?
we / press / +	we press	we pressed
you / be / +	you are	you were
he / be / +	he is	he was
they / be / –	they aren't	they weren't
he / live / –	he doesn't live	he didn't live
he / carry / +	he carries	he carried
they / start / –	they don't start	they didn't start
she / start / +	she starts	she started
she / be / –	she isn't	she wasn't
he / wait / –	he doesn't wait	he didn't wait
we / be / +	we are	we were
she / copy / +	she copies	she copied
I / ask / –	I don't ask	I didn't ask
they / play / ?	Do they play ...?	Did they play ...?

Exercise 5

Hinweise / Ideen Individuelle Antworten (Erfinden erlaubt!). Eventuell als Partnerübungen zuerst mündlich, dann schriftlich oder als Sprech- und Schreibübung gestalten: Die **S** formulieren Nummer um Nummer zuerst mündlich und unmittelbar danach schriftlich.

Workbook Basic Unit 11

Lösung zu b)
6. Did you like the film (on TV / in the cinema / last …)?
7. Was it cold yesterday?
8. Was there anything interesting on television last Sunday?
9. Did you play cards with your friends last night?
10. Did you watch television last Saturday night?

Exercise 6

Hinweise / Ideen

Hier geht es vordergründig um das Erfragen von geschichtlichen Informationen.
Sprachlich ebenso wichtig ist die verständliche Formulierung von Fragen und Antworten.
Die S können zuerst in ein A- und ein B-Team aufgeteilt die Fragen und die Antworten ihrer Seite gemeinsam (mündlich und / oder schriftlich) formulieren und erst anschliessend in Paararbeit die fehlenden Informationen erfragen und die Antworten eintragen.

Lösung Partner A
1. The terrorists destroyed the WTC in September 2001.
2. The film "Titanic" was a hit in the cinemas in 1997.
3. The French Revolution started in 1789.
4. William Shakespeare was born in 1564.
5. Graham Bell invented the telephone in 1876.
6. The Second World War started in 1939.

1. When did the Americans land on the moon?   in 1969
2. When did the Second World War end?   in 1945
3. When did Edmund Hillary and Sherpa Tenzing climb Mount Everest?   in 1953
4. When did Charles Lindbergh cross the Atlantic in a small aeroplane?   in 1927
5. When did ex-Beatle George Harrison die?   in November 2001
6. When was "Harry Potter" a big hit in the cinemas?   in 2001

Lösung Partner B
1. The Americans landed on the moon in 1969.
2. The Second World War ended in 1945.
3. Edmund Hillary and Sherpa Tenzing climbed Mount Everest in 1953.
4. Charles Lindbergh crossed the Atlantic in a small aeroplane in 1927.
5. Ex-Beatle George Harrison died in November 2001.
6. "Harry Potter" was a big hit in the cinemas in 2001?

1. When did the terrorists destroy the WTC?   in September 2001
2. When was the film "Titanic" a hit in the cinemas?   in 1997
3. When did the French Revolution start?   in 1789
4. When was William Shakespeare born?   in 1564
5. When did Graham Bell invent the telephone?   in 1876
6. When did the Second World War start?   in 1939

Language Focus

Ziel Datumsangabe mündlich und schriftlich

Lösung

date	we write	we say
1 / 1 / 2000	1 January 2000	the 1st (first) of January 2000 (two thousand)
15 / 6 / 1963	15 June 1963	the 15th (fifteenth) of June 1963 (nineteen sixty-three)
3 / 3 / 2003	3 March 2003	the 3rd (third) of March 2003 (two thousand and three)
20 / 5 / 2005	20 May 2005	the 20th (twentieth) of May 2005 (two thousand and five)
2 / 12 / 1997	2 December 1997	2nd (second) of December 1997 (nine hundred and ninety-seven)

Unit 11 — Workbook Basic

Exercise 7

Hinweise / Ideen
zu a)
Vertiefungsübung zu den Monatsnamen. Sie eignet sich als stille EA oder als Hausaufgabe, kann aber auch als Wettbewerb im GU gestaltet werden: **L** deckt die Monate in selbst gewählter Reihenfolge am OHP auf, die **S** sprechen, sobald sie die Lösung haben, nach folgendem Muster: *bremeced is d e c e m b e r for December*. Anschliessend wird die Lösung im *Workbook* eingetragen.

zu b)
b) kann schriftlich als Erweiterung zu a) und mündlich als Ausspracheübung von Datumsangaben gelöst werden. Wichtig ist, dass die schriftliche Version keinen Hinweis auf Ordinalzahlen bei den Tagen enthält.
Hinweis: Die amerikanische Schreibweise würde den Monat vor den Tag setzen, was sich auch in der Zahlenversion niederschlägt.

Lösung zu a)
January, February, March, April, May, June, July, August, September, October, November, December

zu b)
1 August 1991, 4 July 1776, 14 July 1789, 8 May 1945, 22 November 1963, 11 September 2001

Erweiterung
Die **S** versuchen herauszufinden, was es mit diesen Daten auf sich hat. Lösung:
700 years of Switzerland, Declaration of Independence, beginning of the French Revolution, end of World War II, Kennedy assassinated in Dallas (see next Unit), terrorist attacks in the US
L kann diese Ereignisse ohne die Daten an die Wandtafel schreiben. Die **S** versuchen dann, sie den Daten zuzuordnen.

Exercise 8

Hinweise / Ideen
Die Projektarbeit in kleinen Arbeitsgruppen angehen. Die Resultate im Schulzimmer aufhängen.

Workbook Basic Unit 12

Unit 12

Language Focus

Ziel unregelmässige *Past*-Formen
Frageformen mit unregelmässigen *Past*-Formen

Hinweis Das selbständige Erarbeiten in diesem *Language Focus* kann für das Erlernen der Formen recht hilfreich sein. Schwächere **S** können zur Lösung der Aufgabe kleine Gruppen bilden.

Lösung

Present	Past	Present	Past	Present	Past	Present	Past
be	was / were	know	knew	become	became	give	gave
come	came	make	made	bring	brought	hit	hit
do	did	say	said	buy	bought	hold	held
get	got	see	saw	fall	fell	sit	sat
go	went	take	took	find	found	wear	wore
have	had						

When	did	I	get	a new English book?	I	got	it last week.
Where	did	you	go	on holiday last year?	I / We	went	to Italy.
When	did	he	have	lunch yesterday?	He	had	lunch at 12 o'clock.
When	did	she	come	to school this morning?	She	came	at 7.30.
How long	did	it	take	to walk to school?	It	took	20 minutes.
What	did	we	see	in the city yesterday?	You	saw	a lot of shops.
What	did	you	say	to your teacher last night?	I	said	"goodbye".
When	did	they	do	their homework?	They	did	it before dinner.

Exercise 1

Hinweise / Ideen Die Übung kann als Spiel mit Zeitlimite gemacht werden: Welches Team bzw. wer innerhalb einer gegebenen Zeit die meisten Formen findet, gewinnt.
Einige Verben stammen aus freiwilligen *Student's Book*-Übungen.
Schnellere **S** können für den Rest der Klasse weitere Verbschlangen ausarbeiten.

Erweiterung - *Past Crossword* (Kopiervorlage Nr. 12a, 12b).
- Die **S** erstellen selbst einen *verb-grid* für andere **S**.

Lösung zu a) were, came, was, sat, went, made, said, hit, brought, fell, took, became, gave, found, did, had
zu b) be, come, be, sit, go, make, say, hit, bring, fall, take, become, give, find, do, have

77

Unit 12   Workbook Basic

Exercise 2

Hinweise / Ideen   Aufbereitung des *Focus*-Textes in EA oder als Hausaufgabe (Hauptgewicht: unregelmässige Verben und Leseverständnis). Zur Kontrolle kann der Text von einem **S** laut vorgelesen werden; dabei wiederholen 1–2 weitere **S** jeweils echoartig die Verbformen.

Lösung zu a)   *came, sat, were, said, came, said, came, hit, brought, fell, died, became, found*
zu b)   *took, wanted, called, walked, took, killed, saw*

Exercise 3

Hinweise / Ideen
zu a) und b)   Vertiefung der negativen *Past*-Formen und der unregelmässigen Verben sowie Kontrolle des Leseverständnisses. Eventuell zuerst im GU die Informationen suchen, dann in EA die Sätze schreiben lassen.

zu c)   Es kann hilfreich sein, wenn die Fragepronomina an der Wandtafel aufgelistet sind.

Bemerkung   Möglichkeit, Personalpronomina in Subjekt- oder Objektformen (in *Ready for English 1*, § 17) neu zu üben.

Lösung
zu a) und b)
1. *President Kennedy and his wife didn't come to Houston, Texas. They came to Dallas, Texas.*
2. *The man didn't have a video camera with him. The man had a film camera with him.*
3. *The limousine didn't take the president to a police station. It took the president to Parkland Hospital.*
4. *Doctors didn't work very fast to save Kennedy's life. They worked very hard to save his life.*
5. *Vice President Johnson didn't become America's second president. He became America's new president.*

zu c)
1. *Where did the Beatles go in their early days?*
2. *When did President John F. Kennedy come to Dallas?*
3. *Who played in the film "Evita"?*
4. *Who worked as a car mechanic?*
5. *Whose videos were a bit like short films?*

Exercise 4

Hinweise / Ideen   Es geht darum, *Past*- und *Present*-Formen zu erkennen. Es dürfte die Arbeit der **S** erleichtern, wenn sie darauf hingewiesen werden, dass klar nach einer *Past*- oder einer *Present*-Form gefragt wird. **L** kann auf einer Folie am OHP die ersten Verbindungen mitzeichnen. Die unregelmässigen Verbformen sind im *Student's Book page 102* aufgelistet.

Lösung zu a)   *went, fall, sit, put, knew, has, did, come, became, found, takes, brought, got, makes, saw, were, (went)*
Verbindet man die Punkte in der richtigen Reihenfolge, so erscheint der Umriss einer elektrischen Gitarre.

zu b)   *eat, begin, catch, drink, drive, flow, give, leave, meet, run, read, sleep, sell, swim, think, tell, wake up*

Workbook Basic   **Unit 12**

Exercise 5

Hinweise / Ideen

Es ist in dieser Übung sehr wichtig, dass die S realisieren, was Mr Boring regelmässig tut *(on a normal day → present simple)* bzw. was gestern ausnahmsweise geschah *(yesterday → past simple)*.
Die Übung ist unterteilt in einen ersten Teil, in dem die S aus der *Past*-Form auf die *Present*-Form schliessen müssen, und einen zweiten Teil mit umgekehrter Aufgabenstellung.
Bei der Kontrolle eignet sich die Übung zum mündlichen Ausgestalten des Inhalts:
Die Sätze werden einander (über)betont gegenübergestellt, indem **S 1** oder eine Kleingruppe den Text *Mr Boring on a normal day* liest und **S 2** oder eine Kleingruppe *Mr Boring yesterday*.
Betonung: *Mr Boring never sleeps late. – Yesterday he got up at eight*, usw.

Lösung

sleeps; gets up; has, has, goes, gives, says; goes, takes, is; comes;
saw, wasn't; were; brought; sat, had, were; made; went, wasn't; got

Exercise 6

Hinweise / Ideen

In dieser Übung werden die S aufgefordert, über sich selber zu sprechen.
Natürlich können auch Antworten erfunden werden.
In schwächeren Klassen kann die Übung zuerst schriftlich vorbereitet werden, evtl. als Hausaufgabe. Mit einer eher kommunikativen Gruppe ist es auch möglich, die ganze Übung zuerst mündlich zu bearbeiten und die Lösung dann als Hausaufgabe schriftlich festzuhalten.

Lösung

1. When did you get up yesterday morning? I got up at …
2. What did you see yesterday? I saw …
3. Where did you have lunch yesterday? I had lunch at …
4. Did you come to school by bicycle? Yes, I did. / Now, I didn't.
5. Did you bring chewing gum to school? Yes, I did. / Now, I didn't.

6. Did you take the bus or the tram after school? I took …
7. Did you go out last night? Yes, I went out. / No, I didn't go out.
8. What did you do last Sunday? I …
9. Did you go out, did you watch television, do your homework or do sports last night? I …
10. Did you go to bed before 11 p.m. yesterday? Yes, I went … / No, I didn't go …

Exercise 7

Hinweise / Ideen

PA mit *information gap*. Ziel ist es, die fehlende Information vom Partner / von der Partnerin zu erhalten.
Wiederum kann es sich lohnen, die Fragen zuerst schriftlich erarbeiten zu lassen, bevor der eigentliche Informationsaustausch stattfindet. Damit bei der Übung wirklich ein Informationsaustausch stattfindet, empfiehlt es sich, vor den eigentlichen Partnerarbeiten die ersten Fragen / Antworten als Beispiele im GU präsentieren zu lassen.

Lösung

Partner A
Fragen:
When was she born? How many sisters did she have? Who did she go to live with?
When did she leave England to go to Rougemont? Where did she work later?
When did she marry Prince Charles? What was the name of her second son? When did Charles and Diana separate? Who did she work with to ban landmines? Where did she die?

Begriffe in den Lücken:
1961, two sisters, her father, 1977, London, in 1981, William, December 1992, Red Cross, Paris

Unit 12 — Workbook Basic

Partner B
Fragen:
Where was she born? How many brothers did she have? When did she go to live with her father? Did she always go to school in England? What was her job later? When did she give birth to her second son? When was she divorced? What did she visit? How did she die?

Begriffe in den Lücken:
near London, one brother, in 1967, Switzerland, kindergarten teacher, 1982, 28 August 1996, AIDA hospitals and Third World countries, in a car accident.

Exercise 8

Hinweise / Ideen

Auch dieses Projekt kann in GA angepackt werden.
Die im *Workbook* aufgeführten Fragen können als Raster für das Starporträt dienen.
Es kann auch sinnvoll sein, die Fragen genauer vorzugeben. Dazu am Beispiel einer Sportlerpersönlichkeit mit der Klasse ein Set von Standardfragen erarbeiten.
Anschliessend können alle **S** ihr eigenes Starporträt mit dem gleichen Frageraster aufbauen.

Erweiterung

Die **S** präsentieren ihr Projekt kurz vor der Klasse.

Workbook Basic   Unit 13

Unit 13

Language Focus

Ziel Gegenüberstellung des *gesprochenen* und des *geschriebenen Present progressive* Singular und Plural. Bedeutungsunterschied von *at the moment* mit Verb im *Present progressive* und *tonight* mit Verb im *Present progressive*: In Kombination mit *at the moment* verweist der Satz auf eine eben stattfindende Handlung, in Kombination mit *tonight* auf eine in der nahen Zukunft geplante Handlung.

Mögliche Lösung

At the moment …

Singular	👄	✏️		
I	'm	am	listening	to a new CD.
you	're	are	sitting	in your chair.
he	's	is	watching	TV.
she	's	is	eating	dinner.
it	's	is	raining	in England.

Plural	👄	✏️		
we	're	are	playing	cards.
you	're	are	doing	this exercise.
they	're	are	speaking	French.

Tonight …

Singular	👄	✏️		
I	'm	am	eating	a cheeseburger.
you	're	are	running	in the street.
he	's	is	writing	a letter to his grandmother.
she	's	is	drinking	Coke.
it	's	is	raining	in Switzerland.

Plural	👄	✏️		
we	're	are	wearing	running shoes.
you	're	are	copying	a new DVD.
they	're	are	making	a lot of noise.

Exercise 1

Ziel a) Zuordnung Verb – Nomen

b) Üben der Verlaufsform in einfachen Fragen und Antworten (Drill).

Hinweise / Ideen Diese Übung eignet sich als Sprech- und Schreib-PA, wobei die S die Fragen und die entsprechenden Antworten Nummer um Nummer zuerst mündlich und unmittelbar danach schriftlich ausformulieren.

Lösung zu a)
1. + f   read a book   5. + b   play cards
2. + d   open a door   6. + g   watch TV
3. + e   ask a question   7. + c   do our English homework
4. + a   wear a pair of jeans

81

Unit 13		Workbook Basic

zu b)
2. What is he doing? — He's opening a door.
3. What is he doing? — He's asking a question.
4. What is she doing? — She's wearing jeans.
5. What are you doing? — I'm playing cards.
6. What are they doing? — They're watching TV.
7. What are you doing? — We're doing our English homework.

Exercise 2

Hinweise / Ideen

Beim Bild handelt es sich um die Zeichnung aus *Unit 7* im *Student's Book 1, page 34*.
Die Handlungen der Personen im Museum sollen hier in Erinnerung gerufen und im *Present progressive* frei ausformuliert werden.
Der Lückentext ist so aufgebaut, dass nicht immer Verbformen eingesetzt werden müssen. Will man das Gewicht auf das *Present progressive* legen, können anschliessend an den Lückentext Sätze (evtl. mit vorgegebenen Verben im Infinitiv als Hilfe) frei geschrieben/ gesprochen werden.

Einstimmung

Why is the museum guard angry? Die S beschreiben, was gerade vor sich geht.
Die Übung kann vorgängig auch mündlich durchgespielt werden.

Variante

Übung als Memoryspiel durchführen: Die S betrachten das Bild (evtl. als Folie auf den OHP gelegt) während 2 Minuten und schreiben dann auf, woran sie sich noch erinnern können.

Mögliche Lösung

*Two boys are playing football in front of the throne. One of the boys is eating ice cream.
A girl is playing with a ball behind the two boys.
A boy is sitting on the floor. He's smoking a cigarette and reading comics.
Somebody is running along the wall. A funny man is standing near the piano and the throne.
A lady and a man are looking at the dog. They are standing near the exit.
The man in a uniform is watching the people.
What is the dog doing? He's making noise. / He's having a pee and barking.*

Exercise 3

Hinweise / Ideen

Diese Übung ist mit dem *Training, Fourth Step,* gekoppelt
(vgl. auch Hinweise zu *Training, Fourth Step*).
Je nach Stärke der Klasse kann L den Tonträger nach jeweils einer oder mehreren Soundeinheiten stoppen.

Vorgehen

1. S hören die Geräusche zum *Training, Fourth Step*, und ordnen diese in der Tabelle den Nummern zu.
2. Anschliessend werden die Geräusche nochmals eingespielt und die Lösungen sprachlich präsentiert. *(Here someone's taking a photo. I think a man is laughing here etc.)*

Lösung

Siehe den Kommentar zum *Student's Book, page 18, Teachers's Book S. 27*.

Exercise 4

Ziel

Sprechen und schreiben über Vorgänge oder Situationen, die in der Gegenwart stattfinden oder für die unmittelbare Zukunft geplant sind.

Hinweise / Ideen zu a)

Je nach Leistungsstärke und Trainingsbedarf kann man sich bei den geschlossenen Fragen *(Are you ...)* mit Kurzantworten begnügen.
Legt man Wert auf ausführliche Antworten, können diese zuerst in EA schriftlich ausformuliert werden und somit als Hilfe / Vorlage für einen mündlichen Durchgang dienen.

Workbook Basic   Unit 13

zu b) Nachdem die Fragen in EA schriftlich vorbereitet worden sind, kann die Übung in PA als Leseübung angegangen werden. Die Übungen a) und b) sind als schriftliche Hausaufgabe oder stille EA geeignet.

Lösung zu a)
1. Yes, it is. / No, it isn't.
2. Yes, it is. / No, it isn't.
3. Yes, she / he is. / No, she / he isn't.
4. Yes, I am. / No, I'm not.
5. I'm answering them aloud. / I'm writing them.
6. Yes, I am. / No, I'm not.
7. I'm doing it at home. / I'm doing it at school.
8. I'm wearing … .
9. I'm eating … .

zu b)
1. Are you sitting at your desk at the moment?
2. Are you doing a maths exercise this evening? / Are you going out this evening?
3. Are you chewing gum right now?
4. Are we singing a song tomorrow morning?
5. Are you working hard right now?

Language Focus

Ziel Erfassen des Unterschieds von *many* und *much*

Mögliche Lösung

How many? (with plural)	How much? (with singular)
a lot of children	a lot of water
many cars	much time
a lot of kids	not much rain

There are a lot of children in classroom number 5 but not many in classroom number 7. We rarely have much money to spend or much time to wait. I can't see many dogs in the park, but many cats in the streets. The guard says: "Please don't make so much noise."

Exercise 5

Hinweise / Ideen Bei dieser freiwilligen Übung liegt das Gewicht grundsätzlich auf den Mengenangaben (siehe Use-Box), die je nach Bedarf im GU mit Hilfe von **L** thematisiert werden können; das Gewicht kann auch auf das Erschliessen der neuen Wörter (*New Words*-Box) gelegt werden, indem **L** (auf dem OHP) die Mengenangaben vorgibt. Auch können die Mengenangaben völlig weggelassen und die Präpositionen wiederholt werden. *(What is there behind / in front of / in, between …)*

Variante Memoryübung: Die **S** betrachten die Gegenstände während einer vorgegebenen Zeit (30 Sekunden bis 1 Minute) und geben dann mit oder ohne Mengenangaben so viel wie möglich wieder. (PA: **S 1** zählt auf, **S 2** kontrolliert bzw. hilft mit dem Buch als Vorlage nach.)

Mögliche Lösung
1. There are a few sandwiches left.
2. There is o lot of chocolate cake left.
3. There is a lot of fruit cake left.
4. There isn't any tea left. / There is no tea left.
5. There are many chocolate chip biscuits left.
6. There is much butter left.
7. There is some apple pie left.
8. There is not much vanilla milkshake left.
9. There is some coffee left.
10. There is some milk left.
11. But there isn't much chocolate milkshake left.

Unit 13 Workbook Basic

Exercise 6

Hinweise / Ideen Die Übung ist progressiv aufgebaut, was bedeutet, dass die S von a) bis d) immer mehr eigene Informationen einbringen müssen.
So kann auch die Unterrichtsform angepasst werden: Teil a) in EA, b) in PA, c) in GA, d) im GU. Nachdem die Wetterberichte je nach Klassenstärke in irgendeiner Unterrichtsform erarbeitet worden sind, können die Texte als Leseübung dienen: S spielen Wetterberichterstatter bzw. TV-Sprecherin. Als Erweiterung kann wie beim Wetterbericht im Fernsehen das zum Publikum gewandte Lesen und Aufschauen geübt werden.

Mögliche Lösung zu a)
Zeichenerklärung: *The sun is shining.*
It's hot. *It's raining.*
It's warm. *It's snowing.*
It's cold. *It's cloudy.*
It's freezing. *Winds are blowing from the east / south / west / north*

zu b) *raining, cloudy, warm, shining, Ireland, wind, north, cold, south*

zu c) *northern, freezing, cold, south, west, rain, snow*

zu d) *In Darwin it's hot and it's raining. On the East coast it's warm. The sun is shining in Sydney. A strong wind is blowing from the south on the South coast. In Perth it's warm and cloudy. It is very hot in Alice Springs.*

zu e) *The sun is shining in Miami and in Los Angeles. In Seattle, the wind is blowing from the north, it's freezing with −3° and it's snowing. It's cold and cloudy in the north. In Chicago and New York, it's raining. It's hot in Miami.*

Exercise 7

Hinweise / Ideen zu a) Dies ist eine Textverständnisübung mit Hauptgewicht auf logischem Füllen der Lücken (siehe Use-Box).
Anschliessend liest L oder lesen starke S den Text abschnittweise vor, die S hören mit oder ohne Textvorlage zu und versuchen den Zusammenhang zu verstehen.
Ziel: Je nach Leistungsstärke der Klasse soll der Inhalt detailliert oder lediglich global verstanden werden.
Der Text kann auch als Lesetext verwendet werden.

Möglichkeiten
- L liest vor, die S wiederholen im Chor, in Gruppen oder in EA; sie geben Echo usw.
- Der Text wird (abschnittweise) aufgeteilt und in GA mit Hilfe von L und mit dem Wörterbuch zum Vorlesen erarbeitet.
- Die S spielen Radioreporter.

Ausbau Ein ähnlicher Text liegt im *Workbook Intensive* als Hörverständnisübung vor; er kann bei Bedarf als weiterführende Aufgabe eingesetzt werden.

Hinweise / Ideen zu b) Textverständnis- oder Hörverständnisübung zur Wetterlage.
Je nachdem, was unter a) für Prioritäten gesetzt worden sind, wird der Text entweder als Textverständnis- (in EA / PA / GA) oder Hörverständnisübung angegangen; hierbei übernimmt L die Rolle des Radioreporters.
Bei leistungsschwächeren Klassen empfiehlt es sich, im ersten Durchgang die Informationen zu sammeln und erst im zweiten Durchgang die Sätze ausformulieren zu lassen.

Erweiterung Schreibübung: Die S verfassen einen aktuellen Wetterbericht (evtl. zu verschiedenen Ländern, Gebieten) und stellen diesen der Klasse vor.

Workbook Basic — Unit 13

Lösung zu a)
listening, looking, singing, raining, offering, dreaming, shining, offering, thinking, offering, shining, snowing, shining, planning, starting

zu b)
*the Florida Keys: It's 32°. The sun is shining.
Lake Tahoe: The sun is shining.
Juneau: It's very cold and it's snowing.
San Diego: The sun is shining and it's very hot.*

Exercise 8

Hinweise / Ideen

Dieses Projekt eignet sich auch für fächerübergreifende Arbeiten. Es können verschiedene Suchaufträge – etwa zum Wetter in Australien oder Japan – mit möglichen Prognosen für die kommenden Tage gegeben werden.

Unit 14

Language Focus

Ziel — Gegenüberstellung der Verlaufsform der Gegenwart *(Present progressive)* und der einfachen Gegenwart *(Present simple)*.

Mögliche Lösung

At the moment,				Normally,			
I	'm	reading	a book in English.	I	read		books in German.
you	're	playing	hockey.	you	play		football.
he	's	eating	an ice cream.	he	eats		an apple.
she	's	listening	to the radio.	she	listens		to a CD.
it	's	raining	in France.	it	rains		in Ireland.
we	're	running	in the building.	we	run		in the streets.
you	're	taking	a shower	you	take		a bath.
they	're	drinking	a milkshake	they	drink		a glass of water.

Exercise 1

Ziel — Üben der Gegenüberstellung von *Present simple* und *Present progressive* in EA.

Hinweise / Ideen — Je nach Leistungsstärke der Klasse kann die Übung entweder zur Illustration und Diskussion der Thematik dienen (die S kennen den Focustext bereits relativ gut und setzen die Formen fast auswendig ein) oder zur Erarbeitung der Thematik (die S kennen den Focustext noch nicht sehr gut und müssen die Formen entsprechend erarbeiten). Die fett gedruckten *keywords* können zur Bildung von (eigenen) Sätzen in der entsprechenden Zeitform an der Wandtafel vorgegeben werden.
Korrekturen anhand des Focustextes.

Lösung — *'m sitting, are flying, are we going, wonder* (verb of feeling, deshalb keine -ing-Form), *are landing, are flying, are, are wearing, often wear, is landing, is coming, is holding, is, 's happening, is rubbing, usually rub*

Exercise 2

Hinweise / Ideen zu a) — Diese Übung kann ganz verschieden angegangen werden. Man kann den S auch eine der Möglichkeiten freistellen.

Möglichkeiten
- Die S korrigieren den Text in EA / PA / GA und vergleichen ihre Lösung anschliessend mit dem Originaltext im *Student's Book*.
- Das *Exercise* wird als Hörverständnisübung angegangen, wobei die S je nach Klassenstärke in einem ersten Durchgang nur unterstreichen, was nicht mit dem Originaltext übereinstimmt; in einem weiteren Durchgang wird (mit oder ohne jeweiliges Anhalten der CD) die Lösung notiert.
- PA: S 1 liest den ‚falschen' Text, S 2 korrigiert mit dem Originaltext als Vorgabe und S 1 notiert die richtige Lösung. (*Last night I had a holiday … – No, it's not "holiday" it's "dream"* usw.)
- Wettbewerb: Wer findet am schnellsten die meisten Ungereimtheiten?

Workbook Basic Unit 14

Hinweise / Ideen zu b)	Wiederholung des Alphabets in verschiedenen Unterrichtsformen.
Möglichkeiten	- Die S buchstabieren den Namen in EA laut vor sich hin. - Die S arbeiten in PA und wechseln sich bei jedem Buchstaben ab. - Sie S arbeiten in Gruppen; ein S buchstabiert jeweils bis zum nächsten *a*. - Diktat des Namens, auf Tempo, mit variierender Lautstärke.
Lösung zu a)	*dream, back, flying, islands, Kiwi, landing, flying, sun, dogs, dogs, landing, rubbing noses, rub noses, Cloud, letters*

Exercise 3

Ziel	Gegenüberstellung des *Present simple* und des *Present progressive*
Hinweise / Ideen	Je nach Leistungsstärke die Lücken im GU und anschliessend in PA besprechen, dann die Lösung in EA einsetzen und mittels Tonträger korrigieren lassen. Am Schluss das Telefongespräch als Leseübung gestalten.

Lösung

	right now	always
Mandy: Hi Kevin? What are you doing?	x	
Kevin: Not much. I'm sitting in the living room with John. We are	x	
watching a video. What about you? Are you working for	x	
school?	x	
Mandy: On Saturday afternoon? Come on. You know, I never		x
work for school on a Saturday. No, I'm getting to go out to	x	
a party tonight with my friends.		
Kevin: Great. So where's the party?		
Mandy: At my friend Jenny's house. She is alone tonight. Her		
parents like opera and classical music. So they often go to		x
concert festivals or to operas in Paris or Berlin. I think,		x
today they are going to Milan to hear Cecilia Bartoli.	x	
Kevin: That's the great diva. She sings in a lot of operas. So what		x
is she singing in Milan at the moment?	x	
Mandy: I don't know. Something called Figaro, I think. But I		x
don't like opera very much, so I don't really know.		x
Anyway, what are you and John watching right now? You	x	
are not watching an opera ...	x	
Kevin: Of course not. We are watching a new film called ...	x	

Exercise 4

Hinweise / Ideen	Die Kurztexte zuerst mündlich im GU / GA besprechen und anschliessend schriftlich formulieren. Nach der Korrektur der Texte können diese zur Repetition der Frageformen dienen. *(When does Cleopatra the Beauty sleep? Who sleeps in the afternoon? When is she getting ready for the cinema? What is she getting ready for? usw.)*

Unit 14 Workbook Basic

Lösung

1. *Frederic the Cat usually drinks milk. Today he is eating sausage.*
   Lilly the Kid usually sits at the table and reads the newspaper. Today she is sitting at the table and drinking coffee.
2. *Napoleon the Tramp usually sits in the park and eats a hamburger. Today he is sitting in the park and drinking a beer.*
   He wears dirty jeans and waits for Frederic. He is wearing dirty jeans and (he) is waiting for Frederic (as always).
3. *Frederic the Cat usually plays the piano like a rock musician and doesn't sing. Today he is singing like an opera singer. And Lilly the Kid is writing a letter.*
   Lilly the Kid usually eats a sandwich and listens to Frederic.

Language Focus

Hinweis

Dieser *Language Focus* wie auch das folgende *Exercise 5* ist für Klassen gedacht, die das unbestimmte Pronomen *one / ones* behandeln möchten.

Mögliche Lösung

George has got two	T-shirts,	a green	T-shirt	and a red	T-shirt.
George has got two	T-shirts,	a green	one	and a red	one.
Mandy has got five	videos,	three French	videos	and two American	videos.
Mandy has got five	videos,	three French	ones	and two American	ones.
Jenny has got three	friends,	an American	friend	and two Swiss	friends.
Jenny has got three	friends,	an American	one	and two Swiss	ones.

Exercise 5

Hinweise / Ideen

Diese freiwillige Übung kann mündlich oder schriftlich angegangen werden, was die Behandlung des unbestimmten Pronomens *one / ones* angeht.
Weiter eignen sich die Kurztexte für verschiedene Diktatformen, z.B. für ein *running dictation* (ein Partner-Wanderdiktat): Ein Text wird mehrfach im Zimmer aufgehängt. **S 1** liest, von einem Zettel zum anderen gehend, einen oder mehrere Sätze und diktiert diese anschliessend **S 2**. **S 2** schreibt das Diktierte nieder, dann wechseln die Rollen. **S 1** korrigiert das Diktat von **S 2**, während **S 2** weitere Sätze von den Zetteln abliest und diese anschliessend **S 1** diktiert, usw.

Lösung

1. *George has got three mountain bikes, a black one and two blue ones.*
2. *He also does a sailing course. There are all kinds of boats, small ones and big ones. George really likes the small ones. He likes the big ones too, but he thinks that the big ones are difficult in bad weather.*
3. *He is a member of two fitness clubs. One is an expensive one, the other one is not so expensive. But the trainers at the expensive one are very nice.*
4. *He goes for a bike ride every day. During the week he goes for short ones, but on Sunday he always has a long one. On Saturdays he sometimes goes for long ones, but normally he goes for a short one.*

Exercise 6

Hinweise / Ideen

Die **S** collagieren und beschreiben nach dem Muster von *Exercise 4* eigene Bilder oder Begebenheiten. Weitere Möglichkeit: **L** kopiert Bilder aus einer Illustrierten und gibt sie an die **S** ab mit dem Auftrag, je einen bis zwei Sätze im *Present progressive* und im *Present simple* dazu zu schreiben. Anschliessend werden die Textchen in der Klasse (vor)gelesen und verglichen.

Revision Workshop 3

Allgemeiner Hinweis zu den Revision Workshops

In der Mitte und am Schluss von *Ready for English 2* steht eine spezielle Einheit, in der keine neuen grammatikalischen Strukturen und nur die nötigsten Wörter eingeführt werden. Der Zweck ist die systematische Wiederholung der wichtigsten Formen und Fertigkeiten aus vorangegangenen *Units*.

Da die Schülerinnen und Schüler möglichst zu Eigenaktivität und zu einer selbständigen Bestandesaufnahme angeregt werden sollen, findet sich sämtliches Arbeitsmaterial im *Workbook*. Das heisst nicht, dass alle Übungen schriftlich gelöst werden müssen. Die Übersicht über den *Revision Workshop 3* auf der folgenden Seite gibt Auskunft über die möglichen Arbeitsformen bei jeder einzelnen Station.

Arbeitsweise — Der *Revision Workshop* kann grundsätzlich auf zwei Arten bearbeitet werden:

1. Klassenverband — Schritt für Schritt bzw. Station für Station, mit Lernkontrolle nach jeder Übung. Dennoch sollten die Übungen wie angegeben in PA, EA oder GA erarbeitet werden. Hörverständnisübungen können im Klassenverband durchgeführt werden. Die einzelnen Stationen müssen nicht unbedingt erst nach Unit 14 erledigt werden, sondern können auch einige Wochen nach Behandlung der jeweiligen Form oder Funktion als Lückenfüller benutzt werden.

2. Workshop — Diese Form wird allen Lehrpersonen empfohlen, die schon etwas Erfahrung mit Workshops haben oder sich auf etwas Neues einlassen wollen. Im Folgenden wird kurz darauf eingegangen, wie ein Workshop aufgebaut werden kann.

Kontrolle — Zur Leistungskontrolle oder zur Eigeneinschätzung der S können die Kopiervorlagen Nr. 27 und 67 *(Control Sheet)* dienen.

Hinweise für den Aufbau eines Workshops

Der Workshop ist aufgebaut wie ein Circuittraining im Sport. Die Stationen sind verteilt im Klassenzimmer aufgebaut, evtl. mit Tafeln bezeichnet. Die Schülerinnen und Schüler gehen zu den einzelnen Stationen und führen die jeweilige Aufgabe nach der aufliegenden Anweisung selbständig aus. Am Ende kontrollieren sie ihren Erfolg selbst und haken die Übung auf dem *Control Sheet* (Kopiervorlage) ab oder machen sie evtl. später nochmals, wenn das Ergebnis nicht befriedigend war. Die Kriterien für die Erfüllung jedes einzelnen Schrittes (z.B. alles richtig, 70 Prozent richtig, höchstens drei Rechtschreibfehler usw.) sollten von der Lehrperson festgelegt und den Schülerinnen und Schülern bekannt gegeben werden. Die Schülerinnen und Schüler arbeiten meist allein, müssen sich aber bei den in der Übersicht mit PA bezeichneten Stationen mit einer Partnerin / einem Partner zusammentun, der / die gerade auch diese Station angelaufen hat. Die Lehrperson fungiert als Kontrollinstanz und Ratgeberin im Hintergrund.

Obschon alle Stationen des *Revision Workshop* im *Workbook* enthalten sind, bedingt eine reibungslose Durchführung etwas Vorbereitung (siehe Übersichtstabelle auf der nächsten Seite).

Für die Durchführung dieses Workshops müssen je nach Leistungsstärke der Klasse zwischen drei und sechs Lektionen eingeplant werden.

Übersicht über den Revision Workshop 3

	Station (Topic)	Sprachliche Struktur	Arbeitsform	Vorbereitung durch L / Material
1.	*Simple Past Forms*	Vergangenheitsform unregelmässiger Verben	EA	—
2.	*Verb Training*			
3.	*Writing*	Verlaufsform der Gegenwart, Gegenwart	EA	—
4.	*Reading*	Textverständnis	EA	Vorbereitung evtl. mündlich mit Hilfe der Grundrisse als Folienkopie
5.	*Combination Crossword*			
6.	*Listening*	Hörverständnis	EA	—
7.	*Questions and Answers*	Fragen und Antworten im *Simple past*	EA/PA	evtl. *Student's Book, page 7*, kopieren und auflegen
8.	*Vocabulary*			

Workbook Basic — **Revision Workshop 3**

Station Simple Past Forms

Lösung

am/are, is	was/were	have	had	say	said
come	came	know	knew	see	saw
go	went	make	made	take	took

become	became	find	found	sit	sat
bring	brought	give	gave	wear	wore
buy	bought	hit	hit		
fall	fell	hold	held		

Station Verb Training

Lösung

Infinitive	Past Tense	Present Simple	Present Progressive
do	we did	we do	we are doing
paint	we paint	we painted	we are painting
come	I came	I come	I'm coming
play	he played	he plays	he's playing
get	they got	they get	they are getting
give	she gave	she gives	she's giving
have	she had	she has	she's having
make	he made	he makes	he's making
say	you said	you say	you are saying
take	it took	it takes	it's taking

bring	we brought	we bring	we are bringing
sit	they sat	they sit	they are sitting
hold	you held	you hold	you are holding
give	I gave	I give	I'm giving
hit	I hit	I hit	I'm hitting
find	we found	we find	we're finding
wear	they wore	they wear	they are wearing
become	she became	she becomes	she's becoming
buy	I bought	I buy	I'm buying
fall	he fell	he falls	he's falling

Station Writing

Mögliche Lösung

1. Today, the teacher's wearing a pullover. He usually wears a jacket.
2. Today, the cat's sitting in front of the door. It usually sits behind the door.
3. Today, two boys are playing American football. They normally play football.
4. Today, a boy is listening to a walkman. He usually listens to a discman.
5. Today, a girl's drinking juice. She usually drinks water.

Zusätzliche Unterschiede:
6. Today, a boy is eating a hamburger. He usually eats a sandwich.
7. Today, two girls are reading on the grass. They normally read on a bank.
8. Today, a woman is cleaning a window. She usually watches the students.

Revision Workshop 3

Workbook Basic

Station Reading

Lösung
- U2: C; A Dream: D; A School Fete: A; Madonna: E; Two Days in November: B

Station Combination Crossword

Lösung
- *running a race, speaking to a friend, dreaming at night, driving a car, playing football, finding the way, doing homework, drinking a glass of water, eating a banana, listening to music, singing a song, blowing from the north, taking a shower, sitting on a chair, touching a vase*
- Das Lösungswort von oben nach unten lautet "READY FOR ENGLISH".

Station Listening

Skript

Jonathan: A simple two-week holiday together, just you and me. That would be so nice. A pretty beach somewhere, but no. It's just not possible.

Melanie: Look Jonathan, it's not my fault that the travel agency went out of business. And I'm also quite mad that we never got a penny back from that holiday arrangement. So be fair, OK?

Jonathan: I know it's not your fault. But why can we never organise our time so we can go away together.

Melanie: Well, why don't we try for next year then?

Jonathan: It's not going to work, Melanie, I'm sure. OK, how about around Easter, April?

Melanie: Sorry, I'm going to the US for four weeks to work for my company in New York. They asked me three months ago.

Jonathan: See, I told you. And you can't make it in May?

Melanie: I think I can. Yes, May's OK for me.

Jonathan: Sorry, it isn't for me, I've just realised. The Local Shakespeare Company is organising a production of Macbeth for June and I promised to help. May is no good. But June would be very good.

Melanie: June? That's a problem for me. We've got the District Tennis Championship, I can't get away. I thought you were busy with the Shakespeare Company.

Jonathan: I'm not acting this year, so no, I would be free. And then I'm taking my mother to a holiday in Ireland in July. So that's no good. So summer is out. How about autumn, October?

Melanie: That's when I go to Spain with my parents. How can they get the best holiday times and we can't …? But how about beginning of September or November?

Jonathan: September is no good because I'm going to that Yoga course in Liverpool. And November, what about November. You said beginning of November, didn't you? – No, I've got Sue and Marc from Canada at my house. I don't like them but they are family and I can't just say: "Hi, nice of you to come, but I'm going on a holiday, see you when I get back." What about August?

Melanie: No, sorry, I can't. I'm doing a language course in Marseille. But, wait a minute, January, how about January?

Jonathan: That's no good at all, sorry. Firstly, I never have any money after Christmas and, secondly, I'm starting a new job on the 5th, so no, that won't be very good. And February is no good either because I'm going on a training course for two weeks.

Melanie: February is no good for me either: I've got my business exams on the 20th. I need to work for that. That leaves December, but …

Jonathan: … that's the busiest time of the year in our shop. There's no way I can take a holiday in December. So that's it, right? No holiday for the two of us. We can only get away if you come to Ireland with me or I come to Spain with you and your dear parents. I don't think I can stand it.

Melanie: Look, your parents are not much fun to be with, either. – Wait a minute, if you haven't got anything on we could go away with each other in …

Jonathan: Yes, of course!

Workbook Basic   **Revision Workshop 3**

Lösung

Melanie	Jonathan
1	
2	2
4	
	5
6	
	7
8	
	9
10	
	11
	12

Station Questions and Answers

Lösung

Where did U2 start their career?
They started it in Dublin.
What was President Kennedy's first name.
His first name was John Fitzgerald.
How do Maori say hello?
They rub noses.
Who wrote a song about the murder of Martin Luther King?
U2 wrote this song.
Whose second album was called "Like a Virgin"?
Madonna's second album.
What sold Christina and Tony at the school fete?
They sold home-made cakes.
When did Prince Charles and Lady Diana separate?
They separated in 1992.
Where did President Kennedy go on 22 November 1963?
He went to Dallas.

Station Vocabulary

Lösung

1. career, 2. gun, 3. juice, 4. island, 5. dream, 6. noise, 7. spring, 8. queue, 9. neck, 10. east, 11. tie

Unit 15

Exercise 1

Hinweise / Ideen — *Exercise 1* ist eine tabellarische Übersicht über die im *Focus* vorgestellten Reisearten. Es ist in stiller EA oder als PA zusammen mit dem *Focus*-Text als Textverständnisübung zu lösen.

Lösung

Air Safari	Railway Travel	Camping Tour
8 days	14 days	10 days
A$ 4260.–	A$ 385.–	A$ 919.–
ten-passenger planes	trains	special coach
max. of 10 in one group	as many as you want	small groups / 6 to 12 people

hotels or farms	sleeping berths	sleeping bag
Great Barrier Reef, Escott Cattle Station, Lawn Hill National Park, Alice Springs, Ayers Rock, Birdsville, Lightning Ridge	unlimited travel from Perth to Cairns	Melbourne / Sydney, Flinder Ranges, Ayers Rock, Alice Springs

Language Focus

Ziel — Erarbeitung der zwei Kategorien des Komparativs. Die **S** sollen das Muster selbst entdecken. Zusätzliche (bekannte) Adjektive: *great, quiet, loud, terrible, funny, boring, lovely*.
Die Regel, die die **S** ableiten sollen: Einsilbige Adjektive und Adjektive auf -y gehören zu *Group 1*, zwei- und mehrsilbige Adjektive zu *Group 2*.
Die orthografischen Regeln dazu sind in § 29 a der Grammatik festgehalten.

Lösung

Group 1	Group 2
harder, smaller, larger, faster, nicer	*more beautiful, more direct, more difficult, more wonderful*

Exercise 2

Hinweise / Ideen — Die **S** üben die Vergleichsformen, indem sie die vorgegebenen Begriffe oder Namen mit den jeweils entsprechenden Adjektiven vergleichen. Zum Teil hängen die Antworten von den Vorstellungen und Ansichten der **S** ab.

zu a) — Die Beispiele können im GU zuerst mündlich durchgegangen werden, um eine gewisse Sicherheit zu gewinnen. Auch über die verschiedenen persönlichen Ansichten kann kurz (auch auf Deutsch) diskutiert werden.

zu b) — Stärkere **S** formulieren ihren Satz in PA mündlich und unmittelbar danach schriftlich oder diktieren einander ihre Beispiele gegenseitig.

Wichtig — Hinweis auf die Schreibweise von *than*.

Workbook Basic
Unit 15

Lösung
1. ... easier than ...
2. A car radio is louder than a walkman.
3. ... more dangerous than ...
4. ... more comfortable ...
5. Commander Wiggles is older than his dog Ben.

1. A golf course is bigger than a tennis court.
2. ... more exciting than ...
3. ... more famous than ...
4. ... more difficult than ...
5. ... stronger than ...

Language Focus

Ziel   Einführung der Steigerungsform *Superlativ*.

Lösung
The Concorde is the fastest passenger plane in the world.
La Brévine is the coldest village in Switzerland.
I think the Matterhorn is the most beautiful mountain in Europe.
Which is the most important city in the world?

Exercise 3

Hinweise / Ideen   Je nach Gutdünken kann diese Übung gleich angegangen werden wie *Exercise 2* (siehe entsprechende Hinweise / Ideen), oder die S können zuerst in EA die Sätze schriftlich formulieren und sich (evtl. mit Zusatznotizen) auf eine anschliessende Begründung vorbereiten. *(For me, the bus is the easiest way to travel **because** we have a bus stop in front of our house etc.)*

Lösung
1. For me, the easiest way to travel is ...
2. For me, the most popular actor is ...
3. The most important thing in my life is ...
4. For me, the greatest person in sports is ...
5. For me, the hardest language to learn is ...
6. For me, the most exciting television programme is ...
7. My biggest problem at the weekend is ...
8. For me, the happiest time of the day is ...
9. For me, the most difficult school subject is ...

Language Focus

Ziel   Veranschaulichung der unregelmässigen Steigerungsformen von *good* und *bad*.

Lösung

Julia Roberts is a	good	actress.
... is a	better	actress.
... is the	best	actress in the world.
Jesse James was a	bad	person.
Al Capone was a	worse	person.
... is / was the	worst	person in the world.

Unit 15 — Workbook Basic

Exercise 4

Ziel Beherrschung der unregelmässigen Steigerungsformen von *good* und *bad*.

Hinweise / Ideen zu a) Die S formulieren eigene Sätze zu den vorgegebenen Begriffen im Superlativ. L kann als Vorlauf die eigenen Beispiele mündlich vorstellen. Die Übung eignet sich als GA, wobei alle S der Gruppe ihre Meinung zuerst mündlich kundtun und anschliessend schriftlich formulieren.

Variante Die Aussagen anderer S aus der Gruppe werden schriftlich festgehalten: *For Sarah, the best book is ...* Anschliessend wird in der Klasse wettbewerbsartig erfragt, wer wohl welche Vorlieben hat. *(Who says "The best book is Harry Potter"?)*

zu b) Die S vergleichen und diskutieren ihre Varianten, möglichst mit Begründungen. Als Hilfe kann L vorgängig zu jedem Beispiel stützende Elemente an der Wandtafel vorgeben.
Beispiel zu 1.: *book: too long; not interesting; I (don't) like comic strips; history books).*
Zu einigen Punkten kann auch (fächerübergreifend) auf Deutsch eingehend diskutiert werden.

Exercise 5

Ziel Hörverständnis, Vergleichsformen, Zahlen erkennen.

Hinweis / Idee Unterschied zwischen *big* und *large*.
Zuerst die Antworten still lesen lassen. Es kann allenfalls schon vor dem Hören spekuliert werden: *Is it possible that Mount Isa is the world's biggest town?*

Skript
Chris: Here's something about Australia. Oh no, that's Austria. Don't go so fast, Mona, I don't have time to read.
Mona: Oh here's something. Look at this picture. It's Sydney.
Chris: Yeah, Sydney Harbour Bridge, the biggest bridge in the world.
Mona: No, not the biggest, stupid, the widest bridge. It's 49 metres wide, and it's got ... let's see, one, two, four, six, eight lanes for cars.
Chris: And two railway tracks besides that.
Mona: It's also very long, more than 500 metres.
Chris: I'm sure the Golden Gate Bridge is longer though ...
Mona: Anything else about Australia? Look under railways. There must be something.
Chris: Yeah, it says here the longest railway line is in Australia.
Mona: I thought that was the Transsiberian.
Chris: No, you're right. It's the longest stretch of railway that is all straight, not a single bend for ... yeah, guess how many kilometres?
Mona: Mmmm ... 200? 500?
Chris: Not quite. 478 kilometres.
Mona: Wow. The driver probably falls asleep every time.
Chris: Did you know that Australia has the world's biggest town?
Mona: Big in what sense?
Chris: Well, big in area. Mount Isa is in Queensland, and it has about 40,000 square kilometres. It says here it's almost as big as Switzerland, not quite, but almost. But it only has 22,000 inhabitants. That's a lot of space for each of them. How many inhabitants has Switzerland got?
Mona: Switzerland? I have no idea. There must be a couple of millions ... two or three?
Chris: Let's check ...

Lösung
1. c) *Sydney Harbour Bridge, erbaut 1932, ist 48,8 m breit und hat eine Spannweite von 502,9 m, die Lichthöhe für Schiffe beträgt 49 m.*
2. b) *Die gerade Strecke zwischen Nurina und Ooldea ist 478 km lang (Linie Adelaide – Perth).*
3. a) *Das Gemeindegebiet von Mount Isa umfasst 40,978 km², die Schweiz ist immer noch ein bisschen grösser (41,295 km²).*

Workbook Basic Unit 15

Language Focus

Ziel Erfassen des Unterschieds zwischen den Fragewörtern *Which* und *What*.

Hinweis *What* fragt offen, aus der ganzen Menge der erhältlichen Dinge: *"What would you like?"*
Which bezieht sich auf eine beschränkte Menge: *"Which of these two bikes is yours?"*

Lösung *Which is your bike? – The red one.*
What is a sleeping berth – It's a bed on a train or a boat.
Which apples do you want? – The cheaper ones, please.
What would you like? – A kilo of bananas, please.

Exercise 6

Hinweis Übung zu den Frageformen mit *Which* und *What*.

Variante Nachdem der Unterschied von *Which* und *What* eingeführt und vertieft worden ist, eignet sich diese Übung bestens als *milling exercise*, indem die S die Fragen nicht auf sich selbst beziehen, sondern mündlich anderen S stellen, die jeweiligen Antworten schriftlich stichwortartig festhalten und erst anschliessend wiederum mündlich oder schriftlich im *Workbook* ausformulieren. *(A green salad is cheaper than a tomato salad. Roger's favourite drink is Red Bull, etc.)* Dieses *Exercise* kann natürlich auch als Festigungsübung des Unterschieds von *Which* und *What* dienen.

Lösung
1. *Which salad is cheaper, …*
2. *What is your favourite drink?*
3. *Which is the best way …?*
4. *Which airline is bigger, …*
5. *What do you think of Harry Potter?*
6. *What did you have for breakfast today?*
7. *Which comic strip character do you like: …?*

Exercise 7

Ziel Adjektive und die Vergleichsformel *as … as* üben. Landeskunde.

Hinweise / Ideen Diese Übung kann als Wettbewerb gestaltet werden: Die S sollen die Antworten zuerst erraten; anschliessend werden die Lösungen mittels Atlas oder Internet in GA/GU gesucht. Diejenigen S, die am meisten richtig geschätzt haben, werden belohnt.

Lösung mit den tatsächlichen Distanzen und Zeiten:
1. c) Perth – Sydney = 3278 km (Luftdistanz)
2. b) Brisbane – Darwin = 3.50 hours
3. a) Melbourne – Sydney = 889 km (Strasse)
4. b) Sidney – Cairns = 53 h
5. a) Australia = 7,686,850 km^2
6. c) Längste gerade Strecke in Australien: 478 km. Genève Aéroport – St. Margrethen = ca. 410 km
7. c) Ayers Rock: 940 m ü. M. Säntis: 2502 m ü. M.

Exercise 8

Ziel Die S beschäftigen sich (auch fächerübergreifend) mit Informationen aus der Geografie.

Hinweise / Ideen zu a) Die Informationen dienen einerseits als Vorgabe zu Aufgabe b), können aber auch zu einem Kurztext ausformuliert und in einem Heft festgehalten werden.

zu b) Die S suchen im Atlas oder im Internet entsprechende Informationen zu einer selbstgewählten Insel und halten diese in einem Heft oder auf einem Plakat im Schulzimmer oder im Schulhaus fest. Natürlich kann anstelle einer Insel auch ein Land gewählt werden, doch ist die Wahrscheinlichkeit grösser, dass die S, vor allem wenn jede(r) S der Klasse eine andere Insel wählt, möglichst viele neue Informationen erhalten.

Unit 16

Exercise 1

Hinweise / Ideen
zu a) Das *Exercise* kann als Hörverständnisübung unter Einsatz des Tonträgers gestaltet werden, oder es dient zur Vertiefung des Focustexts; in diesem Falle setzen die S zuerst in EA / PA / GA mögliche Lösungswörter ein, der Tonträger wird dann zur Korrektur und Ergänzung beigezogen.

zu b) Die S sollten diesen Text nicht vorbereiten, sondern ihn direkt mit dem Hörtext ab Tonträger vergleichen.
Je nach Leistungsstärke der Klasse kann die CD entweder abschnittweise gestoppt oder das Ganze mehrmals abgespielt werden.

Ausbau PA: S 1 liest analog zu b) den Focustext aus dem *Student's Book*, S 2 sagt, was bei b) mit anderen Worten ausgedrückt wird.

Lösung
a) *from, Saturday, young, arrived, last night, by train, down, near, called, canoes, deep, weeks*
b) *hello, bush, supermarket, small, Sweden, bears, new, deep, hard*

Exercise 2

Ziele Aufarbeitung des Focustexts, Üben von Begründungen, Wiederholung einiger Strukturen des Focustexts.

Hinweise / Ideen Je nach Leistungsstärke und je nachdem, wie stark der Focustext verankert ist, kann die Übung mit oder ohne *Student's Book* und in einer beliebigen Unterrichtsform angegangen werden. Die Zuordnung sollte unbedingt mittels Kästchen und nicht mittels Verbindungsstrichen erfolgen, da es ein Ziel dieser Übung ist, dass die S alle Sätze richtig zusammengesetzt laut lesen können. Die Zuordnung in den Kästchen dient also der Vorbereitung zur mündlichen freien Umsetzung.

Lösung *1e, 2d, 3c, 4a, 5b, 6h, 7g, 8f*

Language Focus

Thema *must*, *have to* und *need to* bejaht und verneint; keine Verneinung von *must*

Mögliche Lösung

I: must / have to / need to

I	must	be	at home at 11 o'clock.
You	need to	take	the dog out.
She	has to	buy	a new jacket.
He	must	bring	a coke for lunch.
We	must	write	a letter to grandmother.
You	need to	take	a suitcase.
They	must	find	their books.

II: don't have to / don't need to

I	don't	have to	be	at home at 11 o'clock.
You	don't	need to	take	the dog out.
She	doesn't	have to	buy	a new pair of jeans.
He	doesn't	need to	bring	a coke for lunch.
We	don't	need to	write	a letter to grandmother.
You	don't	need to	buy	a lot of bread.
They	don't	have to	arrive	on time.

Workbook Basic   Unit 16

IV: have to

Last week	I	had to	be	at home at six o'clock every day.
	you	had to	take	the bus to school.
	she	had to	work	very hard.
	we	had to	learn	all the words.

Exercise 3

Hinweise / Ideen zu a) und b)

Es ist wichtig, dass die **S** den Einleitungstext genau erfassen. Möglicher Einstieg:
An der Wandtafel eine Liste von Milchprodukten und Produkten, die keine Milch enthalten, erarbeiten.
Ebenso empfiehlt es sich in schwächeren Klassen, die *New Words*-Box im Voraus zu besprechen, denn die **S** sollten anschliessend fähig sein, die Listen in EA / PA / GA, also möglichst ohne Hilfe von **L**, zu füllen.

zu c)

Dieser Teil der Übung sollte möglichst in EA, als Zusammenfassung von a) und b) erfolgen. Der Text eignet sich auch für eine Diktatform.

Lösung

a) ☺ *apples, bananas, biscuits, chocolate cake, oranges, salad*
   ☹ *hamburgers, salami, sausages, steaks*
b) ☺ *bread, butter, coffee, eggs, French cheese, milk, milkshakes, pop corn, tea*
c) Hi ...,
We have to buy bananas, apples and oranges because my sister really loves fruit.
You don't need to get milkshakes or butter, because she doesn't like things with milk in them.
And – please – you mustn't bring salami, hamburgers or even sausages; she doesn't eat meat, she is vegetarian!

Language Focus

Ziel

much / many / a lot of, *more*, *most* und *little / few*, *less / fewer* und *least / fewest*.
Unterschied zwischen zählbaren und unzählbaren Mengenangaben; Letztere kommen in der Regel nicht im Plural vor.

Lösung

	singular	plural
	There is a lot of forest in Canada.	A lot of people came to the party.
	I haven't got much homework.	How many pupils are there in your class?
comparative	There is often more snow in the Rocky Mountains than in the Alps.	Are there more boys or girls in your class?
superlative	Who has the most milk in their coffee?	Which class in your school has the most pupils?

	singular	plural
	There is only little sunshine in Greenland in winter.	Few tourists know local pubs in Switzerland.
comparative	There is less forest in British Columbia now than in 1950.	In Switzerland, fewer people speak French than German.
superlative	Who has the least money in her bag?	Which is the country with the fewest people?

Unit 16   Workbook Basic

Exercise 4

Hinweise / Ideen Das *Exercise* kann zur Festigung der Strukturen *a lot of / many / much / more* (siehe Begriffe in Klammern) oder zu ihrer Einführung dienen. L kann den Text zuerst mündlich oder auf dem OHP mit der korrekten Lösung präsentieren, um das Thema *zählbar / unzählbar* (siehe *Language Focus*) nochmals aufzuzeigen. Auch können die Lösungen in PA / GA diskutiert werden, evtl. mit Hilfe von Lösungskärtchen (Lücke auf der Vorderseite und Lösung auf der Rückseite), mit denen die S nach jeder gefüllten Lücke ihre Lösung kontrollieren und bei einem Fehler überdenken sollten. (Evtl. absichtlich ein falsches Lösungskärtchen liefern, um die Selbstkontrolle der S zu überprüfen!)

Lösung *much, more, a lot of, many, more, more,*
more, a lot of, many, more

Erweiterung *Canada and Switzerland (Kopiervorlage Nr. 43).*

Exercise 5

Hinweise / Ideen Zuerst das Verständnis sichern und dann die Begriffe in EA nummerieren lassen, damit die S anschliessend ihre Meinung mit den Steigerungsformen ausdrücken können.
Viele Beispiele eignen sich auch zu Kurzdiskussionen, bei denen die S ihre Ansicht begründen, je nach Leistungsstärke auch fächerübergreifend und auf Deutsch.
(I think a dog is more dangerous than a cat because cats can't kill you; but a tiger ...)

Mögliche Lösung
1. *I think a bear is more dangerous than a dog. / I think a bear is the most dangerous animal.*
2. *I think Appenzell is more interesting than Austria. / I think Australia is the most interesting country.*
3. *I think a sleeping berth is more comfortable than a tent. / I think a bed in a dormitory is the most comfortable.*
4. *I think reading is more difficult than counting in English. / I think spelling is the most difficult.*
5. *I think Berne is more rainy than Rome. / I think Vancouver is the most rainy city.*
6. *I think swimming is more relaxing than rafting. / I think walking is the most relaxing activity.*
7. *I think a detective story is more exciting than a love story. / I think a ghost story is the most exciting.*
8. *I think Internet surfing is more boring than computer games. / I think television is the most boring.*

Language Focus

Hinweis Das *Present progressive* wird hier in seiner Funktion als Tempus zur Angabe einer Gegebenheit in der nahen Zukunft nochmals bewusst gemacht (vgl. *Ready for English 1, Unit 10*). Das *Present progressive* wird zusammen mit einer Zeitangabe gebraucht, wenn über ein fixes Arrangement in der nahen Zukunft gesprochen wird.

Lösung
a) *"Right now we're having some problems with the wind. It's very strong."*
    present time, present progressive
b) *"What are your plans for tonight?" – "We're going to Harrison Hot Springs."*
    future time, present progressive

Workbook Basic Unit 16

Exercise 6

Hinweise / Ideen Hörverständnisübung. Der Reiseführer kündigt einige Programmänderungen an.
Die S markieren im ersten Durchgang die entsprechenden Begriffe. Im zweiten Durchgang versuchen sie, die Programmänderungen stichwortartig zu notieren.

Variante Die S spielen in PA / GA selbst Reiseführer und geben Programmänderungen bekannt.

Skript All right, tomorrow is the seventh day of our tour, and it's the most exciting one. We have to start as early as possible, at about 7 o'clock. I'm sorry, that's a change from the printed programme, but we need a little more time.
So we're having breakfast at six. How about that? Well, Max, you don't like the idea, but we have to pick up our canoes at nine o'clock. It's quite a long walk from here to the canoe shop. We've got the rest of the morning to pack everything and to practice a little. Ah, paddling is not as easy as you think!
We're having lunch on Cook Island, not on Bear Island, because there's a girl's camp there and I don't want to lose our boys. So that's another change.
In the afternoon we're paddling up to Joe Lake. It looks like a long way, but we still have enough time for a swim. And we have a short portage there, so we can practice portaging.
Now, at four, we have to make camp. It gets dark early in September. I think we're having soup and sausages for dinner tomorrow.
OK. At night, there may be some bears around, so we have to hang the food in the trees.
Now, isn't that a day full of adventures?

Lösung

~~7.00~~ 6.00	Breakfast at Tea Lake Campground
13.00	Lunch on ~~Bear Island~~ Cook Island
~~17.00~~ 16.00	Arrive at campsite
18.00	~~Steak Dinner~~ Soup and sausage for dinner, evening campfire

Exercise 7

Ziel Üben des *Present progressive* mit Zukunftsbedeutung.

Hinweis Wegen der geplanten Flossreise hat Yolanda ihre Agenda voll von fixen Terminen und kann deshalb ihren Freund nicht treffen. Oder doch?

Vorgehen Die S studieren den Tagesplan in EA und überlegen sich mögliche Fragen.
Anschliessend werden in PA Gespräche geführt. **S 1** spricht in der Rolle von Yolanda, **S 2** in der Rolle von Daniel.
Je nach Leistungsstärke können die Fragen und / oder die Antworten schriftlich vorbereitet, mit Hilfe des Rasters oder lediglich mit der Tagebuchvorlage formuliert werden.

Hilfestellung OHP mit den Vorschlägen aus dem *Workbook*.

Mögliche Lösung

Daniel	Yolanda
Can I see you at 9?	*No, I'm sorry, I'm picking up my flight ticket at 9.*
What about 9.30?	*No, I'm going shopping.*
Oh, perhaps later, at 10?	*No, I'm meeting Margaret at 10.30.*
What about noon then?	*No, I'm meeting Dr. Coleman at 11.00.*
	At 12.00 I'm having lunch with my mother.
You're really difficult. Can I see you at 13.30?	*No, I'm waiting for a phone call from Marco.*
What about 14.30?	*No, Claude is bringing his rucksack at 14.30.*
So let's meet at 15.30?	*No I'm picking up my passport at 15.30.*

Unit 16 Workbook Basic

Exercise 8

Hinweise / Ideen Diese Übung bildet eine Ergänzung zum *Stepping Out* im *Student's Book*. Die S hören ab Tonträger die Information Bild um Bild und formulieren ihre Kurztexte gleich anschliessend. Die Übung kann auch ohne Tonträger direkt mit den vorgegebenen Informationen angegangen werden. Am Schluss können die Kurztexte vorgelesen und / oder gegenseitig korrigiert werden.

Mögliche Lösung
> *The Niagara Falls is a great waterfall. A lot of tourists visit it every year.*
> *It's 57 metres high and on the border with the US.*
> *The Koala bear lives in Australia. They look like teddy bears. They eat leaves*
> *and sleep all day.*
> *On this picture you can see Sydney Tower and Sydney Harbour bridge.*
> *It's 134 metres high.*
> *The Rocky Mountains are very beautiful: blue sky, rocks and white snow.*
> *You can see dangerous Grizzlies.*
> *The Great Barrier Reef is one of the biggest coral reefs in the world.*
> *You can swim and dive in the clear blue sea and see fish.*

Exercise 9

Hinweise / Ideen *Exercise 9* besteht aus Lückentexten, die die Naturphänomene hinter den Experimenten von *Time for a Change* erklären.
Das Ausfüllen der Lücken erlaubt eine Verständniskontrolle: Partnerin A zeigt Partner B, dass sie seine Ausführungen begriffen hat, und umgekehrt.
Diese Übung ist auch für den fächerübergreifenden Unterricht, evtl. für den Immersionsunterricht, konzipiert und kann ebenso auf Deutsch durchgeführt werden.

Lösung
> Experiment 1:
> *above, heavier, lift, air, water, coin, incredible*
>
> Experiment 2:
> *dry battery, bicycle, lemon, pieces, middle, end, metal, into*

Exercise 10

Hinweis Ziel dieses Projekts ist es, dass die S zu Bildern, Postkarten oder Tourismusprospekten aus der eigenen Wohnregion Kurztexte auf Englisch verfassen und präsentieren.

Workbook Basic — Unit 17

Unit 17

Language Focus

Ziel Die Formen des *Past progressive*, gleichzeitig Repetition der *Past*-Formen von *to be* sowie der *Progressive*-Form.

Mögliche Lösung

I	was	doing	my homework.
you	were	listening	to my new Shakira CD.
he	was	working	in the kitchen.
she	was	watching	a football match on TV.
it	was	freezing	on the Jungfraujoch.
we	were	having	our dinner.
you	were	playing	tennis.
they	were	repairing	their bikes.

Exercise 1

Hinweise / Ideen Dieses Exercise hat zwei Ziele: erstens die Verständniskontrolle des *Focus*-Textes und zweitens die praktische Anwendung des *Language Focus*-Themas. Es werden nur *Past progressive*-Formen eingesetzt.
Die **S** vervollständigen den Text zuerst mündlich in der Klasse und anschliessend schriftlich in EA. Die Sätze eignen sich für eine Leseübung. Dabei kann man einen kleinen Wettbewerb durchführen: Wer ohne einen (Aussprache-)Fehler am weitesten kommt, hat gewonnen.

Lösung *The gangsters were not expecting the police. Carla del Monte was listening to music on her discman. Steve "the Thinker" King was reading the novel "Crime and Punishment".*
The Galton Brothers were playing monopoly. Averell Galton was very angry. He said: "It's not fair, I was winning for the first time in my life." There was no shooting because Ramona Zotti was cleaning her machine gun. "Big" Tony Lynch was ironing Ramona's mini-dress. And Johnny "the Bulldozer" Walker was filling smuggled Scotch whisky into bottles.
A policeman said: "He was singing a happy song when we took him to the police car."
Al Bigone and his wife said: "We were watching the news on television." In the hangar, Fred Bull and George Sprite were painting a new number on Al Bigone's aeroplane, and Leonardo da Vicinity was servicing the helicopter when the police arrested them.

Language Focus

Ziel Sensibilisierung auf *gleichzeitige Handlungen*, die beide im *Past progressive* stehen, im Kontrast zu *neu eintretender Handlung*, die im *Past simple* steht. Signalwörter sind *while* bzw. *when*.

Lösung

Something was going on			when	another thing happened.		
I	was having	lunch	when	my friend	came	into the room.
Carla	was listening	to music	when	the police	went	at Bigone's house.
My friend and I	were watching	a video	when	my uncle	phoned.	

Unit 17　　　　　　　　　　　　　　　　　　　　　　　　　　　　　　　Workbook Basic

Something was going on			while	another thing was going on.		
I	was ironing	a mini-dress	**while**	Steve	was	reading a book.
Carla	was listening	to her discman	**while**	the Galtons	were playing	monopoly.
Linda and Laurie	were sitting	in the garden	**while**	Gregory	was sitting	in his room.

Exercise 2

Hinweise / Ideen

Anwendung des *Past simple* und des *Past progressive* in der Gegenüberstellung. Es kann von Vorteil sein, wenn die S sich zuerst darüber klar werden, was die auslösenden Konjunktionen sind (*while:* parallele Handlungen, *when:* neu eintretende Handlung). Um den Unterschied deutlich hervorzuheben, die Sätze bzw. Teilsätze jeweils von zwei S lesen lassen: **S 1** *Past simple*, **S 2** *Past progressive*. Andere Möglichkeit: Die Teilsätze mit verschiedenen Farben unterstreichen oder schreiben lassen.

Lösung

1. *Fred Bull and George Sprite were painting a new number while Leonardo da Vicinity was servicing the helicopter.*
2. *Johnny Walker was singing a song when the police took him to the car.*
3. *Ramona Zotti was cleaning her machine gun while the Galton Brothers were playing monopoly.*
4. *Steve King was reading a book while Tony Lynch was ironing Ramona's mini-dress.*
5. *Mr and Mrs Bigone were watching TV when the police arrested them.*
6. *Averell Galton was winning for the first time in his life when the police came.*

Exercise 3

Hinweise / Ideen

Die S entwickeln in PA oder GA einen Dialog, der den vorgegebenen Begriffen entspricht. Hier werden insbesondere die Frageform und die Verneinung geübt.
An dieser Stelle kann es sinnvoll sein, nochmals auf das *Present simple* zurückzukommen. Wo nötig, können die S im *Focus*-Text nachschauen, was wirklich geschah.

Mögliche Lösung

Watson: *Ramona, what were you doing when the police came?*
Ramona: *I was watching television.*
Watson: *That's not true. You were cleaning your machine gun.*
Tony, what were you doing while the Galton Brothers were playing monopoly?
Tony: *I was ironing Ramona's mini-dress.*
Watson: *Yes, that's true. Carla, what were you doing when the police arrested you?*
Carla: *I was reading a book.*
Watson: *That's not true. You weren't reading a book, you were listening to your discman.*
Johnny Walker, what were you doing while Fred and George were painting a new number?
Johnny: *I was eating pizza.*
Watson: *That's not true. You weren't eating pizza, you were filling Scotch whisky into bottles.*

Erweiterung Rollenspiel

Accusations: **S 1** (wortgewandt) spielt die Rolle der Lehrperson oder einer Chefin / eines Chefs, eine Gruppe von **S** spielt sich selber oder Untergebene. **S 1** macht Vorwürfe im *Past progressive (you were …ing when I came into the room)*, die angeschuldigten **S** müssen sich verteidigen.

Variante

Bei schwächeren Gruppen zuerst ein Skript schreiben lassen.

Workbook Basic   Unit 17

Exercise 4

Hinweis   Ziel ist die praktische Anwendung der *Past progressive*-Formen in einem Gespräch.

Vorgehen   Die S lösen die Aufgabe zuerst in EA (linke Spalte *you*). Dann fragen sie ihren Partner / ihre Partnerin und füllen die rechte Spalte *your partner* in Interviewform aus.
Freiwillig können sie dann noch in der dritten Person über ihre Interviewpartnerin / ihren Partner referieren oder schriftlich berichten.

Erweiterung   Die S lösen die Aufgabe zuerst in EA (linke Spalte *you* möglichst wahrheitsgetreu, die rechte Spalte *your partner* als Vermutung). Anschliessend stellen sie die Lösungen vor und vergleichen in PA ihre Annahmen.

Ausbau   Andere Personen und Tageszeiten wählen. (Als mündliche Übung geeignet.)

Exercise 5

Ziel   Die S finden nach dem Lösen der Aufgabe heraus, wer mit dem Mädchen in den grünen Jeans getanzt hat.

Hinweise / Ideen   Es handelt sich um eine Knobelübung, die erleichtert werden kann, wenn die S die Matrix von *page 69* ausfüllen.

Lösung zu a)
1. The partner of the boy in blue shoes wasn't wearing blue jeans.
2. One boy was wearing green shoes, but he wasn't dancing with the girl in green jeans.
3. One girl was wearing read jeans. She wasn't dancing with the boy in red shoes.
4. Her partner wasn't wearing green shoes.

	girl in red jeans	girl in green jeans	girl in blue jeans
boy in red shoes	*no (3.)*	*yes*	*no*
boy in green shoes	*no (4.)*	*no (2.)*	*yes*
boy in blue shoes	*yes*	*no*	*no (1.)*

zu b)
1. Was the girl in the blue jeans dancing with the boy in the red shoes?
No, she was dancing with the boy in the green shoes.
2. Was the partner of the boy in the blue shoes wearing red jeans?
Yes, she was. (Oder: His partner was wearing red jeans.)
3. Was the boy in the green shoes dancing with the girl in blue jeans?
Yes, he was. (Oder: His partner was wearing blue jeans.)
4. Was the partner of the girl in the red jeans wearing green shoes?
No, he was wearing blue shoes.
5. Who was dancing with the girl in green jeans?
The boy in the red shoes was dancing with her.
(Oder: She was dancing with the boy in the red shoes.)

Exercise 6

Hinweise / Ideen   Erweiterte Memory-Übung: Die S versuchen sich zu erinnern und schreiben, was die Leute auf der Illustration von *Student's Book page 35* gemacht haben.
Zusätzlich können an dieser Stelle nochmals alle bisher vorgekommenen Zeitformen wiederholt und geübt werden. Es empfiehlt sich, für die Zeitformen entsprechende Aufhänger vorzugeben: *Present simple = often / every day; Present progressive = at the moment / tonight; Past simple = yesterday / last week; Past progressive = yesterday between 6 and 8 / while* etc.

Mögliche Lösung

> *Two people were playing tennis.*
> *A boy and a girl were playing ball.*
> *A child was playing in the sand.*
> *Two men were reading.*
> *A man was sleeping. / A man was listening to the radio.*
> *A child was eating two ice creams.*
> *Two people were kissing.*
> *A woman was eating a big ice cream.*

Exercise 7

Hinweise / Ideen

Die S suchen in GA Informationen zu einem der Stichworte.
Bei *FBI* oder beim Stichwort *Prohibition* müssen wahrscheinlich weitere Stichworte in eine Suchmaschine eingegeben werden, z.B *history* oder *American history*, sofern die S das Internet als Informationsquelle benützen möchten.
Die gefundenen Informationen mit Illustrationen zu einem Büchlein zusammenstellen und in der Klasse zirkulieren lassen.

Workbook Basic   Unit 18

Unit 18

Hinweise / Ideen

Die Tabelle soll den S helfen, die wichtigen Erkenntnisse aus dem *Focus*-Text, den *Trainings* und *Exercises* festzuhalten, um einen Überblick über den Fall zu gewinnen.
L oder auch schnelle S können beim Bekanntwerden einer weiteren Information zur Lösung des Falles anregen, dass diese in die Tabelle eingetragen wird.
Dazu kann L im Schulzimmer eine vergrösserte Kopie der Tabelle aufhängen.

Mögliche Lösung zu a)

Lady Mottram died sometime between 6.30 and 11 p.m.
The wound was very small.
The murder weapon was a long pointed object. It was nowhere.
A small piece of peppermint leaf was in the wound.
One thermos flask was full of cold peppermint tea.
The television and the reading light were on.
Professor Mottram's reading glasses were lying on the table.
Ms Witherspoon and Archibald Plumley were watching a film in the Cinema between 7.45 p.m. and 11.30 p.m.
Professor Mottram didn't like his cousin.
He is a professor of anatomy. He needs money. He was working all evening.

Exercise 1

Hinweise / Ideen

Mit diesem *Exercise* sollen die S einen Überblick über die zeitlichen Zusammenhänge des Mordfalls gewinnen. Daraus ergibt sich bereits, dass einzig Prof. Mottram kein Alibi hat für die fragliche Zeit.

Lösung zu a)

Time	I. Witherspoon	from	Basil Mottram	from	A. Plumley	from
until 7.45 p.m.	serving tea to Lady M.	Focus	reading the newspaper	2nd Step	working for his exams	3rd Step
8 until 9 p.m.	going to the cinema	Focus	writing some letters	2nd Step	going to the cinema	3rd Step
after 11.30 p.m.	was sleeping	Focus	was sleeping	2nd Step	–	–
7 a.m.	cleaning the hall, carrying the milk bottles	Focus	heard the television	2nd Step	shaving	3rd Step
9 a.m.	talking to Inspector Bradley	Focus	talking to Detective Hopkins	2nd Step	talking to Inspector Bradley	3rd Step

Mögliche Lösung zu b)

At 7.45 p.m. Ms Witherspoon was serving tea to Lady Mottram. Professor Mottram was reading the newspaper, and Archibald Plumley was working for his exams. From 8 until 9, Ms Witherspoon and A. Plumley were going to the cinema and Basil Mottram was writing some letters. After 11.30 p.m. they were sleeping. At 7 a.m., I. Witherspoon was cleaning the hall and carrying the milk bottles, Prof. Mottram heard the television and A. Plumley was shaving. About 9 a.m., they were all talking to the police.

Unit 18

Language Focus

Ziel Repetition der Verbformen in verschiedenen Tempusformen mit Anwendungshinweisen.
Die S können den *Language Focus* zur besseren Übersicht kolorieren.
Beispiel: die Kästchen links mit zwei verschiedenen hellen Farben, die Kästchen rechts mit den entsprechenden dunklen Farben: links = Tatsachen *(facts)*, rechts = Handlung *(action)*; oben = Gegenwart *(present)*, unten = Vergangenheit *(past)*

Present simple *at present, general fact*
Anwendung
- allgemeine Tatsachen
- Beschreibung von routinemässigen Handlungen

Present continuous *going on at the moment*
Anwendung   Tätigkeiten oder Vorgänge, die zum Gesprächszeitpunkt im Ablaufen begriffen sind.

Simple past *past (fact)*
Anwendung
- abgeschlossene Handlungen in der Vergangenheit
- aufeinander folgende Handlungen in der Vergangenheit (z.B. Geschichte in der Vergangenheit: *He opened a bottle of milk, filled a glass and drank it.*)

Past continuous *period of time in the past*
Anwendung
- länger andauernde Handlung in der Vergangenheit
- zwei parallel ablaufende Handlungen in der Vergangenheit (… *while* …)
- andauernde Handlung, die durch eine neu eintretende Handlung unterbrochen wird (… *when* …)

Lösung

… at present, general fact			… going on at the moment			
I	live	in Olten.	I	am	learning	English.
He	works	in an office.	He	is	working	on a new book.
She	watches	the nine o'clock news.	She	is	listening	to a CD.
It	rains	a lot in Scotland.	It	is	raining	in Basle now.
We	go	by car.	We	are	going	to work by bus today.
You	have	a breakfast early.	You	are	having	breakfast late today.
They	read	newspapers.	They	are	reading	a book.

… past (fact)			… period of time in the past			
I	went	to the cinema last night.	I	was	doing	my homework between 8 and 9.
He	played	guitar when he was younger.	He	was	playing	basketball all day.
She	talked	to Margaret last night.	She	was	talking	to her friend Margaret for an hour.
It	killed	Lady Mottram immediately.	It	wasn't	burning	this morning.
We	watched	the match yesterday.	We	were	watching	TV between 9 and 11 p.m.
You	went	straight to bed at 11.30 p.m. last night.	You	were	sleeping	between 11 p.m. and 6.30 a.m.
They	played	football every day last week.	They	were	playing	football between 2 and 5 p.m. on Sunday.

Workbook Basic Unit 18

Exercise 2

Ziel Repetition der Verbformen

Hinweise / Ideen Wie *Exercises 4* und *6* ist dies eine Übung, die von den **S** gelöst werden kann, sobald die nötige Information vorliegt. Sie gibt zudem Auskunft über die Protagonisten dieses Mordfalls. Die Klasse kann für dieses *Exercise* in vier Gruppen aufgeteilt werden, von denen je eine einen der Protagonisten bearbeitet und die Informationen, wenn diese vollständig sind, in schöner Abschrift an einer Pinnwand aufhängt.

Lösung
Lady Penelope Mottram
didn't go, didn't have, didn't hear, was, wanted, were living / lived
Der Text steht im *Past tense* (Lady Mottram ist bereits tot), der Schlusssatz im *Past progressive* (andauernde Handlung in der Vergangenheit).

Isabella Witherspoon
is, is working, was looking, worked, was not, got
Der Text enthält verschiedene Zeitformen.

Professor Basil Mottram
is, gets, was, doesn't teach, is writing, needs
Der Text enthält verschiedene Zeitformen.

Archibald Plumley
is, is, is working, didn't get, likes, isn't, loses, was living (lived), liked
Der Text enthält verschiedene Zeitformen.

Exercise 3

Hinweise / Ideen Die **S** arbeiten mit einem Notizblock, um die Fragen im *Second Step* ab Tonband zu beantworten. (Vorschläge für das Vorgehen siehe Anmerkungen zum *Second Step* im *Teacher's Book,* Seite 53).
Schwächere **S** können auch versuchen, das *Exercise* mit Hilfe des Skripts (Kopiervorlage Nr. 55) zu bearbeiten.

Lösung
1. *No, he didn't. (She wanted to leave her money to Greenpeace and the WWF.)*
2. *No, they only said "Good morning" etc.*
3. *He said that he was reading the newspaper, writing some letters and working on his new book. At 11 p.m. he made himself a cup of tea in the kitchen and then went to bed.*
4. *He heard Lady Mottram's television. He heard Lady Mottram. She said to Archibald: "Bring me a cup of hot peppermint tea, please."*
5. *Because he heard the television.*
6. *He was eating his breakfast in the dining room.*
7. *No, he didn't. He called the police.*

Exercise 4

Hinweise / Ideen Es handelt sich bei dem Text um eine Zusammenfassung des Verhörs *(Second Step)* mit einigen Fehlern, die Detective Hopkins dabei gemacht hat.
Die **S** sollen diese, eventuell in Gruppen, nach dem Anhören des Verhörs oder gegebenenfalls mit Hilfe des Skripts zum Tonband herausfinden. Die einfachste Variante ist, dass die **S** zuerst den fehlerhaften Text lesen, sich anschliessend stückweise den Dialog anhören und die Fragen zum *Second Step* beantworten. (Siehe auch Varianten zum *Training Second Step.*)

Lösung zu b) Detective Hopkins hat drei Fehler gemacht:
1. *Professor Mottram woke up at seven o'clock, not at six.*
2. *He heard the television, not the radio.*
3. *He was eating breakfast, he was not reading the paper.*
(Detective Hopkins erwähnt in seinem Report nicht, dass sich Professor Mottram vor dem Einschlafen einen Tee gemacht hat.)

Unit 18 Workbook Basic

Exercise 5

Hinweise / Ideen Mit diesen Notizen erhalten die S weitere wichtige Informationen, die zuerst ausgearbeitet werden sollten.

Mögliche Lösung
zu a) *Lady Mottram died between 8.10 and 11.00.*
Plumley und Witherspoon were at the cinema during the time of the murder.

zu b) *Lady Mottram died between 7 and 11 p.m. She was phoning a friend between 7.45 and 8.10.*
Lady Mottram leaves a lot of money to Greenpeace and the WWF. She also leaves some money to Plumley, Witherspoon and Prof. Mottram. Prof. Mottram gets £100,000, Plumley gets £100,000 and Witherspoon gets £10,000.
Prof. Mottram did not have his reading glasses last night.
Prof. Mottram can't publish his book. He needs money.
The doorman at the cinema saw a young couple. They looked like Plumley and Witherspoon. They were very much in love.

zu c) *There was a light on in Plumley's room all evening.*
Plumley has money problems because he plays poker.
He didn't have his regular reading glasses last night. He used a second pair.
He can't publish his book. He needs money.

Exercise 6

Hinweise / Ideen Da das Wort für die Mordwaffe den S nicht geläufig sein dürfte, wird es in dieser Übung eingeführt. Die *clues* sind auch nützlich, wenn man sich den Fall noch einmal vor Augen führen will.
Die S können die *clues* in PA oder GA erarbeiten.

Lösung *winter, object, reading glasses, cold, Earl Grey, peppermint.*
Von oben nach unten ergibt sich das Wort *icicle* (Eiszapfen).

Exercise 7

Hinweise / Ideen Die S sollen mit den Informationen, die sie bisher gewonnen und in *Exercise 1* festgehalten haben, versuchen, den Täter zu ermitteln.

Wichtig Wird in der Tabelle das *Simple present* gebraucht, muss bei den ausformulierten Sätzen das *Simple past* verwendet werden. Steht die -ing-Form, so ist das *Past progressive* zu verwenden.

Mögliche Lösung

Person	Liked / didn't like Lady Mottram	Motive for killing Lady Mottram?	Alibi? For what time?
Isabella Witherspoon	didn't like her	no	cinema, 8 until 11.30 p.m.
Prof. Basil Mottram	didn't like her	Yes, he needs money.	no
Archibald Plumley	liked her	Yes, he needs money.	cinema, 8 until 11.30 p.m.

Professor Mottram killed her.
He wanted her money because he wanted to publish a book about heart problems.
He didn't like her.
The murder weapon was an icicle.
(Die S können das Wort in einem Wörterbuch nachschlagen.)

Workbook Basic

Unit 18

Exercise 8

Hinweise / Ideen

Für alle diese Detektive gibt es Websites. Sie können durch die Eingabe folgender Suchbegriffe gefunden werden: *detective+fiction* „Name des Detektives".
Mit den Informationen und Bildern dieser Websites können die S einzeln oder in Gruppen kurze schriftliche Porträts zusammenstellen, die im Schulzimmer für die Lektüre der ganzen Klasse aufgelegt werden.

Unit 19

Exercise 1

Hinweise / Ideen zu a) — Es geht um eine Verständniskontrolle des Lese-/Hörtextes im *Student's Book*.
Das *Exercise* kann in stiller EA oder als Hausaufgabe gelöst werden. Stärkere S können die falschen Aussagen berichtigen.

zu b) — Die S versuchen den «gescannten» Text trotz den teilweise falsch erkannten Buchstaben zu verstehen. Die richtigen Buchstaben können über die falschen ins *Workbook* geschrieben werden.

Lösung zu a) — 1. yes, 2. no, 3. no, 4. no, 5. no, 6. yes, 7. yes, 8. no

zu b) — Siehe *Student's Book page 50*. Das Problem ist, dass e als c und m als rn erkannt worden sind.

Language Focus

Thema — Ausdrücken verschiedener Grade von Unsicherheit mit den modalen Hilfsverben *may, might, could* und *can't* (negative Sicherheit).

Mögliche Lösung zu a)

He	may	be	at home in bed.
He	may	be	at the doctor's.
He	may	have	a game with the football team.

zu b)

Andy	might	be	on his way to school now.
His bus	might	be	late.
He	could	be	in bed.

zu c)

| "Andy | can't | be | at home because I just tried to phone and nobody answered." |

Exercise 2

Thema — Eine Einsetzübung für modale Hilfsverben. Die S setzen die fehlenden Verben in PA oder GA ein.

Wie bei allen modalen Hilfsverben hängt hier die Auswahl bis zu einem gewissen Grad von der Gewissheit des Sprechers / der Sprecherin ab, wie gut ihr Tipp ist.

Lösung

can
mustn't, could
can, could, should

Exercise 3

Ideen / Hinweise — Diese Übung behandelt das modale Hilfsverb *may* zum Ausdruck einer Möglichkeit; zu lösen ist sie als Hausaufgabe oder in stiller EA.

Es ist wichtig, dass **L** in den *prompts* auf den Gebrauch von *perhaps* hinweist.

Lösung

1. Madonna may / could have plans for another film.
2. There may / could be more people under 18 in China than there are in Europe.
3. Mobile phones may / could make it easier to make friends.
4. Teachers may not always see when pupils cheat in a test.
   (*could* funktioniert im negativen Satz nicht.)
5. It may / could rain in the morning, the sun may / could shine for an hour, then a strong wind may / could start to blow.

Workbook Basic Unit 19

Exercise 4

Thema Repetition von *would like* zum Ausdruck von Wünschen und Präferenzen.

Hinweise / Ideen zu a) Zuerst EA, dann PA. Wenn die S nicht von selbst Gründe angeben, kann L nachfragen.

zu b) als PA-Interview

Exercise 5

Hinweise / Ideen Es ist sinnvoll zu betonen, dass sowohl *can* als auch *may* gebraucht werden können, um auszudrücken, dass etwas möglich oder erlaubt ist. Da *may* eher formell ist, könnte die Übung zuerst den Inhalt einer möglichen Tafel wiedergeben, dann mit *can* die mündliche Information formulieren.

Als Referenz können die Verbotstafeln von Band 1, *Unit 7, Third Step,* gezeigt werden.

Mögliche Lösung
> *In my dream park ...*
> *... I can / may swim in the little lake.*
> *... I can / may use my mountain bike on the grass.*
> *... I can / may bring my own food and have a big picnic.*
> *... I can / may play table tennis on the restaurant tables.*
> *... etc.*

Language Focus

Thema Hier geht es um verschiedene Formen, Ratschläge zu erteilen. Der Gebrauch des Hilfsverbes hängt von der Beziehung zwischen Sprecher/in und Hörer/in ab.

Lösung zu a) *Nancy's mother: C; Kim, a friend of Nancy's: A; Nancy's volleyball coach: B*

zu b)

Affirmative	
A friendly form of advice:	You should learn the words.
A strong form of advice:	You have to learn the words.
A very strong form of advice:	You must learn the words.

Negative	
A friendly form of advice:	You shouldn't smoke cigarettes.
A strong form of advice:	You may not smoke cigarettes.
A very strong form of advice:	You mustn't smoke cigarettes.

Exercise 6

Thema Anwendung des *Language Focus;* Ratschläge geben in immer offenerem Rahmen.

Hinweise / Ideen Aus den Elementen sollen in einem ersten Schritt Verhaltensregeln geformt werden, möglicherweise in PA/GA. Dann schreiben die S in stiller EA die entsprechenden Sätze auf die freien Linien.

Weiterführung Stärkere S sollen sich (evtl. in PA/GA) eigene Regeln einfallen lassen.

Lösung
> *1. – b) ... you should put some cotton wool into your ears.*
> *2. – c) ... you should get a phone card.*
> *3. – e) ... you shouldn't drink any coffee.*
> *4. – f) ... you should switch off your CD player.*
> *5. – d) ... you should buy some white wine.*
> *6. – g) ... you should check your schoolbag.*
> *7. – a) ... you should see a doctor.*

Exercise 7

Thema   Beziehungen zwischen Geschwistern

Hinweise / Ideen   Im ersten Hördurchgang sollen die S, eventuell in PA, nur auf die Namen achten und diese anhand der Hinweise bei den Pfeilen einsetzen.

Im zweiten Durchgang sollen auch noch die fehlenden Wörter (auf die Linien) eingesetzt werden.

Für schwächere S kann das Skript abgegeben werden, anhand dessen die fehlenden Informationen eingesetzt werden können.

Skript

Fiona: I often have fights with my brothers and my sister. I share a room with her. But she always makes ...
Marge: You share a room with whom?
Fiona: With my sister Debbie. She always makes such a mess, and I have to clean it up. My older brother sometimes beats me, but when he does, I bite him. [Pause] I really like my other brother.
Marge: Is he older too?
Fiona: Mike? No, he's younger. When I'm in my room with my sister he often comes in. I think he wants to talk to us, but in the end he just terrorises Debbie. I don't know why.
Marge: Perhaps he doesn't like your sister as much as he likes you?
Fiona: Maybe. Yes, that could be true. But there's something else: a week ago they had a terrible fight in our room. They broke my lamp.
Marge: Who had a fight?
Fiona: Mike and Debbie.
Marge: And what did your older brother do?
Fiona: Patrick? Well, he stopped them. He helped me to repair the lamp.
Marge: I see. Well, Patrick seems to be a pretty helpful brother. Listen, Fiona, why don't you ask your sister if she ...

Lösung zu a)   ■ Debbie, Patrick, Mike

zu b)

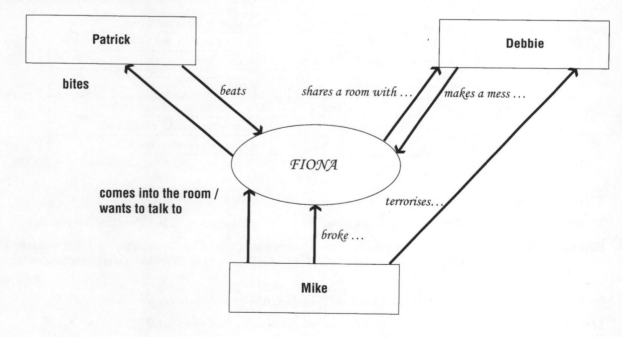

Workbook Basic Unit 19

Exercise 8

Thema Besprechen von Ge- und Verboten, basierend auf Schuluniformregeln.

Ziel Das Ziel ist das richtige Einsetzen der modalen Hilfsverben mit Hilfe der Tabelle.

Hinweise / Ideen Zum Einstieg kann die Klasse in drei Teams aufgeteilt werden. Ein Team bearbeitet je eine Kolonne und präsentiert die Resultate in der Klasse. Zur Erleichterung können die *prompts* *"The students/pupils ... wear ..."* und *"The students/pupils ... bring ... to school"* an die Wandtafel geschrieben werden.

Mögliche Lösung
1. *have to, mustn't*
2. *must, don't have to, mustn't*
3. *have to, doesn't have to, can be, mustn't*
4. *mustn't, should, may*
5. *don't have to, mustn't*

Exercise 9

Thema Praktische schriftliche Anwendung der modalen Hilfsverben

Hinweise / Ideen
zu a) Die S formulieren eventuell in PA oder in kleinen Gruppen Probleme als Brief an *Help*. Diese müssen von **L** am Platz korrigiert werden, bevor sie eingesammelt und neu verteilt werden.

zu b) In einer zweiten Phase werden die Problembriefe verteilt und in PA oder in kleinen Gruppen beantwortet. Diese Ratschläge werden wiederum von **L** korrigiert und dann zusammen mit den Problembriefen im Schulzimmer aufgehängt.

Unit 20

Language Focus

Hinweis — Zusammenfassung zum *Present perfect*

Lösung

Who	has	done	what / who	where / how long, etc.
I	've (have)	informed	the teacher	about the party.
You	've (have)	organised	a CD player.	
She	's (has)	asked	her neighbours	for the lights.
He	's (has)	bought	mineral water.	
It	hasn't (has not)	rained a lot		today.
We	've (have)	invited	our head teacher	to the party.
You	've (have)	done	your homework	in the garden.
They	haven't (have not)	painted	the signs	yet.

Exercise 1

Hinweise / Ideen zu a) — Je nachdem, wie intensiv mit dem *Focus*-Text bzw. den *Trainings* im *Student's Book* gearbeitet worden ist, eignet sich das *Exercise* als Textverständnisübung und sollte daher ohne Textvorlage gelöst werden. Wichtig ist, dass die unregelmässigen Formen (*) entweder aus dem *Focus*-Text gesucht oder vorgängig thematisiert werden.

zu b) — Hier liegt das Gewicht auf den unregelmässigen Verben. Die Übung eignet sich auch als Wettbewerb in PA / GA / GU.

Mögliche Lösung zu a)

has asked, has informed, has looked for, hasn't got, has organised, has asked
has got, has asked
has bought, has got, hasn't told
hasn't painted, hasn't asked

zu b)

F	O	R	G	O	T	T	E	N
	B	O	U	G	H	T		
				T	O	L	D	
			F	O	U	N	D	
					G	O	N	E
B	R	O	U	G	H	T		
				G	O	T		

The present of the verb is "think".

Workbook Basic   Unit 20

Exercise 2

Hinweise / Ideen

Die S sollen nicht einfach die Programmpunkte vom Notizzettel abschreiben, sondern sinngemässe eigene Sätze schreiben und die Tätigkeiten den Personen zuordnen (siehe Lösungen). Es empfiehlt sich, im Vorfeld die unregelmässigen Formen *(buy, tell, get)* nochmals in Erinnerung zu rufen.

Dieses Exercise eignet sich wiederum als Sprech- und Schreibübung, wobei die S Satz um Satz zuerst mündlich und unmittelbar danach schriftlich ausformulieren. So wird die Zuordnung der Personen zu den Tätigkeiten vorweg mündlich nochmals vergegenwärtigt.

Wichtig

Es muss darauf geachtet werden, dass keine Zeitangaben verwendet werden, weil dann *Past simple* stehen müsste.

Mögliche Lösung

1. Has Roy asked Tanya to bring her dance CDs?
2. Has Bridget bought decorations?
3. Has Roy asked Mr Taylor for his barbecue?
4. Has Roy informed the neighbours about the party?
5. Have they invited the teachers?
6. Has Martin told the head teacher about the party?
7. Have they organised the cleaning after the party?
8. Have they painted signs for toilets and the bar?
9. Has Penny got party lights for the room?

Exercise 3

Hinweise / Ideen zu a)

Die S sollen nicht alle Böxchen abhaken, damit bei b) auch negative Antworten gegeben werden müssen.

Bei Bedarf die (unregelmässigen) Verbformen im Voraus repetieren.

Erweiterung zu a)

S 1 zeigt pantomimisch, was bereits gemacht wurde, die übrigen S formulieren die entsprechenden Sätze im *Present perfect*. (In Varianten ist diese Übungsform auch nützlich zur Auffrischung des *Past tense* oder des *Present progressive*.)

Hinweise / Ideen zu b)

Die S formulieren zuerst die Fragen und holen dann in PA Antworten ein, die sie schriftlich festhalten können.

Die Übung eignet sich auch als *milling exercise*, bei dem die S im Zimmer umhergehen und verschiedene Mitschülerinnen und Mitschüler befragen. Je nach Leistungsstärke der Klasse können die Antworten nur mündlich erfolgen oder auch mit den Namen der Befragten festgehalten werden. *(Lena has packed her passport. Peter hasn't turned off all the lights.)*

Lösung zu b)

2. Have you turned off all the lights?
3. Have you locked all the doors?
4. Have you emptied and turned off the fridge?
5. Have you found someone to water the plants?
6. Have you given your holiday address to a friend?
7. Have you packed a first-aid kit?
8. Have you packed your tickets?

Unit 20
Workbook Basic

Exercise 4

Hinweise / Ideen

Dieses *Exercise* ist mit dem *Third Step* im *Student's Book* gekoppelt. Es kann in verschiedenen Durchgängen gelöst werden, z.B. zuerst mündlich im GU, dann in einem zweiten Durchgang mit Abhaken in EA, in einem dritten Durchgang mit Konzentration auf b).

b) sollte zuerst mündlich im GU, dann schriftlich in EA / PA / GA gelöst werden.

Skript

Hello, is that Duke's Drinks Delivery? ...

- Yes. I've got a problem here. We're going to have a party tonight and we didn't think of the drinks. I know it's a little late, but I was wondering if you would be able to deliver some drinks?

- Yes, that's right, for tonight. In an hour? That's great!

- Well, we're going to need some soft drinks, let's say about ten bottles of Coke.

- Yes, that's right. And some water, mineral water, ten bottles, too. No, that's too much. Let's say six.

- Mhm. And then some fruit juice. Orange juice of course, five bottles, some apple juice and some grape juice. Five bottles each.

- Tomato juice? Yes, that's a good idea. Put in three bottles.

- Peanuts? Yes, of course we need peanuts. Let's say five bags. And we need some milk because we're going to make milkshakes.

- Oh, that's too bad. Well, we'll have to go and get it ourselves. Never mind. That's all for the moment.

- Well, umh, can I pay by credit card? Do you accept Visa?

- Okay, the name's Henry J. Bonner, B - O - double N - E - R. ... –
Yes, and the number is 381-7365-035.

- That's right. Thank you very much.

- Oh, the address? It's 78 Pine Grove Drive. That's near Poplar just north of Main Street. There's a garage on the corner ...

Lösung zu a)

Martin has ordered	true	false
- ten bottles of Coke	x	
- some mineral water.	x	
- four kinds of fruit juice.	x	
- peanuts.	x	
- tea and coffee.		x
- milk for milkshakes.		x
- party decorations.		x

zu b)

Martin hasn't ordered tea and coffee, and he hasn't ordered any milk, because Duke doesn't sell milk. Martin hasn't ordered any party decorations.

Workbook Basic

Unit 20

Language Focus

Thema Gebrauch des *Present perfect* und des *Simple past*

Lösung

Has somebody done it? ☑	When did ... do it? ⏱
I've done my homework.	I did it yesterday evening.
He's put all the clothes away.	He put them away this morning.
She's made her bed.	She made it two minutes ago.
Have you brought a barbecue grill?	Yes, I brought it last Monday.
Penny has got the party decorations.	She got them two days ago.
Bridget has bought coloured paper.	She bought them yesterday.
They have told the head teacher about it.	They told it last Wednesday.
You have taken out the empty bottles.	You took them out today.
She's found some comfortable chairs.	She found them this afternoon.
Martin's gone to order some drinks.	He went to order them an hour ago.
Have you seen Roy?	Yes, I saw him this afternoon.
He's forgotten to order them.	He forgot to order the food last year.
Has Penny given back the CDs?	Yes, she gave them back yesterday.
She has read three Harry Potter books.	She read them last summer.
Mary has had a hair cut.	She had it a week ago.
She has been at Figaro's.	She was there a week ago.

Exercise 5

Hinweise / Ideen zu a) Die Fragen werden in EA schriftlich vorbereitet, verglichen, korrigiert und anschliessend mündlich formuliert. Dazu eignet sich vor allem der GU: Die S formulieren zuerst die Frage, halten dann kurz inne, um allen Zeit für die Antworten im Kopf zu geben, dann wird jemand aufgerufen. So wird die *ganze* Klasse gezwungen mitzudenken. Wird der Name der / des S der Frage vorangestellt, fällt diese Intensität weg.

zu b) Hier geht es um die Gegenüberstellung von *Present perfect* und *Simple past*.

Je nach Leistungsstärke müssen vorher die Verbformen und die mündliche Datenangabe nochmals vergegenwärtigt werden.

Für ‚ooops' kann entweder eine Ausrede oder die Formen von *forget* eingesetzt/eingeführt werden.

Variante Man teilt die Klasse in zwei örtlich getrennte Gruppen im Klassenraum. Die eine Gruppe spricht die Sätze im *Present perfect*, die andere die Sätze im *Simple past*. Diese chorartige Gegenüberstellung macht den Unterschied zwischen den beiden Tempusformen und ihrem Gebrauch deutlicher.

Mögliche Lösung zu a)
1. *Have you cleaned the fridge?*
2. *Have you told the milkman about our holiday?*
3. *Have you found out Reggie's holiday phone number?*
4. *Have you reserved tickets for the cinema festival?*
5. *Have you done the dishes?*
6. *Have you phoned the garage about the car?*

zu b)
He has told the milkman about their holiday. He told him early this morning.
He hasn't found out Reggies holiday phone number.
He hasn't bought a box of printer paper.
He has done the dishes from yesterday's party. He did them yesterday after the party.
He has forgotten to phone the garage about the car.
He has reserved tickets for the cinema festival. He has phoned the booking office on May 16.

Unit 20 — Workbook Basic

Exercise 6

Hinweise / Ideen Der Einsatz dieser Übung im Unterricht hängt davon ab, wie die bisherigen Übungen angegangen worden sind und ob **L** das Gewicht auf Mündlichkeit oder Schriftlichkeit, auf eine nochmalige Trainingsphase oder auf eine Anwendungsphase legt.

Lösung zu a)
> *Have you ever lived outside Switzerland? When did you live outside Switzerland?*
> *Have you ever played in a sports team? When did you play in a sports team?*
> *Have you ever worked with handicapped people? When did you work with them?*
> *Have you ever travelled more than a hundred kilometres by bike?*
> *When did you travel more than a hundred kilometres by bike?*
> *Have you ever stayed in a haunted house? When did you stay in this house?*
> *Have you ever gone to Africa? When did you go there?*
> *Have you ever met a famous person? When did you meet this person?*
> *Have you ever eaten frog's legs? When did you eat frog's legs?*

Exercise 7

Ziel Angemessenes Reagieren auf einen situativen Input.

Hinweise / Ideen zu a) Es können mehrere Möglichkeiten genannt / verlangt werden, evtl. auch nach dem Motto *Wer liefert in 1 Minute die meisten sinnvollen Möglichkeiten?*. Andere Möglichkeit: Die Klasse soll versuchen, jeweils mindestens 5, 8 oder 10 Sätze zu finden.

zu b) Je nach Leistungsstärke empfiehlt es sich, dass **L** einige Beispiele mündlich vorgibt oder im GU suchen lässt. Anschliessend formulieren die **S** in EA / PA schriftlich.

Mögliche Lösung zu a)
> *I have drunk the milk.*
> *I have eaten the sausages.*
> *Forgive me! I have broken the glass.*

zu b)
> *1. We're very sorry. We've broken the garage window. We were just playing football.*
> *2. I've moved your moped. It shouldn't stand in front of the shop window.*
> *3. Sandra! You're late. We've gone to the Queen's Hotel already.*
> *4. We've enjoyed ourselves. Thanks!*

Exercise 8

Hinweise / Ideen Dieses *Exercise* ist an *Time for a Change* im *Student's Book* gekoppelt. Die **S** sollten möglichst ungestört in EA am Test im *Student's Book* arbeiten, sich die Buchstaben der für sie zutreffenden Antworten notieren und erst nach Beendigung des Tests die Punktzahl im *Workbook* nachschlagen. An die Auswertung kann sich eine informelle Diskussion über Cliquen oder evtl. Banden im Dorf, im Quartier oder in der Schule anschliessen.

Exercise 9

Hinweise / Ideen Je nach Umfeld kann dieses Projekt in mehreren Klassen, im ganzen Schulhaus und für Eltern durchgeführt oder gar zu einer fächerübergreifenden Projektwoche ausgebaut werden. Dies bedarf einer seriösen Vorbereitung und muss längerfristig geplant werden.

Revision Workshop 4

Allgemeine Hinweise zu den *Revision Workshops*, zu Aufbau, Arbeitsweise und Kontrolle siehe die Ausführungen beim *Revision Workshop 3*, S. 89.

Übersicht über den Revision Workshop 4

	Station (Topic)	Sprachliche Struktur	Arbeitsform	Vorbereitung durch L / Material
1.	*Verb Forms Drill*	Verschiedene Zeitformen in vollständigen Sätzen	EA	—
2.	*Story*	Das *Simple past* regelmässiger und unregelmässiger Verben. Die Übung ist von a) nach c) progressiv aufgebaut.	EA	—
3.	*Writing*	*Present progressive*	EA	— (evtl. Zusatzheft)
4.	*Interview*	*Simple present, Simple past, Present progressive und Past progressive*	PA / GA, vor allem mündlich	Zur mündlichen Vorbereitung: Die beiden Seiten kopieren, die Kärtchen mit den *Prompts* ausschneiden und verteilen. Bei mündlicher Durchführung erfolgt die Kontrolle durch L.
5.	*Reading*	Textverständnis	EA	Vorbereitung evtl. mündlich mit Hilfe der Grundrisse als Folienkopie
6.	*Listening – Numbers*	Hörverständnis, speziell Ziffern und Zahlen	EA	—
7.	*Discussion*	Modale Hilfsverben	EA / PA / GA	—

Revision Workshop 4 — Workbook Basic

Station Verb Forms Drill

Lösung

I don't go to football matches.
We are going to football matches.
Peter went to football matches.
Where they going to football matches?
Have you gone to football matches?

Does Jenny buy a lot of chewing gum?
Are you buying a lot of chewing gum?
We bought a lot of chewing gum.
I was not buying a lot of chewing gum.
Paul has bought a lot of chewing gum.

Does Carol go to school by bus?
I'm not going to school by bus.
We went to school by bus.
Was Marty going to school by bus?
Have you gone to school by bus?

John makes a cup of tea.
I'm making a cup of tea.
Did they make a cup of tea?
Were you making a cup of tea?
Dad has made a cup of tea.

You tell the neighbours about the party.
I'm not telling the neighbours about the party.
Did Joan tell the neighbours about the party?
They were not telling the neighbours about the party.
We haven't told the neighbours about the party.

I don't read an interesting story.
Is Carl reading an interesting story?
We didn't read an interesting story.
Joe was not reading an interesting story.
Have you read an interesting story?

I don't bring dance CDs to school.
Are you bringing dance CDs to school?
Did we bring dance CDs to school?
Joe was bringing dance CDs to school.
Have you brought dance CDs to school?

Station Story

Lösung

zu a) was, lived, had, liked, was, asked, was, went, came, went, was, lived, worked, had, wanted, went, was, didn't want, told, didn't want, went

zu b) lived, heard, was, were, tried, saw, stayed
talked, lived, said, was, helped
went, didn't think, went, were, was

zu c) wrote, didn't hear, came, was, was, went, told, was, tried
wanted, saw, said, worked, wanted, stayed, went, met, took, went, met, fought, fell off, died, got, had, was, wrote

Station Writing

Mögliche Lösung zu a) — *A cat is sitting under a tree. The cat is watching the bird. A bird is flying. The bird is building a nest.*

zu b) — *A man is opening an envelope. A woman is working at the computer. The boss is drinking coffee.*

zu c) — *A boy is running. His ball is rolling away from him. A lorry is coming up the street.*

Station Interview

Lösung

Partner A	Partner B
Questions	Answers
1. watch	
What do you usually watch?	I usually watch the News.
What are you watching at the moment?	I'm watching Eurosports at the moment.
What did you watch last Sunday?	I watched the Flintstones last Sunday.
What were watching yesterday between 8 and 9 p.m.?	I was watching SF2 yesterday between 8 and 9 p.m.
2. read	
What do you normally read?	I normally read the newspaper.
What are you reading now?	I'm reading a horror story at the moment.
What did you read last month?	I read A Day in the Life of Frederic the Cat last month.
What were you reading last night at around 9 p.m.?	I was reading an English text yesterday around 9 p.m.

Partner B	Partner A
Questions	Answers
1. eat	
What do you normally eat for lunch?	I usually eat a sandwich for lunch.
Are you eating right now?	Yes, I'm eating an apple now.
Did you eat an apple yesterday?	No, I didn't. I ate a banana yesterday.
Were you eating last night between 11 and 12 p.m.?	No, I wasn't eating. I was sleeping between 11 and 12 p.m.
2. play	
Do you play the guitar?	No, I don't. I play the piano.
Are you playing with your gameboy now?	No, I'm not playing with my gameboy at the moment.
Did you play at the school sports day last year?	Yes, I played basketball at the school sports day last year.
What were you playing on Saturday between 9 and 10 a.m.?	I was playing tennis on Saturday between 9 and 10 a.m.

Revision Workshop 4

Station Reading
Lösung

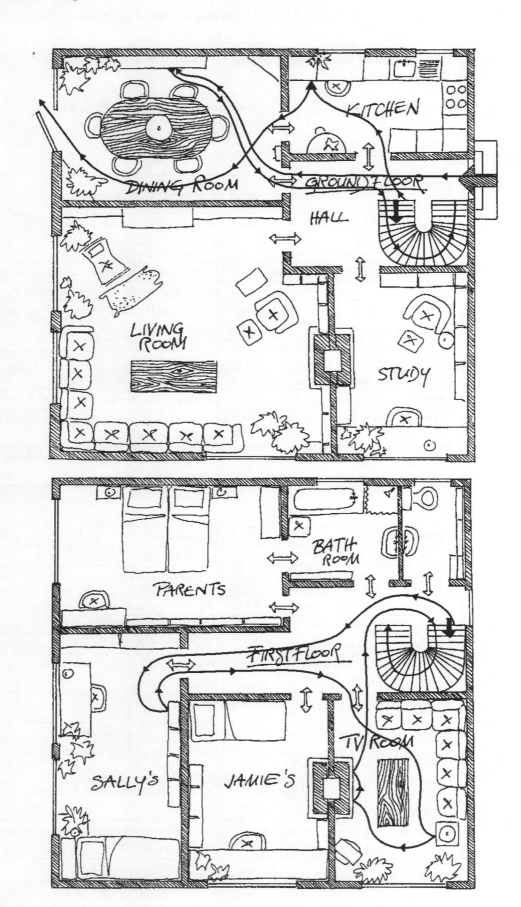

Workbook Basic — Revision Workshop 4

Station Listening – Numbers

Skript

Attractions	Prices
Motor coach sightseeing tour	$A 20 half day; $A 38 full day
Cruise on Sydney Harbour	$A 18 to $A 75
Theatre ticket	$A 13 to $A 58, depending on seats
Concert, opera and ballet ticket	$A 15 to $A 95, depending on seats
Rock concert ticket	$A 22 to $A 49, depending on group
Ticket to a movie	$A 8.50
Entrance to museums	Free to $A 4.50
Entrance to art gallery	Free to $A 5.30
Entrance to Sydney Tower	adults $A 5; children $A 1.50

Station Discussion

Mögliche Lösung

should
– You should try to talk to your teachers.
– You should ask the head teacher for the reasons for some of the rules.

could
– You could go on strike.
– You could ask your parents for help.
– You could organise a protest demonstration.
– You could write to a newspaper.
– On one day you could all wear jeans and leather jackets.

have to
– You have to get out when nobody is watching.
– You have to listen to a discman.
– You have to chew gum when nobody is watching.
– You have to tell the head teacher your names.

shouldn't
– You shouldn't run away from school.
– You shouldn't phone the police.

don't need
– You don't need to write to Amnesty International.

mustn't
– You mustn't smoke in the toilets.
– You mustn't go to cafes before school.

Notes

Workbook

Generelle Bemerkungen

New Words — Im *Workbook* neu eingeführte Wörter sind gemäss der Kennzeichnung im *Vocabulary* im *Student's Book* zu behandeln.

Use-Box — In vielen *Exercises* sind Wörter und Satzteile, die eingesetzt werden müssen, in der *Use*-Box aufgeführt. Je nach Leistungsstärke der Klasse und nach Einschätzung des Schwierigkeitsgrades der Aufgabe sollen die S mit Hilfe dieser Vorgaben arbeiten oder die *Use*-Box mit Post-it-Zetteln abdecken.

Language Focus — Mit Hilfe des *Language Focus* sollen sich die S die Strukturen, die in der nachfolgenden Übung verlangt werden, nochmals vergegenwärtigen. Ein *Language Focus* kann aber auch nach dem Lösen einer Übung, nach dem Abschluss einer oder gar mehrerer *Units* eingesetzt werden, um alle behandelten Strukturen nochmals in Erinnerung zu rufen und zu wiederholen.

Structure Checklist — Am Ende jeder *Unit* findet sich eine *Structure Checklist*. Sie dient den S als Überblick über die verlangten grammatischen Strukturen. Bereits behandelte Teilstrukturen werden in einigen Fällen nochmals aufgeführt. In den Kästchen können die S abhaken, welche Strukturen sie beherrschen.

Grammar — Wie im *Student's Book* sind auch in den *Workbooks* die in Band 2 behandelten grammatischen Strukturen in der *Grammar* aufgelistet. Damit besitzen die S über den Schluss des Schuljahres hinaus eine ihren Kenntnissen entsprechende Englischgrammatik. Anders als im *Student's Book* wurden aber in den *Workbooks* die deutschsprachigen Erklärungen weggelassen, damit die S, in Anleitung durch L, handschriftlich eigene Erläuterungen und Beispielsätze einsetzen können.

Vocabulary — Ebenso wie die Grammatik wird das alphabetisch geordnete Vokabular von Band 2 mit Angabe des Vorkommens in beiden *Workbooks* aufgelistet.

Unit 11

Exercise 1

Hinweise / Ideen — Leseverständnisübung: Durch das Herausfiltern von falscher Information zeigt es sich, ob die S den *Focus*-Text verstanden haben. Der Zugang zur Übung soll der Leistungsstärke der Klasse angepasst werden; er hängt auch damit zusammen, wie intensiv mit dem *Focus*-Text im *Student's Book* gearbeitet wurde.

Die S können sich in EA, PA oder GA mit oder ohne Textvorgabe (*Student's Book page 2*) an die Aufgabe machen. Der *Focus*-Text kann auch (nochmals) als Hörtext abgespielt werden. Die S unterstreichen dabei die Fehler zu a) oder machen Notizen zu b).

Bemerkung — Eine ähnliche Übung wäre mit den freiwilligen *Focus*-Texten denkbar, wobei die S füreinander Texte schreiben könnten, die falsche Informationen beinhalten.

Lösung zu a) — *in Italy, Hollywood, a singer, was very successful, Bird, American, weren't great shows, disco dancer, her albums.*

zu b) —
Madonna was not born in Italy, she was born in Bay City, Michigan.
Hollywood wasn't a good place for a career in music business, but New York was.
At first, she wasn't a singer in dance companies, but she was a dancer.
Her first album wasn't very successful.
Her second album wasn't called "Like a Bird", but "Like a Virgin".
"Like a Virgin" wasn't the beginning of her career as an American pop star, but it was the beginning of her career as an international pop star.
Her concerts were great shows with dancers and lights.
In her early days, Madonna wasn't just a disco dancer, but she was a singer.
Not her albums, but her videos show that she is a good entertainer.

zu c) —
Madonna Louise Ciccone was born in Bay City, Michigan, in 1958. Her dream was to be a star. New York was a good place for a career in the music business. At first, she was a dancer in a number of dance companies. Her first album "Madonna" (1983) wasn't very successful. Her second album, "Like a Virgin", was a big hit and the beginning of her career as an international pop star. Her videos were a bit like short films, and her concerts were great shows with dancers and lights and Madonna in a lot of different dresses. But her films weren't a big success. Her role in the film musical "Evita" was OK, but she isn't a great actress. In the early days she was just a singer, but her videos show that she is a big singer and a good entertainer.

Language Focus

Ziel — *Past*-Formen von *to be*

Lösung

I	was / wasn't	thirteen years old last year.
You	were / weren't	in England for your holidays.
He (my brother / friend)	was / wasn't	born in Neuhausen.
She (my mother / friend)	was / wasn't	born on 4 June 1958.
It (my dog, cat, etc.)	was / wasn't	in school last Monday.
We (my friend and I)	were / weren't	in a big city last week.
You (you and your friends)	were / weren't	in the disco at the weekend.
They (your friends)	were / weren't	tired last night.

Workbook Intensive Unit 11

Who	was	president of the USA in 2001?
How old	were	you in 1995?
What	was	her dream?
When	was	Madonna born?
Where	were	you yesterday?

Exercise 2

Hinweise / Ideen Leseverständnisübung, kann in stiller EA, in PA oder in GA gelöst werden. Der fehlende Text kann in zwei Etappen eingesetzt werden: In einem ersten Durchgang werden die Informationen eingesetzt, in einem zweiten konzentrieren sich die S auf die Verbformen.
Auch dieses *Exercise* kann bei Bedarf als Hörübung angegangen werden. Den Tonträger entweder direkt zum Ausfüllen der Lücken oder zur Korrektur einsetzen.

Lösung *was born, 1958, was, New York, music, dancer, was, was, wasn't, second, hit, pop, were, shows, dresses, her, them, her, her, is, was, singer*

Language Focus

Ziel Frageformen von *to be*
Past-Formen der regelmässigen Verben

Mögliche Lösung

Yesterday	I	listened	to a CD.
Last week	you	played	football with a friend.
When I was 4,	my father	worked	in Berne.
When I was 12,	my	mother liked	Günther Jauch.
Last night	my dog	loved	to go out for a walk.
In 1999	we	needed	new school books.
Yesterday	you	copied	my homework.
Last week	they	tried	to find a good restaurant.

Were	you	at school yesterday?	Yes, / No,	I	was. / wasn't.
Was	she	at home on Sunday?	Yes, / No,	she	was. / wasn't.
Was	he	in Paris yesterday	Yes, / No,	he	was. / wasn't.
Was	it	interesting?	Yes, / No,	it	was. / wasn't.
Were	you	happy with your last English test?	Yes, / No,	we	were. / weren't.
Were	they	at the cinema last Monday?	Yes, / No,	they	were. / weren't.

Did	you	listen to music last night?	Yes, / No,	I	did. / didn't.
Did	he	play the guitar yesterday?	Yes, / No,	he	id. / didn't.
Did	she	watch TV last Monday?	Yes, / No,	she	did. / didn't.
Did	it	rain last night?	Yes, / No,	it	did. / didn't.
Did	we	have homework on Tuesday?	Yes, / No,	you	did. / didn't.
Did	they	go to Zurich last weekend?	Yes, / No,	they	did. / didn't.

Unit 11 | Workbook Intensive

Exercise 3

Hinweise / Ideen zu a) Übung zu den regelmässigen Verbformen im *Simple past*. Die Lösung kann in stiller EA geschehen und anschliessend in PA oder GA verglichen bzw. korrigiert werden.

zu b) Mit den vorgegebenen Informationen allein lässt sich ein recht einfacher Text verfassen. Schnellere S können versuchen, diesen Text mit weiteren Informationen etwas anspruchsvoller zu gestalten.
Die fertigen Texte eignen sich auch zum lauten Vorlesen und zum Formulieren von Fragen in PA: *Where did Larry Mullen Jr. live? Who was the drummer of the band? Etc.*

Lösung zu a) lived in Dublin, needed a good name, sounded like "you, too" or "you two", loved music, but they were also interested in politics, listened to the new Irish band at first, changed in the last years.

zu b)
Larry Mullen Jr. was the drummer of the band.
The new band needed a good name. A friend suggested U2.
Mullen, Hewson, Clayton and Evans loved music, but they were also interested in politics.
"Sunday, Bloody Sunday" was a song about the conflict in Northern Ireland.
At first, mostly people from Ireland, but soon people from all over the world were interested in U2.
There were experiments with dance music and electronic music.
Not all their fans liked the changes.
But nobody can say that U2 is a boring band today.

Exercise 4

Hinweise/Ideen Diese Drillübung eignet sich als stille EA oder als Hausaufgabe, kann aber auch in der Klasse als «Verbtennis» durchgespielt werden:
S 1 liest den gegebenen Teil, S 2 ergänzt die fehlenden Ausdrücke. Sind alle Ausdrücke richtig, liest S 2 einen weiteren vorgegebenen Teil, sonst muss S 2 einen weiteren *serve* von S 1 zurückspielen.

Lösung

Infinitive	Present simple	Past tense
look / she / +	she looks	she looked
watch / he / +	he watches	he watched
love / we / –	we don't love	we didn't love
touch / I / –	I don't touch	I didn't touch
love / you /?	Do you love …?	Did you love …?
play / we / –	we don't play	we didn't play
answer / I / –	I don't answer	I didn't answer
stop / you / +	you stop	you stopped
check / we / +	we check	we checked
brush / they / +	they brush	they brushed
spell / she / –	she doesn't spell	she didn't spell
walk / he / –	he doesn't walk	he didn't walk
turn / she /?	Does she turn …?	Did she turn …?
press / we / +	we press	we pressed
smell / it / +	it smells	it smelled
be / you / +	you are	you were
be / he / +	he is	he was
be / they / –	they aren't	they weren't
live / he / –	he doesn't live	he didn't live

Workbook Intensive   **Unit 11**

carry / he / +	he carries	he carried
start / they / –	they don't start	they didn't start
start / she / +	she starts	she started
return / you / –	you don't return	you didn't return
be / she / –	she isn't	she wasn't
wait / he / –	he doesn't wait	he didn't wait
be / we / +	we are	we were
copy / she / +	she copies	she copied
ask / I / –	I don't ask	I didn't ask
play / they / +	they play	they played

Exercise 5

Hinweise / Ideen   Individuelle Antworten (Erfinden erlaubt!). Als Partnerübungen zuerst mündlich, dann schriftlich oder als Sprech- und Schreibübung gestalten: Die S formulieren Nummer um Nummer zuerst mündlich und unmittelbar danach schriftlich.

Lösung
2. Was it cold yesterday?
4. Did you play cards with your friends last night?
6. Did you like the film (on TV / in the cinema / last ...)?
8. Was there anything interesting on television last Sunday?
10. Did you watch television last Saturday night?

Exercise 6

Hinweise / Ideen   Die S bearbeiten zuerst ihre Fragen und Antworten in stiller EA und erfragen dann die fehlenden Informationen in PA.

Erweiterung   Schnelle S versuchen in Teams, weitere Fragen und Antworten zu formulieren, die sie anschliessend der ganzen Klasse als Quiz abgeben.

Lösung Partner A
1. The terrorists destroyed the WTC in September 2001.
2. The film "Titanic" was a hit in the cinemas in 1997.
3. The French Revolution started in 1789.
4. William Shakespeare was born in 1564.
5. Graham Bell invented the telephone in 1876.
6. The Second World War started in 1939.

1. When did the Americans land on the moon?	in 1969
2. When did the Second World War end?	in 1945
3. When did Edmund Hillary and Sherpa Tenzing climb Mount Everest?	in 1953
4. When did Charles Lindbergh cross the Atlantic in a small aeroplane?	in 1927
5. When did ex-Beatle George Harrison die?	in November 2001
6. When was "Harry Potter" a big hit in the cinemas?	in 2001

Lösung Partner B
1. The Americans landed on the moon in 1969.
2. The Second World War ended in 1945.
3. Edmund Hillary and Sherpa Tenzing climbed Mount Everest in 1953.
4. Charles Lindbergh crossed the Atlantic in a small aeroplane in 1927.
5. Ex-Beatle George Harrison died in November 2001.
6. "Harry Potter" was a big hit in the cinemas in 2001?

1. When did the terrorists destroy the WTC?	in September 2001
2. When was the film "Titanic" a hit in the cinemas?	in 1997
3. When did the French Revolution start?	in 1789
4. When was William Shakespeare born?	in 1564
5. When did Graham Bell invent the telephone?	in 1876
6. When did the Second World War start?	in 1939

Unit 11 — Workbook Intensive

Language Focus

Ziel Datumsangabe mündlich und schriftlich

Lösung

date	we write	we say
1 / 1 / 2000	1 January 2000	the 1st (first) of January 2000 (two thousand)
15 / 6 / 1963	15 June 1963	the 15th (fifteenth) of June 1963 (nineteen sixty-three)
3 / 3 / 2003	3 March 2003	the 3rd (third) of March 2003 (two thousand and three)
20 / 5 / 2005	20 May 2005	the 20th (twentieth) of May 2005 (two thousand and five)
2 / 12 / 1997	2 December 1997	2nd (second) of December 1997 (nine hundred and ninety-seven)

Exercise 7

Hinweise / Ideen zu a) Vertiefungsübung zu den Monatsnamen. Sie eignet sich als stille EA oder als Hausaufgabe, kann aber auch als Wettbewerb im GU gestaltet werden: **L** deckt die Monate in selbst gewählter Reihenfolge am OHP auf, die **S** sprechen, sobald sie die Lösung haben, nach folgendem Muster: *bremeced is d e c e m b e r for December*. Anschliessend wird die Lösung im *Workbook* eingetragen.

zu b) b) zuerst schriftlich lösen als Erweiterung zu a), dann mündlich zum Aussprechen von Datumsangaben. Wichtig ist, dass die schriftliche Version keinen Hinweis auf Ordinalzahlen bei den Tagen enthält.
Hinweis: Die amerikanische Schreibweise würde den Monat vor den Tag setzen, was sich auch in der Zahlenversion niederschlägt.

Erweiterung Als Drill ist ein Partnerspiel denkbar: **S 1** sagt eine Zahl zwischen 1 und 12, **S 2** gibt den entsprechenden Monatsnamen. Bei falscher Antwort oder falscher Aussprache nennt **S 1** eine neue Zahl, sonst ist die Reihe an **S 2**.

Lösung zu a) *January, February, March, April, May, June, July, August, September, October, November, December*

zu b) *1 August 1991, 4 July 1776, 14 July 1789, 8 May 1945, 22 November 1963, 11 September 2001*

zu c) *700 years of Switzerland, Declaration of Independence of the USA, beginning of the French Revolution, end of the Second World War, death of J.F. Kennedy in Dallas, terror attacks in the USA*

Exercise 8

Ziel Eigenständiges Arbeiten mit Geschichtsfragen. Üben der Frageformen (siehe unten).

Hinweise / Ideen Wichtig sind die Frageformen, damit die Formulierung mit *did* vertieft werden kann. Bei den Antworten muss **L** möglicherweise mit unregelmässigen Verbformen helfen. Ist genügend Zeit vorhanden, können die **S**, eventuell in Gruppen, auch Quiz-Poster herstellen, auf denen Bilder und Fragen präsentiert werden. Hier bietet sich auch der fächerverbindende Unterricht an: Die auf den Postern dargestellten Fragen können Themen des Geschichtsunterrichts aufnehmen und vertiefen.

Workbook Intensive

Unit 12

Unit 12

Language Focus

Ziel unregelmässige *Past*-Formen; unregelmässige *Past*-Formen in Fragesätzen

Lösung

Present	Past	Present	Past	Present	Past	Present	Past
be	was / were	do	did	have	had	say	said
become	became	fall	fell	hit	hit	see	saw
bring	brought	find	found	hold	held	sit	sat
buy	bought	get	got	know	knew	take	took
come	came	go	went	make	made	wear	wore

When	did	I	bring	my homework to school?	I	brought	it on Monday.
Where	did	you	go	on holiday last year?	I/We	went	to Italy.
Where	did	he	sit	this morning?	He	sat	near the window.
When	did	she	buy	her new bike?	She	bought	it last month.
How long	did	it	take	to learn these words?	It	took	one hour.
What	did	we	see	in the city yesterday?	You	saw	a lot of shops.
Where	did	you	find	my socks?	I	found	them under your chair.
Where	did	they	come	from?	They	came	from Berne.

Exercise 1

Hinweise / Ideen Dieses *Exercise* kann als Spiel mit Zeitlimite gelöst werden: Welches Team bzw. wer innerhalb einer gegebenen Zeit die meisten Formen findet, gewinnt.

Lösung

m	*a*	*d*	*e*	*s*	o	*s*	x
w	w	*b*	*e*	*c*	*a*	*m*	*e*
e	*e*	*r*	y	*w*	t	*i*	o
r	*n*	*o*	g	a	v	*e*	*d*
e	*t*	*u*	f	*w*	*k*	*c*	h
p	l	*g*	f	*o*	*s*	*a*	e
b	u	*h*	*o*	*r*	*a*	*m*	a
g	*o*	*t*	y	*e*	*t*	*e*	r
i	*k*	*n*	*e*	*w*	*h*	*a*	*d*

Erweiterung – *Past Crossword* (Kopiervorlage Nr. 12a, 12b).

– Die **S** erstellen selbst einen *verb-grid* für andere **S**.

133

Unit 12   Workbook Intensive

Exercise 2

Hinweise / Ideen Aufbereitung des *Focus*-Textes in EA oder als Hausaufgabe (Hauptgewicht: unregelmässige Verben und Leseverständnis). Zur Kontrolle kann der Text von einem S laut vorgelesen werden; dabei wiederholen 1–2 weitere S jeweils echoartig die Verbformen.

Lösung zu a) *came, sat, were, said, came, said, came, hit, brought, fell, died, became, found*

zu b) *got, wanted to take, called, walked, took, killed, saw*

Exercise 3

Hinweise / Ideen Vertiefung der negativen *Past*-Formen und der unregelmässigen Verben sowie Kontrolle des Leseverständnisses. Eventuell zuerst im GU die Informationen suchen, dann in EA die Sätze schreiben lassen.

Bemerkung Möglichkeit, Personalpronomina in Subjekt- oder Objektformen (in *Ready for English 1*, § 17) neu zu üben.

Lösung zu a)
1. *President Kennedy and his wife didn't come to Houston, Texas. They came to Dallas, Texas.*
2. *The man didn't have a video camera with him. The man had a film camera with him.*
3. *The limousine didn't take the president to a police station. It took the president to Parkland Hospital.*
4. *Doctors didn't work very fast to save Kennedy's life. They worked very hard to save his life.*
5. *Vice President Johnson didn't become America's second president. He became America's new president.*

zu b)
1. *No, she didn't. She sang as a background singer.*
2. *No, he didn't. He worked as a lorry driver.*
3. *No, they didn't. They went to Hamburg.*
4. *No, they didn't. They had problems with countries like Russia and Cuba.*
5. *No, they didn't. They saw him as a bad president for their business.*

Exercise 4

Hinweise / Ideen Hier geht es darum, dass die S mit den *Past*- und den *Present*-Formen umgehen können. Die S sollten zuerst darauf aufmerksam gemacht werden, dass es in der Darstellung einige *distractors* hat.
Das Tondokument muss möglicherweise zu Beginn eher langsam, d.h. stückweise abgespielt werden, bis die S die ersten paar Punkte gefunden und verbunden haben. L kann auf einer Folie am OHP die ersten Verbindungen mitzeichnen.
Die unregelmässigen Verbformen sind im *Student's Book page 102* aufgelistet.

Skript
The present is "go". What is the past?
The past is "fell". What is the present?
The past is "sat". What is the present?
The present is "put". What is the past?
The present is "know". What is the past?
The past is "he had". What is the present?
The present is "does". What is the past?
The past is "came". What is the present?
The present is "she becomes". What is the past?
The present is "find". What is the past?
The past is "she took". What is the present?

Workbook Intensive Unit 12

The present is "bring". What is the past?
The present is "it gets". What is the past?
The past is "she made". What is the present?
The present is "see". What is the past?
The present is "we are". What is the past?

Lösung zu a)
went, fall, sit, put, knew, has, did, come, became, found, takes, brought, got, makes, saw, were, (went)
Verbindet man die Punkte in der richtigen Reihenfolge, so erscheint der Umriss einer elektrischen Gitarre.

zu b)
eat, begin, catch, drink, drive, flow, give, leave, meet, run, read, sleep, sell, swim, think, tell, wake up

Exercise 5

Hinweise / Ideen
Es ist in dieser Übung sehr wichtig, dass die S realisieren, was Mr Boring regelmässig tut *(on a normal day → present simple)* bzw. was gestern ausnahmsweise geschah *(yesterday → past simple)*. Haben die S diese Information, sollte die Übung in stiller EA zu lösen sein.
Bei der Kontrolle eignet sich die Übung zum mündlichen Ausgestalten des Inhalts:
Die Sätze werden einander (über)betont gegenübergestellt, indem **S 1** oder eine Kleingruppe den Text *Mr Boring on a normal day* liest und **S 2** oder eine Kleingruppe *Mr Boring yesterday*.
Betonung: *Mr Boring **never sleeps** late. – Yesterday he got up at eight*, usw.

Lösung
sleeps – slept; gets up – got up; has, has – didn't have, didn't have; goes, gives, says – went, said, gave; goes, takes, is – went, took, was; comes – came; doesn't, is – saw, wasn't; are – were; brings – brought; sits, has – sat, had, were; makes – made; goes, is – went, wasn't; gets – got

Exercise 6

Hinweise / Ideen
Bei einer schwächeren Klasse diese Übung zuerst schriftlich vorbereiten lassen, bevor sich die S gegenseitig Fragen stellen. In einer starken Klasse kann das Interview mündlich durchgeführt werden; das schriftliche Festhalten dient dann als Repetition.

Lösung
1. When did you get up yesterday morning? I got up at …
2. What did you see yesterday? I saw …
3. Did you come to school by bicycle? Yes, I did. / Now, I didn't.
4. Did you bring chewing gum to school? Yes, I did. / Now, I didn't.
5. Where did you have lunch yesterday? I had lunch at …
6. Did you take the bus or the tram after school? I took …
7. Did you go out last night? Yes, I went out. / No, I didn't go out.
8. What did you do last Sunday? I …
9. Did you go out, did you watch television, do your homework or do sports last night? I …
10. Did you go to bed before 11 p.m. yesterday? Yes, I went … / No, I didn't go …

Exercise 7

Hinweise / Ideen
PA mit *information gap*. Ziel ist es, die fehlende Information vom Partner / von der Partnerin zu erhalten.
Bei einer schwächeren Klasse kann es sinnvoll sein, die S zuerst die Fragen schriftlich formulieren zu lassen, evtl. in A- und B-Teams.
Damit bei der Übung wirklich ein Informationsaustausch stattfindet, empfiehlt es sich, vor den eigentlichen Partnerarbeiten die ersten Fragen / Antworten als Beispiele im GU präsentieren zu lassen.

Unit 12 — Workbook Intensive

Lösung

Partner A
in 1961, two elder sisters, her parents, at school, in Rougemont, after school, at St. Paul's Cathedral, one year later / in 1982, Third World, December, a television interview, the Prince, 1997, Paris, Althorp

Partner B
near Sandringham, a younger brother, in 1967, a talent for music, Switzerland, in London, in 1981, in 1984, to help people, 1992, her unhappiness in her personal life, the Princess of Wales, for the American Red Cross organisation, in a car accident, England

Exercise 8

Hinweise / Ideen

Die S können sich Informationen über Suchmaschinen im Internet beschaffen, da fast alle Prominenten neben Fan-Websites auch über eine eigene Homepage verfügen.
Die im *Workbook* aufgeführten Fragen können als Grundlage für das Starporträt benützt werden; es ist aber auch möglich, in der Klasse zuerst einen gemeinsamen Fragekatalog zu erstellen. Bei Zeitdruck kann dieses Projekt in GA angepackt werden.

Erweiterung

Arbeitet man in der Klasse mit einem standardisierten Fragekatalog, so kann zusätzlich ein Quiz zu den einzelnen Porträts durchgeführt werden: Die Klasse stellt Fragen und versucht zu erraten, um wen es sich handelt. Als Auflösung das Starporträt aufhängen.

Workbook Intensive Unit 13

Unit 13

Language Focus

Ziel Gegenüberstellung des *gesprochenen* und des *geschriebenen Present progressive* Singular und Plural. Bedeutungsunterschied von *at the moment* mit Verb im *Present progressive* und *tonight* mit Verb im *Present progressive*: In Kombination mit *at the moment* verweist der Satz auf eine eben stattfindende Handlung, in Kombination mit *tonight* auf eine in der nahen Zukunft geplante Handlung.

Mögliche Lösung At the moment …

Singular				
I	'm	am	listening	to a new CD.
you	're	are	sitting	in your chair.
he	's	is	watching	a video.
she	's	is	having	dinner.
it	's	is	raining	in England.

Plural				
we	're	are	playing	cards.
you	're	are	doing	this exercise.
they	're	are	learning	the words of Unit 13.

Tonight …

Singular				
I	'm	am	watching	TV.
you	're	are	running	in the street.
he	's	is	writing	a letter to his grandmother.
she	's	is	drinking	Coke.
it	's	is	snowing	in Switzerland.

Plural				
we	're	are	buying	running shoes.
you	're	are	eating	cheeseburgers.
they	're	are	making	a lot of noise.

Exercise 1

Ziel a) Zuordnung Verb – Nomen

b) Üben der Verlaufsform in einfachen Fragen und Antworten (Drill).

Hinweise / Ideen Diese Übung eignet sich als Sprech- und Schreib-PA, wobei die S die Fragen und entsprechenden Antworten zuerst mündlich und danach schriftlich ausformulieren; es empfiehlt sich dabei, die Beispiele Nummer um Nummer durchzugehen; natürlich können auch alle Beispiele zuerst mündlich und erst dann schriftlich angegangen werden.

Lösung zu a)
1. + f   read a book   5. + b   play cards
2. + d   open a door   6. + g   watch TV
3. + e   ask a question   7. + c   do our English homework
4. + a   wear a pair of jeans

Unit 13　　　　　　　　　　　　　　　　　　　　　　　　　　　　　Workbook Intensive

zu b)
2. What is he doing?　　　　He's opening a door.
3. What is he doing?　　　　He's asking a question.
4. What is she doing?　　　 She's wearing jeans.
5. What are you doing?　　　I'm playing cards.
6. What are they doing?　　 They're watching TV.
7. What are you doing?　　　We're doing our English homework.

Exercise 2

Hinweise / Ideen　　Beim Bild handelt es sich um die Zeichnung aus *Student's Book 1, Unit 7, page 34*.
Die Handlungen der Personen im Museum sollen hier in Erinnerung gerufen und im *Present progressive* frei ausformuliert werden.
Dabei sollen möglichst viele verschiedene Verben und Präpositionen (aus der *Use*-Box) gebraucht werden.

Einstimmung　　*Why is the museum guard angry?* Die S beschreiben, was gerade vor sich geht.
Die Übung kann vorgängig auch mündlich durchgespielt werden.

Variante　　Übung als Memoryspiel durchführen: Die S betrachten das Bild (evtl. als Folie auf den OHP gelegt) während 2 Minuten und schreiben dann auf, woran sie sich noch erinnern können.

Lösung
A boy is smoking a cigarette.
He's sitting on the floor.
He's reading a comic book.
A vase and flowers are lying on the floor.
A boy is touching a vase.
A boy is running.
On a painting two people are smiling.
Someone is playing the piano. He / she is making noise.
A man is standing and smoking.
A boy is wearing a helmet.
A boy is sitting on King Arthur's throne.
Two boys are playing ball. One is eating ice cream. He is leaving the wrapper on the floor.
A girl is playing ball.
A man and a woman are bringing a dog into the museum. The dog is having a pee.
The dog is making noise (barking).

Exercise 3

Hinweise / Ideen　　Diese Übung ist mit dem *Training, Fourth Step*, gekoppelt (vgl. auch Hinweise zu *Training, Fourth Step*).
Je nach Stärke der Klasse kann L den Tonträger nach jeweils einer oder mehreren Soundeinheiten stoppen.

Vorgehen
1. Die S hören die Geräusche zum *Training, Fourth Step*, und ordnen diese in der Tabelle den Nummern zu.
2. Anschliessend werden die Geräusche nochmals eingespielt und die Lösungen sprachlich präsentiert. (*Here someone's taking a photo. I think a man is laughing here etc.*)

Lösung　　Siehe den Kommentar zum *Student's Book page 18, Teacher's Book* S. 27.

Workbook Intensive Unit 13

Exercise 4

Ziel Sprechen und schreiben über Vorgänge oder Situationen, die in der Gegenwart stattfinden oder für die unmittelbare Zukunft geplant sind.

Hinweise / Ideen zu a) Die S können die Fragen auf sich selbst beziehen oder in PA als Interview bearbeiten. Dabei werden die Antworten zuerst mündlich gegeben und anschliessend schriftlich in der 3. Person *(he / she / it)* formuliert.

zu b) Nachdem die Fragen in EA schriftlich oder mündlich vorbereitet worden sind, kann die Übung mündlich in PA angegangen werden.
a) und b) sind als schriftliche Hausaufgabe oder stille EA geeignet.

Lösung zu a)
1. Yes, it is. / No, it isn't.
2. Yes, it is. / No, it isn't.
3. Yes, she / he is. / No, she / he isn't.
4. Yes, I am. / No, I'm not.
5. I'm answering them aloud. / I'm writing them.
6. Yes, I am. / No, I'm not.
7. I'm doing it at home. / I'm doing it at school.
8. I'm wearing ... .
9. I'm eating ... .

zu b)
1. Are you sitting at your desk at the moment?
2. Are you doing a maths exercise this evening? / Are you going out this evening?
3. Are you chewing gum right now?
4. Are we singing a song tomorrow morning?
5. Are you working hard right now?

Language Focus

Ziel Erfassen des Unterschieds von *many* und *much*

Mögliche Lösung

How many? (with plural)	How much? (with singular)
a lot of children	a lot of water
many cars	much time
a lot of kids	not much rain

There are a lot of children in classroom number 5 but not many in classroom number 7. We rarely have much money to spend or much time to wait. I can't see many dogs in the park, but many cats in the streets. The guard says: "Please don't make so much noise."

Exercise 5

Hinweise / Ideen Die S erarbeiten die Übung in PA / GA zuerst mündlich, bevor sie nach einer Kontrollphase (die S wechseln den Partner / die Gruppe; die Übung wird im GU nochmals durchgespielt) alles in EA schriftlich ausformulieren. Auch können die Präpositionen wiederholt werden. *(What is there behind, in front of, in, between ...)*

Variante Memoryübung: **S** betrachten die Gegenstände während einer vorgegebenen Zeit (30 Sekunden bis 1 Minute) und geben dann mit oder ohne Mengenangaben so viel wie möglich wieder. (PA: **S 1** zählt auf, **S 2** kontrolliert bzw. hilft mit dem Buch als Vorlage nach.)

Unit 13 — Workbook Intensive

Mögliche Lösung

1. There are a few sandwiches left.
2. There is some milk left.
3. There is not much strawberry milkshake left.
4. There are many chocolate chip biscuits left.
5. But there is some chocolate milkshake left.
6. There is a lot of chocolate cake left.
7. There is much butter left.
8. There is some apple pie left.
9. There isn't any tea left. / There is no tea left.
10. There is a lot of fruit cake left.
11. There is some coffee left.

Exercise 6

Hinweise / Ideen

Die S fragen gegenseitig in PA nach den fehlenden Wetterinformationen und notieren sich die Antworten.
Es handelt sich um eine PA, bei der zuerst der Teil a) gegenseitig einmal mündlich durchgespielt werden sollte, bevor in einem zweiten Durchgang Teil b) schriftlich angegangen wird.
Zu a): Die S sprechen die ihnen vorliegenden Wetterinformationen einmal mündlich in der Rolle einer «Wetterfee» durch, um sich auf die Fragen vorzubereiten.
Zu b): Möglichkeiten:
- Die S notieren die Antworten zu den gestellten Fragen.
- S 2 präsentiert / wiederholt den Wetterbericht so lange, bis S 1 den Bericht notiert hat.
- Der Bericht wird als Partnerdiktat geliefert.

Anschliessend können die Texte als Leseübung dienen. Die S spielen Wetterberichterstatter oder TV-Sprecherin. Als Erweiterung kann wie beim Wetterbericht im Fernsehen das zum Publikum gewandte Lesen und Aufschauen geübt werden.

Mögliche Lösung Partner A zu a)

Fragen:
Is it raining in Australia today? Is the wind blowing from the north? How cold is it in Alice Springs? Is it hot in the east of Australia? ...
Is it cloudy in Miami? Is the wind blowing from the west in Los Angeles? Is it snowing in New York? Is it cold in Seattle? How cold is it in Chicago? ...

Zeichenerklärung:	The sun is shining.
It's hot.	It's raining.
It's warm.	It's snowing.
It's cold.	It's cloudy.
It's freezing.	Winds are blowing from the east / south / west / north.

zu b)

It's December. It's raining in the east and the north of Australia, but the sun is shining in Melbourne and Sydney. The wind is blowing from the south. It's 35° in Alice Springs. It's warm in the east of Australia. ...
It's March. The sun is shining in Miami. There is no wind blowing in Los Angeles. In New York, it's raining. In Seattle, it's freezing. It's 1° in Chicago. ...

Partner B zu a)

Fragen:
Is it raining in England today? Is the wind blowing from the south in Ireland? How cold is it in Edinburgh? Is it hot in the north of the UK? Is it warm in Belfast? ...
Is it cloudy in Auckland? Is the wind blowing from the north in New Zealand? Is it raining in Alexandra? Is it warm in Dunedin? How cold is it in Wellington? ...

Zeichenerklärung	The sun is shining.
It's hot.	It's raining.
It's warm.	It's snowing.
It's cold.	It's cloudy.
It's freezing.	Winds are blowing from the east / south / west / north.

Workbook Intensive Unit 13

zu b)
> It's October. It's raining in the south of England, but the sun is shining in Liverpool. The wind is blowing from the North in Ireland. It's 15° in Edinburgh. It's cold in Belfast. ...
> It's July. The sun is shining in Auckland. The wind is blowing from the west in New Zealand. It's snowing in Alexandra. It's cold in Dunedin. In Wellington, it's 8°. ...

Exercise 7

Hinweise / Ideen zu a)
Dies ist eine Hörverständnisübung mit Hauptgewicht auf genauem Verstehen der Verben in der Verlaufsform.
Anschliessend kann der Text als Lesetext verwendet werden: Die S spielen Radioreporter, wobei als Erweiterung das relativ schnelle Lesen und / oder das Imitieren des *American English* geübt werden kann.

Hinweise / Ideen zu b)
Leseverständnisübung zur Wetterlage.
Bei leistungsschwächeren Klassen empfiehlt es sich, im ersten Durchgang die Informationen zu sammeln und erst im zweiten Durchgang die Sätze ausformulieren zu lassen.

Lösung zu a)
> *listening, looking, singing, raining, was, dreaming, shining, offering, thinking, offering, leaving, snowing, raining, clearing*

Lösung zu b)
> *Philadelphia: It's 60°. It's raining.*
> *the Florida Keys: It's 90°. The sun is shining.*
> *Lake Tahoe: The sun is shining.*
> *Juneau: It's freezing and it's snowing.*
> *Portland: It's 70° and raining, but the skies are clearing.*
> *San Diego: It's hot, with blue skies.*

Erweiterung
Schreibübung: Die S verfassen einen aktuellen Wetterbericht (evtl. zu verschiedenen Ländern, Gebieten) und stellen diesen der Klasse vor.

Exercise 8

Hinweise / Ideen
Dieses Projekt eignet sich auch für fächerübergreifende Arbeiten. Es können verschiedene Suchaufträge – etwa zum Wetter in Australien oder Japan – mit möglichen Prognosen für die kommenden Tage gegeben werden.

Unit 14

Language Focus

Ziel — Gegenüberstellung der Verlaufsform der Gegenwart *(Present progressive)* und der einfachen Gegenwart *(Present simple)*.

Mögliche Lösung

At the moment,			Normally,		
I	'm	reading	a book in English.	I	read	books in German.
you	're	playing	hockey.	you	play	football.
he	's	eating	an ice cream.	he	eats	an apple.
she	's	listening	to the radio.	she	listens	to a CD.
it	's	raining	in France.	it	rains	in Ireland.
we	're	running	in the building.	we	run	in the streets.
you	're	taking	a shower	you	take	a bath.
they	're	drinking	a milkshake	they	drink	a glass of water.

Exercise 1

Ziel — Üben der Gegenüberstellung von *Present simple* und *Present progressive* in EA.

Hinweise / Ideen — Da es sich um einen Auszug aus dem Focustext handelt, sollte diese Übung kurz nach einer ersten Begegnung mit dem Focustext oder erst nach einer gewissen zeitlichen Distanz dazu angegangen werden. Sonst besteht die Gefahr, dass die **S** den Focustext fast auswendig wiedergeben und sich mit dem Ziel des *Exercise* nicht auseinander setzen müssen.
Die *keywords now, often* usw. können zur Bildung von (eigenen) Sätzen in der entsprechenden Zeitform an der Wandtafel vorgegeben werden.

Variante — Vorbereitung in PA: **S 1** liest den vorgegebenen Satz *(I ... on the back of a Kiwi)*, **S 2** wiederholt den Satz mit eingesetzter Verbform *(I am sitting on the back of a Kiwi)*. Korrekturen anhand des Focustextes.

Lösung — 'm sitting, are flying, are we going, wonder *(verb of feeling, deshalb keine -ing-Form)*, are landing, are flying, are, are wearing, often wear, is landing, is coming, is happening, is rubbing, usually rub, 'm sitting, drive, need *(kommt nie mit -ing-Form vor)*, looks *(Tatsache, deshalb Present simple)*, think, is wearing, usually wear, are flying, are playing, hear *(Verb der Wahrnehmung, deshalb keine -ing-Form)*

Workbook Intensive   **Unit 14**

Exercise 2

Hinweise / Ideen zu a)	Diese Übung kann ganz verschieden angegangen werden. Man kann den S auch eine der Möglichkeiten freistellen.
Möglichkeiten	- Die S korrigieren den Text in EA / PA / GA und vergleichen ihre Lösung anschliessend mit dem Originaltext im *Student's Book*. - Das *Exercise* wird als Hörverständnisübung angegangen, wobei die S je nach Klassenstärke in einem ersten Durchgang nur unterstreichen, was nicht mit dem Originaltext übereinstimmt; in einem weiteren Durchgang wird (mit oder ohne jeweiliges Anhalten der CD) die Lösung notiert. - PA: S 1 liest den ‚falschen' Text, S 2 korrigiert mit dem Originaltext als Vorgabe und S 1 notiert die richtige Lösung. (*Last night I had a holiday … – No, it's not "holiday", it's "dream"*, usw.) - Wettbewerb: Wer findet am schnellsten die meisten Ungereimtheiten?
Lösung	*dream, back, flying, islands, wonder, Kiwi, landing, the capital, flying, cream, noses, cream protects their noses, thin, landing, towards, rubbing noses, rub noses, languages, quite, Cloud, letters, motorbike, don't worry, still flying, sheep, bank clerk looks, shirt, shorts and socks, friendly, bankers, shorts, flying, skyscraper, jumping down, voice, down, school*

Exercise 3

Ziel	Gegenüberstellung des *Present simple* und des *Present progressive*
Hinweise / Ideen	Die S füllen die Lücken in EA aus, vergleichen ihre Lösungen, korrigieren mittels Tonträger und führen anschliessend das Telefongespräch in PA.
Variante	Stärkere S versuchen, den Text sofort mündlich als Telefongespräch zu behandeln und die Lücken dabei sofort zu füllen. Anschliessend in EA schriftlich und am Schluss mittels Tonträger korrigieren.
Lösung	*Mandy:* What are you doing? *Kevin:* I'm sitting / We're watching / Are you working *Mandy:* I never work / I'm getting ready *Mandy:* Her parents like / they often go / I think / they are going *Kevin:* She sings / is she singing *Mandy:* I don't know / I think / I don't like / are you and John watching / You're not watching *Kevin:* We are watching

Exercise 4

Hinweise / Ideen	Die S füllen den Text in EA aus, vergleichen die Lösungen und lesen anschliessend die Bildlegenden in PA mit verteilten Rollen (S 1 *Present simple*, S 2 *Present progressive*).
Variante	PA: S 1 zeigt auf ein Bild, S 2 formuliert den entsprechenden Kommentar mündlich. Anschliessend wird der Kommentar schriftlich in EA festgehalten. Nach der Korrektur der Texte können diese zur Repetition der Fragestellungen dienen. *(When does Cleopatra the Beauty sleep? Who sleeps in the afternoon? When is she getting ready for the cinema? What is she getting ready for?)* usw.
Hinweis	Die S können bereits an dieser Stelle analog zu *Exercise 4* das *Project (Exercise 6)* angehen.

Unit 14 — Workbook Intensive

Lösung

1. *Frederic the Cat usually drinks milk. Today he is eating sausage.*
   Lilly the Kid usually sits at the table and reads the newspaper. Today she is sitting at the table and drinking coffee.
2. *Napoleon the Tramp usually sits in the park and eats a hamburger. Today he is sitting in the park and drinking a beer.*
   He wears dirty jeans and waits for Frederic. He is wearing dirty jeans and (he) is waiting for Frederic (as always).
3. *Frederic the Cat usually plays the piano like a rock musician and doesn't sing. Today he is singing like an opera singer. And Lilly the Kid is writing a letter.*
   Lilly the Kid usually eats a sandwich and listens to Frederic.

Language Focus

Hinweis

Dieser *Language Focus* wie auch das folgende *Exercise 5* ist für Klassen gedacht, die das unbestimmte Pronomen *one / ones* behandeln möchten.

Mögliche Lösung

George has got two	T-shirts,	a green	T-shirt	and a red	T-shirt.
George has got two	T-shirts,	a green	one	and a red	one.
Mandy has got five	videos,	three French	videos	and two American	videos.
Mandy has got five	videos,	three French	ones	and two American	ones.
Jenny has got three	friends,	an American	friend	and two Swiss	friends.
Jenny has got three	friends,	an American	one	and two Swiss	ones.

Exercise 5

Hinweise / Ideen

Diese freiwillige Übung kann mündlich oder schriftlich angegangen werden, was die Behandlung des unbestimmten Pronomens *one / ones* angeht.
Weiter eignen sich die Kurztexte für verschiedene Diktatformen, z.B. für ein *running dictation* (ein Partner-Wanderdiktat): Ein Text wird mehrfach im Zimmer aufgehängt. **S 1** liest von einem Zettel zum anderen gehend einen oder mehrere Sätze und diktiert diese anschliessend **S 2**. **S 2** schreibt das Diktierte nieder, dann wechseln die Rollen. **S 1** korrigiert das Diktat von **S 2**, während **S 2** weitere Sätze von den Zetteln abliest und diese anschliessend **S 1** diktiert, usw.

Lösung

1. *George has got three mountain bikes, a black one and two blue ones.*
2. *He also does a sailing course. There are all kinds of boats, small ones and big ones. George really likes the small ones. He likes the big ones too, but he thinks that the big ones are difficult in bad weather.*
3. *He is a member of two fitness clubs. One is an expensive one, the other one is not so expensive. But the trainers at the expensive one are very nice.*
4. *He goes for a bike ride every day. During the week he goes for short ones, but on Sunday he always has a long one. On Saturdays he sometimes goes for long ones, but normally he goes for a short one.*

Exercise 6

Hinweise / Ideen

Die **S** collagieren und beschreiben nach dem Muster von *Exercise 4* eigene Bilder oder Begebenheiten. Weitere Möglichkeit: **L** kopiert Bilder aus einer Illustrierten und gibt sie an die **S** ab mit dem Auftrag, je einen bis zwei Sätze im *Present progressive* und im *Present simple* dazuzuschreiben. Anschliessend werden die Textchen in der Klasse (vor)gelesen und verglichen.

Revision Workshop 3

Allgemeiner Hinweis zu den Revision Workshops

In der Mitte und am Schluss von *Ready for English 2* steht eine spezielle Einheit, in der keine neuen grammatikalischen Strukturen und nur die nötigsten Wörter eingeführt werden. Der Zweck ist die systematische Wiederholung der wichtigsten Formen und Fertigkeiten aus vorangegangenen *Units*. Da die Schülerinnen und Schüler möglichst zu Eigenaktivität und zu einer selbständigen Bestandesaufnahme angeregt werden sollen, findet sich sämtliches Arbeitsmaterial im *Workbook*. Das heisst nicht, dass alle Übungen schriftlich gelöst werden müssen. Die Übersicht über den *Revision Workshop 3* auf der folgenden Seite gibt Auskunft über die möglichen Arbeitsformen bei jeder einzelnen Station.

Arbeitsweise — Der *Revision Workshop* kann grundsätzlich auf zwei Arten bearbeitet werden:

1. Klassenverband — Schritt für Schritt bzw. Station für Station, mit Lernkontrolle nach jeder Übung. Dennoch sollten die Übungen wie angegeben in PA, EA oder GA erarbeitet werden. Hörverständnisübungen können im Klassenverband durchgeführt werden. Die einzelnen Stationen müssen nicht unbedingt erst nach Unit 14 erledigt werden, sondern können auch einige Wochen nach Behandlung der jeweiligen Form oder Funktion als Lückenfüller benutzt werden.

2. Workshop — Diese Form wird allen Lehrpersonen empfohlen, die schon etwas Erfahrung mit Workshops haben oder sich auf etwas Neues einlassen wollen. Im Folgenden wird kurz darauf eingegangen, wie ein Workshop aufgebaut werden kann.

Kontrolle — Zur Leistungskontrolle oder zur Eigeneinschätzung der S können die Kopiervorlagen Nr. 28 und 68 *(Control Sheet)* dienen.

Hinweise für den Aufbau eines Workshops

Der Workshop ist aufgebaut wie ein Circuittraining im Sport. Die Stationen sind verteilt im Klassenzimmer aufgebaut, evtl. mit Tafeln bezeichnet. Die Schülerinnen und Schüler gehen zu den einzelnen Stationen und führen die jeweilige Aufgabe nach der aufliegenden Anweisung selbständig aus. Am Ende kontrollieren sie ihren Erfolg selbst und haken die Übung auf dem *Control Sheet* (Kopiervorlage) ab oder machen sie evtl. später nochmals, wenn das Ergebnis nicht befriedigend war. Die Kriterien für die Erfüllung jedes einzelnen Schrittes (z.B. alles richtig, 70 Prozent richtig, höchstens drei Rechtschreibfehler usw.) sollten von der Lehrperson festgelegt und den Schülerinnen und Schülern bekannt gegeben werden.

Die Schülerinnen und Schüler arbeiten meist allein, müssen sich aber bei den in der Übersicht mit PA bezeichneten Stationen mit einer Partnerin / einem Partner zusammentun, der / die gerade auch diese Station angelaufen hat. Die Lehrperson fungiert als Kontrollinstanz und Ratgeberin im Hintergrund.

Obschon alle Stationen des *Revision Workshops* im *Workbook* enthalten sind, bedingt eine reibungslose Durchführung etwas Vorbereitung (siehe Übersichtstabelle).

Für die Durchführung dieses Workshops müssen je nach Leistungsstärke der Klasse zwischen drei und sechs Lektionen eingeplant werden.

Revision Workshop 3 — Workbook Intensive

Übersicht über den Revision Workshop 3

	Station (Topic)	Sprachliche Struktur	Arbeitsform	Vorbereitung durch L / Material
1.	*Simple Past Forms*	Vergangenheitsform unregelmässiger Verben	EA	—
2.	*Verb Training*			
3.	*Writing*	Verlaufsform der Gegenwart, Gegenwart	EA	—
4.	*Reading*	Textverständnis	EA	Vorbereitung evtl. mündlich mit Hilfe der Grundrisse als Folienkopie
5.	*Combination Crossword*			
6.	*Listening*	Hörverständnis	EA	—
7.	*Questions and Answers*	Fragen und Antworten im *Simple past*	EA/PA	evtl. *Student's Book page 7*, kopieren und auflegen
8.	*Vocabulary*			

Workbook Intensive Revision Workshop 3

Station Simple Past Forms

Lösung

brought, found, became, wore, fell, bought, held, said, was
came, saw, made, knew, went, gave, hit, sat, took
left, thought, told, ate, began, drank, flew, caught
woke up, slept, met, read, sold, put, ran, drove

Station Verb Training

Lösung

Infinitive	Past Simple	Present Simple	Present Progressive
do	she did	she does	she's doing
hold	we held	we hold	we are holding
sit	they sat	they sit	they are sitting
take	she took	she takes	she's taking
buy	we bought	we buy	we are buying
come	I came	I come	I'm coming
know	you knew	you know	–
have	she had	she has	she's having
bring	he brought	he brings	he's bringing
be	I was	I am	I'm being
go	she went	she goes	she's going
find	we found	we find	we're finding
fall	you fell	you fall	you are falling
wear	they wore	they wear	they are wearing
say	we said	we say	we are saying
make	he made	he makes	he's making
give	I gave	I give	I'm giving
get	she got	she gets	she is getting
see	they saw	they see	they are seeing
put	you put	you put	you are putting
eat	I ate	I eat	I'm eating
read	he read	he reads	he's reading

Station Writing

Mögliche Lösung

1. Today, the cat's sitting in front of the door. It usually sits behind the door.
2. Today, the teacher's wearing a pullover. He usually wears a jacket.
3. Today, two boys are playing American football. They normally play football.
4. Today, a boy is listening to a walkman. He usually listens to a discman.
5. Today, a boy is eating a hamburger. He usually eats a sandwich.
6. Today, a girl's drinking juice. She usually drinks water.
7. Today, two girls are reading on the grass. They normally read on a bank.
8. Today, a woman is cleaning a window. She usually watches the students.

Station Reading

Lösung 1B, 2E, 3F, 4D, 5A, 6C

Revision Workshop 3 — Workbook Intensive

Station Combination Crossword

Lösung

> running a race, speaking to a friend, dreaming at night, driving a car, playing football, finding the way, doing homework, drinking a glass of water, eating a banana, listening to music, singing a song, blowing from the north, taking a shower, sitting on a chair, touching a vase
>
> Das Lösungswort von oben nach unten lautet "READY FOR ENGLISH".

Station Listening

Skript

Jonathan: A simple two-week holiday together, just you and me. That would be so nice. A pretty beach somewhere, but no. It's just not possible.

Melanie: Look Jonathan, it's not my fault that the travel agency went out of business. And I'm also quite mad that we never got a penny back from that holiday arrangement. So be fair, OK?

Jonathan: I know it's not your fault. But why can we never organise our time so we can go away together.

Melanie: Well, why don't we try for next year then?

Jonathan: It's not going to work, Melanie, I'm sure. OK, how about around Easter, April?

Melanie: Sorry, I'm going to the US for four weeks to work for my company in New York. They asked me three months ago.

Jonathan: See, I told you. And you can't make it in May?

Melanie: I think I can. Yes, May's OK for me.

Jonathan: Sorry, it isn't for me, I've just realised. The Local Shakespeare Company is organising a production of Macbeth for June and I promised to help. May is no good. But June would be very good.

Melanie: June? That's a problem for me. We've got the District Tennis Championship, I can't get away. I thought you were busy with the Shakespeare Company.

Jonathan: I'm not acting this year, so no, I would be free. And then I'm taking my mother to a holiday in Ireland in July. So that's no good. So summer is out. How about autumn, October?

Melanie: That's when I go to Spain with my parents. How can they get the best holiday times and we can't …? But how about beginning of September or November?

Jonathan: September is no good because I'm going to that Yoga course in Liverpool. And November, what about November. You said beginning of November, didn't you? – No, I've got Sue and Marc from Canada at my house. I don't like them but they are family and I can't just say: "Hi, nice of you to come, but I'm going on a holiday, see you when I get back." What about August?

Melanie: No, sorry, I can't. I'm doing a language course in Marseille. But, wait a minute, January, how about January?

Jonathan: That's no good at all, sorry. Firstly, I never have any money after Christmas and, secondly, I'm starting a new job on the 5th so no, that won't be very good. And February is no good either because I'm going on a training course for two weeks.

Melanie: February is no good for me either: I've got my business exams on the 20th. I need to work for that. That leaves December, but …

Jonathan: … that's the busiest time of the year in our shop. There's no way I can take a holiday in December. So that's it, right? No holiday for the two of us. We can only get away if you come to Ireland with me or I come to Spain with you and your dear parents. I don't think I can stand it.

Melanie: Look, your parents are not much fun to be with, either. – Wait a minute, if you haven't got anything on we could go away with each other in …

Jonathan: Yes, of course!

Workbook Intensive   **Revision Workshop 3**

Lösung

Melanie		Jonathan
	January	has not money, starts a new job
business exams	February	training course
	March	
goes to the US	April	
	May	helps the Shakespeare Company
District Tennis Championship	June	
	July	takes his mother to a holiday
language course in Marseille	August	
	September	yoga course in Liverpool
goes to Spain with her parents	October	
	November	Sue and Marc from Canada
	December	busy time in the shop

Station Questions and Answers

Lösung

What was Lady Diana's full name?
Princess of Wales
Where was she born?
She was born in Sandringham, England.
What about her family?
She had one brother and two sisters. Her parents separated.
What was her work after school?
She worked as a kindergarten teacher in London.
Who and where did she marry?
She married Prince Charles at St. Paul's Cathedral.
How many children did she have?
She had two sons called William and Henry.
Why did she visit Third World countries?
She visited these countries to help people.
When did she and Prince Charles separate?
They separated in December 1992.
When were they divorced?
They were divorced in 1996.
When and how did she die?
She died in a car accident in Paris, France.

Station Vocabulary

Lösung

1. career, 2. actresses, 3. gun, 4. juice, 5. island, 6. dream, 7. sheep, 8. noise, 9. spring, 10. queue, 11. loaf, 12. guide book, 13. neck, 14. east, 15. tie

Unit 15 — Workbook Intensive

Unit 15

Exercise 1

Hinweise / Ideen — *Exercise 1* ist eine tabellarische Übersicht über die im *Focus* vorgestellten Reisearten. Es ist in stiller EA oder als PA zusammen mit dem *Focus*-Text als Textverständnisübung zu lösen.

Erweiterung — Anschliessend kann **L** einige Fragen im Hinblick auf die einfache Steigerungsform stellen:
Which trip is cheaper, the air safari or the camping tour?
Which tour is longer, the camping tour or the railway travel?
Which touring group is larger, the camping tour group or the air safari group?

Lösung

Air Safari	Railway Travel	Camping Tour
8 days	14 days	10 days
A$ 4260.–	A$ 385.–	A$ 919.–
ten-passenger planes	trains	special coach
max. of 10 in one group	as many as you want	small groups / 6 to 12 people

hotels or farms	sleeping berths	sleeping bag
Great Barrier Reef, Escott Cattle Station, Lawn Hill National Park, Alice Springs, Ayers Rock, Birdsville, Lightning Ridge	unlimited travel from Perth to Cairns	Melbourne / Sydney, Flinder Ranges, Ayers Rock, Alice Springs

Language Focus

Ziel — Erarbeitung der zwei Kategorien des Komparativs. Die **S** sollen das Muster selbst entdecken.
Zusätzliche (bekannte) Adjektive: *great, quiet, loud, terrible, funny, boring, lovely*.
Die Regel, die die **S** ableiten sollen: Einsilbige Adjektive und Adjektive auf -y gehören zu *Group 1*, zwei- und mehrsilbige Adjektive zu *Group 2*.
Die orthografischen Regeln dazu sind in § 29a der Grammatik festgehalten.

Lösung

Group 1	Group 2
harder, smaller, happier (Schreibweise!), bigger (Schreibweise!), nicer	*more beautiful, more direct, more difficult, more famous*

Exercise 2

Hinweise / Ideen — Die **S** üben die Vergleichsformen, indem sie die vorgegebenen Begriffe oder Namen mit den jeweils entsprechenden Adjektiven vergleichen. Zum Teil hängen die Antworten von den Vorstellungen und Ansichten der **S** ab.

Die Übung kann entweder zuerst mündlich und dann schriftlich gemacht werden, indem die **S** in PA ihren Satz mündlich und unmittelbar danach schriftlich formulieren oder indem sie einander ihre Beispiele gegenseitig diktieren.

Wichtig — Hinweis auf die Schreibweise von *than*.

Workbook Intensive — Unit 15

Lösung
1. A golf course is bigger than a tennis court.
2. ... more exciting than ...
3. ... more famous than ...
4. ... more difficult than ...
5. ... easier than ...
6. A car radio is louder than a walkman.
7. ... stronger than ...
8. ... more dangerous than ...
9. ... more comfortable ...
10. Commander Wiggles is older than his dog Ben.

Language Focus

Ziel — Einführung der Steigerungsform *Superlativ*.

Lösung
The world's fastest passenger plane is the Concorde.
The largest island in the world is Greenland.
The Channel Tunnel is the most direct way from England to the Continent.
Which is the most important city in the world?

Exercise 3

Hinweise / Ideen — Je nach Gutdünken kann diese Übung gleich angegangen werden wie *Exercise 2* (siehe entsprechende Hinweise / Ideen), oder die S können zuerst in EA die Sätze schriftlich formulieren und sich (evtl. mit Zusatznotizen) auf ein anschliessendes ‚Streitgespräch' vorbereiten. In PA / GA / GU werden die Meinungen dann vorgetragen und evtl. diskutiert.
*(For me, the most difficult school subject is French **because** of all the different verb forms etc.)*

Lösung
1. For me, the most difficult school subject is ...
2. For me, the most popular actor is ...
3. The most important thing in my life is ...
4. For me, the greatest person in sports is ...
5. For me, the hardest language to learn is ...
6. For me, the most exciting television programme is ...
7. My biggest problem at the weekend is ...
8. For me, the happiest time of the day is ...

Language Focus

Ziel — Veranschaulichung der unregelmässigen Steigerungsformen von *good* und *bad*.

Lösung

Julia Roberts is a	good	actress.
... is a	better	actress.
... is the	best	actress in the world.
Jesse James was a	bad	person.
Al Capone was a	worse	person.
... is / was the	worst	person in the world.

Unit 15 — Workbook Intensive

Exercise 4

Ziel — Beherrschung der unregelmässigen Steigerungsformen von *good* und *bad*.

Hinweise / Ideen zu a) — Die S formulieren eigene Sätze zu den vorgegebenen Begriffen im Superlativ. L kann als Vorlauf die eigenen Beispiele mündlich vorstellen. Die Übung eignet sich als GA, wobei alle S der Gruppe ihre Meinung zuerst mündlich kundtun und anschliessend schriftlich formulieren.

Variante — Die Aussagen anderer S aus der Gruppe werden schriftlich festgehalten: *For Sarah, the best book is ...* Anschliessend wird in der Klasse wettbewerbsartig erfragt, wer wohl welche Vorlieben hat. *(Who says "The best book is Harry Potter"?)*

zu b) — Die S vergleichen und diskutieren ihre Varianten, möglichst mit Begründungen.

Exercise 5

Ziel — Hörverständnis, Vergleichsformen, Zahlen erkennen.

Hinweis / Idee — Unterschied zwischen *big* und *large*.
Zuerst die Antworten still lesen lassen. Es kann allenfalls schon vor dem Hören spekuliert werden: *Is it possible that Mount Isa is the world's largest city?*

Skript

Chris: Here's something about Australia. Oh no, that's Austria. Don't go so fast, Mona, I don't have time to read.
Mona: Oh here's something. Look at this picture. It's Sydney.
Chris: Yeah, Sydney Harbour Bridge, the biggest bridge in the world.
Mona: No, not the biggest, stupid, the widest bridge. It's 49 metres wide, and it's got ... let's see, one, two, four, six, eight lanes for cars.
Chris: And two railway tracks besides that.
Mona: It's also very long, more than 500 metres.
Chris: I'm sure the Golden Gate Bridge is longer though ...
Mona: Anything else about Australia? Look under railways. There must be something.
Chris: Yeah, it says here the longest railway line is in Australia.
Mona: I thought that was the Transsiberian.
Chris: No, you're right. It's the longest stretch of railway that is all straight, not a single bend for ... yeah, guess how many kilometres?
Mona: Mmmm ... 200? 500?
Chris: Not quite. 478 kilometres.
Mona: Wow. The driver probably falls asleep every time.
Chris: Did you know that Australia has the world's biggest town?
Mona: Big in what sense?
Chris: Well, big in area. Mount Isa is in Queensland, and it has about 40,000 square kilometres. It says here it's almost as big as Switzerland, not quite, but almost. But it only has 22,000 inhabitants. That's a lot of space for each of them. How many inhabitants has Switzerland got?
Mona: Switzerland? I have no idea. There must be a couple of millions ... two or three?
Chris: Let's check ...

Lösung

1. c) *Sydney Harbour Bridge, erbaut 1932, ist 48,8 m breit und hat eine Spannweite von 502,9 m, die Lichthöhe für Schiffe beträgt 49 m.*
2. b) *Die gerade Strecke zwischen Nurina und Ooldea ist 478 km lang (Linie Adelaide – Perth).*
3. a) *Das Gemeindegebiet von Mount Isa umfasst 40,978 km², die Schweiz ist immer noch ein bisschen grösser (41,295 km²).*

Workbook Intensive Unit 15

Language Focus

Ziel Erfassen des Unterschieds zwischen den Fragewörtern *which* und *what*.

Hinweis *What* fragt offen, aus der ganzen Menge der erhältlichen Dinge: *"What would you like?"*
Which bezieht sich auf eine beschränkte Menge: *"Which of these two bikes is yours?"*

Lösung *Which is your bike? – The red one.*
What is a sleeping berth – It's a bed on a train or a boat.
Which apples do you want? – The cheaper ones, please.
What would you like? – A kilo of bananas, please.

Exercise 6

Hinweis Übung zu den Frageformen mit *which* und *what*.

Variante Nachdem der Unterschied zwischen *Which* und *What* eingeführt und vertieft worden ist, eignet sich diese Übung bestens als *milling exercise*, indem die S die Fragen nicht auf sich selbst beziehen, sondern mündlich anderen S stellen, die jeweiligen Antworten schriftlich stichwortartig festhalten und erst anschliessend wiederum mündlich oder schriftlich im *Workbook* ausformulieren.
(A green salad is cheaper than a tomato salad. Roger's favourite drink is Red Bull. etc.)

Lösung
1. *Which salad is cheaper, ...*
2. *What is your favourite drink?*
3. *What is a Budget Austrailpass?*
4. *Which (or what) is the best way ...?*
5. *Which airline is bigger, ...*
6. *What do you think of Harry Potter?*
7. *What did you have for breakfast today?*
8. *Which comic strip character do you like: ...?*

Exercise 7

Ziel Adjektive und die Vergleichsformel *as ... as* üben. Landeskunde.

Hinweise / Ideen Diese Übung kann als Wettbewerb gestaltet werden: Die S sollen die Antworten zuerst erraten; anschliessend werden die Lösungen so rasch wie möglich mittels Atlas oder Internet in GA / GU gesucht. Diejenigen S gewinnen, die am meisten und am schnellsten richtig geschätzt haben.

Lösung mit den tatsächlichen Distanzen und Zeiten:
1. c) Perth – Sydney = 3278 km (Luftdistanz)
2. b) Brisbane – Darwin = 3.50 hours
3. a) Melbourne – Sydney = 889 km (Strasse)
4. b) as long as; Sidney – Cairns = 53 h
5. a) as big as; Australia = 7,686,850 km^2
6. c) long, longer; Längste gerade Strecke in Australien: 478 km. Genève Aéroport – St. Margrethen = ca. 410 km
7. c) high, higher, high; Ayers Rock: 940 m ü. M. Säntis: 2502 m ü. M.

Exercise 8

Ziel Die S beschäftigen sich (auch fächerübergreifend) mit Informationen aus der Geografie.

Hinweise / Ideen
zu a) Die Informationen dienen einerseits als Vorgabe zu Aufgabe b), können aber auch zu einem Kurztext ausformuliert und in einem Heft festgehalten werden.
zu b) Die S suchen im Atlas oder im Internet entsprechende Informationen zu einer selbstgewählten Insel und halten diese in einem Heft oder auf einem Plakat im Schulzimmer oder im Schulhaus fest. Natürlich kann anstelle einer Insel auch ein Land gewählt werden, doch ist die Wahrscheinlichkeit grösser, dass die S, vor allem wenn jede(r) S der Klasse eine andere Insel wählt, möglichst viele neue Informationen erhalten.

Unit 16

Exercise 1

Hinweis zu a) Je nachdem, wie stark der Focustext bereits verankert ist, können die S im Vorfeld aus der Erinnerung markieren, was zu viel steht; der Hörtext ab Tonträger dient dann zur Kontrolle und Ergänzung. Das *Exercise* eignet sich aber auch als Hörverständnisübung im herkömmlichen Sinne: Die S markieren, was zu viel steht.

zu b) Die S sollten diesen Text nicht vorbereiten, sondern direkt mit dem Tonträger vergleichen. Im Anhang kann in Erinnerung gerufen werden, was im Originaltext steht.
Je nach Leistungsstärke der Klasse kann die CD entweder abschnittweise gestoppt oder das Ganze mehrmals abgespielt werden.

Ausbau PA: **S 1** liest den Focustext aus dem *Student's Book*, **S 2** sagt, was bei b) mit anderen Worten ausgedrückt wird.

Lösung zu a) *ladies and gentlemen, British Columbia, great, ten, at around 10 p.m., or boat, listen to this, small, somewhere, very, up, That was hard work, only*

zu b) *out West, old school friends, loved, go, the Eastern part, have a look at, Canadian, much, to Western Canada*

Exercise 2

Ziele Aufarbeitung des Focustexts, Üben von Begründungen, Wiederholung einiger Strukturen des Focustexts.

Hinweise / Ideen Je nach Leistungsstärke und je nachdem, wie stark der Focustext verankert ist, kann die Übung mit oder ohne *Student's Book* und in einer beliebigen Unterrichtsform angegangen werden. Die Zuordnung sollte unbedingt mittels Kästchen und nicht mittels Verbindungsstrichen erfolgen, da es ein Ziel dieser Übung ist, dass die S alle Sätze richtig zusammengesetzt laut lesen können. Die Zuordnung in den Kästchen dient also der Vorbereitung zur mündlichen freien Umsetzung.
Stärkere S können auch versuchen, die Sätze direkt mündlich auszuformulieren und lediglich die Lücken schriftlich zu füllen.

Lösung a) is, b) some, c) places, d) wear, e) to, f) water
g) need, h) high, i) liked
1 e, 2 f, 3 d, 4 b, 5 c, 6 a, 7 h, 8 i, 9 g

Language Focus

Thema *must*, *have to* und *need to* bejaht und verneint; keine Verneinung von *must*

Mögliche Lösung I: **must / have to / need to**

I	must	be	at home at 11 o'clock.
You	need to	take	the dog out.
She	has to	buy	a new jacket.
He	must	bring	a coke for lunch.
We	must	write	a letter to grandmother.
You	need to	take	a suitcase.
They	must	find	their books.

Workbook Intensive

Unit 16

II: don't have to / don't need to

I	don't	have to	be	at home at 11 o'clock.
You	don't	need to	take	the dog out.
She	doesn't	have to	buy	a new pair of jeans.
He	doesn't	need to	bring	a coke for lunch.
We	don't	need to	write	a letter to grandmother.
You	don't	need to	buy	a lot of bread.
They	don't	have to	arrive	on time.

IV: have to

Last week	I	had to	be	at home at six o'clock every day.
	you	had to	take	the bus to school.
	she	had to	work	very hard.
	we	had to	learn	all the words.

Exercise 3

Hinweise / Ideen zu a)
Es ist wichtig, dass die **S** den Einleitungstext genau erfassen. Möglicher Einstieg: An der Wandtafel eine Liste von Milchprodukten und Produkten, die keine Milch enthalten, erarbeiten. Ebenso empfiehlt es sich in schwächeren Klassen, die *New Words*-Box im Voraus zu besprechen, denn die **S** sollten anschliessend fähig sein, die Listen in EA / PA / GA, also möglichst ohne Hilfe von **L**, zu füllen.

zu b)
Die **S** versuchen, ihre Vorschläge mit Hilfe der *Use*-Box zu kommentieren und allenfalls auch zu diskutieren. *(Biscuits have got milk powder but I think it is OK because she likes sweets so much etc.)* Dieser Teil der Übung kann auch im GU erfolgen, wobei **L** dann das Gespräch entsprechend steuert. *(Hasn't chocolate cake got milk in it? etc.)*

zu c)
Dieser Teil der Übung sollte möglichst in EA, als Zusammenfassung von a) und b) erfolgen. Die Texte können anschliessend gegenseitig vorgelesen werden und / oder als Diktatvorlage dienen.

Lösung zu a)
☺ *apples, bananas, biscuits, chocolate cake, honey, oranges, salad*
☻ *brown bread, butter, coffee, corn flakes, eggs, French cheese, margarine, milk, milkshakes, pop corn, tea, white bread*
☹ *hamburgers, salami, sausages, steaks*

Language Focus

Ziel
much / many / a lot of, more, most und little / few, less / fewer und least / fewest.
Unterschied zwischen zählbaren und unzählbaren Mengenangaben; Letztere kommen in der Regel nicht im Plural vor.

Lösung

	singular	plural
	There is a lot of forest in Canada.	A lot of people came to the party.
	I haven't got much homework.	How many pupils are there in your class?
comparative	There is often more snow in the Rocky Mountains than in the Alps.	Are there more boys or girls in your class?
superlative	Who has the most milk in their coffee?	Which class in your school has the most pupils?

Unit 16 — Workbook Intensive

	singular	plural
	There is only little sunshine in Greenland in winter.	Few tourists know local pubs in Switzerland.
comparative	There is less forest in British Columbia now than in 1950.	In Switzerland, fewer people speak French than German.
superlative	Who has the least money in her bag?	Which is the country with the fewest people?

Exercise 4

Hinweise / Ideen

Die S nummerieren die Begriffe zuerst in EA, um nachher ihre Meinung mit den Steigerungsformen ausdrücken zu können. Je nach Bedarf können die ‚positiven' Steigerungsformen nochmals geübt und angewendet und / oder die weniger bekannten ‚negativen' Steigerungsformen *less* und *least* eingeführt und geübt werden.
Viele Beispiele eignen sich auch zu Kurzdiskussionen, wobei die S ihre Ansicht begründen können. *(I think a cat is less dangerous than a dog because cats can't kill you; but a tiger ...)*

Mögliche Lösung

1. I think a bear is more dangerous than a dog. / I think a cat is the least dangerous animal.
2. I think Australia is more popular than Austria. / I think Alaska is the least popular region.
3. I think a bed in a dormitory is the most comfortable. / I think a tent is the least comfortable.
4. I think spelling is more difficult than reading. / I think counting is the least difficult.
5. I think Vancouver is more rainy than Berne. / I think Rome is the least rainy city.
6. I think swimming is less relaxing than walking. / I think rafting is the least relaxing activity.
7. I think a ghost story is more exciting than a detective story. / I think a love story is the least exciting.
8. I think television is more boring than Internet surfing. / I think computer games are the least boring.

Exercise 5

Hinweise / Ideen

Das *Exercise* kann zur Festigung der Strukturen *a lot of / many / much / more* (siehe *Use*-Box) oder zu ihrer Einführung dienen. L kann den Text zuerst mündlich oder auf dem OHP mit der korrekten Lösung präsentieren, um das Thema zählbar / unzählbar (siehe *Language Focus*) nochmals aufzuzeigen. Auch können die Lösungen in PA / GA diskutiert werden, evtl. mit Hilfe von Lösungskärtchen (Lücke auf der Vorderseite und Lösung auf der Rückseite), mit denen die S nach jeder gefüllten Lücke ihre Lösung kontrollieren und bei einem Fehler überdenken sollten. (Evtl. absichtlich ein falsches Lösungskärtchen liefern, um die Selbstkontrolle der S zu überprüfen!)

Lösung

more, a lot, few, many, more, the fewest, fewer, most
most, little, few, less, more, most
many, more, least, little

Erweiterung

Canada and Switzerland (Kopiervorlage Nr. 43).

Language Focus

Hinweise

Das *Present progressive* wird hier in seiner Funktion als Tempus zur Angabe einer Gegebenheit in der nahen Zukunft nochmals bewusst gemacht (vgl. *Ready for English 1, Unit 10*).
Das *Present progressive* wird zusammen mit einer Zeitangabe gebraucht, wenn über ein fixes Arrangement in der nahen Zukunft gesprochen wird.

Lösung

a) *"Right now we're having some problems with the wind. It's very strong."*
   present time, present progressive
b) *"What are your plans for tonight?" – "We're going to Harrison Hot Springs."*
   future time, present progressive

Workbook Intensive Unit 16

Exercise 6

Hinweise / Ideen — Hörverständnisübung. Der Reiseführer kündigt einige Programmänderungen an. Die S markieren im ersten Durchgang die entsprechenden Begriffe. Im zweiten Durchgang versuchen sie, die Programmänderungen stichwortartig zu notieren.

Variante — Die S spielen in PA / GA selbst Reiseführer und geben Programmänderungen bekannt.

Skript — All right, tomorrow is the seventh day of our tour, and it's the most exciting one. We have to start as early as possible, at about 7 o'clock. I'm sorry, that's a change from the printed programme, but we need a little more time.
So we're having breakfast at six. How about that? Well, Max, you don't like the idea, but we have to pick up our canoes at nine o'clock. It's quite a long walk from here to the canoe shop. We've got the rest of the morning to pack everything and to practice a little. Ah, paddling is not as easy as you think!
We're having lunch on Cook Island, not on Bear Island, because there's a girl's camp there and I don't want to lose our boys. So that's another change.
In the afternoon we're paddling up to Joe Lake. It looks like a long way, but we still have enough time for a swim. And we have a short portage there, so we can practice portaging.
Now, at four, we have to make camp. It gets dark early in
September. I think we're having soup and sausages for dinner tomorrow.
OK. At night, there may be some bears around, so we have to hang the food in the trees. Now, isn't that a day full of adventures?

Lösung

~~7.00~~ 6.00	Breakfast at Tea Lake Campground
13.00	Lunch on ~~Bear Island~~ Cook Island
~~17.00~~ 16.00	Arrive at campsite
18.00	~~Steak Dinner~~ Soup and sausage for dinner, evening campfire

Exercise 7

Ziel — Üben des *Present progressive* mit Zukunftsbedeutung.

Hinweis — Wegen der geplanten Flossreise hat Yolanda ihre Agenda voll von fixen Terminen und kann deshalb ihren Freund nicht treffen. Oder doch?

Vorgehen — Die S studieren den Tagesplan in EA und überlegen sich mögliche Fragen.
Anschliessend werden in PA Gespräche geführt. **S 1** spricht in der Rolle von Yolanda, **S 2** in der Rolle von Daniel.
Je nach Leistungsstärke können die Fragen und / oder die Antworten schriftlich vorbereitet, mit Hilfe des Rasters oder lediglich mit der Tagebuchvorlage formuliert werden.

Hilfestellung — OHP mit den Vorschlägen aus dem *Workbook*.

Mögliche Lösung

Daniel	Yolanda
Can I see you at 9?	No, I'm sorry, I'm picking up my flight ticket at 9.
Oh, perhaps later, at 10?	Okay, but only for twenty minutes. I'm meeting Margaret at 10.30 because of my dog.
What about noon then? You're really difficult.	I'm having lunch with my mother then.
Can I see you before work, at half past three?	At half past three? I'm really sorry, I'm picking up my passport then. The office closes at four.
Okay, so let's meet after 9, at 9.30.	I'm sorry, but I'm going shopping then. I need a sleeping bag, a hat and sunglasses.

Unit 16   Workbook Intensive

What about 11 o'clock?	I told you that I'm having an appointment with Dr. Coleman at 11.
I see. And what are you doing after lunch?	I'm waiting for a phone call from Marco at 13.30, and at 14.30 Claude is bringing his rucksack. But we could meet at 14.00 ...

Exercise 8

Hinweise / Ideen

Je nachdem, wie intensiv das dazugehörige *Stepping Out* im *Student's Book* bearbeitet worden ist, kann der Hörtext als kurze Wiederholung dienen oder auch als Informationslieferant.
Die S können auf einem Beiblatt Notizen aufnehmen und die Kurztexte anschliessend im *Workbook* ausformulieren.
Andere Möglichkeit: den Tonträger nach jedem Bild stoppen, die S formulieren ihre Kurztexte direkt Bild um Bild.

Mögliche Lösung

The Niagara Falls is a great waterfall, 57 metres high on the border with the US. A lot of tourists visit it every year.
The Koala bear is nice, small and cuddly. It looks like a teddy bear. It eats leaves and sleeps all day.
On this picture you can see Sydney Tower and Sydney Harbour bridge. It's 134 metres high.
The Rocky Mountains are very beautiful: blue sky, rocks and white snow.
You can see dangerous Grizzlies.
The Great Barrier Reef is one of the biggest coral reefs in the world. You can snorkel and dive in the clear blue sea.

Exercise 9

Hinweise / Ideen

Exercise 9 besteht aus Lückentexten, die die Naturphänomene hinter den Experimenten von *Time for a Change* erklären.
Das Ausfüllen der Lücken erlaubt eine Verständniskontrolle: Partnerin A zeigt Partner B, dass sie seine Ausführungen begriffen hat, und umgekehrt.
Diese Übung ist auch für den fächerübergreifenden Unterricht, evtl. für den Immersionsunterricht, konzipiert und kann ebenso auf Deutsch durchgeführt werden.

Lösung

Experiment 1:
above, heavier, lift, air, water, coin, incredible

Experiment 2:
dry battery, bicycle, lemon, pieces, middle, end, metal, into

Exercise 10

Hinweis

Ziel dieses Projekts ist es, dass die S zu Bildern, Postkarten oder Tourismusprospekten aus der eigenen Wohnregion Kurztexte auf Englisch verfassen und präsentieren.

Workbook Intensive Unit 17

Unit 17

Language Focus

Ziel — Die Formen des *Past progressive*, gleichzeitig Repetition der *Past*-Formen von *to be* sowie der *Progressive*-Form.

Mögliche Lösung

I	was	doing	my homework.
you	were	listening	to my new Shakira CD.
he	was	working	in the kitchen.
she	was	watching	a football match on TV.
it	was	freezing	on the Jungfraujoch.
we	were	having	our dinner.
you	were	playing	tennis.
they	were	repairing	their bikes.

Exercise 1

Hinweise / Ideen — Dieses Exercise hat zwei Ziele: erstens die praktische Anwendung des *Language Focus*-Themas und zweitens die Verständniskontrolle des *Focus*-Textes. Es wird nur nach *Past progressive*-Formen gefragt.
Die S vervollständigen den Text mündlich oder schriftlich in EA. Wird der Text in erster Linie mündlich angegangen, können die S versuchen, die Sätze ohne Denkpausen direkt zu lesen. Je nach Leistungsstärke kann den S dazu im Vorfeld kurz Zeit zum stillen (mündlichen) Studium eingeräumt werden.

Lösung — *The gangsters were not expecting the police. Carla del Monte was listening to music on her discman. Steve "the Thinker" King was reading the novel "Crime and Punishment".
The Galton Brothers were playing monopoly. Averell Galton was very angry. He said: "It's not fair, I was winning for the first time in my life." There was no shooting because Ramona Zotti was cleaning her machine gun. "Big" Tony Lynch was ironing Ramona's mini-dress. And Johnny "the Bulldozer" Walker was filling smuggled Scotch whisky into bottles.
A policeman said: "He was singing a happy song when we took him to the police car."
Al Bigone and his wife said: "We were watching the news on television." In the hangar, Fred Bull and George Sprite were painting a new number on Al Bigone's aeroplane, and Leonardo da Vicinity was servicing the helicopter when the police arrested them.*

Language Focus

Ziel — Sensibilisierung auf *gleichzeitige Handlungen*, die beide im *Past progressive* stehen, im Kontrast *zu neu eintretender Handlung*, die im *Past simple* steht. Signalwörter sind *while* bzw. *when*. Auf (pro-)gymnasialer Stufe kann L darauf aufmerksam machen, dass die Signalwörter nicht immer ganz zuverlässig sind.

Lösung

Something was going on			when	another thing happened.		
I	was having	lunch	when	my friend	came	into the room.
Carla	was listening	to music	when	the police	went	into Bigone's house.
My friend and I	were making	a lot of noise	when	our teacher	came	into the classroom.

Unit 17 Workbook Intensive

Something was going on			while	another thing was going on.		
I	was ironing	a mini-dress	while	Steve	was	reading a book.
Carla	was listening	to her discman	while	the Galtons	were playing	monopoly.
Fred and George	were painting	a new number	while	Johnny Walker	was filling	bottles with whisky.

Exercise 2

Hinweise / Ideen

Anwendung des *Past simple* und des *Past progressive* in der Gegenüberstellung.
Um den Unterschied deutlich hervorzuheben, die Sätze bzw. Teilsätze jeweils von zwei **S** lesen lassen: **S 1** *Past simple*, **S 2** *Past progressive*.

Lösung

1. Fred Bull and George Sprite were painting a new number while Leonardo da Vicinity was servicing the helicopter.
2. Johnny Walker was singing a song when the police took him to the car.
3. Ramona Zotti was cleaning her machine gun while the Galton Brothers were playing monopoly.
4. Steve King was reading a book while Tony Lynch was ironing Ramona's mini-dress.
5. Mr and Mrs Bigone were watching TV when the police arrested them.
6. Averell Galton was winning for the first time in his life when the police came.

Exercise 3

Hinweise / Ideen

Die **S** entwickeln in PA oder GA einen Dialog, der den vorgegebenen Begriffen entspricht. Hier werden insbesondere die Frageform und die Verneinung geübt. Dieser Dialog kann anschliessend als Rollenspiel aufgeführt werden.

Mögliche Lösung

Watson: Ramona, what were you doing when the police came?
Ramona: I was watching television.
Watson: That's not true. You were cleaning your machine gun.
Tony, what were you doing while the Galton Brothers were playing monopoly?
Tony: I was ironing Ramona's mini-dress.
Watson: Yes, that's true. Carla, what were you doing when the police arrested you?
Carla: I was reading a book.
Watson: That's not true. You weren't reading a book, you were listening to your discman.
Johnny Walker, what were you doing while Fred and George were painting a new number?
Johnny: I was eating pizza.
Watson: That's not true. You weren't eating pizza, you were filling Scotch whisky into bottles.

Erweiterung Rollenspiel

Accusations: **S 1** (wortgewandt) spielt die Rolle der Lehrperson oder einer Chefin / eines Chefs, eine Gruppe von **S** spielt sich selber oder Untergebene. **S 1** macht Vorwürfe im *Past progressive (you were ...ing when I came into the room)*, die angeschuldigten **S** müssen sich verteidigen.

Variation

Bei schwächeren Gruppen zuerst ein Skript schreiben lassen.

Workbook Intensive Unit 17

Exercise 4

Hinweis	Ziel ist die praktische Anwendung der *Past progressive*-Formen in einem Gespräch.
Vorgehen Variante 1	Die S lösen die Aufgabe zuerst in EA (linke Spalte *you*). Dann fragen sie ihren Partner / ihr Partnerin und füllen die rechte Spalte *your partner* in Interviewform aus.
Ausbau	Die Informationen über den Interviewpartner / die Interviewpartnerin schriftlich festhalten.
Variante 2	Die S lösen die Aufgabe zuerst in EA (linke Spalte *you* möglichst wahrheitsgetreu, die rechte Spalte *your partner* als Vermutung. Anschliessend stellen sie die Lösungen vor und vergleichen in PA ihre Annahmen.
Ausbau	Andere Personen und Tageszeiten wählen. (Als mündliche Übung geeignet.)

Exercise 5

Ziel	Die S finden nach dem Lösen der Aufgabe heraus, wer mit dem Mädchen in den grünen Jeans getanzt hat.
Hinweise / Ideen	Es handelt sich um eine Knobelübung, die erleichtert werden kann, wenn die S die Matrix von *page 69* ausfüllen.
Lösung zu a)	1. The partner of the boy in blue shoes wasn't wearing blue jeans. 2. One boy was wearing green shoes, but he wasn't dancing with the girl in green jeans. 3. One girl was wearing read jeans. She wasn't dancing with the boy in red shoes. 4. Her partner wasn't wearing green shoes.

	girl in red jeans	girl in green jeans	girl in blue jeans
boy in red shoes	no (3.)	yes	no
boy in green shoes	no (4.)	no (2.)	yes
boy in blue shoes	yes	no	no (1.)

zu b)	1. Was the girl in the blue jeans dancing with the boy in the red shoes?
	    No, she was dancing with the boy in the green shoes.
	2. Was the partner of the boy in the blue shoes wearing red jeans?
	    Yes, she was. (Oder: His partner was wearing red jeans.)
	3. Was the boy in the green shoes dancing with the girl in blue jeans?
	    Yes, he was. (Oder: His partner was wearing blue jeans.)
	4. Was the partner of the girl in the red jeans wearing green shoes?
	    No, he was wearing blue shoes.
	5. Who was dancing with the girl in green jeans?
	    The boy in the red shoes was dancing with her.
	    (Oder: She was dancing with the boy in the red shoes.)

Exercise 6

Hinweise / Ideen	Erweiterte Memory-Übung: Die S versuchen sich zu erinnern und schreiben, was die Leute auf der Illustration von *Student's Book page 35* gemacht haben. Zusätzlich können an dieser Stelle nochmals alle bisher vorgekommenen Zeitformen wiederholt und geübt werden. Es empfiehlt sich, für die Zeitformen entsprechende Aufhänger vorzugeben: *Present simple = often / every day; Present progressive = at the moment / tonight;* *Past simple = yesterday / last week; Past progressive = yesterday between 6 and 8 / while etc.*

Unit 17   Workbook Intensive

Mögliche Lösung
> *Two people were playing tennis.*
> *A boy and a girl were playing ball.*
> *A child was playing in the sand.*
> *Two men were reading.*
> *A man was sleeping. / A man was listening to the radio.*
> *A child was eating two ice creams.*
> *Two people were kissing.*
> *A woman was eating a big ice cream.*

Exercise 7

Hinweise / Ideen

Die S suchen einzeln oder in Gruppen Informationen zu einem der Stichworte.
Bei *FBI* oder beim Stichwort *Prohibition* müssen wahrscheinlich weitere Stichworte in eine Suchmaschine eingegeben werden, z.B *history* oder *American history*, sofern die S das Internet als Informationsquelle benützen möchten.
Die gefundenen Informationen können illustriert und in Kurzvorträgen präsentiert werden.

Workbook Intensive   Unit 18

Unit 18

Exercise 1

Hinweise / Ideen

Die Tabelle soll den **S** im Laufe von *Unit 18* helfen, die wichtigen Erkenntnisse aus dem *Focus*-Text, den *Trainings* und *Exercises* festzuhalten, um einen Überblick über den Fall zu gewinnen.
Die **S** sollten dementsprechend die neu gewonnenen Informationen in die Tabelle einsetzen.
Als Alternative kann **L** die Tabelle auch mit den **S** im GU ausfüllen.

Mögliche Lösung zu a)

Lady Mottram died sometime between 6.30 and 11 p.m.
The wound was very small.
The murder weapon was a long pointed object. It was nowhere.
A small piece of peppermint leaf was in the wound.
One thermos flask was full of cold peppermint tea.
The television and the reading light were on.
Professor Mottram's reading glasses were lying on the table.
Ms Witherspoon and Archibald Plumley were watching a film in the Cinema between 7.45 p.m. and 11.30 p.m.
Professor Mottram didn't like his cousin.
He is a professor of anatomy. He needs money. He was working all evening.

zu b)

Time	I. Witherspoon	from	Basil Mottram	from	A. Plumley	from
until 7.45 p.m.	serving tea to Lady M.	Focus	reading the newspaper	2nd Step	working for his exams	3rd Step
8 until 9 p.m.	going to the cinema	Focus	writing some letters	2nd Step	going to the cinema	3rd Step
after 11.30 p.m.	was sleeping	Focus	was sleeping	2nd Step	–	–
7 a.m.	cleaning the hall, carrying the milk bottles	Focus	heard the television	2nd Step	shaving	3rd Step
9 a.m.	talking to Inspector Bradley	Focus	talking to Detective Hopkins	2nd Step	talking to Inspector Bradley	3rd Step

Language Focus

Ziel

Repetition der Verbformen in verschiedenen Tempusformen mit Anwendungshinweisen.
Die **S** können den *Language Focus* zur besseren Übersicht kolorieren. Beispiel:
die Kästchen links mit zwei verschiedenen hellen Farben, die Kästchen rechts mit den entsprechenden dunklen Farben: links = Tatsachen *(facts)*, rechts = Handlung *(action)*; oben = Gegenwart *(present)*, unten = Vergangenheit *(past)*

Present simple   *at present, general fact*
Anwendung   - allgemeine Tatsachen
                            - Beschreibung von routinemässigen Handlungen

Present continuous   *going on at the moment*
Anwendung   Tätigkeiten oder Vorgänge, die zum Gesprächszeitpunkt im Ablaufen begriffen sind.

Simple past — *past (fact)*
Anwendung
- abgeschlossene Handlungen in der Vergangenheit
- aufeinander folgende Handlungen in der Vergangenheit
(z.B. Geschichte in der Vergangenheit: *He opened a bottle of milk, filled a glass and drank it.*)

Past continuous — *period of time in the past*
Anwendung
- länger andauernde Handlung in der Vergangenheit
- zwei parallel ablaufende Handlungen in der Vergangenheit
(... while ...)
- andauernde Handlung, die durch eine neueintretende Handlung unterbrochen wird (... when ...)

Lösung

... at present, general fact			... going on at the moment			
I	live	in Olten.	I	am	learning	English.
He	works	in an office.	He	is	working	on a new book.
She	watches	the nine o'clock news.	She	is	reading	the newspaper.
It	rains	a lot in Scotland.	It	is	raining	now.
We	go	by train or by car.	We	are	sitting	in the classroom.
You	do	the housework everyday.	You	are	eating	breakfast at the moment.
They	read	the NZZ.	They	are	wearing	jeans.

... past (fact)			... period of time in the past			
I	went	to the cinema last night.	I	was	doing	my homework between 8 and 9.
He	played	tennis last Saturday.	He	was	playing	basketball all day.
She	watched	TV in the evening.	She	was	talking	to her friend Margaret on the phone.
It	killed	Lady Mottram immediately.	It	wasn't	burning	this morning.
We	bought	food for the party.	We	were	watching	TV between 9 and 11 p.m.
You	went	straight to bed at 11.30 p.m. last night.	You	were	working	between 11 p.m. and 6.30 a.m.
They	lost	a lot of money.	They	were	playing	football between 2 and 5 p.m. on Sunday.

Workbook Intensive Unit 18

Exercise 2

Ziel Repetition der Verbformen

Hinweise / Ideen Wie *Exercises 4* und *6* ist dies eine Übung, die von den S gelöst werden kann, sobald die nötige Information vorliegt. Sie gibt zudem Auskunft über die Protagonisten dieses Mordfalls.

Lösung

Lady Penelope Mottram
didn't go, didn't have, didn't hear, was, wanted, were staying
Der Text steht im *Past tense* (Lady Mottram ist bereits tot), der Schlusssatz im *Past progressive* (andauernde Handlung in der Vergangenheit).

Isabella Witherspoon
is, is working, was looking, worked, was not, got
Der Text enthält verschiedene Zeitformen.

Professor Basil Mottram
is, gets, was, doesn't teach, is writing, needs
Der Text enthält verschiedene Zeitformen.

Archibald Plumley
is, is, is working, didn't get, likes, isn't, loses, was living (lived), liked
Der Text enthält verschiedene Zeitformen.

Exercise 3

Hinweise / Ideen Die S arbeiten mit einem Notizblock, um die Fragen im *Second Step* ab Tonband zu beantworten. (Vorschläge für das Vorgehen siehe Anmerkungen zum *Second Step* im *Teacher's Book*, Seite 53).

Lösung
1. No, he didn't, because she wanted to leave her money to Greenpeace and the WWF.
2. Yes, they were, but they only said "Good morning" etc.
3. Professor Mottram was reading the newspaper. Then he was writing some letters and he was working on his new book. At 11 p.m. he made himself a cup of tea in the kitchen and then went to bed.
4. When he heard Lady Mottram's television, he put on his stereo and listened to Mozart music. After 9 p.m., he heard Lady Mottram say to Archibald: "Bring me a cup of hot peppermint tea, please."
5. Because he heard the television at seven o'clock in the morning.
6. He was eating his breakfast in the dining room.
7. No, he didn't. He called the police.

Exercise 4

Hinweise / Ideen Es handelt sich bei dem Text um eine Zusammenfassung des Verhörs *(Training Second Step)* mit einigen Fehlern, die Detective Hopkins dabei gemacht hat. S sollten diese nach dem Anhören des Verhörs *(Training Second Step)* oder gegebenenfalls mit Hilfe des Skripts zum Tonband herausfinden. Die einfachste Variante ist, dass die S zuerst den fehlerhaften Text lesen, anschliessend stückweise den Dialog anhören und die Fragen zum *Training Second Step* beantworten. (Siehe Varianten zum *Training Second Step*.)

Lösung zu b) Detective Hopkins hat drei Fehler gemacht:
1. Professor Mottram woke up at seven o'clock, not at six.
2. He heard the television, not the radio.
3. He was eating breakfast, he was not reading the paper.
(Detective Hopkins erwähnt in seinem Report nicht, dass sich Professor Mottram vor dem Einschlafen einen Tee gemacht hat.)

Unit 18 — Workbook Intensive

Exercise 5

Hinweise / Ideen

In diesem *Exercise* ergibt sich die Möglichkeit, Frageformen und den Gebrauch von Fragewörtern zu repetieren.
PA: **S 1** stellt **S 2** die *Open questions* von *Exercise 5A*, die mit den vorliegenden Stichwörtern formuliert werden müssen. **S 2** gibt die Antworten anhand der Stichwörter auf dem eigenen Blatt (in ganzen Sätzen) und stellt dann seinerseits die *Open questions* von *Exercise 5B*. Zuerst sollten die **S** die Fragen unter *Open questions* ausarbeiten.

Mögliche Lösung

5A Why did / does Professor Mottram need money? He can't publish his book (without money).
Why did / does Archibald Plumley need money? He has got money problems because he often plays poker.
Why did Prof. Mottram think (that) Plumley was working all evening? Because there was a light in Plumley's room all evening.
When did Professor Mottram lose his reading glasses? He lost them last night.
5B (from) When (until when) did Lady Mottram talk to a friend? (She was talking to a friend) between 7.40 and 8.10 p.m.
When did she die? She died between 7 and 11 p.m.
Who gets money from Lady Mottram? How much do they get?
Plumley gets £100,000, Prof. Mottram gets £100,000, Isabella Witherspoon gets £10,000 and the rest goes to Greenpeace.
Did Plumley and Witherspoon watch a film in the cinema? Yes, the doorman saw them.

Exercise 6

Hinweise / Ideen

Da das Wort für die Mordwaffe den **S** nicht geläufig sein dürfte, wird es in dieser Übung eingeführt. Die *clues* sind auch nützlich, wenn man sich den Fall noch einmal vor Augen führen will.

Lösung

winter, object, reading glasses, cold, Earl Grey, peppermint.
Von oben nach unten ergibt sich das Wort *icicle* (Eiszapfen).

Exercise 7

Hinweise / Ideen

Die **S** sollen mit den Informationen, die sie bisher gewonnen und in *Exercise 1* festgehalten haben, versuchen, den Täter zu ermitteln.

Wichtig

Wird in der Tabelle das *Simple present* gebraucht, muss bei den ausformulierten Sätzen das *Simple past* verwendet werden.
Steht die *-ing*-Form, so ist das *Past progressive* zu verwenden.

Mögliche Lösung

Person	Liked / didn't like Lady Mottram	Motive for killing Lady Mottram?	Alibi? For what time?
Isabella Witherspoon	didn't like her	no	cinema, 8 until 11.30 p.m.
Prof. Basil Mottram	didn't like her	Yes, he needs money.	no
Archibald Plumley	liked her	Yes, he needs money.	cinema, 8 until 11.30 p.m.

Professor Mottram killed her.
He wanted her money because he wanted to publish a book about heart problems.
He didn't like her.
The murder weapon was an icicle.
(Die **S** können das Wort aus *Exercise 6* ableiten.)

Workbook Intensive   Unit 18

Exercise 8

Hinweise / Ideen   Für alle diese Detektive gibt es Websites. Sie können durch die Eingabe folgender Suchbegriffe gefunden werden: *detective+fiction* „Name des Detektives".
Mit den Informationen und Bildern dieser Websites können die S einzeln oder in Gruppen kurze schriftliche Porträts zusammenstellen, die im Schulzimmer für die Lektüre der ganzen Klasse aufgelegt werden.

Unit 19

Exercise 1

Hinweise / Ideen
zu a) Es handelt sich hier um eine Übung zum Testen des Lese-/Hörverständnisses. Die S können den Text einzeln oder in Gruppen zu entziffern versuchen.

zu b) Als weitere Aufgabe versuchen die S zu beschreiben, was das Problem beim Scannen war.

Lösung Siehe *Student's Book page 50*.

Language Focus

Thema Ausdrücken verschiedener Grade von Unsicherheit mit den modalen Hilfsverben *may, might, could* und *can't* (negative Sicherheit).

Mögliche Lösung
zu a)

He	may	be	at home in bed.
He	may	be	at the doctor's.
He	may	have	a game with the football team.

He	may	be	on a holiday.
He	may	be	late.

zu b)

Andy	might	be	on his way to school now.
His bus	might	be	late.
He	could	be	in bed.

zu c)

"Andy	can't	be	at home because I just tried to phone and nobody answered."

Exercise 2

Ideen / Hinweise Eine Einsetzübung für modale Hilfsverben, lösbar in EA oder als Hausaufgabe. Möchte man auf die mögliche Auswahl der Modalverben besonderes Gewicht legen, kann die Übung in PA/GA angegangen werden mit dem Ziel, zu besprechen (evtl. auf Deutsch), welches Modalverb welche Wirkung hat oder hätte.

Wie bei allen modalen Hilfsverben hängt hier die Auswahl bis zu einem gewissen Grad von der Sicherheit des Sprechers / der Sprecherin ab, wie gut der gemachte Ratschlag ist.

Lösung zu a)
can
mustn't, could
can, could, should

zu b) *would, might, shouldn't, can*

Exercise 3

Thema Diese Übung behandelt das modale Hilfsverb *may* zum Ausdruck einer Möglichkeit; zu lösen ist sie als Hausaufgabe oder in stiller EA.

Als Alternative kann die Übung zuerst mündlich gelöst werden. S 1 wählt einen der gegebenen Sätze, S 2 formuliert ihn um unter Verwendung eines Hilfsverbes. Schnelle S können versuchen, weitere analoge Sätze zu bilden.

Workbook Intensive Unit 19

Lösung
> 1. Madonna *may / could* have plans for another film.
> 2. There *may / could* be more people under 18 in China than there are in Europe.
> 3. Mobile phones *may / could* make it easier to make friends.
> 4. Teachers *may* not always see when pupils cheat in a test.
>   (*could* funktioniert im negativen Satz nicht.)
> 5. It *may / could* rain in the morning, the sun *may / could* shine for an hour, then a strong wind *may / could* start to blow

Exercise 4

Thema Repetition von *would like* zum Ausdruck von Wünschen und Präferenzen.

Hinweise / Ideen zu a) Zuerst EA, dann PA. Wenn die S nicht von selbst Gründe angeben, kann L nachfragen.

zu b) als PA-Interview

Exercise 5

Hinweise / Ideen Es ist sinnvoll zu betonen, dass sowohl *can* als auch *may* gebraucht werden können, um auszudrücken, dass etwas möglich oder erlaubt ist. Da *may* eher formell ist, könnte die Übung zuerst den Inhalt einer möglichen Tafel wiedergeben, dann mit *can* die mündliche Information formulieren.

Als Referenz können die Verbotstafeln von Band 1, *Unit 7, Third Step,* gezeigt werden.

Mögliche Lösung
> In my dream park ...
> ... I can / may swim in the little lake.
> ... I can / may use my mountain bike on the grass.
> ... I can / may bring my own food and have a big picnic.
> ... I can / may play table tennis on the restaurant tables.
> ... etc.

Language Focus

Thema Hier geht es um verschiedene Formen, Ratschläge zu erteilen. Der Gebrauch des Hilfsverbes hängt von der Beziehung zwischen Sprecher/in und Hörer/in ab.

Lösung zu a) *Nancy's mother: C;   Kim, a friend of Nancy's: A;   Nancy's volleyball coach: B*

zu b)

Affirmative	
A friendly form of advice:	You should learn the words.
A strong form of advice:	You have to learn the words.
A very strong form of advice:	You must learn the words.

Negative	
A friendly form of advice:	You shouldn't smoke cigarettes.
A strong form of advice:	You may not smoke cigarettes.
A very strong form of advice:	You mustn't smoke cigarettes.

Unit 19　　　　　　　　　　　　　　　　　　　　　　　　　　　　Workbook Intensive

Exercise 6

Thema　Anwendung des *Language Focus;* Ratschläge geben in immer offenerem Rahmen.

Hinweise / Ideen zu a)　Aus den Elementen sollen Verhaltensregeln geformt werden.

zu b)　Die S sollen sich (evtl. in PA) eigene Regeln einfallen lassen.

Lösung
1. – b) … *you should put some cotton wool into your ears.*
2. – c) … *you should get a phone card.*
3. – e) … *you shouldn't drink any coffee.*
4. – f) … *you should switch off your CD player.*
5. – d) … *you should buy some white wine.*
6. – g) … *you should check your schoolbag.*
7. – a) … *you should see a doctor.*

Exercise 7

Thema　Beziehungen zwischen Geschwistern

Hinweise / Ideen zu a)　Im ersten Hördurchgang sollen die S nur auf die Namen achten und diese anhand der Hinweise bei den Pfeilen einsetzen.

zu b)　Im zweiten Durchgang sollen auch noch die fehlenden Wörter (Linien) eingesetzt werden.

zu c)　Kann in Form eines kleinen Aufsatzes als Hausaufgabe gelöst werden.

Skript

Fiona: I often have fights with my brothers and my sister. I share a room with her. But she always makes …
Marge: You share a room with whom?
Fiona: With my sister Debbie. She always makes such a mess, and I have to clean it up. My older brother sometimes beats me, but when he does, I bite him. [Pause] I really like my other brother.
Marge: Is he older too?
Fiona: Mike? No, he's younger. When I'm in my room with my sister he often comes in. I think he wants to talk to us, but in the end he just terrorises Debbie. I don't know why.
Marge: Perhaps he doesn't like your sister as much as he likes you?
Fiona: Maybe. Yes, that could be true. But there's something else: a week ago they had a terrible fight in our room. They broke my lamp.
Marge: Who had a fight?
Fiona: Mike and Debbie.
Marge: And what did your older brother do?
Fiona: Patrick? Well, he stopped them. He helped me to repair the lamp.
Marge: I see. Well, Patrick seems to be a pretty helpful brother. Listen, Fiona, why don't you ask your sister if she …

Lösung zu a)　*Debbie, Patrick, Mike*

Workbook Intensive Unit 19

zu b)

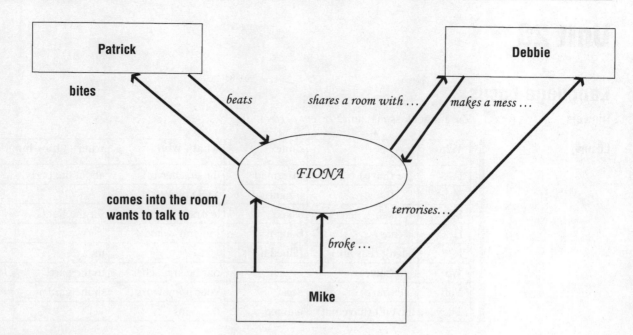

Exercise 8

Thema Besprechen von Ge- und Verboten, basierend auf Schuluniformregeln.

Hinweise / Ideen Als Einstieg kann in der Klasse anhand der Tabelle besprochen werden, welches die Regeln sind.

Die eigentliche Einsetzübung kann anschliessend in stiller EA oder als Hausaufgabe gelöst werden.

Mögliche Lösung
1. have to wear, mustn't wear
2. must wear, don't have to wear, may not wear
3. have to wear, doesn't need to be, can be, mustn't come
4. mustn't bring, should be, may be
5. don't need to wear, mustn't wear

Exercise 9

Thema Ausformulierung von Verbotstafeln mit Modalverben

Hinweise / Ideen Als einfacher Text, eventuell als Hausaufgabe.

Darauf hinweisen, dass sich hinter der -ing-Form das Hauptverb versteckt, das im Modalsatz verwendet werden muss.

Exercise 10

Thema Praktische schriftliche Anwendung der modalen Hilfsverben

Hinweise / Ideen zu a) In Form eines kleinen Aufsatzes als Hausaufgabe lösen; die Aufsätze müssen von L am Platz korrigiert werden, bevor sie eingesammelt und neu verteilt werden.

zu b) In einer zweiten Phase wird die Klasse in Paare oder Kleingruppen aufgeteilt.
Jede Gruppe erhält zwei bis drei Problembriefe, die sie zu beantworten versucht.
Diese Ratschläge werden wiederum von L korrigiert und dann zusammen mit den Problembriefen im Schulzimmer aufgehängt.
Je nach Klasse ist es wichtig, dass nur die engsten Freunde / Freundinnen (best friends) die Probleme zu sehen bekommen, weil die Chance grösser ist, dass interessante Texte entstehen. Die Texte dürfen auch anonym abgegeben werden. Wenn im Einverständnis mit der Klasse die Texte öffentlich gemacht werden sollen, bietet sich eine Wandzeitung an mit den anonymen Beiträgen (mit Schreibmaschine oder Computer geschrieben).
Als Zusatz können die Problembriefe und die Antworten der Kopiervorlage Nr. 62a und b behandelt werden.

Unit 20

Language Focus

Hinweis Zusammenfassung zum *Present perfect*

Lösung

Who	has	done	what / who	where / how long, etc.
I	've (have)	informed	the teacher	about the party.
You	've (have)	organised	a CD player.	
She	's (has)	asked	her neighbours	for the lights.
He	's (has)	bought	mineral water.	
It	hasn't (has not)	rained a lot		today.
We	've (have)	invited	our head teacher	to the party.
You	've (have)	done	your homework	in the garden.
They	haven't (have not)	painted	the signs	yet.

Exercise 1

Hinweise / Ideen zu a)

Bei diesem *Exercise* handelt es sich um eine Textverständnisübung, bei der möglichst ohne Textvorlage gearbeitet werden sollte, und um eine schriftliche Übung zur Vertiefung der Verbformen im *Present perfect*. Die **S** sollen aus der Erinnerung und mit Hilfe der *Use*-Box Sätze im *Present perfect* üben. Das Hauptgewicht liegt noch bei den regelmässigen Verbformen, nur die Perfektform von *buy* ist bei Bedarf vorgängig anzugeben.
Je nachdem, wie intensiv mit dem *Focus*-Text bzw. den *Trainings* im *Student's Book* gearbeitet worden ist, eignet sich das *Exercise* auch als Hörverständnisübung. Vorgehen: Den *Focus*-Text ab Tonträger abspielen oder in irgendeiner Unterrichtsform vortragen. Die **S** ordnen die *prompts* in der *Use*-Box mit 1 (= Roy), 2 (= Penny) und 3 (= Bridget) den Sprecherinnen und Sprechern zu und lösen die Aufgabe dann schriftlich.

zu b) Hier liegt das Gewicht auf den unregelmässigen Verben. Die Übung eignet sich auch als Wettbewerb in PA / GA / GU.

Mögliche Lösung zu a)

1. Roy has asked for dance CDs, he has informed the neighbours about the noise, he has looked for a CD player, he has organised a team to clean up and he has asked Mr Taylor for the barbecue.
2. Penny has asked her dad for the big speakers, she has asked her neighbour for the party lights, but she hasn't got any party decorations yet.
3. Bridget has organised the party decorations, she has bought lots of coloured paper and she has talked to her sister.

zu b)

F	O	R	G	O	T	T	E	N
	B	O	U	G	H	T		
				T	O	L	D	
			F	O	U	N	D	
					G	O	N	E
B	R	O	U	G	H	T		
				G	O	T		

The present of the verb is "think".

Workbook Intensive Unit 20

Exercise 2

Hinweise / Ideen

Die S sollen nicht einfach die Programmpunkte vom Notizzettel abschreiben, sondern sinngemässe eigene Sätze schreiben und die Tätigkeiten den Personen zuordnen (siehe Lösungen). Es empfiehlt sich, im Vorfeld die unregelmässigen Formen *(buy, tell, get)* nochmals in Erinnerung zu rufen.

Dieses *Exercise* eignet sich wiederum als Sprech- und Schreibübung, wobei die S Satz um Satz zuerst mündlich und unmittelbar danach schriftlich ausformulieren. So wird die Zuordnung der Personen zu den Tätigkeiten vorweg mündlich nochmals vergegenwärtigt.

Wichtig

Es muss darauf geachtet werden, dass keine Zeitangaben verwendet werden, weil dann *Past simple* stehen müsste.

Mögliche Lösung

1. *Has Bridget bought decorations?*
2. *Has Roy asked Mr Taylor for his barbecue?*
3. *Has Roy informed the neighbours about the party?*
4. *Has anybody invited the teachers?*
5. *Has Martin told the head teacher about the party?*
6. *Have they organised the cleaning after the party?*
7. *Has anybody painted signs for toilets and the bar?*
8. *Has Penny got party lights for the room?*

Exercise 3

Hinweise / Ideen

Transferübung zum *Present perfect* im Zusammenhang mit Verrichtungen, die erledigt werden müssen. Nachdem die Broschüre in EA / GU vervollständigt worden ist, eignet sich die Übung als PA, aber vor allem auch als *milling exercise*, bei dem die S im Zimmer umhergehen, verschiedene Mitschülerinnen und Mitschüler befragen und die Antworten je nach Leistungsstärke (frei) notieren können. *(Paul has packed his passport, Lena hasn't packed hers. Pascal hasn't packed anything etc.)*

In leistungsschwächeren Klassen können auch die Fragen zuerst schriftlich ausformuliert werden, worauf jeweils nur eine Antwort eingeholt wird.

Auch können die (unregelmässigen) Verbformen im Voraus thematisiert werden.

Erweiterung zu a)

S 1 zeigt pantomimisch, was bereits gemacht wurde, die übrigen S formulieren die entsprechenden Sätze im *Present perfect*. (In Varianten ist diese Übungsform auch nützlich zur Auffrischung des *Past tense* oder des *Present progressive*.)

zu b)

Dieser Teil des *Exercise* kann auch als offenes Rollenspiel gestaltet werden.

Mögliche Lösung zu a)

- *Buy a travel insurance.*
- *Leave your keys with a neighbour.*

Lösung zu b)

Fragen:
1. *Have you turned off all the lights?*
2. *Have you locked all the doors, including the back door?*
3. *Have you emptied and turned off the fridge?*
4. *Have you found someone to water the plants?*
5. *Have you given someone your holiday address?*
6. *Have you packed a first-aid kit?*
7. *Have you bought a travel insurance?*
8. *Have you left your keys with a neighbour?*

Unit 20 — Workbook Intensive

Exercise 4

Hinweise / Ideen

Dieses *Exercise* ist mit dem *Third Step* im *Student's Book* gekoppelt und bietet eine Notizfläche zur Lösung der Hörverständnisübung.
Je nachdem, wie intensiv die Übung im *Student's Book* bereits mündlich angegangen worden ist, kann sie im *Workbook* entweder (vor allem in EA) zur Wiederholung und Festigung eingesetzt werden oder es kann aus der Erinnerung abgehakt, verglichen bzw. kontrolliert und / oder direkt zu b) übergegangen werden.
b) sollte zuerst mündlich in PA/GA, dann schriftlich in EA gelöst werden.

Skript

Hello, is that Duke's Drinks Delivery? ...
- Yes. I've got a problem here. We're going to have a party tonight and we didn't think of the drinks. I know it's a little late, but I was wondering if you would be able to deliver some drinks?
- Yes, that's right, for tonight. In an hour? That's great!
- Well, we're going to need some soft drinks, let's say about ten bottles of Coke.
- Yes, that's right. And some water, mineral water, ten bottles, too. No, that's too much. Let's say six.
- Mhm. And then some fruit juice. Orange juice of course, five bottles, some apple juice and some grape juice. Five bottles each.
- Tomato juice? Yes, that's a good idea. Put in three bottles.
- Peanuts? Yes, of course we need peanuts. Let's say five bags. And we need some milk because we're going to make milkshakes.
- Oh, that's too bad. Well, we'll have to go and get it ourselves. Never mind. That's all for the moment.
- Well, umh, can I pay by credit card? Do you accept Visa?
- Okay, the name's Henry J. Bonner, B - O - double N - E - R. ... –
Yes, and the number is 381-7365-035.
- That's right. Thank you very much.
- Oh, the address? It's 78 Pine Grove Drive. That's near Poplar just north of Main Street. There's a garage on the corner ...

Lösung zu a)

Martin has ordered	true	false
- ten bottles of Coke	x	
- some mineral water.	x	
- four kinds of fruit juice.	x	
- peanuts and crisps	x	
- tea and coffee.		x
- milk for milkshakes.		x
- party decorations.		x

zu b)

Martin has only ordered peanuts, no crisps. He hasn't ordered tea and coffee, and he hasn't ordered any milk, because Duke doesn't sell milk. Martin hasn't ordered any party decorations.

Workbook Intensive Unit 20

Language Focus

Thema Gebrauch des *Present perfect* und des *Simple past*

Lösung

Has somebody done it? ☑	When did … do it? 🕐
I've done my homework.	I did it yesterday evening.
He's put all the clothes away.	He put them away this morning.
She's made her bed.	She made it two minutes ago.
Have you brought a barbecue grill?	Yes, I brought it last Monday.
Penny has got the party decorations.	She got them two days ago.
Bridget has bought coloured paper.	She bought them yesterday.
They have told the head teacher about it.	They told it last Wednesday.
You have taken out the empty bottles.	You took them out today.
She's found some comfortable chairs.	She found them this afternoon.
Martin's gone to order some drinks.	He went to order them an hour ago.
Have you seen Roy?	Yes, I saw him this afternoon.
He's forgotten to order them.	He forgot to order the food last year.
Has Penny given back the CDs?	Yes, she gave them back yesterday.
She has read three Harry Potter books.	She read them last summer.
Mary has had a hair cut.	She had it a week ago.
She has been at Figaro's.	She was there a week ago.

Exercise 5

Hinweise / Ideen zu a) Die Fragen werden in EA schriftlich oder mündlich kurz vorbereitet und anschliessend mündlich formuliert. Dazu eignet sich vor allem der GU: Die S formulieren zuerst die Frage, halten dann kurz inne, um allen Zeit für die Antworten im Kopf zu geben, dann wird jemand aufgerufen. So wird die *ganze* Klasse gezwungen mitzudenken; wird der Name der / des S der Frage vorangestellt, fällt diese Intensität weg.

Ausbau Die Dialoge können auch sketchartig aufgeführt werden; dabei die Fragen und evtl. auch die Antworten entsprechend scharf, provokativ, laut, verdattert, mit einem Akzent usw. sprechen.

zu b) Hier geht es um die Gegenüberstellung von *Present perfect* und *Simple past*.

Für *ooops* kann entweder eine Ausrede gefunden oder es können die Formen von *forget* eingesetzt bzw. eingeführt werden.

Varianten Man teilt die Klasse in zwei örtlich getrennte Gruppen im Klassenraum. Die eine Gruppe spricht die Sätze im *Present perfect*, die andere die Sätze im *Simple past*. Diese chorartige Gegenüberstellung macht den Unterschied zwischen den beiden Tempusformen und ihrem Gebrauch deutlicher.

Ausbau Entschuldigungen oder Ausreden finden (Achtung: wenn nötig ins *Simple past* wechseln!)

Mögliche Lösung zu a)
1. *Have you cleaned the fridge?*
2. *Have you told the milkman about our holiday?*
3. *Have you found out Reggie's holiday phone number?*
4. *Have you reserved tickets for the cinema festival?*
5. *Have you done the dishes?*
6. *Have you brought the empty bottles back to the supermarket?*
7. *Have you bought a box of printer paper?*
8. *Have you phoned the garage about the car?*

Unit 20

Workbook Intensive

zu b)

> He has told the milkman about their holiday. He told him early this morning.
> He has found out Reggies holiday phone number. He found out three days ago.
> He hasn't bought a box of printer paper.
> He has done the dishes from yesterday's party. He did them yesterday after the party.
> He has forgotten to phone the garage about the car.
> He has brought the empty bottles back to the supermarket. He brought them back yesterday when he went shopping for the party.
> He has reserved tickets for the cinema festival. He has phoned the booking office on May 16.

Exercise 6

Hinweise / Ideen

Der Einsatz dieser Übung im Unterricht hängt davon ab, wie die bisherigen Übungen angegangen worden sind und ob L das Gewicht auf Mündlichkeit oder Schriftlichkeit, auf eine nochmalige Trainingsphase oder auf eine Anwendungsphase legt.

Lösung zu a)

> Have you ever eaten frog's legs? When did you eat frog's legs?
> Have you ever climbed a mountain? When did you climb this mountain?
> Have you ever gone to America? When did you go there?
> Have you ever stayed in a haunted house? When did you stay in this house?
> Have you ever lived outside Switzerland? When did you live outside Switzerland?
> Have you ever met a famous person? When did you meet this person?
> Have you ever travelled more than a hundred kilometres by bike? When did you travel more than a hundred kilometres by bike?

Exercise 7

Ziel

Angemessenes Reagieren auf einen situativen Input.

Hinweise / Ideen zu a)

Es können mehrere Möglichkeiten genannt / verlangt werden, evtl. auch nach dem Motto *Wer liefert in 1 Minute die meisten sinnvollen Möglichkeiten?*. Andere Möglichkeit: Die Klasse soll versuchen, jeweils mindestens 5, 8 oder 10 Sätze zu finden.

zu b)

Die Bilder können auch als Anlass zu Kurzgeschichten (in einem Beiheft niederschreiben) dienen.

Mögliche Lösung zu a)

> I have drunk the milk.
> I have eaten the sausages.
> Forgive me! I have broken the glass.

zu b)

> 1. We're very sorry. We've broken the garage window. We were just playing football.
> 2. I've moved your moped. It shouldn't stand in front of the shop window.
> 3. Sandra! You're late. We've gone to the Queen's Hotel already.
> 4. We've enjoyed ourselves. Thanks!

Exercise 8

Hinweise / Ideen

Dieses *Exercise* ist an *Time for a Change* im *Student's Book* gekoppelt. Die S sollten möglichst ungestört in EA am Test im *Student's Book* arbeiten, sich die Buchstaben der für sie zutreffenden Antworten notieren und erst nach Beendigung des Tests die Punktzahl im *Workbook* nachschlagen. An die Auswertung kann sich eine informelle Diskussion über Cliquen oder evtl. Banden im Dorf, im Quartier oder in der Schule anschliessen.

Exercise 9

Hinweise / Ideen

Je nach Umfeld kann dieses Projekt in mehreren Klassen, im ganzen Schulhaus und für Eltern durchgeführt oder gar zu einer fächerübergreifenden Projektwoche ausgebaut werden. Dies bedarf einer seriösen Vorbereitung und muss längerfristig geplant werden.

Revision Workshop 4

Allgemeine Hinweise zu den *Revision Workshops*, zu Aufbau, Arbeitsweise und Kontrolle siehe die Ausführungen beim *Revision Workshop 3*, S. 145.

Übersicht über den Revision Workshop 4

	Station (Topic)	Sprachliche Struktur	Arbeitsform	Vorbereitung durch L / Material
1.	*Verb Forms Drill*	Verschiedene Zeitformen in vollständigen Sätzen	EA	—
2.	*Story*	Das *Simple past* regelmässiger und unregelmässiger Verben. Die Übung ist von a) nach c) progressiv aufgebaut.	EA	—
3.	*Writing*	*Present progressive*	EA	— (evtl. Zusatzheft)
4.	*Interview*	*Simple present, Simple past, Present progressive und Past progressive*	PA / GA, vor allem mündlich	Zur mündlichen Vorbereitung: Die beiden Seiten kopieren, die Kärtchen mit den *prompts* ausschneiden und verteilen. Bei mündlicher Durchführung erfolgt die Kontrolle durch L.
5.	*Reading*	Textverständnis	EA	Vorbereitung evtl. mündlich mit Hilfe der Grundrisse als Folienkopie
6.	*Listening – Numbers*	Hörverständnis, speziell Ziffern und Zahlen	EA	—
7.	*Discussion*	Modale Hilfsverben	EA / PA / GA	—

Revision Workshop 4   **Workbook Intensive**

Station Verb Forms Drill

Lösung

> I don't go to football matches.
> We are going to football matches.
> Peter went to football matches.
> Where they going to football matches?
> Have you gone to football matches?

> Does Jenny buy a lot of chewing gum?
> Are you buying a lot of chewing gum?
> We bought a lot of chewing gum.
> I was not buying a lot of chewing gum.
> Paul has bought a lot of chewing gum.

> Does Carol go to school by bus?
> I'm not going to school by bus.
> We went to school by bus.
> Was Marty going to school by bus?
> Have you gone to school by bus?

> John makes a cup of tea.
> I'm making a cup of tea.
> Did they make a cup of tea?
> Were you making a cup of tea?
> Dad has made a cup of tea.

> You tell the neighbours about the party.
> I'm not telling the neighbours about the party.
> Did Joan tell the neighbours about the party?
> They were not telling the neighbours about the party.
> We haven't told the neighbours about the party.

> I don't read an interesting story.
> Is Carl reading an interesting story?
> We didn't read an interesting story.
> Joe was not reading an interesting story.
> Have you read an interesting story?

> I don't bring dance CDs to school.
> Are you bringing dance CDs to school?
> Did we bring dance CDs to school?
> Joe was bringing dance CDs to school.
> Have you brought dance CDs to school?

Station Story

Lösung zu a)
> was, died, wrote, was, was, was, didn't have, had, was, lived, was, was, became, loved, was, asked, was left, went, came, went, was, lived, worked, had, wanted, went, was, didn't want, threw, went, disappeared, didn't want, left

zu b)
> lived, studied, heard, is, thought, heard, forgot, were, tried, went, saw, was, talked, said, was, helped, went, forgot, went, was, were, thought, was

Mögliche Lösung zu c)
> wrote, told, waited, got, was, said, was, said, was, went, told, was, had, went, met, said, worked, wanted, went, saw, took, went, found, fell, got, had, was, wrote

Workbook Intensive   **Revision Workshop 4**

Station Writing

Mögliche Lösung zu a)   A cat is sitting under a tree. The cat is watching the bird. A bird is flying. The bird is building a nest.

zu b)   A man is opening an envelope. A woman is working at the computer. The boss is drinking coffee.

zu c)   Two boys are talking. Some girls are playing volleyball. One boy is eating a banana. A girl is reading a book. zu d) A boy is running. His ball is rolling away from him. A lorry is coming up the street.

Station Interview

Lösung

Partner A	Partner B
Questions	Answers
1. watch	
What do you usually watch?	I usually watch the News.
What are you watching at the moment?	I'm watching Eurosports at the moment.
What did you watch last Sunday?	I watched the Flintstones last Sunday.
What were you watching yesterday between 8 and 9 p.m.?	I was watching SF2 yesterday between 8 and 9 p.m.
2. read	
What do you normally read?	I normally read the newspaper.
What were you reading last night at around 9 p.m.?	I was reading an English text yesterday around 9 p.m.
What are you reading now?	I'm reading a horror story at the moment.
What did you read last month?	I read A Day in the Life of Frederic the Cat last month.
3. go	
Were you going to the disco when I saw you?	No, I was going to hockey practice when you saw me.
Where do you usually go on Saturday night?	I often go to the cinema.
Where are you going now?	I'm going home right now.
Did you go to the cinema last Saturday?	No, I didn't. Last Saturday, I went to the football match.

Revision Workshop 4 — Workbook Intensive

Partner B — Questions	Partner A — Answers
1. eat	
Did you eat an apple yesterday?	No, I didn't. I ate a banana yesterday.
Are you eating right now?	Yes, I'm eating an apple now.
What do you normally eat for lunch?	I usually eat a sandwich for lunch.
Were you eating last night between 11 and 12 p.m.?	No, I wasn't eating. I was sleeping between 11 and 12 p.m.
2. play	
Are you playing with your gameboy now?	No, I'm not playing with my gameboy at the moment.
Do you play the guitar?	No, I don't. I play the piano.
Did you play at the school sports day last year?	Yes, I played basketball at the school sports day last year.
What were you playing on Saturday between 9 and 10 a.m.?	I was playing tennis on Saturday between 9 and 10 a.m.
3. phone	
Do you usually phone your friends in Lausanne?	I phone them every Sunday.
Were you phoning somebody yesterday between 9 and 10?	No, I wasn't. My brother was phoning his girlfriend between 9 and 10 yesterday.
Did you phone your teacher from home yesterday?	No, I didn't. I phoned him / her from a phonebox yesterday.
Are you phoning your grandmother at the moment?	No. I'm phoning my uncle at the moment.

Workbook Intensive

Station Reading
Lösung

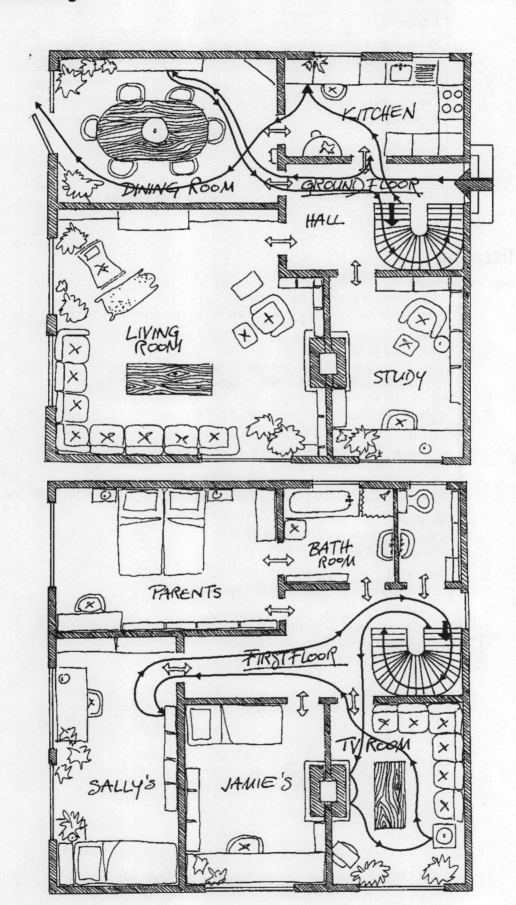

Revision Workshop 4 — Workbook Intensive

Station Listening – Numbers

Skript

Attractions	Prices
Motor coach sightseeing tour	$A 20 half day; $A 38 full day
Cruise on Sydney Harbour	$A 18 to $A 75
Theatre ticket	$A 13 to $A 58, depending on seats
Concert, opera and ballet ticket	$A 15 to $A 95, depending on seats
Rock concert ticket	$A 22 to $A 49, depending on group
Ticket to a movie	$A 8.50
Entrance to museums	Free to $A 4.50
Entrance to art gallery	Free to $A 5.30
Entrance to Sydney Tower	adults $A 5; children $A 1.50

Station Discussion

Mögliche Lösung

should
– You should try to talk to your teachers.
– You should ask the head teacher for the reasons for some of the rules.

could
– You could go on strike.
– You could ask your parents for help.
– You could organise a protest demonstration.
– You could write to a newspaper.
– On one day you could all wear jeans and leather jackets.

have to
– You have to get out when nobody is watching.
– You have to listen to a discman.
– You have to chew gum when nobody is watching.
– You have to tell the head teacher your names.

shouldn't
– You shouldn't run away from school.
– You shouldn't phone the police.

don't need
– You don't need to write to Amnesty International.

mustn't
– You mustn't smoke in the toilets.
– You mustn't go to cafes before school.

Inhaltsverzeichnis

Kopiervorlagen

Anweisungen			**185**
Unit 11	1	Fill in the Gaps I	**187**
	2	Fill in the Gaps II	
	3	Verb Training	
	4	History Quiz	
Unit 12	5	Two Days in November	**191**
	6	Fill in the Gaps	
	7	Verb Training I	
	8	Verb Training II	
	9	Question Cards	
	10	Verb Diagram	
	11	Verb Bingo	
	12a	The Past Crossword	
	12b	Verb Cards	
	13	The Club of Dead Rock'n'Roll Stars	
Unit 13	14	A School Fete	**201**
	15	Check Your Vocabulary!	
	16a	Questions and Answers	
	16b	Questions and Answers	
	17	True or False?	
	18	Dialogue Snap	
	19	What Are You Doing?	
	20	Verb Training	
Unit 14	21a	Fill in the Gaps	**209**
	21b	Fill in the Gaps	
	22	Verb Training	
	23	Script: The White Lady	
	24	The White Lady	
	25	The Phantom on the Wall	
	26	Shadows	
Revision Workshop 3	27	Control Sheet Revision Workshop Basic	**216**
	28	Control Sheet Revision Workshop Intensive	
Unit 15	29	Map of Australia	**218**
	30	Yes or No?	
	31	Fill in the Gaps I	
	32	Fill in the Gaps II	
	33	Switzerland Quiz Partner A and B	
	34	Cue Cards: Nonsense Comparisons	
	35a	The Island Quartet	
	35b	The Island Quartet	
	35c	The Island Quartet	
	36	Australia Quiz	
	37	Quiz	
	38	World Records	
	39a	Everybody Knows That …	
	39b	Everybody Knows That …	

Inhaltsverzeichnis

Unit 16	40	Fill in the Gaps	**232**
	41	Is this Text Correct?	
	42	Match the Questions and the Answers	
	43	Canada and Switzerland	
	44	The Weather in New Zealand	
	45	Danger – Your Safety?	
Unit 17	46	Fill in the Gaps I	**238**
	47	Fill in the Gaps II	
	48	Fill in the Gaps III	
	49	Is this Text Correct?	
	50	What Were They Wearing?	
Unit 18	51	Fill in the Missing Verbs	**243**
	52	Fill in the Missing Words	
	53	What Are the Correct Questions?	
	54	Questions and Answers	
	55	Script: Second Step	
	56	Puzzle Text	
	57	Three Stories	
Unit 19	58	Fill in the Verbs	**250**
	59	Fill in the Gaps	
	60	What's the Name of the Game?	
	61	The Story of an Escape	
	62a	Can You Help Me?	
	62b	(Can You Help Me?)	
Unit 20	63	What Have They Done?	**256**
	64	Fill in the Gaps	
	65	Kim's Game	
	66	Going to Camp	
Revision Workshop 4	67	Control Sheet Revision Workshop Basic	**266**
	68	Control Sheet Revision Workshop Intensive	

Anweisungen

Nr. 3 / Verb Training
Pro Gruppe ein Set *Verb Training*-Karten verteilen. Die **S** mischen die Karten und bilden einen Stapel. An der Wandtafel die Zeichen: +, ?, und – anbringen. **L** zeigt auf eines der drei Zeichen. Die **S** schreiben den korrekten Satz im *Simple past* für die oberste Karte auf und legen ihn zusammen mit der Verbkarte auf dem Gruppentisch ab. Nachdem alle Karten aufgebraucht sind, untersuchen die **S** die aufliegenden Sätze der anderen Gruppen auf Fehler.

Nr. 7 / Verb Training I
Verfahren wie oben bei Nr. 3 beschrieben oder auch eine Variante wählen: **L** zeigt auf eines der drei Zeichen; die **S** formulieren ihre Sätze in der Gruppe mündlich. Die Kontrolle erfolgt im GU. Anschliessend geben die **S** ihre Karte weiter im Kreis der Gruppe. Andere Möglichkeit: Die **S** arbeiten mit dem ganzen Blatt und formulieren die Sätze von links oben nach rechts unten oder in einer anderen Richtung "Slalom fahrend".

Nr. 9 / Question Cards
Die **S** erhalten je eine Karte, wandern im Zimmer umher und stellen den anderen **S** die auf den Karten formulierten Fragen. Die Antworten lauten entweder kurz *Yes, I did* bzw. *No, I didn't* oder länger, z.B. *Yes, I played football yesterday*, um das Üben der Past-Formen zu intensivieren.

Nr. 10 / Verb Diagram
Mit dieser Vorlage können nochmals die *Present-* und *Past-*Formen im positiven, negativen und Fragesatz geübt werden. **L** nennt dabei ein Verb und zeigt am OHP auf eine leere Position auf dem Blatt, z.B. auf der Seite *Answer* auf die *2nd Person Singular, Past, Verb Positive*. Die **S** schreiben die richtige Verbform hinein.

Nr. 11 / Verb Bingo
Alle **S** haben ein Kärtchen vor sich und kreisen darauf vier Verben ein. **L** nennt nun Verben im *Past simple*. Wer auf seinem Kärtchen das aufgerufene Verb eingekreist hat, kann es streichen. Gewonnen hat, wer zuerst alle eingekreisten Zahlen streichen kann.

Nr. 34 / Cue Cards: Nonsense Comparisons
Die *Cue Cards* kopieren, zerschneiden und in einem Behälter vermischen. PA: Jedes Paar zieht zwei oder vier Karten muss dann einen Vergleich der genannten Gegenstände herstellen, auch wenn das Wortpaar scheinbar nichts Gemeinsames hat. Beispiel: *An island is bigger than a bicycle.* Variante: Das Paar erhält alle *Cue Cards* in einem Couvert, zieht jeweils zwei heraus und formuliert die Vergleichssätze.

Nr. 35 / The Island Quartet
Das Spiel soll die **S** darauf hinweisen, wie vielfältig und weltumspannend die englische Sprachgemeinschaft ist. Im GU versuchen herauszufinden, um welche Inseln es sich handelt. Lösung von oben nach unten: New Zealand, Jamaica, Hawaii, Ireland (Eire).
Die Spielregeln folgen dem bekannten Quartettspiel: Die **S** bilden Vierergruppen. Jede Gruppe erhält ein Spiel von 16 Karten (Vorlagen Nr. 35 b und c). Jeder / jede **S** muss versuchen, von den anderen **S** der Gruppe so schnell wie möglich vier Karten zu der gleichen Insel zu erbeten. Um dies sprachlich auszuweiten, nicht nur sagen *I need New Zealand from …*, sondern mit den fehlenden Informationen auf den Kärtchen arbeiten und den Gebrauch von *have got* repetieren. Der Dialog kann folgendermassen verlaufen: **S 1**: *Have you got the size of Ireland, S 2? S 2: No, I'm sorry, I haven't. – Have you got the size of Jamaica, S 3? S 3: Yes, I have. S 2: How big is Jamaica? S 3: It's 10,991 square kilometres. Here you are.*

Nr. 41 Match the Questions and the Answers
Die **S** bekommen eine Frage oder eine Antwort, lernen sie einigermassen auswendig und machen sich auf die Suche nach der vorhergehenden oder nachfolgenden Antwort bzw. Frage. Einige Kärtchen können mehrmals vorkommen. Anschliessend stellen sich die **S**-Paare oder -Gruppen in der Reihenfolge des Interview-Texts auf und sprechen das Interview in ihrer Version.

Nr. 44 / Danger – Your Safety?
Diese Texte können Collage-artig in ein Beiheft eingetragen werden. Sie eignen sich auch für eine Übersetzung ins Deutsche, die aufzeigen soll, dass nicht wörtlich übersetzt werden darf und dass auch der Satzbau in der einen Sprache stark von dem in der anderen abweicht.

Nr. 56 Puzzle Text
Die **S** nummerieren die Sätze in EA. **S 1** liest den ersten Satz, **S 2** fährt mit dem zweiten Satz fort usw.

Nr. 57 / Three Stories
Die **S** versuchen in GA, die Sätze in der richtigen Reihenfolge den Titeln zuzuordnen. Anschliessend liest jede Gruppe eine Geschichte vor. Der Rest der Klasse beurteilt, ob die Geschichte korrekt zusammengesetzt wurde.
Variante: Die Klasse in drei Gruppen aufteilen. Jeder Gruppe wird ein Titel zugeteilt. Die Gruppen müssen nun versuchen, die Sätze zu ihrem Titel in der richtigen Reihenfolge zu finden.

Nr. 61 / The Story of an Escape
Übung zum Leseverständnis mit Modalverben; Schreibaktivität zur Wiederholung der Vergangenheit.

Nr. 62 / Can You Help Me?
Es handelt sich um etwas gekürzte Texte aus Beratungskolumnen englischer Teenagerzeitschriften. Die Texte unter Kleingruppen verteilen. Textarbeit mit dem

Anweisungen

Wörterbuch. Variante: Die kopierten Anfragen und die Antworten werden einzeln ausgeschnitten. Die S versuchen, die passenden Paare wieder zusammenzufügen.

Nr. 65 / Kim's Game

Von der Vorlage eine Folie anfertigen. Die Gegenstände einzeln ausschneiden und einige davon auf dem OHP präsentieren. L fordert die S auf, sich 30 Sekunden lang die Gegenstände und deren Lage zu merken. Dann wird der OHP ausgeschaltet, L verschiebt Gegenstände oder ersetzt sie durch andere und schaltet den OHP wieder ein. L: *What have I just done?* S: *You've moved the ticket (to the left / right / middle / top / bottom)*. Oder: *You've changed one / two / three pictures*. L: *Which ones?* Hat man viele Gegenstände auf der Folie platziert, sollte man sie nummerieren. S: *You've changed picture number 5, 9 and 13*. Oder: *The tie is new.*

Gegenstände können auch rotiert oder gewendet (Spiegelbild!) werden. Einige Gegenstände in Reserve behalten, so dass auch welche hinzugefügt werden können. Variante: Natürlich können die S das Spiel auch selber in Gruppen spielen, am besten mit realen kleinen Gegenständen (*pen, pencil, scissors, book etc.*), die auf einem Tisch verteilt werden.

Nr. 66 / Going to Camp

Die vier Karten enthalten dieselben Anweisungen in vertauschter Reihenfolge. Jeweils vier S bilden eine Gruppe, jede / jeder erhält eine Karte. Es geht darum, Fragen im *Present perfect* zu bilden und Antworten darauf zu geben. Dabei sollte darauf geachtet werden, dass jede Frage nur einmal gestellt wird. Ziel ist, herauszufinden, was bereits erledigt wurde und was nicht. Noch nicht erledigt wurde lediglich *Make sure the water near the camp site is OK for drinking.*

Fill in the Gaps I

I Madonna

Madonna Louise Ciccone _____ born in Bay City, Michigan, on 16 August 1958.
Her _____ was to be a star and New York _____ a good place for a career in the _____ business.
At first, she was a _____ in a number of dance companies, then she was a background singer.
Her first album "Madonna" (1983) _____ very successful, but her second album "Like a Virgin" (1984) was a big _____.
This was the beginning of her career as an international pop star.
Her videos _____ a bit like short films and her concerts were great shows with dancers and lights and Madonna in a lot of different _____. But were her films a success? No, most of them _____. Her role in the film musical "Evita" _____ bad, but she isn't a great actress. In the early days Madonna was just a singer, but her new videos _____ that she is also a good entertainer.

II U2

It was the _____ 1976, the time of punk and of loud aggressive _____ and a time of young people with no future. Larry Mullen Jr. _____ 14 years old. He lived in Dublin and his interest was music, rock music. He _____ a drummer and he wanted to play in a band. So he _____ around for other musicians at his high school in Dublin. Three students joined him: Paul Hewson (Bono) was a _____, David Evans (The Edge) was a guitarist and Adam Clayton was a bass player.
The new band needed a good _____. A friend suggested U2. Why _____ they like it? Because it sounded like "you, too" or "you two" and it _____ the name of a submarine and a spy plane.
Most punk groups _____ other bands but U2 tried to find a new style. The four school-friends _____ music, but they were also interested in politics.
Their first albums _____ good, but their first big hit was "Sunday, Bloody Sunday" in 1983, a _____ about the conflict in Northern Ireland.
Who _____ to the music of this new Irish band? At first, mostly people from Ireland, but soon people from all over the _____ were interested in U2.
"Pride (In the Name of Love)", a song about the murder of Martin Luther King, was a big success.
_____ their style change in the last years? Yes, experiments with electronic music and dance music _____ important for U2. Not all their fans _____ the changes, but nobody can say that U2 is a boring band.

Fill in the Gaps II

III Elvis Presley

For the Beatles, for Bruce Springsteen and for many _____ people in his days he was "The King". For American parents he was shocking, bad for their _____ and their daughters, a terrible _____ for the clean American life style.
Elvis Aaron Presley _____ in Tupelo, Mississippi in 1935. He was a truck _____.
His first record was "My Happiness", a _____ for his mother's birthday.
Elvis Presley's music was a mixture of black music like gospel and blues and _____ music like Country and Western, and his _____ was aggressive and sexy. Elvis was the _____ really big rock'n'roll star, the _____ teenage rebel ...
In the sixties Presley was a soldier in the US _____. Then, in his later life there _____ problems: his huge success _____ good for him. At the _____ of forty Elvis wasn't a good-looking singer any more. He was very _____. His death in August 1977 was the result of too many cheeseburgers and too many _____.

IV The Beatles

They were _____ young men from Liverpool and they were full of new _____.
Teenagers George Harrison, Paul McCartney, John Lennon and Ringo Starr liked American rock'n'roll. But the beginning wasn't _____: the Beatles started to play in Liverpool, then in Hamburg. They _____ hard and learned a lot. Lennon and McCartney _____ also good songwriters. Back in England they _____ to work with manager Brian Epstein. He liked their music but he also liked the _____ young men and _____ them a lot in their career.
After their _____ single "Love Me Do" almost all their singles were top hits. The sixties were the time of Beatlemania: Teenage girls all over Great _____ and the United States started to go wild at their _____.
In 1966 the Beatles were tired of touring. There was only one more concert in 1969 for the film "Let It Be" but the police _____ that.
For the next four _____ the Beatles released a lot of albums, all different in style and music.
In 1970 there was _____ between Paul McCartney and John Lennon because of Lennon's new wife Yoko Ono. That was the end of the Beatles as a group. In 1980 Mark Chapman killed John Lennon in _____. George Harrison died in 2001.

Verb Training

look schoolbag	watch TV	hate gangster
welcome friend	return 5 o'clock	start training
pass sugar	press button	listen rock music
start match	love soap operas	walk park
play games	answer questions	turn crossing
touch vase	ask way	follow road
look out window	check phone numer	play instrument
wait station	like teacher	brush hair
listen folk songs	hate school	live America

Supplement: Training

(4) Unit 11

History Quiz

Form correct sentences with the prompts and tick the correct box. If a statement is false, write down the correct answer in a short sentence.

	True	False
Terrorists / destroy / the World Trade Center / in 1998.	☐	☐

Correct statement: _____

_____

The first modern Olympic Games / be / in 1933. ☐ ☐

Correct statement: _____

_____

The 'Titanic' / start / her journey / in 1912. ☐ ☐

Correct statement: _____

_____

Graham Bell / invent / the telephone / in 1945. ☐ ☐

Correct statement: _____

_____

The First World War / end / in 1915. ☐ ☐

Correct statement: _____

_____

Mark Chapman / kill / John Lennon / in 1915. ☐ ☐

Correct statement: _____

_____

Princess Diana / marry / Prince Charles / in 1981. ☐ ☐

Correct statement: _____

_____

Columbus / discover / the New World / in 1291. ☐ ☐

Correct statement: _____

_____

Supplement: Stepping Out

(5) Unit 12

Two Days in November ...

Put the verbs in brackets into the past tense.

I Elm Street

On 22 November 1963 President John F. Kennedy and his wife Jackie _____ (come) to Dallas, Texas. It _____ (be) a normal visit, but then ...
On their tour through Dallas the president and his wife _____ (sit) in an open limousine. The limousine _____ (turn) from Houston Street into Elm Street and _____ (go) past a small hill. But what _____ (happen) next? We know some things because a man _____ (have) a film camera with him and _____ (make) a film of the scene:
At 12.31 there _____ (be) three or four shots. Some people _____ (say) that the shots _____ (come) from a big building. Other people _____ (say) that the shots _____ (not come) from the building, but from a car park.
One bullet _____ (hit) Kennedy in the head; he _____ (bring) his hands up to his neck and _____ (fall) forward. The limousine _____ (take) the president to Parkland Hospital at great speed. Doctors at the hospital _____ (work) very hard to save Kennedy's life, but it _____ (be) too late. Kennedy _____ (die) in hospital and Vice President Johnson _____ (become) America's new president ninety-nine minutes after the shots.
At about 14.30 the police _____ (arrest) a man called Lee Harvey Oswald. He _____ (work) in the big building on Elm Street. In the building the police _____ (find) Oswald's gun ...

Now check with the text in your book and fill the words which you did not know into the list below:

Present Tense	Past Tense
....	....
....	....
....	....
....	....
....	....
....	....
....	....
....	....
....	....
....	....
....	....
....	....

Supplement: Focus

Fill in the Gaps!

Who was Lee Harvey Oswald?

Lee Harvey Oswald had an _____ life. He was a soldier and he was always in trouble in the army and later with the _____. He was also a communist and that was a _____ in America in those days. Perhaps he didn't _____ President Kennedy's policies towards Cuba because at that time the Americans had problems with communist _____ like Russia and Cuba.
Early in 1963 Oswald bought two guns. His _____ took a photograph in their garden. On it he _____ a black uniform and he _____ his new guns up in the air.

II The Dallas Police Department

Two days after his arrest the _____ got Oswald out of his cell in the Dallas Police Department. They _____ to take him to another cell. A man called Jack Ruby _____ up to Oswald and the policeman.
He took a gun out of his _____ and killed Oswald. Millions of Americans _____ this on television. Nobody knew how Jack Ruby got into the _____ …

The questions

There are _____ questions about President Kennedy's death. Did all the shots come from the _____ building on Elm Street? Did some of them come from a _____? How many shots _____ there? Did Oswald act _____? Kennedy was a popular _____ but some conservative politicians didn't like his _____. The Mafia didn't want him as a president because he and his _____ Robert were very anti-crime. Some people _____ that Oswald didn't work _____ or that he didn't kill the president. They _____ that a big organisation wanted President Kennedy dead. Was this the Mafia or an anti-Communist group? And why did Jack Ruby _____ Oswald? Some people think that Ruby _____ connections with the Mafia. Others say that he didn't …
What really _____ on 22 November 1963? There are still a lot of questions and not many _____ answers.

Verb Training I

buy	know	become
pizza	TV programme	gangster

go	take	eat
home	suitcase	biscuit

do	make	become
homework	mistake	film star

wear	have	get
T-shirt	brunch	paper

read	write	go
book	exercise	home

drink	bring	know
water	animal	answer

hear	hear	take
dog	answer	instrument

sit	meet	get
floor	teacher	T-shirt

come	leave	go
disco	school	America

Supplement: Training

Verb Training II

Put the verbs into the correct tense.

Infinitive	Past tense (positive)	Past tense (negative)
bring	She	
hear	We	
sell	She	
go	You	
sleep	I	
become	He	
have	We	
come	It	
know	You	
take	It	
do	He	
make	I	
wear	She	
meet	We	
get	You	
run	They	
give	We	
sit	I	
be	He	

Question Cards

Did you play football yesterday? Did you go to the disco last week? Did you smoke last night? Did you like Charlie Chaplin? Did you ride a bike last Sunday?	Didn't you give me your book? Why did you like her/him? Where did you have brunch? When did you like school? Where did you smoke?
Did you drink whisky last night? Did you feed dogs at the zoo? Did you write a letter yesterday? Did you speak Italian last week? Did *you* leave ice-cream wrappers on the floor?	When did you drive a car? Why did you like Otto? When did you go home? When did you drink coke? When did you get up early?
Did you help your friends yesterday? Did you like your last holiday? Did you eat a banana yesterday? Did you listen to DRS3 last night? Did you read a book last week?	Where did you eat fish? Didn't you write songs? Didn't you speak Welsh? Did you smell something? When did you wear a hat?
Did you watch TV yesterday? Did you get up before 6 o'clock? Did you swim last winter? Did you like your kindergarten? Did you eat a banana last week?	Why did you sit in a basket? When did you drink beer? When did you go to a concert? Where did you play cricket? When did you follow a team?
Did you drink fruit juice yesterday? Did you live in Germany last year? Did you read a book last night? Did you play tennis yesterday? Did you eat fish yesterday?	Where did you sit on a throne? When did you meet a film star? When did you run 5000 m? Where did you take a photo? Where did you sing a song?
Did you help your friends last week? Did you walk in the park last night? Did you give him a record yesterday? Did you play football yesterday? Did you go to the cinema last night?	When did you play basketball? How did you go to a concert? Where did you meet Americans? When did you eat lemons? When did you run to school?

Supplement: Training

(10) Unit 12

Verb Diagram

	Answer							Question (Who? Where? How? When? etc.)							
Present				**Past**				**Present**					**Past**		
"to be" positive	"to be" negative	Verb positive	Verb negative	"to be" positive	"to be" negative	Verb positive	Verb negative	"Who ...?"	"to be" positive	"to be" negative	Verb positive	Verb negative	"Who ...?"	"to be" positive	"to be" negative	Verb positive	Verb negative

2nd Person sing.

3rd Person sing.

Supplement: Training

Verb Bingo

hold	bring	wear
give	buy	become
see	sit	say

make	know	fall
sit	say	take
become	wear	bring

see	be	do
make	go	find
buy	have	get

get	go	give
sit	know	buy
do	fall	see

fall	say	get
make	sit	see
have	know	go

do	go	wear
see	buy	become
bring	take	know

wear	sit	make
know	get	have
bring	be	see

become	bring	fall
come	hold	see
make	do	buy

become	bring	fall
know	get	have
wear	be	see

bring	be	take
come	hold	see
make	do	buy

go	sit	make
know	get	have
bring	be	see

become	bring	fall
wear	sit	make
hold	do	buy

Supplement: Training

The Past Crossword

Rules

1. Three to four students get a grid and a set of verb cards.
2. Each student gets three cards, the rest are left in a pile in the middle.
3. The first student takes one of the three words and writes its past form *in pencil* into the grid (across or down). The word must contain one of the letters already on the grid (start with "Ready for English").
4. Every correct word gets the number of points noted on the card. If a student doesn't get the spelling right, she / he loses the same number of points.
5. If a student has a card with an asterisk (*), she / he can start somewhere new and doesn't have to use letters already on the grid.
6. If a student can't continue, she / he misses a turn.
7. For every card put down, the student must take a new one from the pile in the middle.
8. The game ends when nobody can continue anymore or when all the cards are used up.

(12b) Unit 12

Verb Cards

become (2)	bring (2)	sleep (2)	change (1)
eat (3)	come (2)	copy * (1)	drink (3)
die (1)	do (2)	get (1)	give (2)
go (2)	have (1)	hear (2)	write (3)
kill (1)	know (2)	like (1)	listen * (1)
live (2)	love (1)	make (2)	meet (2)
move (1)	play (2)	put (2)	rain (1)
leave (3)	start (1)	stay * (1)	stop * (1)
take (2)	run (3)	wear (3)	work * (1)

Score card

	Player 1	Player 2	Player 3	Player 4
Score				

Supplement: Training Second Step

The Club of Dead Rock'n'Roll Stars

Who was it?

The King was born on 8th January 1935 in East Tupelo. His parents were farm labourers and quite poor. He became a truck driver. In 1953 he recorded *My Happiness* for his mother's birthday. It was a song in his typical mixture of Country & Western, Gospel, Blues and Rock'n'Roll. Other hits included *Heart Break Hotel*, *Hound Dog* and *Love Me Tender*. From 1958 to 1960 the rock'n'roll singer did his army service as a soldier in Germany, but his fans did not forget him. For young people he was a rebel, a hero and an idol. He made rock'n'roll popular and also very sexy. America was shocked by his dance style. In the late Sixties he made a comeback and sang in Las Vegas and Hawaii in very glamourous clothes and with big orchestras.
But there were two big problems in his life: his manager "Colonel" Parker and pills. Parker used his position as a manager to make a lot of money and he helped the singer to get his pills. On 16th August 1977 they found the King in his bedroom in Graceland. There were over 30 different types of medicine and pills in his fat body. He died on the same day.

He grew up in Liverpool with his aunt Mimi. He was a very aggressive young man and had two interests in life: rebellion and rock'n'roll. As a teenager he played in several bands in Liverpool until he formed the Beatles with Paul McCartney, George Harrison and, after some changes, Ringo Starr on drums. He wrote a lot of songs with McCartney but also two books of nonsense poetry. But he often got into trouble because he said just what he felt. When he said that the Beatles were more popular than Jesus, the American public went wild: radio stations organised fires to burn Beatles records and posters. It got so bad that he flew to New York and in a press conference took back what he said.
His life changed when he met Yoko Ono, a Japanese artist. His music became more experimental and together with Yoko he organised demonstrations for peace. 1975 to 1980 were his "house-husband" years. He looked after Yoko's and his son Sean. In 1980 he produced the album *Double Fantasy* with Yoko. He seemed a new and happier man. On the evening of 8th December 1980 Mark Chapman shot him as he and his wife Yoko walked into his apartment house in New York. He died in hospital half an hour later.

She was a white girl with a very black voice. She was born in Texas on 19th January 1943, the daughter of a Texaco oil company director. But she preferred music to her parents' life style. For several years she travelled through the States and sang in clubs and bars. In 1967 she was a big hit at the Monterey Pop Festival and got a record contract with CBS. She recorded three albums. But her lifestyle was a problem: she drank very much, almost a litre of whisky a day, she gave a lot of concerts, too many perhaps, and she had a lot of unhappy affairs with men. As a result she was very lonely.
In 1970 she recorded her last album, *Pearl*, with her biggest hit *Me and Bobby McGhee*, but she didn't hear the finished album. On 4th October she died in a motel room of an overdose of heroin. She left $2500. It was her last wish that her friends had a party with that money. The film *The Rose* with Bette Middler tells her story.

For guitarists, there is nobody like him: he took the sound of guitars to new extremes, he played his instrument with his mouth, he produced screaming feedback. Born on 27th November 1942, in Seattle, Washington, he played for many black stars of the Fifties and early Sixties, Little Richard and also Ike and Tina Turner, for example. In 1966, Chas Chandler, a British manager, brought him to London, found a bass player and a drummer for him and built him up as a star. Some of his hits were *Hey Joe* and *Purple Haze*, a song about drugs.
All the stars of his time loved him, he was a big hit, he got $100,000 for a concert, but he was very lonely and unhappy. He also experimented with drugs and alcohol. On 18th September 1970 he died in a hotel room in London. The press thought it was because of hard drugs, but he had had too much to drink and some sleeping tablets. Before he died he made several phonecalls because he wanted to talk to somebody, anybody. But there was nobody to talk to …

He was born in 1945 in St. Ann, Jamaica. His father was a British officer, his mother ran a food shop. He is important in rock culture for two things: he became the first famous reggae musician and he was a Rastafarian. Rastafarians or Rastas have a very unusual hairstyle called dreadlocks. They believe that they come from the old people of Israel. They don't live in Israel or Africa any more because they became slaves to the Western world. In many ways he and his Reaggae music were typical for this idea. Reaggae is music of protest from the ghettos of Jamaica. In 1976 he said: "I don't sing about politics, I sing about freedom."
Some of his hits were *Stir It Up*, *I Shot the Sheriff* and *No Woman No Cry*. He was a star in Jamaica already in the Sixties and early Seventies, but in America and the rest of the world he and his music didn't really become famous until Eric Clapton did *I Shot the Sheriff* in 1973. But after that Rastas became popular in the Western world, and young white people also played reggae and copied the dreadlocks. He died in Miami on 11th May 1981 of a brain tumor. For Jamaicans it was a very sad day: their national hero was dead.

There were a lot of punk bands in London in the Seventies, but everybody knew the Sex Pistols. Their show was rude, their songs anti-everything and the dance style of their fans was absolutely crazy. This dance was called pogo and its creator was the bass player of the band. Pogo is very simple: you just jump up and down to the rhythm of punk rock, especially the music of the Sex Pistols.
In 1978 the band broke up and he started a solo career. He had a hit with a punk version of the Frank Sinatra hit *My Way*. But he became famous because of another story: on 12th October 1978 his girl friend Nancy Spungen died after a wild night in room 100 of the Chelsea Hotel in New York. The police arrested him for murder, but released him on bail. He died of an overdose of heroin on 2nd February 1979. The film *Sid And Nancy: A Love Story* (1986) tells the sad story of the these two punkers' lives and deaths.

Jimi Hendrix, Janis Joplin, John Lennon, Bob Marley, Elvis Presley, Sid Vicious

(14) Unit 13

A School Fete

Put the verbs in brackets into the correct form.

I Let's dance

Hello and welcome to the Bedford Park School Fete. It _____ (not rain) any more, it _____ (clear up) and the sun _____ (shine). It looks like a nice day, doesn't it? So what _____ (go on) ? The school band _____ (play). A lot of people _____ (listen) to the music and they _____ (have) a really good time. But there aren't many people dancing yet. So go over there, have a good time and DANCE!
And please don't forget our coffee shop. At the moment some people _____ (sit) at the tables in front of the coffee shop and only a few people _____(wait) in the queue.
Are you hungry? Go over there and eat something. There aren't any hot meals but Christina and Tony have got a lot of sandwiches and ice creams too, in many different flavours. Is there anything else? Oh, yes, they _____ (sell) home-made cakes, too. They're something special! Go and taste them!
Or is anybody thirsty? Our sixth formers Cathy and Brian _____ (serve) any alcoholic drinks, but there are a lot of different fruit juices and there is tea.
Wait a minute! Two boys _____ (smoke) behind the toilet. Stop it right there, boys!
By the way, Greg and Sharon _____ (take) pictures. So smile!
And what _____ (go) on in the sports field? Some people over there _____ (laugh) and making a lot of noise.
Ah yes, the three girl finalists _____ (run) the 80 m race and Danny, our school champion _____ (ride) his bicycle over the first part of the obstacle course ...

Now check with the text in your book.

Supplement: Focus 201

(15) Unit 13

Check Your Vocabulary!

Fill in the gaps

I Let's dance

Hello and _____ to the Bedford Park School Fete. It isn't _____ing any more, it's clearing up and the _____ is shining. It looks like a nice _____, doesn't it?
So what's going on? The school band is _____ing. A lot of people are _____ing to the music and they're having a really good time. But there aren't many _____ dancing yet. So go over there, have a good time and DANCE!
And please don't _____ our coffee shop. At the moment some people are sitting at the _____ in front of the coffee shop and only a few people are _____ing in the queue.
Are you hungry? Go over there and _____ something. There aren't any hot _____ but Christina and Tony have got a lot of _____ and ice creams too, in many different flavours.
Is there anything else? Oh, yes, they are selling home-made _____, too. They're something special! Go and taste them!
Or is anybody _____? Our sixth formers Cathy and Brian aren't serving any alcoholic _____, but there are a lot of different _____ juices and there is tea.
Wait a minute! Two boys are smoking behind the _____. Stop it right there, boys!
By the way, Greg and Sharon are _____ing pictures. So smile!
And what is going on in the sports field? Some people over there are _____ing and making a lot of _____.
Ah yes, the three girl finalists are running the 80 m _____ and Danny, our school champion is riding his _____ over the first part of the obstacle course ...

Now check with the text in your book and write the words which you didn't know into the list below!

Words to learn:

English	German
....	....
....	....
....	....
....	....
....	....
....	....
....	....
....	....
....	....

(16a)   **Unit 13**

Questions and Answers

Here are some answers. What are the questions?

1. _____
   No, it isn't raining any more.

2. _____
   Yes, the sun is shining.

3. _____
   The school band is playing.

4. _____
   A lot of people are listening to the music.

5. _____
   Yes, they're really having a good time.

6. _____
   No, they aren't dancing yet.

7. _____
   Yes, some people are sitting in front of the coffee shop.

8. _____
   No, only a few people are waiting in the queue.

9. _____
   Christina and Tony are selling home-made cakes.

10. _____
    No, Cathy and Brian aren't serving any alcoholic drinks.

11. _____
    They're serving a lot of different fruit juices and tea.

12. _____
    The two boys are smoking (behind the toilet).

13. _____
    Greg and Sharon are taking pictures.

14. _____
    The three girl finalists are running the 80 m race.

Note: The two copy sheets 16a and 16b can be combined using one half from the first and one half from the second sheet to avoid one student only doing questions and one student only doing answers.

Supplement: Training

(16b) Unit 13

Questions and Answers

Here are some questions. What are the answers?

1. Is it raining at the moment?

2. Is the sun shining?

3. Who is playing?

4. Are any people listening to the music?

5. Are they having a good time?

6. Are the people dancing?

7. Are any people sitting in front of the coffee shop?

8. Are many people waiting in the queue?

9. What are Christina and Tony doing/selling?

10. Are Cathy and Brian serving any alcoholic drinks?

11. What are they serving?

12. What are the two boys behind the toilet doing?

13. What are Greg and Sharon doing?

14. What are the three girl finalists doing?

Note: The two copy sheets 16a and 16b can be combined using one half from the first and one half from the second sheet to avoid one student only doing questions and one student only doing answers.

Supplement: Training

True or False?

A school fete

Are the following statements true or false? Correct the false statements using negative sentences.

1. It is raining.

2. The moon is shining.

3. The school orchestra is playing.

4. A lot of people are dancing to the music.

5. They're really having a terrible time.

6. They aren't listening to the music.

7. A lot of people are waiting in the queue.

8. Cathy and Brian are selling their home-made cakes.

9. Christina and Tony are serving alcoholic drinks.

10. Two boys are chewing tobbaco behind the toilet.

11. Greg and Sharon are painting portraits.

12. Some people over there are very quiet.

13. The three girl finalists are running the 100 m race.

14. Our school champion Danny is riding his motorbike.

Supplement: Training

Dialogue Snap

II At the coffee shop

Now, here we are at Christina and Tony's coffee shop. Christina, how is business?

We're doing fine. Look at the queue! Tony is just making some fresh sandwiches. Hey, Tony, don't put so much butter on the bread!

OK, OK. There isn't much bread left, anyway.

Of course, there is. It's over there. Two loaves of brown bread and one big loaf of white bread

---

I can see you've got a lot to do and not much time for an interview. Is there anything important you'd like to say?

Well, yes. Hello everybody! We've still got a lot of fruit cake and some apple pie. There isn't much chocolate cake left, I'm afraid, but you can have chocolate-chip biscuits.

Christina, there isn't much milk left, so they can't have any milk shakes or milk in their tea ...

Or you can try one of Tony's sandwiches in a minute. So, come to the coffee shop, sit down and have a cup of tea or coffee, or a milkshake ...

Yes, well ... I can see business is going well for Christina and Tony. They're a great team. Thanks for the interview.

Tony! There are five bottles of milk right behind you! ... Really!

What Are You Doing?

Follow the order and say what you are doing.

| Please open the door! |
| Please sit on your desk! |
| Stand on your chair, please! |
| Please dance! |
| Open all the windows, please! |
| Count from 10 to 0, please! |
| Please open your mouth! |
| Look out of the window, please! |
| Draw a picture of a fish, please! |
| Open and shut the cupboard, please! |
| Knock on the door, please! |
| Please stand in front of the blackboard! |
| Open and shut your workbook, please! |
| Read from a newspaper, please! |
| Eat a banana, please! |
| Touch a vase, please! |
| Run to the door, please! |

| Clean a window, please! |
| Play with a ball, please! |
| Play an instrument, please! |
| Sing a song, please! |
| Stand in a corner, please! |
| Walk around the classroom, please! |
| Point at a poster, please! |
| Please open your schoolbag! |
| Wash your hands, please! |
| Fill a glass with water, please! |
| Please brush your hair! |
| Spell your name, please! |
| Listen to your friend, please! |
| Go to sleep, please! |
| Say "Hello" to your friends, please! |
| Read a text, please! |
| Please go home! |

Supplement: Training

Verb Training

Put the verbs into the correct tense.

Infinitive	Past tense (positive)	Present progressive
bring	She	
write	We	
sit	They	
go	You	
drink	I	
come	It	
take	He	
do	We	
wear	She	
run	He	
give	You	
sell	They	
eat	We	
buy	I	

Key:

bring	She brought	She is bringing
write	We wrote	We are writing
sit	They sat	They are sitting
go	You went	You are going
drink	I drank	I am drinking
come	It came	It is coming
take	He took	He is taking
do	We did	We are doing
wear	She wore	She is wearing
run	He ran	He is running
give	You gave	You are giving
sell	They sold	They are selling
eat	We ate	We are eating
buy	I bought	I am buying

A Dream

Fill in the gaps. Put the verbs in brackets into the correct form.

Last night I had a dream. I _____ (not usually remember) my dreams but I remember this one. I think a lot of things in my dream were wrong. Here's my dream:
I _____ (sit) on the back of a Kiwi. We _____ (fly) over two big islands and a lot of small ones. It _____ (look) like a volcanic wonderland. There are a lot of craters and some springs _____ (boil). Where _____ we _____ (go), I wonder? The bird says: "Welcome to New Zealand. In five minutes we _____ (land) in Dunedin, the capital.
Now we _____ (fly) over a beach. A lot of people _____ (lie) in the sun. On the beach there are also some dogs. They _____ (wear) straw hats and sunglasses. Some also have green cream on their noses. "Dogs very _____ (often wear) hats and sunglasses because of the sun," the bird says. "The green cream _____ (protect) their noses." Now the Kiwi _____ (land) on the beach. A man _____ (come) towards us.
He _____ (hold) a fish in his hands. "This is Hohepa or Joseph in English. He's a Maori," says the Kiwi. What _____ (happen)? Hohepa _____ (rub) noses with me. "That's normal," says the Kiwi, "Maoris _____ (usually rub) noses when they say hello. And they _____ (dive) into the water and _____ (catch) fish just with their hands. Isn't that clever?
You know, some Maoris _____ (speak) two languages. One is English, the other one is their old language, quite an interesting one.
Hohepa has got a 'motopaika'. That's the Maori word for motorbike. I _____ (sit) on the back seat, Hohepa _____ (drive) it – on the left. "Don't worry, in New Zealand we _____ (drive) on the left," says the Kiwi. He _____ (still fly) over our heads. As we _____ (travel) along, we _____ (see) thousands of sheep.
Oh, I _____ (need) some money. There is a bank by the side of the road. The bank clerk _____ (look) very strange, I think: he _____ (wear) a shirt and tie with – shorts and socks, white ones. He is very friendly. "This is very typical," says the Kiwi, "bankers _____ (usually wear) shorts in summer."
Now I _____ (fly) on the back of the Kiwi again. There is a skyscraper under us. Some people _____ (jump) off ... and they survive!
"This is called rap jumping. A lot of tourists _____ (come) here to walk down the walls," the bird says. Just then I _____ (hear) a voice. "Come down Sheila, you're late for school ...!"

Supplement: Focus

A Dream

Fill in the gaps using the verbs in the box below. Put them in the correct tense.

Last night I had a dream. I _____ usually _____ my dreams but I remember this one. I think a lot of things in my dream were wrong. Here's my dream:

I _____ on the back of a Kiwi. We _____ over two big islands and a lot of small ones.

It _____ like a volcanic wonderland. There are a lot of craters and some springs _____. Where _____ we _____, I wonder? The bird says: "Welcome to New Zealand. In five minutes we _____ in Dunedin, the capital.

Now we _____ over a beach. A lot of people _____ in the sun. On the beach there are also some dogs. They _____ straw hats and sunglasses. Some also have green cream on their noses. "Dogs very often _____ hats and sunglasses because of the sun," the bird says. "The green cream _____ their noses." Now the Kiwi _____ _____ on the beach. A man _____ towards us.

He _____ a fish in his hands. "This is Hohepa or Joseph in English. He's a Maori," says the Kiwi.

What _____? Hohepa _____ noses with me. "That's normal," says the Kiwi, "Maoris usually _____ noses when they say hello. And they _____ into the water and _____ fish just with their hands. Isn't that clever?

You know, some Maoris _____ two languages. One is English, the other one is their old language, quite an interesting one.

Hohepa has got a 'motopaika'. That's the Maori word for motorbike. I _____ on the back seat, Hohepa _____ it – on the left. "Don't worry, in New Zealand we _____ on the left," says the Kiwi.

He _____ still _____ over our heads. As we _____ along we _____ thousands of sheep.

Oh, I _____ some money. There is a bank by the side of the road. The bank clerk _____ very strange, I think: he _____ a shirt and tie with – shorts and socks, white ones. He is very friendly. "This is very typical," says the Kiwi, "bankers usually _____ shorts in summer."

Now I _____ on the back of the Kiwi again. There is a skyscraper under us. Some people _____ off ... and they survive!

"This is called rap jumping. A lot of tourists _____ here to walk down the walls," the bird says. Just then I _____ a voice. "Come down Sheila, you're late for school ...!"

> **USE**
>
> boil, catch, come (2x), dive, drive (2x), fly (4x), go, happen, hear, hold, jump, land (2x), lie, look (2x), need, protect, not remember, rub (2x), see, sit (2x), speak, travel, wear (4x)

Verb Training

Put the verbs into the correct tense.

Infinitive	Simple past	Present progressive
come	she	
paint	we	
play	they	
hit	you	
wear	I	
hold	he	
sit	they	
buy	she	
give	he	
find	I	
know	you	
become	it	
bring	I	
fall	we	
go	they	
get	you	
think	she	
read	he	
eat	we	
begin	it	

Script: The White Lady

Sheila Batts, Supernatural Studies Institute.
Case: The White Lady. Tape protocol Nr. 34,
4 March.

Now we know some more things about the White Woman. We know what she wears. It's a long white dress from the 18th century. We also know that she has white hair. She's not very old: she looks about forty to forty-five.
She stands at the top of the stairs in Kilmichael House. Then she goes down the stairs and comes back up again. She looks very sad and often lifts her hands up in the air. Sometimes she goes up and down the stairs for an hour or more.
I wanted to find out more about the White Woman. So, today I read a lot of old books and letters in Kilmichael library. This is what I found out about the story of the White Lady:
Lady Elizabeth Kilmichael was a very hard woman. She hated the people of the Isle of Arran and the people hated her. She also had three big and very dangerous dogs.
In the year 1720, there was very little food and a lot of people didn't have anything to eat. We can see from old books and records that 25 children died of hunger in that year. The story goes that many people came to Kilmichael House and asked for help or food. But Lady Elizabeth never gave them anything.
One evening in the winter of 1720 a young woman came to Kilmichael House. She had a small baby with her. The baby was hungry and the woman asked for some milk. She came up the stairs and fell on her knees. Lady Elizabeth told her to go away. But the woman didn't go away, so Lady Elizabeth called her dogs. The woman tried to run away and fell backwards down the stairs.
Both the mother and the baby were dead. Lady Elizabeth laughed and went to bed. But when she got up the next morning her hair was white as snow. From then on she didn't eat or drink anymore. She also didn't speak anymore. Three days later two people saw her down at the beach. They were the last people to see her. She disappeared and never came back. Nobody saw her again, nobody found her dead body.
From time to time, especially on cold nights, she stands at the top of the stairs.
I want to find out more about Lady Elizabeth tomorrow in the town library.

Sheila Batts, Supernatural Studies Institute.
Case: The White Lady. Tape protocol Nr. 37,
7 March.

Tonight is a very cold, windy night. It seems a good night for the White Lady. Pauline West, the hotel manageress and I are waiting in the bedroom next to the stairs. We can hear the clock in the hall. It's midnight. There's something down in the hall, it looks like a woman …

The White Lady

a) Listen and find the missing information:
Student A: fill in the gaps marked with an (A)
Student B: fill in the gaps marked with a (B)

The date of the first tape protocol (no _____ [A]) is _____ (B)
The white woman wears _____ (A) from the _____ (B) century.
She has _____ (A) hair. She is not very old: she looks about _____ (B) to _____ (B).
She stands at the top of the _____ (A) in Kilmichael house. Then she goes _____ (B).
She looks very _____ (A) and often lifts her hands up in the _____ (B).
Sometimes she goes up and down for _____ (A).
Lady _____ (B) Kilmichael was a very hard woman.
She _____ (A) the people of the Isle of Arran and they _____ (B) her.
She had three big and very dangerous _____ (B).
In the year _____ (A), there was very little food.
_____ (B) children died of hunger in that year.
Lady Elizabeth never _____ (A) the hungry people anything.
One evening a _____ (B) came to Kilmichael House.
The young woman had a _____ (A) with her.
She asked for some _____ (B).
Lady Elizabeth _____ (A) her to go away.
The woman didn't go away, so Lady Elizabeth called _____ (B).
The woman fell backwards down the _____ (A).
Both the mother and the _____ (B) were dead.
But Lady Elizabeth _____ (A).
The next morning her hair was _____ (B). From then on she didn't _____ (A) or _____ (B) or _____ (A) anymore.
Three days later two people saw her _____ (B).
_____ (A) saw her again, _____ (A) found her dead body.
The White Lady usually appears _____ (B).

b) Now ask each other questions to find the missing information.

The Phantom on the Wall

In Bisham Hall in Berkshire there is an interesting ghost, Dame Elizabeth Hoby. She was a friend of Queen Elizabeth I (1558–1603) and was a very intelligent woman. Her son William died from a brain disease when he was a child.

Elizabeth did not know of this disease and often beat him because she thought that he was very stupid. Now she can't find rest and haunts her old home.

Her picture hangs in the Great Hall of Bisham Abbey. The ghost looks like the negative of that picture. Her hands and face are dark, but her dress is so white that it shines.

Admiral Vansittart bought the Hall in the 1890s.

He did not believe in ghosts, but something very strange happened to him one night. He was in the Great Hall near Dame Elizabeth's picture.

"Someone is standing beside me", he thought. He turned around and saw Dame Elizabeth, but when he turned again and looked at her picture, there was nothing there …

Supplement: Reading Corner

Shadows

With a little bit of practice you can amuse your friends. All you need is a bright light, a blank wall and your two hands.

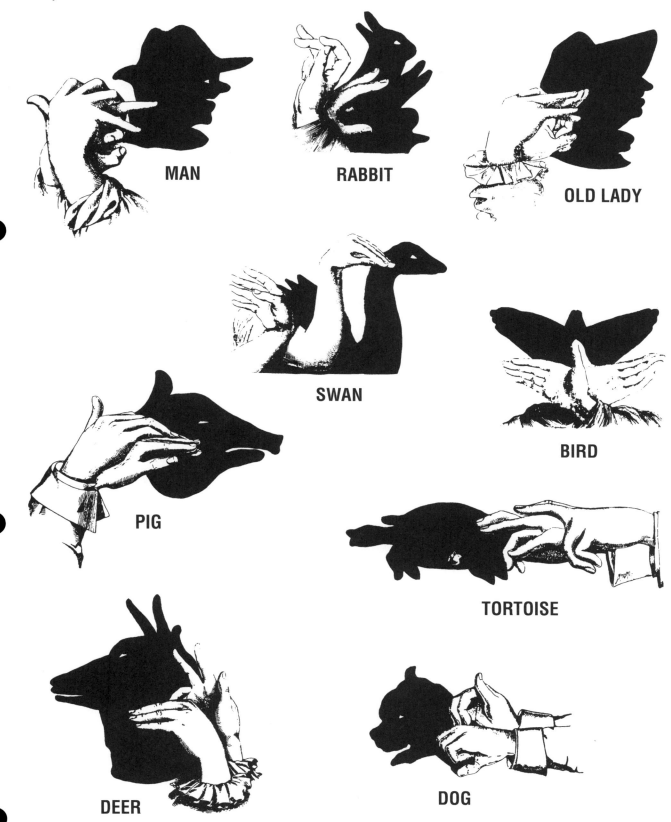

CONTROL SHEET Revision Workshop 3		
Student's name : _____	Score:	Points to repeat:
Station Simple Past Forms _____ correct forms out of 16 or 36	_____	_____ _____ _____
Station Verb Training _____ correct forms out of 28 or 48	_____	_____ _____ _____
Station Writing _____ correct sentences out of 10	_____	_____ _____ _____
Station Reading _____ correct answers out of 5	_____	_____ _____ _____
Station Combination Crossword _____ correct answers out of 15	_____	_____ _____ _____
Station Listening _____ correct entries out of 12	_____	_____ _____ _____
Station Questions and Answers _____ correct questions out of 8 _____ correct answers out of 8	_____	_____ _____ _____
Station Vocabulary _____ correct keywords out of 11	_____	_____ _____ _____

CONTROL SHEET Revision Workshop 3		
Student's name : _____	Score:	Points to repeat:
Station Simple Past Forms _____ correct forms out of 18 or 34	_____	_____ _____
Station Verb Training _____ correct forms out of 66	_____	_____ _____
Station Writing _____ correct sentences out of 10	_____	_____ _____
Station Reading _____ correct answers out of 6	_____	_____ _____
Station Combination Crossword _____ correct answers out of 15	_____	_____ _____
Station Listening _____ correct entries out of 12	_____	_____ _____
Station Questions and Answers _____ correct questions out of 10 _____ correct answers out of 10	_____	_____ _____
Station Vocabulary _____ correct keywords out of 15	_____	_____ _____

Map of Australia

Yes or No?

Air safari

	true	false
1. Australia is an island.	☐	☐
2. Australia isn't a continent.	☐	☐
3. Europe is larger than Australia.	☐	☐
4. Australia hasn't got a very good rail network.	☐	☐
5. On an air safari you travel by plane.	☐	☐
6. Outback is an Australian word for beach.	☐	☐
7. On this air safari, you always stay on farms.	☐	☐
8. Cairns is more beautiful than Sydney.	☐	☐
9. Sydney is more exciting than Cairns.	☐	☐

Adventure camping tour

1. On an adventure tour you go to the outback.	☐	☐
2. The big four-wheel drive coaches ravel on the main roads only.	☐	☐
3. Old people cannot go on this adventure tour.	☐	☐
4. Young people like this type of tour very much.	☐	☐
5. You sometimes have to prepare dinner on this trip.	☐	☐
6. You can wear a mini-dress on this tour if you want.	☐	☐
7. If your suitcase is heavier than 16 kg, you have to take a second suitcase.	☐	☐
8. You don't have to buy a sleeping bag for the adventure tour.	☐	☐

Australia by train

1. The most expensive way to travel in Australia is by train.	☐	☐
2. Travelling by train is easy.	☐	☐
3. Perth and Cairns are small cities.	☐	☐
4. With the Budget Austrailpass you don't have to buy any tickets.	☐	☐
5. You cannot travel between Perth and Cairns with the Budget Austrailpass.	☐	☐
6. A sleeping berth is more comfortable than a normal seat.	☐	☐
7. You can have a bath on some trains.	☐	☐
8. You can eat warm meals on every train.	☐	☐

Supplement: Focus

Fill in the Gaps I

Find the correct word from the box below to fill in. Be careful: You have to use the comparative or the superlative.

Which is the _____ way to travel in Australia?

Air safari

Australia is a huge island continent. It is _____ than all the countries of Europe together.
An air safari is the _____ and _____ way to get to the Australian outback.
An eight-day air safari takes you from Cairns to Sydney, Australia's _____ and _____ city.

Australia by train

The _____, _____ and _____ way to see Australia is by train.
Modern, air-conditioned trains run between the _____ cities from Perth in the west to Cairns in the far north.
For even _____ comfort, you can reserve a sleeping berth on the train. There are showers and toilets at the end of every car. _____ trains have dining or buffet cars.
Australia, the land down under, offers you a great experience on its trains!

Adventure camping tours

A camping tour can be a wonderful way to see Australia. Our special four-wheel drive coaches are robust enough to travel on the _____ bush roads. Our tours are open to travellers of all ages, but they are _____ with people under 35.

USE
beautiful, big, comfortable, direct, easy, exciting, fast, good, great, large, many, popular, relaxing, wild

Fill in the Gaps II

Fill in the missing words.

Which is the best _____ to travel in Australia?

Air safari
Australia is a _____ island _____. It is larger than all the countries of Europe together. There are great _____s between the cities, and the trains and roads are not as good as in many _____ countries.
An air safari is the _____est and most _____ way to get to the Australian outback. You fly from place to place in a small ten_____ aeroplane.
Our eight-day air safari _____s you from Cairns to Sydney, Australia's most _____ and most beautiful _____.
On the way from Cairns to Sydney you stay at farms and small but _____ hotels. Our air safaris take you to the Great Barrier Reef, Escott Cattle Station, Lawn Hill National Park, Alice Springs, Ayers Rock, Birdsville and Lightning Ridge.

Australia by train
The easiest, most _____ and most comfortable way to see Australia is by train. Modern, air-conditioned trains _____ between the bigger cities from Perth in the west to Cairns in the far north. With the Budget Austrailpass you can _____ unlimited travel on all Australian trains. A 14-day _____ costs $A 385.
For even greater _____, you can _____ a sleeping berth on the train. There are showers and _____ at the end of every car. _____ trains have dining or buffet cars. Australia, the land down under, offers you a great _____ on its trains!

Adventure camping tours
Do you like _____ trips? This 10-day camping _____ is a wonderful way to see Australia. Our special four-wheel drive _____es are tough enough to travel on the wildest bush roads. Our tours are open to _____s of all _____s, but they are most _____ with younger people (under 35). We travel in small _____s (6 to 12 people) and passengers usually _____ with the camp tasks: they put up the _____s and _____ the meals.
Comfortable _____ are important, and you can bring one _____ of maximum 16 kg. The price _____s touring, meals, _____ and camping equipment.

Supplement: Focus

Switzerland Quiz / Partner A

Ask your partner questions to complete the information on your sheet.

1. The _____ (high) point in Switzerland is the **Dufourspitze**.
   It's _____ high.
2. The _____ (long) river in Switzerland is the _____.
   It's **375 kilometres** long.
3. The _____ (big) lake in Switzerland is the Neuenburgersee.
   It's _____ in size.
4. The _____ (low) point in Switzerland is the _____.
   It's **193 metres** above sea level.
5. The _____ (long) tunnel in Switzerland is the **Simplon tunnel**.
   It's _____ long.
6. The _____ (tall) Swiss woman is from the canton of _____.
   In 1992, she was **1.96 metres** tall.
7. The _____ (large) city in Switzerland is **Zurich**.
   About _____ live there.
8. The _____ (old) Swiss football team is _____.
   It was founded in **1879**.

Switzerland Quiz / Partner B

Partner B: Ask your partner questions to complete the information on your sheet.

1. The _____ (high) point in Switzerland is the _____.
   It's **4,634 metres** high.
2. The _____ (long) river in Switzerland is the **Rhine**.
   It's _____ long.
3. The _____ (big) lake in Switzerland is the _____.
   It's **218.3 square kilometres** in size.
4. The _____ (low) point in Switzerland is the **Lago Maggiore**.
   It's _____ above sea level.
5. The _____ (long) tunnel in Switzerland is the _____
   It's **19.823 kilometres** long.
6. The _____ (tall) Swiss woman is from the canton of **Solothurn**. In 1992, she was _____ tall.
7. The _____ (large) city in Switzerland is _____.
   About **350,000 people** live there.
8. The _____ (old) Swiss football team is **FC St. Gallen**.
   It was founded in _____.

Cue Cards: Nonsense Comparisons

fish	cinema	credit card
waitress	umbrella	apple
passenger	guitar	muesli
mini-dress	kitchen	record
door	gun	ghost
rain	boat	party
friends	nose	island
travel	tea	bicycle
hat	train	meal

The Island Quartet

The first island

Name: Dutch for "new country in the sea"
Population: English, Scottish, Irish origin, 257,770 Maori
Languages: English, Maori
Famous person: Kiri Te Kanawa (an opera singer)
Record: the world's steepest street (in Dunedin)

The second island

Name: *Chaymaka* = "well watered"
Population: 77% black, 19% mulattoes
Language: English
Famous person: Bob Marley (a reggae musician)
Record: the fastest hurricane (300 km/h, Hurricane "Gilbert" in 1988)

The third island

Name: *Aloha State*
Population: Polynesian;
a large part of Japanese origin
Languages: English, Pidgin dialect
Famous person: Robbie Naish (a surfer)
Record: the world's biggest active volcano

The fourth island

Name: *Poblacht Na h'Eireann*
Population: 7.5 million people from this island live as immigrants in North America
Languages: Gaelic, English
Famous person: Sinead O'Connor (a pop singer)
Record: Europe's highest cliff (Achill Head on Achill Island), 668 m

The Island Quartet

New Zealand
Size: 268,103 km²
Inhabitants: _____
Largest city: _____
Distance from
nearest continent: _____

Jamaica
Size: 10,991 km²
Inhabitants: _____
Largest city: _____
Distance from
nearest continent: _____

New Zealand
Size: _____
Inhabitants: 3,400,000
Largest city: _____
Distance from
nearest continent: _____

Jamaica
Size: _____
Inhabitants: 2,400,000
Largest city: _____
Distance from
nearest continent: _____

New Zealand
Size: _____
Inhabitants: _____
Largest city: Auckland (778,000)
Distance from
nearest continent: _____

Jamaica
Size: _____
Inhabitants: _____
Largest city: Kingston (663,000)
Distance from
nearest continent: _____

New Zealand
Size: _____
Inhabitants: _____
Largest city: _____
Distance from
nearest continent: about 1600 km

Jamaica
Size: _____
Inhabitants: _____
Largest city: _____
Distance from
nearest continent: about 650 km

(35c) Unit 15

The Island Quartet

Hawaii	**Ireland**
Size: 16,705 km²	Size: 70,283 km²
Inhabitants: _____	Inhabitants: _____
Largest city: _____	Largest city: _____
Distance from nearest continent: _____	Distance from nearest continent: _____

Hawaii	**Ireland**
Size:	Size: _____
Inhabitants: 965,000	Inhabitants: 3,700,000
Largest city: _____	Largest city: _____
Distance from nearest continent: _____	Distance from nearest continent: _____

Hawaii	**Ireland**
Size: _____	Size: _____
Inhabitants: _____	Inhabitants: _____
Largest city: Honolulu (365,000)	Largest city: Dublin (1,100,000)
Distance from nearest continent: _____	Distance from nearest continent: _____

Hawaii	**Ireland**
Size: _____	Size: _____
Inhabitants: _____	Inhabitants: _____
Largest city: _____	Largest city: _____
Distance from nearest continent: 4,300 km	Distance from nearest continent: about 80 km

Australia Quiz

Cities in Australia

Which number is it on the map?

- [ ] Melbourne
- [ ] Perth
- [ ] Sydney
- [ ] Alice Springs
- [ ] Darwin
- [ ] Cairns
- [ ] Port Douglas
- [ ] Adelaide
- [ ] Brisbane

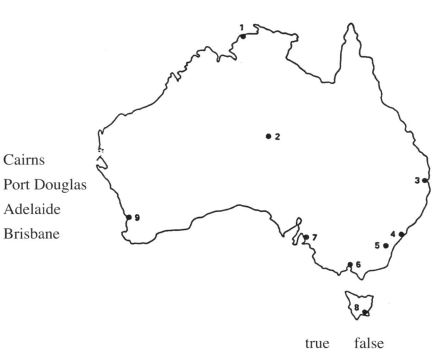

True or false?

	true	false
1. There are a lot of mountains in Australia.	☐	☐
2. The Indian Ocean is east, the Pacific Ocean is west of Australia.	☐	☐
3. Australians drive on the left.	☐	☐
4. Australian currency (money) is in pounds.	☐	☐

Which one is correct?

1. Tasmania is
   - [ ] a) an island
   - [ ] b) a city
   - [ ] c) a river

2. The capital of Australia is
   - [ ] a) Sydney
   - [ ] b) Melbourne
   - [ ] d) Canberra

3. The first people in Australia were
   - [ ] a) Maoris
   - [ ] b) Aboriginals
   - [ ] c) Indians

4. A lot of early white settlers were
   - [ ] a) American soldiers
   - [ ] b) Welsh farmers
   - [ ] c) British prisoners

5. Probably the most famous Australian animals are
   - [ ] a) possums
   - [ ] b) kangaroos
   - [ ] c) kiwis

Supplement: Additional Material

Quiz

Fill in the boxes with the letters for the correct answers from "Stepping Out" in the Student's Book, page 32.

1. The smallest continent in the world is …
   - ☐ … Europe.
   - ☐ … Australia.
   - ☐ … Greenland.

2. The fastest rapper is Tung Twista with …
   - ☐ … 597,
   - ☐ … 88 or
   - ☐ … 1,537 syllables per minute.

3. The biggest train station in Europe is in …
   - ☐ … Leipzig.
   - ☐ … Zurich.
   - ☐ … Milan.

4. The world's longest river is …
   - ☐ … the Rhine.
   - ☐ … the Amazon.
   - ☐ … the Nile.

5. The most expensive shoes (in 1999) cost …
   - ☐ … US$ 937.
   - ☐ … US$ 23,800.
   - ☐ … US$ 7,500.

6. The highest point in the world (Mount Everest) is …
   - ☐ … 8,888 metres above sea level.
   - ☐ … 7,000 m.
   - ☐ … 8,830 m.

7. The most expensive film (up to 2001) was …
   - ☐ … Modern Times with Charlie Chaplin.
   - ☐ … Titanic with Kate Winslet and Leonardo di Caprio.
   - ☐ … Terminator II with Arnold Schwarzenegger.

8. The first comic was published in …
   - ☐ … 1956.
   - ☐ … 1896.
   - ☐ … 1786.

9. How many women did the greatest kisser in the world, A.E. Wolfram, kiss in 8 hours?
   - ☐ 81
   - ☐ 801
   - ☐ 8,001

10. The biggest party in the world took place in London's Hyde Park with …
    - ☐ … 160,000 children.
    - ☐ … 160,000 policemen.
    - ☐ … 160,000 punks.

World Records

Make sentences using the superlative.

1. small continent / world / Australia
   _____

2. fast rapper / Tung Twista / with 597 syllables per minute
   _____

3. big train station in Europe / in Leipzig
   _____

4. world's long river / the Nile
   _____

5. expensive shoes to buy in 1999 / cost / US$ 23,800
   _____

6. high point in the world (Mount Everest) / 8,830 m
   _____

7. expensive film to produce (up to 2001) / Titanic with Kate Winslet and Leonardo di Caprio
   _____

8. first comic / published / in 1896
   _____

9. Wolfram / kiss / 8,001 women in 8 hours
   _____

10. big party in the world / take place in London's Hyde Park with 160,000 children
    _____

Supplement: Stepping Out

(39a) Unit 15

Everybody Knows That ...

a) What does your partner think? Write questions, ask him / her and note down the answers, ticking the box.

Example: city / far / west: ☑ Berne ☐ St. Gallen
Which city is farther west: Berne or St. Gallen?

1. city / far / south: ☐ Paris ☐ New York

2. tall: ☐ Eiffel Tower ☐ Empire State Building

3. animal / fast: ☐ sheep ☐ dog

4. fattening: ☐ glass of orange juice (2 dl) ☐ glass of milk (2 dl)

5. small: ☐ Liechtenstein ☐ Monaco

6. large: ☐ St. Peter's (Vatican) ☐ the Taj Mahal in India

7. instrument / sound high: ☐ the tenor saxophone ☐ guitar

8. near to the earth: ☐ Venus ☐ Mars

9. close to the sun: ☐ Neptune ☐ Uranus

10. old: ☐ the Sphinx in Egypt ☐ Stonehenge in England

11. long: ☐ the Nile ☐ the Mississippi

12. big: ☐ Boeing 747 ☐ Concorde

Key: 1 New York, 2 Empire State Building, 3 dog, 4 glass of milk, 5 Monaco, 6 Taj Mahal, 7 guitar, 8 Venus, 9 Uranus, 10 Sphinx, 11 Nile, 12 Boeing 747

Supplement: Stepping Out

(39b)   Unit 15

Everybody Knows That ...

a) Now write down the answer to the question of part a).
Example: city / far / west: ☑ Berne   ☐ St. Gallen
– Berne is farther west than St. Gallen.

1. _____

2. _____

3. _____

4. _____

5. _____

6. _____

7. _____

8. _____

9. _____

10. _____

11. _____

12. _____

Supplement: Stepping Out

Fill in the Gaps

Fill in the missing words.

I Radio Report

Hi folks! This is Joan Bensen from CHWK Radio, Chilliwack, with a Saturday _____ special. A group of _____ people from Switzerland _____d in Chilliwack last night, but not by car or _____. They are drifting down the Fraser River on two _____ rafts.

They _____d out near the source of the Fraser, in a place called Lucerne. That's near Jasper National Park. They had to _____ canoes at the beginning because the river is not _____ enough there. Then they built their rafts in Prince George. They _____ five weeks to _____ to Chilliwack.

But why come to Canada to drift _____ a river? It's a long story: Some years ago, a _____ friends went down the River Rhine in Europe on their _____ rafts. They _____d it so much that they _____d to travel down the St. Lawrence River in Eastern Canada. They wanted to _____ the Great Lakes, Toronto with the CN Tower, Montreal and French-speaking Quebec City. But there were the Niagara Falls _____ Lake Erie and Lake Ontario. They were _____ a little too _____ for them. So the Swiss _____d to come out West.

II Interview

JB: Hi Marco, welcome _____ Chilliwack. So what kind of material did you use to _____ your rafts? Did you cut down trees in the _____?

M: No, we _____t a lot of _____ from a sawmill, and we used 64 oil drums. There are two _____ on one raft and a big table with a fireplace on the _____. So we can cook our _____ meals while we are drifting.

JB: And what did you _____ from Switzerland? What are the most _____ things for you and your friends?

M: Anti-mosquito spray – just kidding ... There are very few insects _____ here, actually. No, I _____ it is rain jackets and the good old Swiss Army knives.

JB: Isn't the river quite _____ in some places? Do you _____ life-jackets?

M: Of course we do. And we _____ be good _____s, too! In fact, it's _____ dangerous here than _____ north. There aren't as many rapids as _____ there. Sometimes we _____ into the trees. Now we're having some _____s with the wind. It's very strong.

Is this Text Correct?

Huckleberry Finn listened to the Saturday afternoon special on CHWK Radio and took notes. Unfortunately he made some mistakes. Can you correct his mistakes?

Drifting down the Fraser River

Hi folks! This is Joan Bensen from CHWK Radio, Chilliwack, with a Sunday evening special. A group of young people from Sweden arrived in Chilliwack last night, but not by car or train. They are drifting down the Red River on two wooden boats.

They started out near the source of the Fraser, in a place called Lausanne. That's near Yellowstone National Park. They had to use canoes at the beginning because the river is not deep enough there. Then they built their rafts in Prince George. They took four weeks to get to Chilliwack.

But why come to Canada to drift down a river? It's a short story: Some years ago, a few friends went down the River Rhine in America on their own rafts. They liked it so much that they decided to travel down the St. Lawrence River in Western Canada. they wanted to see the Big Lakes, Quebec City with the CN Tower, Montreal and French-speaking Toronto. But there were the Victoria Falls between Lake Erie and Lake Ontario. They were just a little too high for them. So the Swedish decided to come out North.

Match the Questions and the Answers

This is the interview of Joan Benson with Marco. Can you match Joan's questions with Marco's answers?

JB: Well, Marco, thank you very much for talking to us. I hope you have a good trip to Vancouver. 1	M: Yes, the people here are very friendly, but there are far fewer people in British Columbia than in Switzerland. 2
JB: What are your plans for tonight? 3	M: Thank you. 4
JB: Oh, I see. You must meet a lot of interesting people on your trip. 5	M: Of course we do. And we must be good swimmers, too! In fact, it's less dangerous here than further north. There aren't as many rapids as up there. Sometimes we crash into the trees. Right now we're having some problems with the wind. It's very strong. 6
JB: Isn't the river quite dangerous in some places? Do you wear life-jackets? 7	M: We're going to Harrison Hot Springs. We all need a nice warm bath. 8
JB: What can you do about it? 9	M: Oh, we bought a lot of wood from a sawmill, and we used 64 oil drums. There are two tents on one raft and a big table with a fireplace on the other. So we can cook our own meals while we are drifting. 10
JB: Marco, what kind of material did you use to build your rafts? 11	M: Not much. We just have to wait and see. Perhaps we can drift a little further tomorrow. 12

Canada and Switzerland

Canada is of course more than 240 times larger than Switzerland, but there are also things that are similar. Few other countries have as many high mountains as Switzerland and Canada. In both countries, there is more than one official language, English and French in Canada, German, French, Italian and Romansh in Switzerland. There are fewer French speakers in Canada than English speakers. In Switzerland there are more German speakers than French speakers.

In Canada most people live along the border with the United States. That's where most of the big cities are. But there are also some quite big cities, Saskatoon and Edmonton, further north in the provinces Saskatchewan and Alberta. Of course, Switzerland has got some bigger cities, but they are not as big cities as Toronto, Montreal and Vancouver. All of them have more than one million inhabitants. The fewest people live in the far north, in the so-called Territories (Yukon and Northwest). In Switzerland we can say the same about the high Alps.

Most tourists know little about the east of Canada, the Maritime Provinces. This is also an interesting part of Canada. A few of the people there still speak an old French dialect. In French-speaking Switzerland, dialects are less important. Both countries have one or more "big brothers": for the Canadians, this is the United States. And for the Swiss? Well, most people would say, Germany, France and Italy.

Last but not least, Canada is very active as a member of the United Nations. Switzerland has only been a member of the UN since 2002.

True or false?

	True	False
Most big cities in Canada are in the north.	☐	☐
Switzerland is an active member of the United Nations.	☐	☐
Some Canadians are French speakers.	☐	☐
Some of the French Canadians live in the Maritime Provinces.	☐	☐
Canada doesn't have a border with the United States in the north.	☐	☐
Switzerland is smaller than Canada.	☐	☐
There are no really high mountains in Canada.	☐	☐
Canada's "big brother" is France.	☐	☐
In Canada there are two official languages.	☐	☐

Supplement: Workbook Basic Exercise 4
Workbook Intensive Exercise 5

The Weather in New Zealand

a) *Compare the maximum temperatures in the four cities.*
   Say: Auckland is **hotter** in … than in … .
   … is the hottest **month** in … .

maximum	Auckland	Wellington	Christchurch	Dunedin
January	23	20	22	19
July	14	11	11	10

b) *Compare the minimum temperatures in the four cities.*
   Say: Wellington is **colder** than … .
   … is the **coldest** month in … .

maximum	Auckland	Wellington	Christchurch	Dunedin
January	16	13	12	11
July	8	6	1	3

c) *Look at the rain in the four cities.*
   Say: … is **drier** than … .
   … is the **driest** month in … .

days with rain	Auckland	Wellington	Christchurch	Dunedin
January	8	7	7	11
July	15	14	9	10
per year	140	124	85	119

d) *Compare the hours of sunshine in the four cities.*
   Say: … has **more/less** sunshine than … in … . / per year.
   … has **the most/the least** sunshine in … . / per year.

hours per day	Auckland	Wellington	Christchurch	Dunedin
January	7.6	7.5	6.8	5.8
July	4.5	3.4	4.0	3.5
hours per year	2153	2007	1970	1679

Danger – Your Safety?

Camping

Bears are attracted to campgrounds by food. Keep food locked in your vehicle or suspended 10 ft. (3 meters) above ground and 4 ft. (1.5 meters) horizontally from post or tree trunk. A clean camp is generally your best protection. Always be aware of the possibility of the presence of bears, especially at night. Lock up your camping gear and other equipment to prevent its being stolen.

Wildlife

Park animals are wild and dangerous. Bears and other animals are aggressive and unpredictable. Small animals may transmit disease. View animals from a safe distance or from your car. Feeding or molesting wildlife is prohibited.

Traffic: drive gently

Park roads are designed for slow speed. Do not block traffic when viewing wildlife or scenery. Drive defensively. Bicycles and motorcycles present a special hazard. Lock your car when you leave it – even for a short time.

Backcountry travel: permits required

Backcountry travel by foot, horseback or boat presents many dangers. Cold, deep water is a special hazard to fishermen and boaters. Always check with a ranger before entering the backcountry. When leaving your vehicle, do not invite theft by leaving valuable items in plain view. Lock your car.

Thermal areas

Thermal areas are dangerous. Boiling water. Unstable ground. Thin crusts may conceal hot pools. Keep children under control. No pets. Stay on designated trails or boardwalks.

Fill in the Gaps I

Police Arrest Al Bigone's Gang

Put the verbs in brackets into the correct tense (Present or Simple past).

Yesterday at 10 p.m. Inspector Elliot Lomond and the Chicago police _____ (go) into Al Bigone's headquarters. They _____ (arrest) many members of the gang of Chicago's biggest crime boss.

The raid on the headquarters, a warehouse with a luxury apartment in the Docks, _____ (be) a complete surprise. The gangsters _____ (be not) expecting the police. Carla del Monte _____ (not hear) anything: she was listening to Elvis Presley's Jailhouse Rock on her discman. Steve 'the Thinker' King was reading a book called *Crime and Punishment*.

The Galton Brothers _____ (not realise) what was going on because they were playing monopoly on their computer. Averell Galton _____ (be) very angry. He _____ (say): "It _____ (be) not fair. I was winning for the first time in my life."

But the police _____ (be) also very lucky. There _____ (be) no shooting, perhaps because Ramona Zotti was cleaning her machine gun at the time of the raid. Her boyfriend, 'Big' Tony Lynch, _____ (not have) his gun ready because he was ironing Ramona's mini-dress. Even Johnny 'the Bulldozer' Walker _____ (be) no problem. He _____ (be) filling bottles with smuggled Scotch whisky. A policeman _____ (say): "He was singing a very happy song when we _____ (take) him to the police car."

Al Bigone and his wife _____ (be) very surprised. "We were watching the News at Ten on television when we _____ (hear) the noise. But we _____ (think) the boys _____ (be) just having a good time."

Next to the apartment the police _____ (find) a big hangar. There the service crew men _____ (be) working very hard. Two mechanics, Fred Bull and George Sprite, _____ (be) painting a new number on Al Bigone's aeroplane while Leonardo da Vicinity, the top technician, _____ (be) servicing the helicopter.

Fill in the Gaps II

Police Arrest Al Bigone's Gang

Put the verbs in brackets into the Past progressive.

Yesterday at 10 p.m. Inspector Elliot Lomond and the Chicago police went into Al Bigone's headquarters. They arrested many members of the gang of Chicago's biggest crime boss.
The raid on the headquarters, a warehouse with a luxury apartment in the Docks, was a complete surprise. The gangsters _____ not _____ (expect) the police. Carla del Monte did not hear anything: she _____ (listen) to Elvis Presley's Jailhouse Rock on her discman. Steve 'the Thinker' King _____ (read) a book called *Crime and Punishment*.
The Galton Brothers did not realise what _____ (go on) because they _____ (play) monopoly on their computer. Averell Galton was very angry. He said: "It's not fair. I _____ (win) for the first time in my life."
But the police were also very lucky. There was no shooting, perhaps because Ramona Zotti _____ (clean) her machine gun at the time of the raid. Her boyfriend, 'Big' Tony Lynch, did not have his gun ready because he _____ (iron) Ramona's mini-dress. Even Johnny 'the Bulldozer' Walker was no problem. He _____ (fill) bottles with smuggled Scotch whisky. A policeman said: "He _____ (sing) a very happy song when we took him to the police car."
Al Bigone and his wife were very surprised. "We _____ (watch) the News at Ten on television when we heard the noise. But we thought the boys _____ just _____ (have) a good time."
Next to the apartment the police found a big hangar. There the service crew men _____ (work) very hard. Two mechanics, Fred Bull and George Sprite, _____ (paint) a new number on Al Bigone's aeroplane while Leonardo da Vicinity, the top technician, _____ (service) the helicopter.

Supplement: Focus

Unit 17

Fill in the Gaps III

Police Arrest Al Bigone's _____

Use the words in the box below to fill in the gaps.

Yesterday at 10 p.m. Inspector Elliot Lomond and the Chicago _____ went into Al Bigone's _____. They arrested many _____ of the gang of Chicago's biggest crime boss.

Complete _____

The raid on the headquarters, a warehouse with a _____ apartment in the Docks, was a _____ surprise. The gangsters were not expecting the police. Carla del Monte did not hear anything: she was listening to Elvis Presley's Jailhouse Rock on her discman. Steve 'the Thinker' King was reading a book _____ *Crime and Punishment.*
The Galton Brothers did not _____ what was going on because they were playing monopoly on their computer. Averell Galton was very _____. He said: "It's not _____. I was winning for the first time _____."

Lucky _____

But the police were also very lucky. There was no shooting, perhaps _____ Ramona Zotti was cleaning her machine _____ at the time of the raid. Her _____, 'Big' Tony Lynch, did not have his gun _____ because he was ironing Ramona's mini-dress. Even Johnny 'the Bulldozer' Walker was no _____. He was filling _____ with smuggled Scotch whisky. A policeman said: "He was singing a very happy _____ when we took him to the police _____."
Al Bigone and his wife were very surprised. "We were watching the News at Ten on _____ when we heard the _____. But we thought the boys were just having a good time."

Aeroplane and Helicopter Ready

Next to the _____ the police found a big hangar. There the service _____ men were working very hard. Two _____, Fred Bull and George Sprite, were painting a new _____ on Al Bigone's aeroplane while Leonardo da Vicinity, the top technician, was _____ the helicopter.

> **USE**
> angry, apartment, because, bottles, boyfriend, called, car, complete, crew, fair, gang, gun, headquarters, in my life, luxury, mechanics, members, noise, number, police, police, problem, ready, realise, servicing, song, surprise, television

Is this Text Correct?

This text was in another newspaper, but the reporter made a lot of mistakes. Can you correct them?

Police Arrest Al Capone's Gang

Yesterday at 10 p.m. Inspector Elliot Ness and the Chicago police went into Al Capone's headquarters. They arrested many members of the gang of Chicago's biggest crime boss.

Complete Surprise

The raid on the headquarters, a supermarket with a luxury apartment in the Rocks, was a complete surprise. The gangsters were not expecting the police. Carla del Monte did not see anything: she was listening to Elvis Presley's *Jailhouse Rock* on her sofa. Steve 'the Drinker' King was reading a book called *Wine and Punishment*.
The Galton Sisters did not realise what was going on because they were playing 'Scotland Yard' on their mobile phone. Averell Galton was very hungry. He said: "It's not fair. I was winning for the first time in my life."

Lucky Police

But the police were also very lucky. There was no footing, perhaps because Ramona Zotti was cleaning her plastic gun at the time of the raid. Her boyfriend, 'Big' Tony Lynch, did not have his revolver because he was ironing Ramona's evening dress. Even Johnny 'the Bulldozer' Walker was no problem. He was filling boats with smuggled Scotch whisky. A policeman said: "He was ringing a very happy song when we took him to the police car."
Al Capone and his wife were very happy. "We were catching the News at Ten on television when we heard the noise. But we thought the boys were just having a good time."

Aeroplane and Helicopter Ready

Next to the garage the police found a big hangar. There the service crew men were talking very hard. Two pop stars, Fred Bull and George Coke, were painting a new name on Al Capone's aeroplane while Leonardo da Vicinity, the top technician, was flying the helicopter.

Supplement: Focus

What Were They Wearing?

Colour the clothes of these two teenagers. Show your partner the picture for one minute. Then ask your partner questions.

Example: Was the boy wearing a hat?
What colour were the girls' shoes?

T-shirt: _____

jeans: _____

jacket: _____

scarf: _____

schoolbag: _____

socks: _____

shoes: _____

Supplement: Training

Fill in the Missing Verbs

Put the verbs in brackets into the correct tense (Present, Present progressive, Simple past or Past progressive).

Who killed Lady Mottram?

Lady Penelope Mottram _____ (be) dead. She _____ (die) of a heart wound on 16th January between 6.30 p.m. and 11 p.m. The wound _____ (be) very small, but it _____ (kill) Lady Mottram immediately.

The murder weapon, a long pointed object, _____ (be) nowhere. Mr Sanderby, the police expert, _____ (find) a small piece of a peppermint leaf in the wound. There _____ (be) two thermos flasks in Lady Mottram's room. One had Earl Grey tea in it. The other one, next to Lady Mottram's chair, was full of cold peppermint tea. There _____ (be) Earl Grey tea in her cup.

Inspector Bradley of Scotland Yard _____ (talk) to Isabella Witherspoon, the household help. She _____ (find) the body.

Bradley: How _____ (find) the body?
Ms Witherspoon: I _____ (clean) the hall. Then I _____ (hear) the milkman. I _____ just _____ (carry) the milk bottles in when I _____ (hear) the television in Lady Mottram's drawing room.
Bradley: _____ (be) that unusual?
Witherspoon: Yes, Lady Mottram only _____ (watch) the Nine o'clock News on BBC 1 in the evening. She never _____ (watch) anything else.
Bradley: And what _____ the room _____ (look) like?
Witherspoon: Lady Mottram _____ (sit) in her chair. First I _____ (think) she _____ (sleep), but then I _____ (see) that her eyes _____ (be) open. And there _____ (be) some blood on the front of her dress, but not very much.
Bradley: _____ you _____ (notice) anything unusual about the room?
Witherspoon: Well, the television _____ (be) on – BBC 1, I think. Her reading light _____ (be) on, but the fire in the fireplace _____ (not burn).
Bradley: This pair of glasses _____ (lie) on the table next to the thermos flask. Are they Lady Mottram's glasses?
Witherspoon: No, they _____ (be) Professor Mottram's reading glasses.
Bradley: I _____ (be) sorry, but I _____ (have) to ask this question. What _____ you _____ (do) last night between dinner and midnight?
Witherspoon: Well, I _____ (bring) Lady Mottram her evening tea, Earl Grey, at about a quarter to eight. I _____ (leave) the thermos flask on the little table next to her chair. She _____ (talk) to her friend Margaret on the phone.
I _____ (say) good night and then I _____ (go) out to the cinema to _____ (see) the new Tom Cruise film with – with a – friend.
I _____ (come) back at 11.30 and _____ (go) straight to bed.

(52)   Unit 18

Fill in the Missing Words

Use the words in the box below.

Who killed Lady Mottram?

_____ Penelope Mottram was dead. She died of a heart _____ on 16th January between 6.30 p.m. and 11 p.m. The wound was very small, but it killed Lady Mottram _____.
The _____ weapon, a long _____ object, was nowhere. Mr Sanderby, the police _____, found a small piece of a peppermint _____ in the wound. There were two thermos flasks in Lady Mottram's room. One had Earl Grey tea in it. The other one, next to Lady Mottram's chair, was full of cold peppermint tea. There was Earl Grey tea in her _____.

Inspector Bradley of Scotland Yard is talking to Isabella Witherspoon, the _____ help. She found the body.

Bradley: How did you find the _____?
Ms Witherspoon: I was cleaning the _____. Then I heard the milkman. I was just carrying the _____ bottles in when I heard the television in Lady Mottram's _____.
Bradley: Is that _____?
Witherspoon: Yes, Lady Mottram only watches the Nine o'clock News on BBC 1 in the evening. She never watches anything _____.
Bradley: And what did the room look like?
Witherspoon: Lady Mottram was sitting in her chair. First I thought she was sleeping, but then I saw that her eyes were _____. And there was some blood on the _____ of her dress, but not very much.
Bradley: Did you _____ anything unusual about the room?
Witherspoon: Well, the television was on – BBC 1, I think. Her reading _____ was on, but the _____ in the fireplace wasn't burning.
Bradley: This pair of _____ was lying on the table next to the thermos flask. Are they Lady Mottram's _____?
Witherspoon: No, they are Professor Mottram's reading glasses.
Bradley: I'm sorry, but I have to ask this question. What were you doing last night between dinner and _____?
Witherspoon: Well, I brought Lady Mottram her evening tea, Earl Grey, at about a quarter to eight. I left the thermos flask on the _____ table next to her chair. She was talking to her friend Margaret on the _____. I said good night and then I went out to the cinema to see the new Tom Cruise film with – with a – friend. I came back at 11.30 and went _____ to bed.

USE

body, cup, drawing room, else, expert, fire, front, glasses, glasses, hall, household, immediately, Lady, leaf, light, little, midnight, milk, murder, notice, open, phone, pointed, straight, unusual, wound

244   Supplement: Focus

What Are the Correct Questions?

Complete Inspector Bradley's questions.

Who killed Lady Mottram?

Bradley: _____ you find the body?

Ms Witherspoon: I was cleaning the hall. Then I heard the milkman. I was just carrying the milk bottles in when I heard the television in Lady Mottram's drawing room.

Bradley: _____ unusual?

Witherspoon: Yes, Lady Mottram only watches the Nine o'clock News on BBC 1 in the evening. She never watches anything else.

Bradley: And _____ the room look like?

Witherspoon: Lady Mottram was sitting in her chair. First I thought she was sleeping, but then I saw that her eyes were open. And there was some blood on the front of her dress, but not very much.

Bradley: _____ notice anything unusual about the room?

Witherspoon: Well, the television was on – BBC 1, I think. Her reading light was on, but the fire in the fireplace wasn't burning.

Bradley: This pair of glasses was lying on the table next to the thermos flask. _____ Lady Mottram's glasses?

Witherspoon: No, they are Professor Mottram's reading glasses.

Bradley: I'm sorry, but I have to ask this question. _____ last night between dinner and midnight?

Witherspoon: Well, I brought Lady Mottram her evening tea, Earl Grey, at about a quarter to eight. I left the thermos flask on the little table next to her chair. She was talking to her friend Margaret on the phone. I said good night and then I went out to the cinema to see the new Tom Cruise film with – with a – friend. I came back at 11.30 and went straight to bed.

(54) Unit 18

Questions and Answers

Can you match Inspector Bradley's questions to the answers of Ms Witherspoon?

Bradley:

1. Did you notice anything unusual about the room?
2. I'm sorry, but I have to ask this question. What were you doing last night between dinner and midnight?
3. How did you find the body?
4. And what did the room look like?
5. This pair of glasses was lying on the table next to the thermos flask. Are they Lady Mottram's glasses?
6. Is that unusual?

Ms Witherspoon:

a) Lady Mottram was sitting in her chair. First I thought she was sleeping, but then I saw that her eyes were open. And there was some blood on the front of her dress, but not very much.
b) Yes, Lady Mottram only watches the Nine o'clock News on BBC 1 in the evening. She never watches anything else.
c) Well, the television was on – BBC 1, I think. Her reading light was on, but the fire in the fireplace wasn't burning.
d) I was cleaning the hall. Then I heard the milkman. I was just carrying the milk bottles in when I heard the television in Lady Mottram's drawing room.
e) Well, I brought Lady Mottram her evening tea, Earl Grey, at about a quarter to eight. I left the thermos flask on the little table next to her chair. She was talking to her friend Margaret on the phone. I said good night and then I went out to the cinema to see the new Tom Cruise film with – with a – friend. I came back at 11.30 and went straight to bed.
f) No, they are Professor Mottram's reading glasses.

Question number ...

1) matches answer ☐   3) matches answer ☐   5) matches answer ☐

2) matches answer ☐   4) matches answer ☐   6) matches answer ☐

Script: Second Step

Hopkins: Did you like Lady Mottram?
Mottram: No, I did not like my cousin very much.
Hopkins: Why not?
Mottram: Because she wanted to leave all her money to Greenpeace and the World Wildlife Fund and all those green idiots. Last summer we had a big argument about this. Now we are talking to each other again – you know, "Good morning", but that's all. And another thing: She always has her radio and television on so damn loud. How can I work with all that noise?
Oh, well! Poor girl! Thank God, it was a quick death. With a wound like that you are dead immediately.
Hopkins: How do you know that?
Mottram: I'm a professor of anatomy, actually. I would know something like that, wouldn't I?
Hopkins: Yes, of course, you would. Well – errm – and what were you doing last night after dinner?
Mottram: Between 7.30 and 8.00 I was reading the newspaper. Then I wrote some letters. At 9 o'clock that blasted television came on, so I put on my stereo – Mozart. Then I can't hear Penelope's television. From about 9 to 11 I was working on my new book. At 11 I went to the kitchen to make myself a cup of tea. Then I went to bed.
Hopkins: Did anything unusual happen? What about Mr Plumley and Ms Witherspoon?
Mottram: Ms Witherspoon went out at a quarter to 8. I don't know where. After 9 o'clock Archibald went into Penelope's room. She was suffering from a cold. When he opened the door, she said to him: "Bring me a flask of hot peppermint tea, please."
Hopkins: Did Mr Plumley stay at home last night?
Mottram: Yes, he was working for his exams.
Hopkins: What happened this morning?
Mottram: I usually wake up at 8, but this morning I heard Penelope's television at 7 o'clock. Later, when I was eating my breakfast in the dining room, I heard a scream from Ms Witherspoon. She came out of Penelope's drawing room and said: "Don't go in there, Professor. Lady Mottram is dead." So I called the police.
Hopkins: Did you go into your cousin's drawing room yesterday or this morning?
Mottram: No, Ms Witherspoon closed the door, and then the people from the police came. But I never go in there anyway, never.
Hopkins: Well, Professor, thank you very much. – Oh, are these your glasses?
Mottram: Oh – errm – yes, they are. Thank you. I thought I had them last night.

Puzzle Text

Can you order the sentences of this story?

A very strange story

a) A father and his son were travelling home by car.
b) A helicopter took the boy to the hospital.
c) When they were going over a bridge, the father lost control of the car.
d) "I'm sorry. I cannot operate on this patient. He is my son."
e) It was clear that a very difficult operation was necessary to save the boy's life.
f) It was snowing and a strong wind was blowing.
g) It went over the side and fell into the river. The father died immediately.
h) The nurses brought him into the operating theatre.
i) The son didn't die, and a helicopter took the boy to the nearest hospital.
j) Then the doctor came in, looked at the boy and said:

The correct order is:

Three Stories

Do you remember these titles from the Stepping Out?

A	**Dangerous Trains**
B	**A Slow Grand Prix**
C	**An Easy Holiday**

The texts to these three stories are all mixed up. Can you find out which sentences belong to which title?

☐ After my first day at the beach I switched off the light in my hotel room.

☐ The train line between Thornington and Washam has two train tracks.

☐ Both trains entered the tunnel, both trains were going in the opposite direction.

☐ Both trains were travelling very fast – and – there was no accident.

☐ But Bill Grates had an idea.

☐ But the prize was not for the fastest car in the race, it was for the slowest car.

☐ But there is a high mountain with a tunnel on that line.

☐ Another train was travelling from Washam to Thornington.

☐ He organised a Formula 1 Grand Prix with a prize of $100,000.

☐ He told the drivers what to do and the race was as fast as any other, perhaps even a bit faster.

☐ "How can we run this race?

☐ I walked the 4 meters to my bed and was in bed before it was dark.

☐ I was having a great time and I took things easy.

☐ In the tunnel there is not enough room for two tracks.

☐ It was going from Thornington to Washam.

☐ Last summer I was on holiday in Italy.

☐ One afternoon a train went into the tunnel.

☐ One of the drivers said to Mr Gates:

☐ Bill Grates is very rich and a bit strange.

☐ We'll all just go slower and slower and the race will never finish."

☐ What did Mr Grates think of?

Supplement: Stepping Out

Fill in the Verbs

Use the verbs in the box below. Sometimes more than one verb is correct.

Problem page

Hi there,

My name is Andy and I've got a problem. I fancy this girl called Carla. She's not in my class but I see her in the computer lessons. She's great and I _____ ask her out. My problem: I am very shy. I always go red when I talk to people, especially girls. Sometimes I think of something clever to say, but when I talk to the girl, I _____ get the words out. It _____ be because I'm not very good-looking: I'm skinny and my hair is very thick. I _____ do anything with it. My parents are old hippies and they like my hair long, I don't. I _____ it short. I'm also not very sporty. I'm only good at computer things and that's not very interesting for a girl, is it?

Carla has got a lot of friends and she sometimes smiles when I walk past. Perhaps I _____ say something to her, but there are always girls around her. I just _____ talk to her alone. _____ you help?

Andy, Lancaster

USE
can, can't (3x), could, may, would like/'d like, would love to/'d love to

Fill in the Gaps

Problem page

Hi there,
_____ is Andy and I've got a problem. I _____ this girl called Carla. She's not in my class but I see her in the computer _____. She's great and I'd love to _____ her out. My problem: I am very _____. I always go red when I _____ to people, _____ girls. Sometimes I think of something _____ to say, but when I talk to the girl, I can't get the words out. It may be because I'm not very _____: I'm _____ and my hair is very thick. I can't do anything with it. My _____ are old hippies and they like my _____ long, I don't. I'd like it short. I'm also not very sporty. I'm only _____ at computer things and that's not very _____ for a girl, is it? Carla has got a lot of friends and she sometimes _____ when I walk past. Perhaps I could _____ something to her, but there are always girls around her. I just can't talk to her _____.
Can you _____?
Andy, Lancaster

Dear Andy,
I had the same _____, but there is a way out: you must _____ to her. Find out where she _____. Then you can _____ for her and _____ her out for an ice-cream or something.
Jessica

Dear Andy,
I know a lot _____ computers and I _____ them interesting – and I'm a girl. You mustn't think that girls are not very good with computers. Ask her for "help" with a computer problem. It could be a good _____, you know ...
Alice

Dear Andy,
You are good with computers, _____? Can you send her a _____ in your computer class? Or could you ask one of her friends for Carla's e-mail _____? Then send her a _____ e-mail and ask her to go out to the cinema. And you should talk to your parents _____ your hair.
Colin

What's the Name of the Game?

Reginald Tackle is a sports teacher. He's having a bad dream. Yesterday, he explained the rules of three ball games to his pupils. Now they are all mixed up in his dream. Can you find out the names of the games? Which rules belong to which games?

1. The ball must never touch the ground.
2. There must be eleven players in each team.
3. Only seven players can be on the field at the same time.
4. After two passes you must play the ball into the other team's field.
5. The field players must not touch the ball with their hands except when they throw it in from the sideline.
6. The ball may touch the net, but not when you are serving.
7. There is a small semicircle around the goal.
8. If you foul a player in the semicircle around the goal, the other team gets a penalty kick.
9. Only the goalkeeper may stand in the semicircle.
10. After every set you must change sides.
11. The goalkeeper may touch the ball with his / her hands, but only in the penalty area.
12. Players must not carry the ball in their hands while they are running.

Game A: _____ rule number ☐ ☐ ☐ ☐

Game B: _____ rule number ☐ ☐ ☐ ☐

Game C: _____ rule number ☐ ☐ ☐ ☐

Key:

The three games are: football (rule number 2., 5., 8., 11.) handball (rule number 3., 7., 9., 12.) volleyball (rule number 1., 4., 6., 10.)

The Story of an Escape

Read the following story first, then do the two tasks below.

'Big' Tony Lynch is in prison now. The prison is in an old castle. He would like to get out, but his cell is on the sixth floor.

In a cake from Ramona Zotti, there is a knife. There are two long ropes hanging from the high ceiling of his cell. But he needs both ropes to escape. So he has to climb the ropes and cut them as high up as he can. But the ceiling is so high that if he cuts one rope off near the top he can't jump to the floor without breaking his legs. Tony thinks about the problem for a few days. Suddenly he finds a way to get almost all of the ropes. What does he have to do? Tony: "My idea is really clever. First of all, I must tie the ends of the two ropes together. Then I climb the top of one rope. Let's say this is Rope A. When I'm at the top I cut Rope B about half a metre below the ceiling. Then I have to tie the short rest into a loop.

Now I can put one arm through the loop and hang there while I'm cutting Rope A near the ceiling. But I mustn't drop Rope A! Then I can pass Rope A through the loop and pull it until the knotted ends are at the top.

Now I can climb down the double rope, pull it until it comes down. I can tie it to the window frame and climb down from the sixth floor. Bye-bye!"

a) Draw a sketch of the situation before and during the escape.

b) Now you are Tony. Tell the story of your escape to your friend Al Bigone. Use the past tense.
   Example: My idea **was** really clever. First of all, **I had to** tie ...

Supplement: Trainig

Can You Help Me?

OH, BROTHER

I'm a 16 year old boy. Our family lives in a small house so I share a room with my 11-year old younger brother. I just hate it! The worst thing is that he goes through my things. My girlfriend and I write each other e-mails and I'm sure he sometimes reads them. My parents tell me that I should delete them.
I print them out and delete the e-mails, but he finds the prints and reads them. What can I do? I feel I just haven't got a private life anymore.
An angry teenager, Romford

I'm sure you're not the only one with a nosy younger brother or sister. Well, for all of you with such a problem the easy answer is a box with a lock. You can buy them in stationers like W. H. Smiths. Put your private things in there, lock it and take the key with you. Everybody needs a private life. You don't have to share everything with everybody, and certainly not with nosy little brothers (or sisters).

I DON'T WANT A BOYFRIEND

My friends at school all want to have a boyfriend. They only seem interested in that. They always talk about boys, about how they fancy this one or that one and wonder if those boys want to go out with them. Some of my mates have got boyfriends and for a while they may get on OK but then they have fights and break up. Afterwards they never have a good word for their ex-boyfriends.
I like to talk to boys and have a laugh with them but I just don't want a boyfriend. Some of my mates say that I don't mean that, I only say it because boys don't ask me out. But they do ask me out and I say no to them. I don't think it's wrong that I don't want a boyfriend – so why do my friends give me the feeling that I am really strange?
Girl, single, 16

*Don't let your friends give you that feeling. But perhaps you show them that you think they are silly when they get excited over a boy, so they get angry with you. And perhaps they are just saying what they think, just as you are saying what you think. Some girls are very interested in boys, and they want to have a boyfriend; there is nothing wrong with that. I know you are not interested in boys and that's OK too. But it can be fun to fancy a boy and to wonder "will I see him today or not", but it can also be very sad when he doesn't react.
Perhaps you are not ready for a relationship with a boy yet, that's fine. You are still young and relationships at your age rarely last very long. So don't listen to your friends, but don't look down on them either …*

I'M SO BROKENHEARTED

Please help me. I feel so down I don't think I can ever feel happy again. Two weeks ago my girl-friend of 3 months dumped me: she doesn't want to go out with me anymore, but she still wants to be friends. I thought we were really happy but I now know that she wanted to dump me a long time ago. I feel brokenhearted; every day I get up and feel sad and depressed. It gets worse when I see her, because I try to be happy and friendly so she sees that I'm still a nice person. My mother tells me that there are lots of fish in the sea and that I should go out more. But I just want to be alone so I don't even go out with my old friends …
Jason, 17, Sheffield

It is never easy to accept it when your girlfriend or your boyfriend dumps you. It doesn't matter much how it happens or why it happens, it still hurts. It can be even harder when your ex isn't horrible about it and says he / she still wants to be friends. But at the moment you need time away from her so you can sort yourself out. Don't live in hope that she may change her mind because you're still "a nice person", but you must get over her and the hurt. And remember one thing: you are still the same person you were three months ago. Your relationship is over, but not your life. Your mum is right: there are a lot of other people out there. Let your friends help you get over your broken heart. Perhaps you may not feel like it but the best way out of the situation is to have fun with friends. Sitting at home and thinking about the relationship will not make you feel better.

I'M IN LOVE WITH A POP STAR

I'm 15 years old and very much in love with Jason from Robbie Williams. I cry myself to sleep every night because I know he's somewhere without me and he's having a great time. I also know he will never go out with me. I think about him all the time. I listen to his records, buy every magazine and cover my bed-room with pictures of him. My friends like him too, but I don't think they realise how terrible I feel. We went to a concert a few weeks ago but I left early because I felt so terrible: all those girls screaming and wanting to be near him.
I know it's stupid, but I just can't get him out of my head. Please help me.
A Robbie Williams Fan, Glasgow

I think there are probably a lot of people in the world like you. When I was your age I felt the same about Cat Stevens, so I really understand how you feel. It may help you to know that these feelings go away after a while and that you can look back with nice memories and not feel sad and confused any longer. One day you will realise that the pain isn't so strong anymore. Don't get me wrong, I'm not saying that your feelings for Robbie are not real, because they are. But one day you will start a relationship with someone and you'll find that real love is something that develops between two people when they get to know each other. But don't push your feelings for Robbie away; they're nothing to be ashamed of. Accept them and one day you'll find that you can still be a fan and it doesn't have to take over your whole life.

I DON'T WANT TO HURT HIM

I'm 16 years old and I feel very sorry for a male friend of mine. He's not very good-looking. I know that sounds horrible, but it's true. He has pretty bad acne and most of the time he really acts like a complete idiot, perhaps because he wants attention, but he has a heart of gold. I know he fancies me and would like to go out with me because he tells his friends and sometimes my best friend. I think he really would like to have a girlfriend, because in the last two weeks he asked out four girls. They all said no and then he came to me and told me that he loves me from the bottom of his heart. I don't want to hurt his feelings but I could never go out with him. How can I tell him so that he doesn't get hurt?
Helen, Durham

It is very hard to say "no" and not hurt the person, but it's important to learn to do it. It helps you if someone says no to you. From your letter I get the feeling that you can work this situation out, because you really like this boy and don't want to hurt him. I think one of his problems is that he wants a girlfriend too much. This can make a person look stupid and unattractive. But you must tell him that you don't want to be his girlfriend. Tell him in a way that you could understand and live with if you were in his shoes. You can also tell him why, because that may help him, but you don't have to explain your feelings in detail. Just tell him that you want to be friends with him. This way you can be kind and tell him that you like him. In any case never say "yes" when you mean "no". It's much worse to give someone false hope just because you haven't got the courage to say "no".

ACNE

I'm a 16 year old boy. I wouldn't be bad-looking, but my problem is that I have about 19 spots on my face. In the last 6 months I lost two girlfriends, and I'm sure its because of my spots. I've tried all kinds of things, but nothing works.
So now I don't go out anymore so that people can't see me. I feel horrible and ugly. All I want is clean skin. My parents tell me that acne disappears when you're older, but I want to be happy now. Please help!
David, Halifax

*One of the biggest problem about acne is that you think you look unattractive because of it. You look at your face much more critically than other people: you can see that you have 19 spots, but I don't think anybody else can. You probably try to pick them and that makes the problem worse. So what can you do? You can use antibacterial lotions to clean your skin. Cream and, for girls, a lot of make-up, makes the problem worse because it covers your skin and fills your pores. What sometimes helps is a change of diet. Many of our western foods are too rich and fatty. Try to eat fruit and lightly cooked vegetables instead of fast food, drink natural fruit juices instead of coke and most important of all, don't smoke. In most cases (70%) acne will go away after about 8 weeks. In the other cases see a doctor.
But remember, spots or no spots, you are what and who you are ...*

MY STOMACH STICKS OUT

Until I was 13 I was very thin, but then I put on a lot of weight (I'm 16 now). I'm not exactly fat, but my stomach sticks out. My mother says that when I grow older I will lose all this puppy fat. But I don't think it is puppy fat because I was so thin as a child. I cry about it at night and sometimes I go to the toilet and try to be sick. It really depresses me. What can I do?
Nicole, Dorchester

Your Mum is absolutely right. The most important thing is to stop worrying. When you are in puberty your body changes from a child's body to a woman's. So you start filling out all over your body. It's only natural to have a bit of a round tummy. A lot of girls have problems with that. The most important thing is: don't try to make yourself sick – it's very very dangerous and you could get very ill. You could even die from this. What you can do is exercise, swimming, cycling or yoga. This may make your muscles firmer and stronger and your stomach look a little flatter.

I FANCY THIS BOY

I know this boy called Gary. He lives near me, and he's really good-looking. I really fancy him and sometimes I get the feeling that he likes me too, but I don't know. He's got a girlfriend, you see, and so all my friends say I'm crazy to like him. But last time I saw him he put his arm around me all the time and when I sat down he came and put his head on my shoulder. In fact, he acted like a boyfriend. I'm really lost because I don't know how he feels about me. Does he want to go out with me or is he just doing all this for fun? I don't want to ask him because he might laugh at me or tell me that he doesn't like me. I'm so sad that sometimes I want to kill myself.
Miserable, Birmingham

*Gary sounds like a flirty type. I think he may probably really like you, but I don't think it is a good idea to get carried away over him. Let him take the first step. Then you can see how he really feels. But think about this: he is flirting with you but he already has a girlfriend. Could you trust him as your boyfriend?
When you are young many things seem worse than they are. The smallest thing can seem like the worst problem in the world. Believe me, it isn't. Talk to older friends and they will tell you they felt the same at your age. And when you tell someone about your problem, you can see it in perspective and it may then be easier to find a way out.*

What Have They Done?

Who has or hasn't done what? Look at the Focus II text for help.

The afternoon before the party

Martin

_____
_____
_____

Roy

_____
_____
_____

Penny

_____
_____
_____

Bridget

_____
_____
_____

Fill in the Gaps

Put the verbs in brackets into the present perfect or the past simple.

The morning after the party

The morning after the party, Bridget talks to her sister on the phone:
"You know that yesterday _____ (be) our end-of-the school-year party. Some friends and I _____ (organise) the party for our class, and we _____ (invite) the teachers. The neighbours _____ (go) away for the whole weekend because of the noise. They _____ (go) on a trip to Paris. So I'm sure we _____ (have) more fun at the party last night.
The party rooms _____ (be) decorated like an amusement park.
There _____ (be) lights and colourful decorations all over the room.
We _____ (have) hamburgers and sausages. We _____ (dance) a lot and _____ (get) very thirsty. Two hours after the beginning of the party, the soft drinks finally _____ (arrive). It _____ (be) a delivery service and they _____ (bring) the drinks to the wrong address first.
But now it's Sunday morning at eleven, and you should see the mess. No one _____ (take) away the decorations yet. The balloons _____ (lose) most of their air – it's a sad picture. Martin _____ (move) the comfortable chairs out of the chill-out room. Mike and Susan _____ (start) to clean up the room. Joe _____ (put) the empty bottles into his mother's car. Roy _____ (bring) back Mr Taylor's barbecue and _____ (give) back the CD player. Penny _____ (put) the big speakers in the car. Someone _____ (clean) the windows of the party room. A girl and a boy _____ (move) the table back to the class room.
Everyone seems very tired. Just imagine I only _____ (sleep) three hours last night!
I _____ (wake up) at eight o'clock when two dogs _____ (start) making an awful noise."

Key:

was, organised, invited, have gone, went, had, were, were, had, danced, got, arrived, was, brought, has taken, have lost, has moved, have started, has put, has brought, has given, has cleaned, have moved, slept, woke up, started

Kim's Game

Going to Camp

Have the camp organisers thought of all the things on the lists below?

Camp Organiser 1

- write down the addresses of all the parents (if something happens)
- buy food for the first day ✓
- ask the farmer about milk and eggs for the camp
- bring maps of the region
- check that the tents are OK ✓
- draw a plan of the route to the camp site for visitors
- find out the phone number of the nearest doctor ✓
- get bicycle repair kit
- make a list of all the equipment (ropes, torches, compass, etc.)
- ask the farmer for permission to camp on his land ✓
- make sure the lights on the bicycles are OK
- make sure the water near the camp site is OK for drinking
- buy some plastic sheets for kitchen tent
- organise some wood to build a kitchen
- put new strings on the guitar
- send the rucksacks to the nearest train station
- tell the postman about the address of the camp

✓ = You have done that.

Camp Organiser 2

- write down the addresses of all the parents (if something happens)
- tell the postman about the address of the camp ✓
- put new strings on the guitar ✓
- buy some plastic sheets for kitchen tent
- organise some wood to build a kitchen
- make sure the water near the camp site is OK for drinking
- make sure the lights on the bicycles are OK ✓
- make a list of all the equipment (ropes, torches, compass, etc.)
- get bicycle repair kit ✓
- send the rucksacks to the nearest train station
- find out the phone number of the nearest doctor
- ask the farmer for permission to camp on his land
- draw a plan of the route to the camp site for visitors
- check that the tents are OK
- buy food for the first day
- bring maps of the region ✓
- ask the farmer about milk and eggs for the camp

✓ = You have done that.

Camp Organiser 3

- ask the farmer for permission to camp on his land
- find out the phone number of the nearest doctor
- check that the tents are OK
- draw a plan of the route to the camp site for visitors ✓
- buy food for the first day
- bring maps of the region
- send the rucksacks to the nearest train station ✓
- put new strings on the guitar
- get bicycle repair kit
- make sure the lights on the bicycles are OK
- write down the addresses of all the parents (if something happens) ✓
- make sure the water near the camp site is OK for drinking
- tell the postman about the address of the camp
- make a list of all the equipment (ropes, torches, compass, etc.)
- organise some wood to build a kitchen ✓
- buy some plastic sheets for kitchen tent
- ask the farmer about milk and eggs for the camp

✓ = You have done that.

Camp Organiser 4

- bring maps of the region
- get bicycle repair kit
- make sure the lights on the bicycles are OK
- make a list of all the equipment (ropes, torches, compass, etc.) ✓
- ask the farmer for permission to camp on his land
- find out the phone number of the nearest doctor ✓
- tell the postman about the address of the camp ✓
- check that the tents are OK
- buy food for the first day
- put new strings on the guitar
- write down the addresses of all the parents (if something happens)
- draw a plan of the route to the camp site for visitors
- send the rucksacks to the nearest train station
- organise some wood to build a kitchen
- buy some plastic sheets for kitchen tent ✓
- make sure the water near the camp site is OK for drinking ✓
- ask the farmer about milk and eggs for the camp ✓

✓ = You have done that.

Supplement: Stepping Out

CONTROL SHEET Revision Workshop 4		
Student's name : _____	Score:	Points to repeat:
Station Verb Forms Drill _____ correct forms out of 35	_____	_____ _____ _____
Station Story a) _____ correct forms out of 21 b) _____ correct forms out of 17 c) _____ correct forms out of 27	_____	_____ _____ _____
Station Writing _____ correct sentences out of 10	_____	_____ _____ _____
Station Interview _____ correct questions out of 8 _____ correct answers out of 8	_____	_____ _____ _____
Station Reading ☐ correct burglar's route ☐ incorrect burglar's route	_____	_____ _____ _____
Station Listening – Numbers _____ correct entries out of 15	_____	_____ _____ _____
Station Discussion _____ correct answers out of 6	_____	_____ _____ _____

CONTROL SHEET Revision Workshop 4		
Student's name: _____	Score:	Points to repeat:
Station Verb Forms Drill _____ correct forms out of 35	_____	_____ _____ _____
Station Story a) _____ correct forms out of 34 b) _____ correct forms out of 23 c) _____ correct forms out of 28	_____	_____ _____ _____
Station Writing _____ correct sentences out of _____	_____	_____ _____ _____
Station Interview _____ correct questions out of 12 _____ correct answers out of 12	_____	_____ _____ _____
Station Reading ☐ correct burglar's route ☐ incorrect burglar's route	_____	_____ _____ _____
Station Listening – Numbers _____ correct entries out of 15	_____	_____ _____ _____
Station Discussion _____ correct answers out of _____	_____	_____ _____ _____